DANCE OF THE BUTTERFLIES

Bunches of butterflies, here and there, flutter wildly in the air.
So many different colors and hues, among the flowers and trees.
By nature, they don't depend upon the music of strings and reeds.
Mindlessly they dance about, aloft on the breezes of spring.

Emperor Saga (786-842), *Bunka shūreishū*

DANCE OF THE BUTTERFLIES

CHINESE POETRY

FROM THE JAPANESE COURT TRADITION

*Translated and Edited with
Introductions and Commentaries by*

JUDITH N. RABINOVITCH

AND

TIMOTHY R. BRADSTOCK

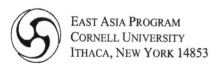

EAST ASIA PROGRAM
CORNELL UNIVERSITY
ITHACA, NEW YORK 14853

The Cornell East Asia Series is published by the Cornell University East Asia Program (distinct from Cornell University Press). We publish affordably priced books on a variety of scholarly topics relating to East Asia as a service to the academic community and the general public. Standing orders, which provide for automatic notification and invoicing of each title in the series upon publication, are accepted.

If after review by internal and external readers a manuscript is accepted for publication, it is published on the basis of camera-ready copy provided by the volume author. Each author is thus responsible for any necessary copy-editing and for manuscript formatting. Address submission inquiries to CEAS Editorial Board, East Asia Program, Cornell University, Ithaca, New York 14853-7601.

Number 125 in the Cornell East Asia Series
Copyright © 2005 by Judith N. Rabinovitch and Timothy R. Bradstock. All rights reserved
ISSN 1050-2955
ISBN-13: 978-1-885445-35-3 hc / ISBN-10: 1-885445-35-0 hc
ISBN-13: 978-1-885445-25-4 pb / ISBN-10: 1-885445-25-3 pb
Library of Congress Control Number: 2005922989

23 22 21 20 19 18 17 16 15 14 13 12 11 10 09 08 05   9 8 7 6 5 4 3 2 1

CONTENTS

PREFACE

No one today questions the central importance of Chinese literature and aesthetics in the development of the Japanese literary arts. Chinese literary traditions, versification in particular, formed the very foundations of Japanese court literature, providing a means by which the sophisticated literary concepts, rhetoric, techniques, and aesthetics of China could be introduced to the Japanese court. Without this activity and the support it received at the highest levels, the aristocratic literary mind would have evolved quite differently. The importation of Chinese books into Japan commenced around the fifth century, a process which was given considerable impetus by extended visits to the Japanese court by Chinese officials, scholars, and priests, and corresponding journeys to the capital city of Chang'an by members of the Japanese elite eager to study in China. By around 750, the impact of Chinese civilization upon Japan had reached remarkable proportions; the appeal of Chinese literary traditions, notably various genres of Chinese poetry (*shi*), later called *kanshi* ("Chinese verse"), intensified under the continued patronage of the emperor and high nobility. The actual term *kanshi* appears to have first come into use in the 1880s, to distinguish the genre from the newly emerging native form known as *shintaishi*, "new-style verse" (later called *jiyūshi* "free verse," or just *shi*). Prior to this time, *kanshi* were simply known as *shi*, or less commonly, *karauta* (or *kara no uta*, "Chinese poems"), the latter term earliest seen in *Tosa nikki* (tenth century).

The present volume focuses on the *kanshi* written during the Nara and Heian periods but includes as well some of the earliest extant Chinese poems dating back to the Ōmi court period (667–72) and centering upon the reigns of emperors Tenji (Tenchi) and Kōbun (formerly Prince Ōtomo), both early *kanshi* poets of distinction. A small number of selections preserved in the first *kanshi* anthology, *Kaifūsō* (751), whose works span the years 672–751, represents this foundational period of *kanshi* practice. Many other compositions were lost during the Jinshin Disturbance, which broke out in 772. Throughout the Heian age, *kanshi* versification and *kanbun*

ix

prose composition remained at the forefront of literary activity among males of privilege at court, with a few female nobles and court ladies also participating. Yet the study of literature written in Chinese during the court period remains relatively undeveloped, especially in the West. Recent decades have seen a number of outstanding contributions to *kanshi* studies, although relatively few translations have been produced compared to the corpus of translated *waka* from the same period.

We would like to make special mention of the following works, which have furthered our understanding of *kanshi*: Konishi Jin'ichi, *A History of Japanese Literature* (3 vols., 1984–91); Helen C. McCullough, *Brocade by Night: 'Kokin Wakashū' and the Court Style in Classical Japanese Poetry* (1985); Robert Borgen, *Sugawara no Michizane and the Early Heian Court* (orig. pub. 1986); Sonja Arntzen, *Ikkyū and the Crazy Cloud Anthology: A Zen Poet of Medieval Japan* (1986); and Marian Ury, *Poems of the Five Mountains* (1977). Other important works include Burton Watson, *Japanese Literature in China* (2 vols., 1975); J. Thomas Rimer and Jonathan Chaves, *Japanese and Chinese Poems to Sing: The* Wakan rōei shū (1997); Ivo Smits, *The Pursuit of Loneliness: Chinese and Japanese Nature Poetry in Medieval Japan, ca. 1050–1150* (1995); and Jonathan Pollack, *The Fracture of Meaning: Japan's Synthesis of China from the Eighth Through the Eighteenth Century* (1986). We also want to acknowledge the valuable contributions made by Stephen Addiss in his study *Tall Mountains and Flowing Waters: The Arts of Uragami Gyokudō* (1987), and a recent publication on a modern *kanshi* poet by Addiss, Chaves, and Rimer titled *Old Taoist: The Art, Poetry, and Life of Kodōjin (1865–1944)*, published in 2000.

The present volume was preceded by our two earlier publications: *An Anthology of* Kanshi (*Chinese Verse*) *by Japanese Poets of the Edo Period (1603–1868)*, published in 1997, and *The* Kanshi *Poems of the Ozasa* Tanzaku *Collection: Late Edo Life through the Poetry of Kyoto Townsmen* (2002). Deepening interest in *kanshi* generated by our previous endeavors led us to delve back further into the classical age, this anthology being the outcome. Our translations aim to preserve some semblance of the Chinese poetic form. Besides striving to remain faithful to the original language, we have also tried to achieve a euphonic effect similar to the prosodic rhythm of the Chinese line. This has been accomplished by providing, as far as possible, an accented syllable in the English for every character per line in the original. We have not attempted to make the lines rhyme, so as to avoid compromising accuracy and creating infelicitous auditory effects. In all of our efforts to date, we acknowledge our substantial debt to others in the field, whose translations, commentaries, and other writings have inspired us to try to bring this appealing genre to a wider audience.

LIST OF POEMS BY TITLE

Below, listed either by their title or by the poet's introduction, are all of the poems translated in this volume, these taken from fourteen anthologies, which are presented in chronological order. The number at the left margin is the original poem number in the anthology. Title notes and other explanatory material appended by the original poets to poem titles, as well as the ranks and secondary titles of the poets, are omitted from this list.

KAIFŪSŌ (POETIC GEMS CHERISHING THE STYLES OF OLD), COMPILED 751

xii

RYŌUN SHINSHŪ (THE NEW CLOUD-TOPPING COLLECTION), COMPILED
814

***KEIKOKUSHŪ* (COLLECTION OF VERSE FOR BRINGING ORDER TO THE REALM), COMPILED CA. 827**

KANKE BUNSŌ (THE SUGAWARA LITERARY DRAFTS), COMPILED 900, AND
KANKE KŌSHŪ (THE SECOND SUGAWARA COLLECTION), COMPILED 903,
POETRY BY SUGAWARA NO MICHIZANE (845-903)

FUSŌSHŪ (ANTHOLOGY OF POETRY FROM OUR LAND), COMPILED CA. 995–98

HONCHŌ MONZUI (LITERARY GEMS FROM OUR COURT), COMPILED CA.
1060

HONCHŌ ZOKU MONZUI (FURTHER LITERARY GEMS FROM OUR COURT), COMPILED CA. 1140

HOSSHŌJI DONO GYOSHŪ (A COLLECTION OF POEMS BY THE LORD OF HOSSHŌJI), COMPILED 1145

HONCHŌ MUDAISHI (POEMS FROM OUR COURT WITHOUT ALLUSIVE TITLES), COMPILED 1162–64

TITLE ABBREVIATIONS

BKSRS   *Bunka shūreishū*, in Kojima Noriyuki, annot., *Kaifūsō, Bunka shūreishū, Honchō monzui.* Nihon koten bungaku taikei, 69. Tokyo: Iwanami Shoten, 1964.

FSS   *Fusōshū*, in Kawamata Keiichi, ed., *[Shinkō] Gunsho ruijū* 126, vol. 6. Tokyo: Naigai Shoseki Kabushiki Kaisha, 1931.

HCMDS   *Honchō mudaishi*, in Honma Yōichi, annot., *Honchō mudaishi zenchūshaku*, 3 vols. Shintensha chūshaku sōsho, vols. 2, 4, 7. Tokyo: Shintensha, 1992–94.

HCMZ   *Honchō monzui*, in Kojima Noriyuki, annot., *Kaifūsō, Bunka shūreishū, Honchō monzui.* Nihon koten bungaku taikei, 69. Tokyo: Iwanami Shoten, 1964. See also SNKBT, below, for a newer annotated text of HCMZ.

HCRS   *Honchō reisō*, in Kawaguchi Hisao and others, annot., *Honchō reisō kanchū.* Tokyo: Benseisha, 1993.

HDG   *Hosshōji dono gyoshū*, by Fujiwara no Tadamichi, in *[Shinkō] Gunsho ruijū* 126, vol. 6. Tokyo: Naigai Shoseki Kabushiki Kaisha, 1931.

HZM   *Honchō zoku monzui*, in Nakatsuka Eijirō and others, eds., Nihon bungaku taikei, 24. Tokyo: Kokumin Tosho Kabushiki Kaisha, 1927.

KFS   *Kaifūsō*, in Kojima Noriyuki, annot., *Kaifūsō, Bunka shūreishū, Honchō monzui.* Nihon koten bungaku taikei, 69. Tokyo: Iwanami Shoten, 1964.

xxv

KKBS   *Kanke bunsō*, in Kawaguchi Hisao, annot., *Kanke bunsō, Kanke kōshū*. Nihon koten bungaku taikei, 72. Tokyo: Iwanami Shoten, 1966.

KKKS   *Kanke kōshū*, in Kawaguchi Hisao, annot., *Kanke bunsō, Kanke kōshū*. Nihon koten bungaku taikei, 72. Tokyo: Iwanami Shoten, 1966.

KKS   *Keikokushū*, in Kojima Noriyuki, annot., *Kokufū ankoku jidai no bungaku: Kōnin-, Tenchō-ki no bungaku o chūshin to shite*, vol. 2 (bk. 3), pt. I; vol. 2 (bk. 3), pt. II; vol. 3 (pt. I); vol. 3 (pt. II); and vol. 3 (pt. III). Tokyo: Hanawa Shobō, 1985–98.

NKBT   *Nihon koten bungaku taikei* series. See KFS, BKSRS, HCMZ, KKBS, and KKKS, above, and SRS, below.

RUS   *Ryōunshū*, in Kojima Noriyuki, annot., *Kokufū ankoku jidai no bungaku: Kōnin-, Tenchō-ki no bungaku o chūshin to shite*, vol. 2 (bk. 2). Tokyo: Hanawa Shobō, 1979.

SNKBT   *Honchō monzui*, in Ōsone Shōsuke, Kinpara Tadashi, and Gotō Akio, annot., *Honchō monzui*. Shin Nihon koten bungaku taikei, 27. Tokyo: Iwanami Shoten, 1992.

SRS   *Seireishū*, in Watanabe Shōkō and Miyasaka Yūshō, annot., *Sangō shiki, Seireishū*. Nihon koten bungaku taikei, 71. Tokyo: Iwanami Shoten, 1965.

INTRODUCTION

INTRODUCTION

Chinese graphs probably first came to the attention of the Japanese elite around the start of the Common Era, when artifacts etched with Chinese characters began to appear on the Japanese archipelago. In the early centuries of the first millennium A.D., Chinese coins, official seals, and somewhat later, from around the fourth century, swords and ceremonial bronze mirrors forged on the continent found their way to Japan. The mirrors were given as gifts or souvenirs to Japanese who visited China, and before long, these were being crafted in Japan as well. The Japanese swords and mirrors were richly engraved with Chinese graphs. The inscriptions were often written in hybrid Chinese styles, sometimes with a Korean flavor, suggesting authorship by Korean immigrants, who were resident in Japan from around the fifth century and often served as scribes and Chinese language experts. Going further ahead in time, the Chinese inscriptions we encounter appear even more naturalized, bearing an increasing number of common Japanese words and place-names, not to mention fragmentary Japanese grammatical locutions and honorific expressions.[1] These artifacts, many of which have been excavated from burial tumuli in recent years, are important historical records, predating the first surviving paper records by centuries and attesting to the high prestige and growing use of Chinese in the official life of the developing Japanese state.

Having yet to devise a native writing system, Japanese court scribes began to study Chinese prose in earnest under Korean and Chinese tutelage, intent on adopting Chinese as the language of officialdom, scholarship, and the priesthood. By the late fifth century, some two centuries before a provisional system for writing Japanese was developed, scribes of the Yamato court, mainly well-educated men of Chinese and Korean origin, were beginning to exchange documents with China and use Chinese to compose

---

1. For a detailed description of these early stone and metal objects, called *kinseki*, and their various Chinese-style language forms, see Christopher Seeley, *A History of Writing in Japan* (Leiden, New York: E.J. Brill, 1991), pp. 16–39.

4

accounts, official dispatches, and other public records. Chinese had emerged as Japan's first written official language in what was truly a bilingual court described by Leo J. Loveday as a "diglossic bilingual setting," where spoken Chinese had been "seriously studied, under native Chinese teachers" for several centuries. This bilingualism, Loveday explains, prevailed at least until the tenth century, after which time those diglossic characteristics persisted to a greater or lesser degree, but without oral bilingualism, down until the mid-twentieth century.[2]

By the early seventh century, as the Tang dynasty (618–907) was becoming established in China, Japanese intellectuals were able to read and write Chinese with a fair degree of skill. By the end of that same century, they were composing *kanshi* with growing confidence, if not originality, and had begun to imitate the so-called modern-style regulated verse forms popular from the early Tang dynasty. The acquisition of books from China was an indispensable element in the learning of Chinese and gaining knowledge from the continent, but it is unclear when the first such texts arrived in Japan. Two early eighth-century histories written in Japan tell how in the late third century two Korean scribes, Achiki and Wani, were dispatched to Japan by the king of Paekche bearing Chinese books, but this dating is thought to be erroneous and should probably be moved forward to the early fifth century. Achiki and Wani may also have served as Chinese language tutors to the crown prince, although early accounts of their activities differ.[3] In any event, Japanese envoys who were sent to the Chinese court down through the ninth century customarily brought books back to the Japanese court, helping to build libraries of Chinese books containing thousands of volumes.

According to the ninth-century Japanese bibliography *Nihon koku genzai sho mokuroku* (Catalog of Books Found in Japan, ca. 890), a source not considered exhaustive in its listings, there were some 17,345 volumes (1,579 titles) catalogued in Japan at this time, not counting Buddhist works. Some believe that a similar quantity of material may already have been present in the Japanese court as early as Nara times (710–84), among them works such as the anthology *Wen xuan* (Selections of Refined Literature, compiled ca. 530), various histories, collections of famous anecdotes, poetics, lexicons, classified encyclopedias, guides to Chinese composition, and

2. Leo J. Loveday, *Language Contact in Japan: A Socio-linguistic History* (Oxford: Oxford University Press, 1996), pp. 31–32.
3. See Seeley, pp. 4–6, for a discussion of the historical passages dealing with these events. *Kojiki* (A Record of Ancient Matters, 712) indicates that Wani brought to the Japanese court such books as the *Thousand-Character Classic* and the *Analects of Confucius*, but as Seeley observes, the former work was not compiled until the end of the fifth century, casting doubt upon the reliability of this account. Not all scholars believe that these two scribes really existed See Seeley, p. 6, note 10.

manuals on rhyming.[4] Among the Chinese poets represented in the catalog are Bo Juyi, Yuan Zhen, Liu Yuxi, and Wang Wei, all from the Tang dynasty.[5] Remarkably, less than ten percent of the titles listed in this source are extant today.

It is not known when the Japanese first attempted to write Chinese poetry, but a conservative estimate would be the middle of the seventh century, around the time of Prince Ōtomo (Ōtomo no Miko, 648–72), generally regarded as Japan's earliest *kanshi* poet.[6] By Prince Ōtsu's day, the Japanese male elite had achieved a degree of skill in writing formal Chinese styles under the tutelage of Chinese and Korean teachers. Despite the pronounced dissimilarities between the Japanese and Chinese languages, the Japanese were determined to gain proficiency in Chinese, even before possessing the means to write their own language.

Why Chinese? By the end of the sixth century, when the sinification process was well underway in Japan, China was the most advanced civilization in the world, its intellectual, philosophical, and artistic traditions long and distinguished and its vast empire now united once more under the rule of a single all-powerful emperor. Thus, the Japanese aspired to emulate the Chinese experience in all areas of endeavor, from law and philosophy to belles lettres and the fine arts. Without the ability to read Chinese texts and to communicate with visiting Chinese scholars, tutors, scribes, priests, and state guests, there could be no rapid progress toward the established national goal of building a Chinese-style bureaucratic state possessing comparable material and intellectual strength. The Chinese language was also essential for diplomatic communications with Korea and the kingdom of Parhae (Ch. Bohai) in Manchuria as well. Furthermore, as Burton Watson notes, Japanese officials had to be able to compose an appropriate Chinese verse on command at diplomatic functions in order to earn the respect of their continental counterparts. One has to admire these early poets, Watson writes, "for their determination to transcend their insularity and participate to some degree in the larger sphere of Sinitic culture."[7]

Chinese poetics and versification were never totally separate from the theory and practice of native Japanese poetry, and we must be careful not to

---

4. Honma Yōichi, annot., *Nihon kanshi* (Osaka: Izumi Shoin, 1996), pp. 254–55.

5. See J. Thomas Rimer and Jonathan Chaves, trans., *Chinese Poems to Sing: The* Wakan rōei shū (New York: Columbia University Press, 1997), p. 16.

6. *Nihon shoki* (Chronicles of Japan, 720), book 30, records that the practice of composing Chinese verse in Japan "had its origin" with Prince Ōtsu (663–86), but it is clear from the literary record that Ōtsu was not the first Japanese *kanshi* poet. See William George Aston, trans., *Nihongi: Chronicles of Japan from the Earliest Times to A.D. 697* (Rutland, Vt. and Tokyo: Charles E. Tuttle Company, 1972; orig. pub. 1896), vol. 2, p. 383.

7. Burton Watson, trans., *Japanese Literature in Chinese: Poetry and Prose in Chinese by Japanese Writers of the Early Period*, vol. 1 of 2 (New York and London: Columbia University Press, 1975), pp. 4–6.

6

imagine large conceptual barriers and impervious boundaries between the two traditions, which did not in reality exist. As Thomas LaMarre points out, even the poetics of the *Kokinshū* collection, a product of the golden age of the Heian court, displays "a constant evocation of doubleness, ceaselessly conjoining 'Japanese' and 'Chinese' forms" and a tendency "to design styles and modes that especially recall those of the Six Dynasties, [the] Sui Dynasty, and the early T'ang." Moreover, he also reminds us that the "prestige of kana writing" more generally (both in the Heian court and beyond) "would derive not from its autonomy from mana [Chinese graphs] but from its proximity to mana."[8]

In a cultural milieu where the elite emulated Chinese literary forms for the sake of self-cultivation and the development of the nation, the study of the Chinese classics and the pursuit of *kanshi* composition soon gained an important place at the center of Japanese court life. The oldest surviving *kanshi* dates from the reign of Emperor Tenji (Tenchi, r. 668–71), a Sinophile who wrote *kanshi* himself and believed that literature could serve as an instrument for bringing order to the state and elevating its cultural level. The preface to *Kaifūsō* records that Emperor Tenji, who had established his court in present day Ōtsu (in old Ōmi province to the east of modern Kyoto), enjoyed sufficient leisure to entertain men of letters, holding great banquets at which Chinese poetry was composed, much of it unfortunately lost.[9] *Nihon shoki* (720), book 25, relates that Tenji's predecessor, Emperor Kōtoku (r. 645–54), also "loved men of learning" and that he dispatched an official envoy to the Tang court to obtain "numerous books and precious objects."[10] This interest stemmed from the belief that by studying the Chinese classics, scholar-officials would be able to develop critical understandings of a more sophisticated nature, these applicable not only to the immediate pursuit of the Chinese literary arts but to the development of Japanese social institutions, statecraft, and native literary endeavors as well.

Some have speculated that back in Tenji's time most of the best *kanshi* composed at court were likely written by scholars and scribes of Korean and Chinese descent.[11] Nevertheless, the first anthology of *kanshi* poetry, *Kaifūsō* (751), preserves a number of competent poems by ethnic Japanese from the same period, many of whom were probably educated in the newly established Daigakuryō (the court academy or university). In fact, of the sixty-four poets represented in *Kaifūsō* only about one-fifth appear to be of

8. Thomas LaMarre, *Uncovering Heian Japan: An Archaeology of Sensation and Inscription* (Durham and London: Duke University Press, 2000), pp. 14–15, 29–31.
9. See the translation of the preface in Ryusaku Tsunoda, Wm. Theodore de Bary, and Donald Keene, comps., *Sources of Japanese Tradition*, vol. 1 of 2 (New York and London: Columbia University Press, 1958), p. 89.
10. See Aston, *Nihongi*, vol. 2, pp. 195, 247.
11. Helen Craig McCullough, *Brocade by Night: 'Kokin Wakashū' and the Court Style in Japanese Classical Poetry* (Stanford: Stanford University Press, 1985), p. 87.

continental ancestry, and of these poets most were active in the early eighth century.

During Tenji's reign, there emerged a consciousness of *kanshi* as the preeminent public verse form, accompanied by a growing awareness of the nature and significance of literary language and poetic precedent. Although detailed historical information is lacking, it appears that this critical consciousness developed in a court circle or salon of some kind, utilizing knowledge acquired from studying the vast literature of China's Six Dynasties (222–589), Sui (589–618), and early Tang periods. The ornate and formal palace poetry of the sixth and seventh centuries was to become especially important in the Japanese court, profoundly influencing the styles of both *kanshi* and *waka*. Crown Prince Ōtomo, who later ruled as Emperor Kōbun (r. 671-72), as well as Princes Ōtsu and Nagaya (684–729), were at the forefront of *kanshi* writing in their respective times, all composing competently, and at times even commendably, in the courtly style of the late Six Dynasties.[12] For these literati steeped in Chinese tradition, albeit from afar, the language and literature of China had become central to their conception of themselves as writers and intellectuals. Indeed, as one reads the anthologized verse composed at the early Nara poetry gatherings held by Prince Nagaya and his circle of poets, one is struck by the seeming routineness of writing Chinese verse as a social art by this time. In order to receive the respect of his peers, a literatus had to pit his *kanshi* writing skills against those of the others present and to display confidently his familiarity with Chinese letters, all the while consuming generous amounts of wine.

These earliest literary compositions have for the most part been lost, apart from the small number—just over one hundred poems—that have come down to us in *Kaifūsō*. Despite the derivative and at times amateurish quality of the poems, the anthology nonetheless deserves our attention as the first collection of *kanshi*. Its very compilation suggests the rising status of the *kanshi* genre and the interest of certain mid-eighth century courtiers in preserving the earliest examples of the tradition. The number of surviving *kanshi* from between the seventh and twelfth centuries, a figure of around 3,500, is doubtless just a fraction of the original volume of verse produced during this period. "New" poems continue to come to light, as seen, for example, in the mid-twentieth century discovery of some 460 verses written on the back of an old manuscript of Fujiwara no Munetada's (1062-1141) courtier diary *Chūyūki*, a text provisionally named *Chūyūki*

---

12. On this early period and the influence of Six Dynasties and later poetic styles, we are indebted to Konishi Jin'ichi, *A History of Japanese Literature*, Volume One: *The Archaic and Ancient Ages*, trans. Aileen Gatten and Nicholas Teele (Princeton: Princeton University Press, 1984), and Konishi Jin'ichi, *A History of Japanese Literature*, Volume Two: *The Early Middle Ages*, trans. Aileen Gatten (Princeton: Princeton University Press, 1986).

8

burui shihai kanshishū (Collection of Poems Written on the Reverse of *Chūyūki*).

A significant proportion of *Kaifūsō*'s poems are formal, occasional pieces, many written at banquets and outings and celebrating the prosperity of the realm or extolling the emperor's virtue—standard fare in palace verse, much of which was written extemporaneously and on imperial command, as the following poem illustrates:

> Lying ill, my hair already white,
> Feeling as if about to leave the world,
> When to my surprise there came an imperial command
> To accompany His Majesty on a spring visit to the Park.
> From pine-treed cliffs gurgling falls descend;
> By bamboo banks new flowers come into bloom.
> I am just a simple rustic type,
> Undeservedly asked to ride in the attendants' carriage.

—"A Poem Written in Response to an Imperial Order to Accompany the Imperial Procession" (KFS 18), by Middle Counselor Ōmiwa no Asomi Takechimaro, Junior Third Rank

Kaifūsō poems like the above seem to display a budding creative confidence and a measure of lyricism. Donald Keene observes that "few poems described specifically Japanese scenes" and that "most of the *Kaifūsō* poems are hardly more than pastiches of familiar Chinese imagery."[13] However, some poems, even if owing a conspicuous debt to Chinese models, exhibit a modest charm and a pleasingly unpretentious spirit, transcending mere imitation and providing insights into the social milieu of the poets. While it is true that *Kaifūsō* poets rely heavily on Chinese images, themes, and allusions, it is perhaps too sweeping to assert categorically that the poems lack "convincing expressions of personal feeling" or that such expressions necessarily "adhere closely to Chinese models," as one scholar has stated.[14]

Under the enthusiastic patronage of Emperor Saga (786–842; r. 809–823) and his coterie, the study of Chinese poetry and the composition of *kanshi* in the court achieved a level of official support and prestige never again equaled in the history of Japanese court literature. Deeply immersed in Chinese studies and a poet in his own right, Saga believed that Chinese literature and learning were essential elements in the building of a Japanese state and indispensable tools for the adaptation of Chinese civilization to

13. Donald Keene, *Seeds in the Heart: Japanese Literature from the Earliest Times to the Late Sixteenth Century* (New York: Henry Holt and Co., 1993), p. 77.
14. McCullough, p. 93.

Japanese soil. Courtiers viewed versification as an essential social grace, an embellishment that beautified human relations and enhanced the dignity of formal public occasions. Chinese poetic forms could also effectively convey certain ideas and literary effects alien to, or at least uncommon in, the more narrowly circumscribed native tradition. Political matters, life among the peasantry, the miseries of poverty and illness, and even death itself are examples of *kanshi* topoi that would generally have been out of place in *waka* written during the Heian period, when the thematic range further narrowed.

Saga's ardent efforts to promote Chinese literary activity ushered in a golden half century of Japanese *kanshi* versification. During this period, the status of *waka* decreased and the composition of native verse became less common at formal events, although by no means vanishing entirely.[15] That one looks in vain for a first-rate *waka* talent of this period, someone who could have breathed new life into the native verse forms, suggests that the vogue for Chinese letters had so eclipsed the writing of *waka* that talented poets chose to put their best efforts into *kanshi* instead. This remarkable mania for *kanshi* led to the compilation of three imperially sponsored anthologies of Chinese verse between 814 and 827, the court determined to preserve for posterity the best verse of the age. Most of the poems contained in these anthologies are post–Nara works: of the 147 poets whose poems are preserved therein, only about a tenth were active before 780, suggesting that literary tastes had changed to the point where contemporary styles were preferred, or that the editors were largely interested in preserving the works of recent poets, themselves included in some cases. Overall, the artistic quality, variety, the volume of poems, and the sheer number of poets encountered in these anthologies represent a distinct advance over *Kaifūsō*, which appeared more than a half a century earlier. We note also a higher level of creativity in the use of words and phrases, which were either adapted from Chinese poetic sources or invented by the Japanese themselves.[16]

The *kanshi* of Saga and his fellow poets employ two recurrent settings: the imperial palace, with its adjoining gardens, and the Kayō (Kaya) Imperial Retreat on the Yodo River, where the emperor and his courtiers went to relax, drink wine, write verse, and enjoy such pursuits as flower-viewing, fishing, and bird-watching. It was in this refined imperial environment that the early Heian art of *kanshi* composition developed, culminating in the production of the three anthologies alluded to above, which collectively contain about 1,550 poems. These works are *Ryōun shinshū* (The New

15. Konishi, II, p. 59. See also pp. 59–66 for examples of *waka* written in this period.

16. A valuable study of Japanese diction and various sensory and other kinds of expressions seen in *kanshi* from Saga's time can be found in Sugano Hiroyuki, *Heian shoki ni okeru Nihon kanshi no hikaku bungakuteki kenkyū* (Tokyo: Taishūkan, 1988), pp. 182–262.

Cloud-Topping Collection, 814), *Bunka shūreishū* (Anthology of Splendid Literary Flowerings, 818), and *Keikokushū* (Collection of Verse for Bringing Order to the Realm, ca. 827). Although the first two of these anthologies have survived largely intact, *Keikokushū,* the largest of the three, suffered the loss of fourteen of its original twenty *maki* (chapters). Despite its grandiose title, suggesting a political or didactic intent (which is in fact rarely in evidence among the surviving poems), *Keikokushū* shows by far the broadest thematic and imaginative range.

In the poetry of these three anthologies and in subsequent Heian collections, we observe the continued imprint of the polished, aristocratic beauty of the poetry written during the late Six Dynasties and early Tang periods, with its genteel elegance, ornateness, and mannered style. We encounter elaborate metaphors, witty conceits, and elegant indirection of a sort that favors subtle shades of lyrical expression over impassioned declaration. The following spring banquet poem (HCRS 12), written by Fujiwara no Michinaga on the theme "fallen petals dancing above the water," well illustrates this almost overly refined court style:

> Petals fall as cool spring breezes blow across the pond;
> Dancing along, over the water, to the sound of warblers singing.
> Above the flow, charming as jeweled hairpins in disarray;
> Along the banks, looking as airy as sleeves of light silk gauze.
> Easily mistaken for powdered dancers as they whirl by the bay at dusk;
> Hard to tell from court musicians as they drift across the waves.
> Today we rejoice that the ways of old prevail here once again:
> His Majesty favors us with a visit, returning to the district of Pei.

One common literary device, present in the above verse, is "oblique" (*yipang*) reasoning, sometimes characterized by contrived deductive processes applied to natural principles and phenomena. Typically, the poet reaches "logical conclusions" on the basis of natural circumstances apparent to him, drawing inferences that are either self-evident or else display a studied naivete or contrived misapprehension. This may be seen in the above poem where the poet pretends to mistake petals for powdered dancers in the distance, probably just for the sake of being able to include this elegant image in the poem.

Nara and early to mid-Heian *kanshi* are often characterized by an impersonal tone, as is seen in RUS 81, "Going over Shinano Pass," by Sakanoue no Imiki Imatsugu. This poem shows a restraint often associated with Six Dynasties verse and a somewhat detached quality, considering the personal plight of the poet, lost as he is in the winter wilderness and unable to find his home:

Boulder on boulder, perilously steep;
Treacherous path, twisting, winding around.
I have lost my way in the snow in this far-off place.
My horse treads through low-hanging clouds.
The crags are cold—hard for flowers to bloom;
The valleys are deep—early it grows dark.
Where is my old home village to be found?
The traveler's mind grows ever more confused.

While the Six Dynasties court style persisted throughout the ninth century as the dominant mode in *kanshi*, its formalism and conceptual conventions were increasingly counterbalanced in Japan by the artistic pull of Bo Juyi (772–846) and, to a far lesser extent, other mid- and late-Tang poets. Such movement is seen, for example, in the emerging shades of personalism, experimentation with more mundane, even indecorous subject matter, plainer language, and a gradual deepening of the artistic imagination. However, far from trying to imitate a single poet's style or diction, the poets in Saga's circle eclectically adapted for their own use "patchworks of phrases and conceptions borrowed from Chinese sources of all periods,"[17] using whatever captured their fancy and served their artistic purposes. Even in the poetry of Sugawara no Michizane (845–903), where the linguistic and expressive influence of Bo Juyi is especially marked, Michizane asserts his own style, personal character, and sense of his native surroundings, limiting himself to what is a most selective and somewhat idiosyncratic adaptation from Bo Juyi's poetic works. Konishi Jin'ichi observes that "whenever scholars of Japanese literature have happened upon Chinese shih diction analogous to that in Japanese shih, they have tended to label the Japanese shih diction a borrowing or transposition from the Chinese. Yet it is only in exceptional instances that a given expression can be shown to have been based on specific diction."[18] These observations hold true not only for ninth century *kanshi* but also for many of those written in subsequent centuries.

A significant proportion of *kanshi* from the early Heian period are formal and public in character, their topoi mostly tasteful, characteristics that were carried forward into the poetry of subsequent centuries. Court *kanshi* tend to favor such themes as enjoying nature and the four seasons, where, as in the Chinese tradition, nature "is what it is by virtue of itself," to use James Liu's words, representing an absolute value unconnected to a theological belief in a creator and being neither adversarial nor benign.[19] As Liu observes, "[T]he Chinese mind seems content to accept Nature as a fact,

17. McCullough, p. 170.
18. Konishi, II, p. 12.
19. James J.Y. Liu, *The Art of Chinese Poetry* (Chicago: The University of Chicago Press, 1966, Phoenix Ed.; orig. pub. 1962), p. 49.

without searching for a *primum mobile*," seeing itself as co-existing with nature and being a part of its endless cycles of birth, flourishing, and decay.[20]

Second in importance to poetry describing nature is occasional verse, typically written at formal events such as imperial banquets and during court excursions to famous scenic spots. Wine-drinking and flower-viewing are typical topoi in such verse. As in Tang poetry, friendship and separation are also recurrent poetic concerns. Following Six Dynasties palace poetic models, the treatment of romantic love in *kanshi* tends to be conventionalized and impersonal, and poems of this sort are less frequent than in the Chinese poetic tradition.[21] Other themes and subjects include grieving for the dead, the sufferings of loneliness, the nostalgia of the traveler, and the evanescence of life, important concerns in Chinese verse as well. The theme of homesickness occurs plentifully throughout the poetry of China, poets always retaining a deep sense of attachment to the provincial family home, even if they spent most of their lives elsewhere. Such sentiments also color the poetry of Japanese exiles and travelers, although for most of the poet-courtiers of the Nara and Heian periods, who belonged to a hereditary elite, home was generally the capital or the surrounding area. However, the Japanese courtier when serving in the capital is often seen to write longingly of the bucolic charms of a leisured life in rural seclusion, where the mind is free of mundane concerns and at one with nature, a theme which owes much to the Chinese eremitic tradition.

A further major *kanshi* subgenre with Chinese origins is historical musings, including "poems recalling antiquity" (*huaigu shi*) and "poems on history" (*yongshi shi*), in which the moral examples set by rulers and ancient worthies are glorified or an important historical event is recalled, often for the sake of comparison with a particular situation in the poet's own life or in contemporary society. The Japanese poet sometimes employs such historical allusions to suggest that he cannot possibly live up to the examples set by the Chinese ancients, in what are largely *pro forma* expressions of modesty. It is a telling commentary on the strength of the influence of Chinese culture upon the Japanese at this time that historical poems almost invariably draw upon the exemplary traditions of Chinese rulers, worthies, and military heroes rather than those of their Japanese counterparts.

The range of topoi seen in *kanshi* may seem somewhat limited in scope but evidently provided sufficient diversity to satisfy the creative whims of Japanese *kanshi* poets for centuries to come. Although *kanshi* permit the treatment of certain subjects that were out of bounds in the Heian *waka* tradition, others such as war, political affairs, sex, and natural calamities are

---

20. Ibid.
21. Ibid., pp. 57–58, for a discussion of the importance of love as a theme in Chinese poetry.

uncommon even in *kanshi*. We have translated two exceptional poems by Shimada no Tadaomi (828–92?) from his private anthology *Denshi kashū* (The Shimada Poetry Collection) that refer to prohibition laws and measures for economic retrenchment, but these are atypical among Heian *kanshi*. Works by literati (*bunjin*) and courtier-officials are the norm in court *kanshi*, although one finds a sprinkling of poems by Buddhist priests, old recluses, and, in rare instances, foreigners, Buddhist nuns, and women of the court. We have discovered only five *kanshi* poetesses in our extensive reading of Nara and Heian *kanshi*: Empress Kōken (r. 749–58), Emperor Saga's daughter Princess Uchiko (Uchiko Naishinnō or Uchishi, 804–47), Ōtomo Uji no Hime (also known as Hime Ōtomo Uji, fl. ca. 810–24), Nun Yamato (?–?), and a little-known lady-in-waiting in Saga's court named Kore (no) Uji no Onna (or Korenaga [no] Uji no Onna, ?–?). There are also a fair number of poems by obscure minor provincial poet-officials, whose names alone are known to us.

The nature and variety of poetic forms in *Kaifūsō* and subsequent collections is a complicated issue that requires some explanation. The prosodic structures of *kanshi*, not to mention the poetic language, imagery, topoi, and even the occasions for composition, generally followed Chinese conventions, no new poetic genres appearing in Japan. Most of the poems in the present volume are cast in various subgenres of the Chinese *shi*, a genre that in traditional Chinese society played a complex, multi-purpose role with both aesthetic and social dimensions. As Stephen Owen explains, it was never a "'pure art' in the western sense" but instead "was bound both to occasion and to concepts of poetry as the expression of inner nature or as a vehicle for the enduring principles of the civilization."[22] However, during the seventh and eighth centuries, as the Tang dynasty unfolded, "poetry was transformed," in Owen's words, "from a minor diversion to an art that fully embodied these private, social, and cultural values."[23] This appreciation of the value of *shi* poetry not only as a social phenomenon—a functional tool of social interaction and the transmission of cultural values—but also as a refined art form was fully embraced by Japanese literati.

Shi mainly denotes occasional lyrical poetry, typically in five- or seven- character lines and featuring end rhyme in alternate lines. This genre dates back in China to at least the ninth century B.C. and constitutes one of five Chinese poetic forms.[24] *Shi* includes (1) *siyan shi* ("verse with four

---

22. Stephen Owen, *The Great Age of Chinese Poetry: The High T'ang* (New Haven and London: Yale University Press, 1981), p. 3.
23. Ibid.
24. The other four are the *sao* (elegiac verse, ca. 400 B.C.–200 B.C.), *fu* (the rhapsody or prose-poem, flourishing ca. 150 B.C. to A.D. 600), *ci* (lyrical songs in mixed meter, fl. ca. 850–1300), and *sanqu* (the dramatic lyric), popular during the Yuan dynasty (1280–1368). See Kang-i Sun Chang, *The Evolution of Chinese Tz'u Poetry from Late Tang to Northern Sung* (Princeton: Princeton University Press, 1980), pp. 210–12.

14

words per line"), associated with the *Book of Songs* (*Shi jing*); (2) *yuefu* (J. *gafu*, "ballads"), a variety of poetry typically possessing a folk or pseudo-folk quality, which appeared in China during the second century B.C. and flourished until the late sixth century; (3) *gushi* (J. *koshi* or *kotai-shi*, "old-style poetry"), which was popular in China ca. A.D. 200–900 and accounts for the vast majority of poems in *Kaifūsō*; and (4) *jinti shi* (J. *kindaishi*, "modern-style verse"), which arose in the sixth century and came to maturity in the Tang.[25] The latter two varieties, described more fully below, were especially favored by the Japanese, most of the poems of the *kanshi* tradition falling into these genres.

"Old-style poetry" only came to be known as such after the introduction of "modern" regulated verse in the early Tang period, and "old-style" verse in fact continued to be written throughout the Tang. As Sugano points out, this old style, which includes the *zayan* (*zatsugon*, see below), *ge* (*uta*), *yin* (*gin*), *yin* (*in*), and various other quasi-*yuefu* type poems, was especially conducive to the composition of forthright, personal poems rich in lyricism and sentiment, because it was relatively unfettered by complex prosodic rules.[26] In *koshi*, the number and length of lines are not prescribed, and rules related to tonal prosody were only occasionally followed. Normally, the even-numbered lines rhymed, and poets could employ more than one rhyme sound in the verse. Five- or seven-character lines were the norm.

One common subgenre of *koshi* was the aforementioned *zatsugon* (also known as *zasshi* or *zattai*), a wide-ranging category of poems in various (*zatsu* "miscellaneous") styles and in non-regulated verse form. Some *zatsugon* are described as being "mixed-meter shih,"[27] but they are certainly not always written in mixed meter, that is, with lines of varying length. The *zatsugon* made its first appearance in the three early ninth-century court anthologies, where examples account for about 14 percent of the total corpus of poems.[28] Thereafter, this subgenre was to remain a popular novelty throughout the history of *kanshi* composition in Japan. Although poets writing *zatsugon* with irregular lineation had to pay close attention to end-rhyme variation and the felicitous arrangement of lines of varying length in the poem, they were not burdened by the complicated tonal prosody rules inherent in the "modern" verse forms—in other words, they coped with "a set of problems different from those found in verse of more set forms," as Konishi notes.[29]

25. See ibid., where a summary of the characteristics of the five major genres of traditional Chinese poetry may be found.
26. Sugano, pp. 107–8, 115–16.
27. Following Konishi's terminology, II, p. 7.
28. Kawaguchi Hisao, *Heian-chō Nihon kanbungakushi no kenkyū*, vol. 1 (*jō*) (Tokyo: Meiji Shoin, 1975, rev. exp. 3rd ed; orig. pub. 1959), p. 23.
29. Konishi, II, p. 8.

Jinti shi comprised three distinct subgenres: *lüshi* (J. *risshi*, "regulated verse"), *jueju* (J. *zekku*, "broken-off lines"), and *pailü* (J. *hairitsu*, "extended regulated verse"), which collectively came to constitute the mainstream of *kanshi* composition from the ninth century on. Japanese anthologies, beginning with *Ryōunshū*, show a clear preference for the *lüshi*, these being octaves with five or seven character lines, the longer line length being the preferred model. The *jueju*, or quatrain, was the shortest variety of "modern-style" verse and consisted of four lines of uniform length, either in five or seven characters. This form was less common than the octave in Heian *kanshi*.

The longest and least common variety among the "modern" verse types is the *pailü*, which consisted of an unrestricted number of couplets. As their skill and confidence increased, Japanese poets such as Priest Kūkai (774–835) began to experiment with writing longer *pailü*, some of their compositions running to a hundred lines or more. However, the longer the poem, the greater the likelihood of tonal error (from the standpoint of orthodox Chinese prosody). At the same time, in longer poems in particular, *kanshi* poets tend to lapse into peculiar Japanese idiosyncrasies—syntactical features and expressions found only in the Chinese written in Japan.[30] We have provisionally identified as *pailü* most of the Heian *kanshi* longer than eight lines, recognizing that these do not necessarily adhere to all of the tonal prosody rules for regulated verse. Without careful reconstruction of the tonal patterns in these poems, it is difficult to determine whether any given Heian long poem is truly a *pailü* or simply an extended *gushi*. This may be why modern editions do not always identify the specific genre of these longer poems.

Chinese scholars codified the rules of *lüshi* during the seventh century, with the prosodic conventions centering upon a fixed scheme in which rhyming characters were always in the level tone, and the same rhyme sound was maintained throughout the verse. In the pentasyllabic varieties of regulated verse, the poet was expected to implement end-rhyme in the even-numbered lines; but in the longer heptasyllabic compositions, the first line could also be included in the rhyme scheme. Incorporated in specific positions throughout the octave were certain fixed patterns of alternating (that is, level vs. deflected) tone sequences, with verbal parallelism employed in the middle two couplets so as to produce, ideally, antithetical couplets. Overall, the effect of these patterns of variation was one of euphonic, rhythmic contrast and repetition of tones, not only within a single line but also between key correlated words in a couplet, as seen in the diagram on the following page, which depicts tonal variations typically found in regulated verse.

---

30. On the matter of Japanese linguistic idiosyncrasies, see Kojima Noriyuki, comp. and annot., *Ōchō kanshisen*, Iwanami Bunko 30-036-1 (Tokyo: Iwanami Shoten, 1987), pp. 467–68.

A DIAGRAM OF TONAL PATTERNS
IN REGULATED VERSE

THE PENTASYLLABIC REGULATED OCTAVE

Note: "–"denotes level tone, "+," deflected tone, a comma represents a pause, and "*," rhyme.[31]

(A type)
– –, – + + (or, – –, + + – *)
+ +, + – – *
+ +, – – +
– –, + + – *
– –, – + +
+ +, + – – *
+ +, – – +
– –, + + – *

(B type)
+ +, – – + (or, + +, + – – *)
– –, + + – *
– –, – + +
+ +, + – – *
+ +, – – +
– –, + + – *
– –, – + +
+ +, + – – *

THE HEPTASYLLABIC REGULATED OCTAVE

(A type)
– –, + +, + – – * (or, – –, + +, – – +, without rhyme)
+ +, – –, + + – *
+ +, – –, – + +
– –, + +, + – – *
– –, + +, – – +
+ +, – –, + + – *
+ +, – –, – + +
– –, + +, + – – *

(B type)
+ +, – –, + + – * (or, + +, – –, – + +, without rhyme)
– –, + +, + – – *
– –, + +, – – +
+ +, – –, + + – *
+ +, – –, – + +
– –, + +, + – – *
– –, + +, – – +
+ +, – –, + + – *

31. These diagrams, with some notational differences, are based on Liu, pp. 26–27.

The composition of *jueju* was subject to rules of tonal parallelism similar to those seen in *lüshi* but with some softening of the requirements for verbal parallelism. Although in effect only half of a *lüshi*, the *jueju* was considered artistically complete in itself, capable of carrying the "matter and weight" of an octave twice its length, as James R. Hightower explains, this by virtue of its power of "conciseness and concentration," which relied heavily on the use of connotation and allusion.[32] In the five-character line type, end rhyme, which was always implemented using the same tonal category, was found in the even lines; but in the seven-character type, the first line could also carry a rhyme-word, even one with a deflected tone. A six-character variety also existed but is rarely seen. The *pailü* is similar to the *lüshi* in its tonal requirements and is characterized by the use of strict parallelism in all but the opening and final couplets. Its principal feature is that it had no specified length but needed to be at least ten lines long. Japanese examples down through history usually confine themselves to a rather short twelve lines. In the *pailü*, five- and, less often, seven-character lines are the norm. There was one additional freedom: poets could alter the original rhyme-word, thereby minimizing monotony.

Scholars disagree concerning the extent to which poets adhered to the prosodic requirements of regulated verse in the Heian *kanshi* anthologies. Kojima's research indicates that although there are about seventy *Ryōunshū* poems possessing modern-style features, only about one in seven of them is truly compliant—amounting to perhaps a dozen.[33] Sugano's findings are generally consistent with those of Kojima, concluding that the regulated verse of "the majority" of ninth-century poets fell short in the correctness of its tonal prosody, because the poets were not sufficiently skilled in the deployment of Chinese tones.[34] The data of Kojima and Sugano conflict with those of Inoguchi Atsushi, who, at least with respect to *Ryōunshū*, writes that its poems "adhere strictly to the rules of *kindaishi* verse."[35] Konishi similarly asserts that "nearly all" of the poems in *Ryōunshū* and the other two early ninth-century anthologies "either preserve the tonal patterns of the 'modern' form or endeavor to do so," with "only a few egregious violations."[36]

---

32. See James R. Hightower, *Topics in Chinese Literature: Outlines and Bibliographies*, Harvard-Yenching Institute Studies, vol. 3 (Cambridge: Harvard University Press, 1966), p. 69.
33. Kojima Noriyuki, annot., *Kokufū ankoku jidai no bungaku: Kōnin-, Tenchō-ki no bungaku o chūshin to shite (hohen* exp. ed.), vol. 2 (bk. 2) of 9 vols. incl. one vol. suppl. (Tokyo: Hanawa Shobō, 1968–2002), p. 1292.
34. Sugano, pp. 103–4.
35. Inoguchi Atsushi, *Nihon kanbungaku shi* (Tokyo: Kadokawa Shoten, 1984), p. 111.
36. Konishi, II, p. 8. On the same page Konishi appears to contradict himself. In an apparent reference to the poetry of the early ninth century he says, "The Japanese poetic circles of this time were not yet ready to concern themselves with the tonal patterns of T'ang shih."

As these divergent views suggest, scholars appear to have different standards concerning what constitutes "compliance" or "attempted compliance" with the rhyming conventions and tonal rules of regulated verse. One scholar's assessment that a given collection shows "few egregious violations" might be countered by an opposing view that even a few errors are too many and that compliance has not been achieved. A further complexity is that even in China the master poets themselves did not always fully adhere to the prosodic requirements, no doubt causing some Japanese critics to be reluctant to hold native poets to the most rigorous standards.

The period after the three major early Heian anthologies is only slightly less murky on the question of compliance with tonal prosody conventions. The few Japanese scholars who have grappled with the problem of prosodic adherence generally do not explain their methodologies and standards for evaluation, often rendering impressionistic judgments that consist mostly of generalities rather than comprehensive and systematic data. Moreover, their writings do not indicate which rhyme and tonal reference sources they took to be the principal texts consulted by Heian *kanshi* poets.[37] The present authors have already begun to compile data on the works of several leading Heian poets. However, a systematic survey would be a large-scale undertaking, requiring analysis not only of rhyme words but also the tone (often governed by considerations of usage and syntax) of every character in every poem in the sample and is thus beyond the scope of the present study.

One of the more detailed investigations into Heian tonal prosody has been conducted by Kinpara Tadashi in *Heian-chō kanshibun no kenkyū*. He cites the findings of Matsura Tomohisa, which indicate that regulated verse contained in such anthologies as *Fusōshū*, *Honchō reisō*, *Denshi kashū*, *Kanke bunsō*, *Kanke kōshū*, and *Honchō mudaishi* show an almost flawless adherence to the Tang rules of tonal prosody, allowing for occasional textual variations.[38] In his own investigation, however, Kinpara concludes that it would be wrong to assert, as Matsura does, that tonally "non-compliant" (*hakaku*) *kindaishi* are almost non-existent in *Fusōshū* and later collections, as well as in individual collections such as *Denshi kashū*, the ninth-century

---

37. Although little information exists regarding the use of rhyme manuals (of both Chinese and Japanese origin) in the Heian court, one may speculate that most poets probably utilized tonal-category identifications based directly or indirectly upon the *Qieyun* (J. *Setsuin*, compiled 601), an early Chinese rhyme-category manual. This work in turn was the model for later influential manuals such as *Guangyun* (J. *Kōin*), compiled in 1008. These rhyme-category handbooks and writing guides of various sorts supplied suitable rhyme characters for each of the traditionally designated rhyme categories and were probably consulted alongside such Japanese composition manuals as *Sakumon daitai* (Basics of Composition, comp. by Fujiwara no Munetada [1062–1141] and others).

38. Kinpara Tadashi, *Heian-chō kanshibun no kenkyū* (Fukuoka: Kyūshū Daigaku Shuppansha, 1981), p. 385.

anthology of Shimada no Tadaomi's verse.[39] However, he grants that the works of Tadaomi and Michizane show a generally high level of compliance. On the other hand, the poetry of Ōe no Masahira, who was active about a century later, shows a far higher frequency of tonal prosodic errors, with content and expression taking precedence over matters of tonal prosody.[40] Three of the more common errors seen in the regulated octaves of Tadaomi, Michizane, and Masahira involve the use of the same tone category (*inmoku*) in the second and fourth positions in a line, the use of a different tone category in the second and sixth positions, and the sandwiching of a single level-tone word between two deflected tones, the so-called "single-level" (*kohei*) fault.[41] Tang and Song poets considered the latter error so egregious that it is seldom seen in works of that period.[42]

One factor contributing to the commission of errors in rhyme and tonal prosody in *kanshi* composition was the Japanese practice of decoding Chinese poetry (whether *kanshi* or *shi*) using a special sort of Japanese literary translation technique, instead of following Chinese word order and readings. This technique, called *kundoku* (reading by Japanese semantic gloss), dates at least as far back as the time of Priest Kūkai[43] and grew more and more prevalent as the Heian period progressed, becoming the norm. The resulting verse, while providing the literal meaning of the poem in translationese, possessed none of the aural qualities of Chinese poetry, namely, rhyme, tonal alternation, and linear uniformity, which the original poet had labored to achieve in the first place. In other words, the poem, once recited using the *kundoku* method, bore little aural (or structural) resemblance to the verse as written. The poet's expectation that his poem would likely be read using *kundoku* may well have served as a disincentive to take pains over the implementation of rhyme and the correct placement of Chinese level and oblique tones. Kinpara suggests that because of the use of *kundoku*, tonal prosody considerations must have been seen as an abstract and contrived set of constraints, one that could not possibly be observed by all Japanese poets at all times.[44] In this connection, however, Burton Watson reminds us that Chinese poets themselves often violated the "modern" rules to some extent,[45] making for a standard of comparison that was itself not perfect.

In summary, it is difficult make to an accurate assessment regarding the overall level of conformity to the rules of tonal prosody in regulated verse during the Nara and Heian periods. Individual *kanshi* poets show varying

39. Ibid., p. 386.
40. Ibid., pp. 370–81.
41. Ibid., p. 379.
42. Ibid., pp. 379–80.
43. Ibid., p. 387, note 1.
44. Ibid., p. 354.
45. Burton Watson, *Chinese Lyricism: Shih Poetry from the Second to the Twelfth Century* (New York and London: Columbia University Press, 1971), p. 111.

degrees of compliance within their own corpora, and thus a large sample comprising hundreds of Nara and Heian *kanshi* by numerous poets would need to be analyzed in order to yield statistically valid findings. Such a study would require uniform standards of assessment, these utilizing as criteria specific rules of regulated verse. Rhyme and tonal categories should not be the only points for attention; it would also be instructive to assemble data on levels of compliance with other *jinti shi* requirements, including those related to parallelism and word repetition.

The gross structure and thematic layout of Japanese regulated verse is somewhat easier to discern. In Heian *kanshi* the structure of the *lüshi* (regulated octave) presents the following scheme: typically, the poem begins with a presentation of the topic in the first couplet, and if the poem is a *kudai*-type verse, which borrows a line from a Chinese poem as the title or "topic" of the poem, that line will be at least partially incorporated into the first couplet. There often follows in the second couplet an expatiation on the content of the first, a restatement of sorts. In the third couplet, we typically find an allusive or metaphorical elaboration of the theme. The second and third couplets are ideally parallel in their internal construction. The final couplet usually provides a personal reflection or conclusion: either the poet's reaction to what he has witnessed or a moment of discovery, elation, or regret. Some *kanshi* poets became so focused upon the technical dictates of parallelism that constructing parallel couplets as artfully as possible became almost an end in itself, detracting from the overall literary appeal of the verse. At its best, however, parallelism works to bind the poem together, lending a certain structural unity and aesthetic richness. Indeed, it is often in the parallel couplets that the poet seems to place his most lyrical sentiments.

Considering the inherent difficulties of composing in verse forms so fettered by prosodic rules and other conventions, and the fact that the poets were writing in what was essentially for them a foreign language, it is remarkable how quickly poets of a truly high caliber emerged in Japan. The first individual who comes to mind is Priest Kūkai (774–835), who spent several years studying Buddhism in China and was one of the true pillars of Chinese literary studies in this important formative age. Kūkai is best known today as the founder of the Shingon sect of Buddhism, but he was also a first-rate *kanshi* poet and scholar of Chinese poetic theory. Kūkai's collection of largely Buddhist Chinese poetry and prose, *Seireishū* (The Spirit and Mind Collection, compiled ca. 827–35), remains a classic in the Chinese literary tradition of the Heian court and bears testimony to his belief in the high value of Chinese letters in imparting Buddhist doctrine.

In the years following Kūkai and Emperor Saga, the period roughly corresponding to the Jōwa era (834–48), Japanese poets took a great interest in the works of two highly-acclaimed Middle Tang poets, Bo Juyi and Yuan Zhen (779–831). A collection of poetry by Bo and Yuan is thought to have found its way to Japan before the middle of the ninth century, probably sometime between 824 and 838; the oral transmission of Bo's poetry might have taken place somewhat earlier still.[46] Further volumes of Bo's poetry also reached Japan, among them, *Boshi wenji* (*Hakushi monjū*, The Collected Works of Master Bo, compiled 845), a massive self-edited compilation of Bo's works. By contrast, the works of the illustrious High Tang poets Li Bo (701–62) and Du Fu (712–70), and the Middle Tang poet Han Yu (768–824) received scant attention in Japan until the early Edo period.[47] Bo's vivid, colloquial idiom, his accessible diction, his honest emotional tone, and professed social concerns were enthusiastically embraced and emulated by Japanese literati with apparently little of the ambivalence, even contempt, evinced by some Chinese scholars towards his writing. As Jonathan Chaves writes, Bo's diction was typically seen as being "too easy, or vulgar, inadequately subtle or allusive to be considered refined."[48] In any event, his style gradually came to have a major impact upon the *kanshi* written in Japan. Whereas Kojima sees the literary influence of Bo Juyi as being almost immediate and at times striking, evident, for example, in the poetry of Ono no Takamura (802–852) written during the period 834–848, Konishi believes that it took about forty years for Japanese *kanshi* poets to begin to compose poetry discernably colored by Bo's style.[49] However one chooses to date the onset of a palpable Bo influence upon the composition of *kanshi*, it is undeniable that the introduction into Japan of Bo Juyi's poetry was a watershed in Japanese literary history, one that affected *kanshi* tastes, themes, diction, and style for centuries, while shaping the artistry of *waka* as well.

It is difficult to summarize the essential literary contribution, let alone define the style, of a poet as versatile as Bo. Perhaps his most notable

46. Accounts differ concerning the exact titles and nature of the works first imported as well as the person or persons responsible for their introduction into Japan. See Konishi, II, pp. 150–51, and Rajyashree Pandey, *Writing and Renunciation in Medieval Japan: The Works of Poet-Priest Kamo no Chōmei*, Michigan Monograph Series in Japanese Studies, 21 (Ann Arbor: The University of Michigan Press, 1998), p. 14.

47. See Konishi, II, pp. 150–55 for a discussion of the curious special popularity of Bo and the relative lack of awareness in Japan of High Tang masters such as Du Fu. In this regard, Chaves, in *Japanese and Chinese Poems to Sing*, p. 17, points out that the first "comprehensive, well-edited collection" of Du Fu's poetry did not even appear in China until 1039.

48. Rimer and Chaves, p. 19.

49. See Kojima, *Ōchō kanshisen*, pp. 462–63, and Konishi, II, pp. 150–51. When we speak of the "Bo style" in the context of Japanese *kanshi*, a caveat is in order, because few Japanese poets (Konishi later goes so far as to say *no* ninth-century poets except Michizane—see Konishi, II, p. 167) who were "influenced" by Bo had a thorough understanding of his range and complexity. Most poets narrowly conceived this style as residing merely in simplicity and plainness of diction. Even among modern Japanese scholars there is a marked difference of opinion as regards what constitutes "noticeable" Bo influence: is it enough for the diction of a given poem to show a debt to Bo, or must the style and subject matter of the poem also display his imprint?

achievement in China was to bring poetry to the populace at large, making it comprehensible to persons from all social backgrounds, including the illiterate.[50] This was accomplished by clarifying and simplifying diction, incorporating humbler, more ordinary vocabulary into the basic literary language of *shi*, and by striving to achieve realistic and genuine portrayals of human affairs, their seamier side included. Bo did not shrink from writing satirical poems that pointed to social inequities and political abuses, in a style that, while didactic, seemed fresh and heartfelt. Although seldom emulated by later Japanese poets, Bo's *fengyu* (satirical and didactic admonitions) were the works which he most hoped would be remembered, being written, he asserted in a letter dated 815 to his friend and fellow poet Yuan Zhen, "for the purpose of saving the world."[51]

Religio-spiritual aspirations, especially the achievement of peace of mind through reclusion, are further themes encountered in Bo's works: Japanese courtiers often saw the pursuit of a Buddhist lifestyle, detached from the pressures and temptations of the mundane world, as the path to emotional well-being. It was this yearning for spiritual liberation in quiet seclusion, expressed in language both simple and direct, that so engaged the imagination of Japanese literati in the Heian period, especially during the eleventh and twelfth centuries. We need to remember that the life of a scholar-official was not necessarily one of ease and comfort. The scholar always depended heavily upon the continued favor of his political superiors in order to have a successful career in the bureaucracy and thus lacked real professional security. Accordingly, as the Heian period advances, we find a growing incidence of poets lamenting their failure to win prestigious posts and expressing the desire to abandon the quest for glory and wealth.

From the mid-ninth to the early tenth centuries, vibrant and prolific *kanshi* activity both within and without the court continued unabated, with such poets as Miyako no Yoshika (834–79), Shimada no Tadaomi, Sugawara no Michizane, and Ki no Haseo (845–912) becoming particularly prominent. It was during this time that the Heian *kanshi* reached its creative zenith. These four poets were all devotees of Bo Juyi—Michizane was especially in his debt—yet each achieved a distinctive personalism and voice in his verse.

Michizane's contributions to the development of the Heian *kanshi* are particularly significant. Although he continued to write a fair proportion of his verse in the elegant older styles already discussed, he, more than any of his peers, can be credited with propagating the contemporary Bo-inspired style, while managing to express his own poetic personality and give new

50. Wu-chi Liu and Irving Yucheng Lo, eds., *Sunflower Splendor: Three Thousand Years of Chinese Poetry* (Bloomington and Indianapolis: Indiana University Press, 1975), p. 568.
51. Ibid., p. 568. According to Pandey, p. 15, among the Japanese, "there was no interest at all in Po's (*sic*) political poetry."

meaning to certain words and phrases borrowed from Bo. Michizane was already a *kanshi* poet of the first order when he was exiled and sent to live in Dazaifu, in 901. No longer able to attend the formal court banquets and poetry competitions to which he had been accustomed, he managed to find during this period, as in an earlier period as governor of distant Sanuki, many new sources of poetic inspiration. Indeed, the bitter experience of living in these remote places during his final years lifted Michizane to unparalleled lyrical heights in his *kanshi*, which were forever to stand as a yardstick by which later verse is measured. His approximately 700 surviving compositions have earned him literary immortality. They also illuminate many aspects of the world he inhabited—provincial and court life, literary aesthetics and religion, social relationships, and political affairs— with a level of detail and sharpness of personal insight unmatched in the literature of this age.

Other private collections of works in Chinese from this period include Miyako no Yoshika's poetic corpus, *Toshi bunshū* (The Miyako Literary Collection, ca. 879), of which only three *maki* survive, and *Denshi kashū*, an anthology of poems by Shimada no Tadaomi, which is among the best yet most underappreciated of *kanshi* collections. Tadaomi's down-to-earth language, the novelty of many of his themes, and the endearing, if at times quirky, personality that emerges in clear relief above his words lend this collection a special flavor and distinctiveness. A collection of works by Ki no Haseo, titled *Kikeshū* (The Ki Collection, compiled early tenth century), has been lost except for a single *maki* of prose.

The tenth century was an age of continued confidence where *kanshi* composition was concerned. An anthology representative of this period's finest works and yet even remoter than *Denshi kashū* in the collective consciousness of Japanese literary historians is *Fusōshū*, whose title means "Anthology of Poetry from Our Land." This collection, completed around 996 and presented to Emperor Ichijō, includes in its present form *kanshi* from as far back as the 930s. Originally, it contained works by some seventy-six leading poets spanning more than a century, but only two *maki* survive today, with a total of 104 poems. Although a crowning achievement in terms of the technical quality and lyrical depth seen in many of its poems, *Fusōshū* has received little scholarly attention, perhaps because of textual corruption suffered early on and the loss of much of the original material. The surviving poems have never been properly annotated, and formidable textual problems remain. Intensely private at times and often too obscure to be fully comprehensible, the poetry of *Fusōshū* offers considerable lyrical interest, while posing substantial challenges to anyone prepared to brave its daunting text.

As Japan entered the glorious age of Michinaga, Sei Shōnagon, and Lady Murasaki, *kanshi* composition maintained its popularity undiminished in the upper echelons of society. Nonetheless, the freshness and innovation present in earlier works is now harder to find, although the urge to employ simpler diction and plainer vocabulary is still detectable in many poems of this age. Watson observes that the revolutionary influence of Bo Juyi "on the whole displaced earlier models and styles" in the Japanese court.[52] However, the *kanshi* from this period characteristically displays an uneven and eclectic synthesis of styles, one combining the intimacy and plainness of poets like Bo and the mannered ornateness of late Six Dynasties court poetry. One example of this synthesis is seen in Tachibana no Tameyoshi's poem "From All Around Pleasant Breezes Arise" (HCRS 48), where the poet writes of wind drying the "trickles of sweat" flowing in his sleeves, this earthy image following a somewhat refined depiction of the pleasures of enjoying the cool in a pondside pavilion. Overall, however, the synthesis was one which on balance favored the elegant aestheticism of the Six Dynasties palace style, and graceful, decorous poetry constituted the mainstream of Heian *kanshi* down through the eleventh century.

Eleventh-century *kanshi* are typified by an almost flowery prettiness—a lustrous surface beauty—evident in both diction and theme, and, in the better poems, an overall sensory appeal not unlike the *waka* from the same age. At their worst—and it is not hard to find mediocre examples—the *kanshi* lack freshness and seem cloyingly overripe, lapsing sometimes into simplistic diction and failing to rise above conceptual triteness. As Konishi observes, the Japanese *kanshi* poet in the tenth and eleventh centuries "found it greatly moving to discern a minute quality of freshness within repetitions of similar expression."[53] That is to say, most poets were content to remain largely within the thematic and technical confines of their peers and predecessors, only inching their toes over the stylistic boundaries to express themselves as individuals. As Konishi explains, Fujiwara no Kintō (966–1041), whom he considers the premier *shi* poet of his time, achieved succcess "not by creating his own style, but by manipulating most skillfully the commonest contemporary tone," composing, along with his contemporaries, plain-style poetry that Konishi observes could be compared to "a vintage wine diluted with water."[54]

Honchō reisō (Poetic Masterpieces from Our Court, ca. 1010), whose poems date from approximately 990 to 1010, preserves the largest body of mid-Heian *kanshi*, its appearance coinciding with the peak of Fujiwara fortunes and courtly glory. In its many polished, graceful *kanshi*, almost all pleasant to read if seldom emotionally compelling, we can enjoy the charming self-portraits created by some of the leading men of the day, most notably Fujiwara no Michinaga and his son-in-law Emperor Ichijō. Michinaga

52. Watson, *Japanese Literature in Chinese*, p. 10.
53. Konishi, II, p. 171.
54. Ibid., p. 243.

stands out as a representative poet of this period, albeit hardly one of the highest order. While his verse tends to lack lyrical power and thematic originality, it nonetheless has much that is appealing, especially the sensuousness of its descriptions of the ambient scents and shades of color in both the Heian palace and the surrounding countryside. The following excerpt from HCRS 5, a spring poem which shows Michinaga reveling in a shower of petals as he journeys down the river, displays this sensitivity to the beauty of nature:

> In the forest flowers are falling, branches growing bare.
> I see them spread in vast profusion, blanketing the boat with pink.
> Night, we moor by peach-blossom banks, rosy raindrops whirl;
> Spring, heading out from willow dikes, sent off by a willow-down breeze.
>
> . . . .
>
> Absorbed in all the opulent beauty, we halt our oars for a spell:
> Interest piqued, I shall live out my days as an old reciter of verse.

Another literary work important to our understanding of Japanese *kanshi* poetics in the mid-Heian period is an anthology of Chinese and Japanese poems and couplets titled *Wakan rōeishū* (Japanese and Chinese Poems to Sing, compiled by Fujiwara no Kintō, ca. 1013). The extemporaneous writing and chanting of occasional poems at formal social events and poetry competitions was a common affair, but, as Donald Keene notes, the difficulty of composing such *kanshi* on the spot meant that as the Heian period advanced, "impromptu" offerings increasingly took the form of compositions prepared ahead of time.[55] In preparing these poems and single couplets for recitation, poets consulted handy couplet reference works, among them *Wakan rōeishū*. Sugano observes that Heian *kanshi* poets possessed an "inordinate interest" in couplets, reading and appreciating them as complete creations in their own right.[56] This interest had its origins in China, where both poets and critics alike commonly extracted key couplets from poems for study and enjoyment, almost as if they were independent literary creations. Japanese poets, Sugano explains, not only extracted couplets from whole poems for study and appreciation, but also composed individual couplets, adding titles to them and even sometimes referring to these creations as "*shi*," as if to proclaim their literary autonomy and poetic integrity on a formal level.[57]

In *Wakan rōeishū*, some 588 couplets (234 from Chinese *shi* and 354 from Japanese *kanshi*) by more than 40 *kanshi* poets and 20 Tang poets

---

55. Keene, p. 342.
56. Sugano, pp. 56–57.
57. Ibid., pp. 61–65.

have been collected and arranged according to seasonal and other conventional categories and, significantly, are aligned with 216 *waka* on kindred topoi. The most commonly excerpted *waka* poet is Ki no Tsurayuki, with 26 poems. Of the Chinese poets represented in *Wakan rōeishū*, Bo Juyi is the overwhelming favorite, with 135 couplets drawn from his corpus. Yuan Chen distantly follows Bo, with 11 couplets. Wang Wei is barely represented and Li Bo entirely absent, their long-standing popularity in China by this time notwithstanding.[58] The lack of contact between Japan and China after the termination of exchange missions in the ninth century doubtless helps explain the curious absence of certain influential Chinese poets from this work, especially those active during the tenth century.

The conscious intermingling of the *waka* and *kanshi* traditions is also seen in such whole-verse literary anthologies as *Shinsen Man'yōshū* (The Newly Compiled *Man'yōshū*, compiled 893). This work provides Chinese translations in heptasyllabic quatrains for the *waka* poem selections, these mostly taken from a single twenty-round *waka* poetry contest (*utaawase*) which took place around 890. Writes Konishi about this interesting "symbolic contact" between the two poetic media: "The experiment of translating waka into shih was based on an assumption that the two forms shared certain traits . . . An awareness of features shared by both waka and shih contributed in no small way to the emerging conviction that waka and shih had equal literary merit."[59] The compilers likely believed that juxtaposing the two renditions (which often significantly diverged from each other) was a useful means for displaying conceptual and other differences in these traditions and perhaps showing the Japanese reader how various native expressions could be turned into suitable poetic equivalents in Chinese.

Wakan rōeishū helped popularize some of the themes, the diction, and the rhetorical conventions of Chinese poetry, thereby facilitating their seamless, almost unconscious integration into the very fabric of *waka*. This collection also had a profound influence upon subsequent medieval Japanese prose genres, from war tales, Noh drama, and travel essays to later *kanshi*. *Wakan rōeishū* was the subject of continuous study throughout the medieval age and inspired a succession of kindred works cataloging exemplary poems intended to serve as recitation pieces and composition models.

Leaving the spirited period of *Honchō reisō* and *Wakan rōeishū*, we now turn to Fujiwara no Akihira (989?–1066) and his influential private compilation *Honchō monzui* (Literary Gems from Our Court, compiled ca. 1060). Akihira was evidently not much of a poet himself. His bureaucratic career, too, was less successful than one might expect given his academic credentials, perhaps on account of academic indiscretions committed on

58. The data have been gathered from Kawaguchi Hisao, *Wakan rōeishū zen'yaku chū*, Kōdansha Gakujutsu Bunko, 325 (Tokyo: Kōdansha, 1982), pp. 625–29.
59. Konishi, II, p. 209.

two separate occasions.[60] Long ranked beside *Kaifūsō, Bunka shūreishū,* and Michizane's *Kanke bunsō* as a canonical Japanese classic, *Honchō monzui* contains both *kanshi* and *kanbun* (prose selections in Chinese) dating mainly from the tenth and early eleventh centuries, with some from as far back as 810. *Honchō monzui*'s prose sections contain a wealth of rather utilitarian but stylistically exemplary pieces such as memorials to the throne, historical documents, letters, and petitions, all of which are collectively indicative of the central role *kanbun* continued to play in public life. Some seventy authors are featured. As Keene observes, writings by members of the Sugawara and Ōe families are particularly numerous; the absence of Fujiwara literati among the important writers of *Honchō monzui*, as well as a lack of works by Buddhist priests, points to "the preponderant importance of two scholarly families, the Ōe and the Sugawara" and "a Confucian bias to the editorial process."[61] Female poets are also absent, although this was hardly for reasons of editorial bias: educated women by this time mainly wrote in Japanese, being taught, it seems, to view the pursuit of Chinese studies as a male endeavor.

Honchō monzui overall is more noteworthy as a repository of exemplary Japanese *kanbun* pieces than as a collection of verse, having only forty-three poems (including *fu*) in its fourteen *maki*. Perhaps for reasons of familiarity, Akihira selected already well-known poems for this collection: by Ōsone Shōsuke's calculation, 88 percent of the poems in *Honchō monzui* are the full texts of *kanshi* excerpted as couplets in *Wakan rōeishū*.[62] The overall emotional tone of these poems seems subdued, particularly alongside the better *kanshi* found in contemporaneous private collections, leaving the reader with the distinct impression that the editor of this work was interested primarily in documenting form and genre. Among the poems there are some thematically unusual items, including several vulgar and satirical pieces of a kind not seen in other Heian collections. Considering that in Heian *kanshi* one rarely finds allusion to any body part more private than the face, one is taken aback to discover among these stately and formal writings the pornographic "Tettsuiden" (Biography of Iron Hammer) and the graphic sexual rhapsody "Danjo kon'in no fu" (Rhyme-prose on the Marriage of a Man and a Woman). A desire to preserve as many literary forms and varieties of subject matter as possible may have motivated Akihira's inclusion of such anomalous pieces.

---

60. For details concerning these scandals, see our biography of Akihira in the appendix, or see Ōsone Shōsuke and others, comp., *Kanshi, kanbun, hyōron,* Kenkyū shiryō Nihon koten bungaku, vol. 11 (Tokyo: Meiji Shoin, 1984), p. 32.
61. Keene, pp. 344–45.
62. As cited in Kojima Noriyuki, comp., *Kaifūsō, Bunka shūreishū, Honchō monzui,* Nihon koten bungaku taikei, 69 (Tokyo: Iwanami Shoten, 1964), p. 32.

Another important *kanshi* collection, the earliest known manuscript of which dates from about 1130, is *Chūyūki burui shihai kanshishū*, a work mentioned earlier. This is a compilation of court *kanshi*. Lost for centuries, it was rediscovered through the efforts of Kawaguchi Hisao around 1950. This compilation has been tentatively attributed to Fujiwara no Munetada (1062–1141), who is thought to have recorded the poems on the back of his *Chūyūki* diary manuscript, a work originally more than 200 *maki* in length and covering the years 1087–1138. Preserved in this collection are some 455 *kanshi* (three-quarters of them heptasyllabic regulated octaves) by 241 poets. About 80 percent of the poems are *kudaishi* (poems with allusive verse titles), and all were composed between 1004 and 1126. Of particular interest is the fact that two-thirds of the poets in this collection are entirely unknown to us from any other work. Among them are 25 members of the Fujiwara family, the best-represented family in the collection, with some 127 poems in the extant portion. The original text apparently had at least 28 *maki*, of which only 6 have survived. Each *maki* appears to have been divided into numerous topical categories (at least 46 in the case of *maki* 7, for example), an indication that this was originally a work of enormous scale and scope.[63]

A further distinctive feature of this collection is the grouping together of poems composed on the same occasion, typically a poetry gathering at the palace, a temple, or a private home. The poetry has been somewhat uncharitably characterized in one source as "plain [in diction] and stereotypical (*ruikei teki*) in conception" and "not displaying a particularly high level of polish."[64] However, the collection is by no means devoid of interest and appeal and deserves to be included in any discussion of late Heian *kanshi*. Time and space constraints have made it necessary for us to defer a more detailed examination and treatment of this anthology to some future time.

The last major monument in the Heian *kanshi* tradition is *Honchō mudaishi* (Poems from Our Court Without Allusive Titles), compiled 1162–64 with the involvement of Fujiwara no Tadamichi (1097–1164). Tadamichi was a regent and a leading poet and patron of *kanshi*; some of his *kanshi* are translated below in the section devoted to his anthology *Hosshōji dono gyoshū* (A Collection of Poems by the Lord of Hosshōji). Judging from the often somber tone of the poetry in *Honchō mudaishi*, these were anxious times for the court, not surprising when one considers that the Hōgen and Heiji uprisings (1156 and 1159–60, respectively) had recently ended. A conspicuous emotional undercurrent in the collection is concern on the part

63. An excellent summary of the features of this anthology may be found in Kawaguchi Hisao, *Heian-chō Nihon kanbungaku-shi no kenkyū*, vol. 3 (*ge*) (Tokyo: Meiji Shoin, 1988, rev. exp. 3rd ed.; orig. pub. 1959), pp. 815–44.
64. Ōsone Shōsuke and others, comp., *Nihon koten bungaku daijiten* (Tokyo: Meiji Shoin, 1998), p. 820.

of many poets about the possibility of being excluded from political life, either through losing one's court post or being unable to gain one in the first place. Numerous poems embrace the theme of career failure and reveal a sense of personal worthlessness. These concerns are accompanied—and in some cases alleviated—by a deepening Buddhist consciousness. A further characteristic of the poetry in *Honchō mudaishi*, one reminiscent of late Tang verse, is an appreciation for the faded *sabi*-like beauty of nature in decline, delicately and unobtrusively observed by the poet, who, in the words of Konishi, focuses on "a fading reality, while evoking an underlying beauty superior to that of reality."[65]

Technically, we note a relative simplicity in diction and rhetoric, as well as a reduced reliance upon the use of Chinese allusions. The subject matter is more distinctively Japanese, showing a richness of local color and an enhanced degree of lyricism. In the poetry of Priest Renzen, Fujiwara no Tadamichi, and others, we see an interest in sustained description of mundane events and objects not unlike that seen in the poetry of the Northern Song period: *Honchō mudaishi* poets write on a wide range of everyday, even vulgar, subjects, such as prostitutes, peasants, itinerant peddlers, merchants, diviners, domestic animals, and insects. The following verse composed by Priest Renzen during an extended sea voyage, titled "A Humorous Poem About Life on the Boat, Written While Moored at Port," HCMDS 506, reveals the fineness of quotidian detail and freshness of local color seen in the best poems of *Honchō mudaishi*:

All quiet here on the boat, I lie with my head on my arms.
Everything I see and hear so hard to put into words.
The cook secretly sneers at me as she boils my nighttime medicine.
All the boatmen feel upset, for at breakfast there's not enough food.
My two sutra volumes I put in a bag, and then I hang it up;
I sweep the stern, then put in place my portable Buddhist altar.
I seek no riches anywhere, keeping just a worn-out broom.
During our journey the grain has run out; the basket sits there empty.
The wind fills our sails as we travel along, clear skies into the distance.
At every port I long for home; the autumn is suddenly cold.
Surely those two sons of mine are laughing at their father:
"Whatever possessed him to journey so far, over the Western Sea?"

The local color and personalism of this particular collection aside, Kojima Noriyuki observes that the *kanshi* tradition by this time was "shedding

65. Konishi Jin'ichi, *A History of Japanese Literature*, Volume Three: *The High Middle Ages*, trans. Aileen Gatten and Mark Harbison (Princeton University Press, 1991), p. 7; note that pp. 7–9 contain a number of translations of *Honchō mudaishi* poems not included in our anthology

a dying light."[66] While it is true that during the thirteenth century court interest in *kanshi* abated and thematic innovation seems to have waned, the genre was by no means moribund. Collections of reasonable size were still being assembled, an example being *Inokuma kanpaku ki shihai kaishi* (Pocket-paper [Poems] Recorded on the Reverse of the Diary of Regent Inokuma [Konoe no Iezane, 1179–1242]), which contains poetry written between 1197 and 1211.[67] Yet much of the verse was now casting a paler light, the aesthetics more restrained and subdued and the poetry rarely rising to the moments of vigor seen in the best *kanshi* of earlier centuries. The *kanshi* tradition, hitherto cultivated in the reflected glow of Chinese precedents and models, was now artistically more self-contained and had become more inclined to follow its own conventions and preferences. Chinese poems were still composed in large numbers, most of them along the stylistic lines of *Honchō mudaishi*. Courtier diaries of this period make frequent reference to *kanshi* composition events, suggesting that there was no significant decrease in the volume of production during the Kamakura age. The existence of various technical manuals on *kanshi* composition, including couplet source books, compendia of antonyms and poetic expressions, and other such reference works, points to the undiminished "luxuriance of the *kanshi* forest," as one scholar has put it,[68] a forest now only dimly glimpsed from what little of it has survived.

66. Kojima, *Ōchō kanshisen*, p. 468.
67. Other small extant fragments of the diary include entries dating from the years 1217–35. Some 350 poems, mostly *kudai* compositions, are recorded on the back of the manuscript. The term *kaishi* (*futokorogami*, literally, "paper carried at the breast") in the provisional title of this anthology refers to a special folded *washi* paper carried at the chest inside the *kimono*. The paper most often used was *danshi* (made from mulberry fiber) or *sugiharagami*, another mulberry-fiber variety. *Kaishi* was used to record *kanshi* and *waka* poetry for formal presentation. The stylistic layout of the poems recorded thereon gradually came to be formally prescribed, according to poetic genre and the gender of the poet. There were also special traditions found within individual families.
68. Honma, *Nihon kanshi*, p. 262.

POETRY TRANSLATIONS

KAIFŪSŌ (POETIC GEMS CHERISHING THE STYLES OF OLD)

Kaifūsō is the earliest known anthology of *kanshi* and one of the earliest extant works of Japanese literature. A small collection of predominantly occasional verse spanning the period 672–751, it was compiled privately and bears an anonymous preface dated 751/11. Numerous theories have arisen concerning the compiler's identity, with Ōmi no Mifune (722–85), Isonokami no Yakatsugu (729–81), Prince Shirakabe (Emperor Kōnin, 709–81) and Fujiwara no Satsuo (?–?) being among the possibilities suggested. The *Nihon koten bungaku taikei* edition of *Kaifūsō* comprises 116 *kanshi*, a number smaller than the figure of 120 stated in the original preface. An additional three unnumbered (*bangai*) poems, possibly of later origin, are also present.

The *Kaifūsō* preface indicates that Emperor Tenji had recognized the value of belles lettres as a force "to regulate customs and bring culture to the people," believing that nothing could surpass learning as a means "to cultivate virtues and make oneself resplendent in them."[69] Thus, he promoted *kanshi* composition, establishing a Chinese-style literary culture among the aristocracy that would endure for centuries. Aware of the loss of literary works that had occurred during the Jinshin Disturbance of 672, the compiler of *Kaifūsō* was evidently keen to see the best works of his age preserved. In the preface to the collection he laments, "Many more than a hundred were the pieces of chiseled prose and exquisite calligraphy. But with the passage of time, disorders reduced all these writings to ashes." He adds, "Since my reason for making this anthology was to keep from oblivion the poetry of the great men of former days, I think it is proper to call the collection *Kaifū*—Fond Reminiscences."[70] Notwithstanding the compiler's

---

69. As translated in *Sources of Japanese Tradition*, vol. 1, p. 89.
70. Ibid., pp. 89–90. Earlier, on page 88, the compilers render the title of the anthology as "Fond Recollections of Poetry," as do Donald Keene (*Seeds of the Heart*, p. 74), and Ivo Smits,

34

stated wish to preserve for posterity the poetry in this collection, *Kaifūsō* appears to have been lost, or was otherwise out of circulation, for some two centuries after its compilation. In fact, all extant Edo manuscripts descend not from any edition close in time to the original *Kaifūsō* but from a now lost and probably incomplete Heian text, dated 1041.[71] The compiler arranged the poems roughly in chronological order and by poet. Twenty-one of the sixty-four poets represented are known to us also from the early *waka* anthology *Man'yōshū* (ca. 759). The preface indicates that for each of the sixty-four there was supposed to be an introductory biography, providing the poet's full name, court post, rank, and place of birth. However, in the 1041 text we find biographical sketches for only nine poets. Thus, we may conjecture that the manuscript either suffered damage or underwent editorial revision, losing most of the biographies in the process, or perhaps the missing biographies were never present in the first place. Three-quarters of the poets were courtiers, mostly holders of the fourth and fifth ranks, with a handful of priests, nobles, and one emperor included as well. Persons of Korean and Chinese ancestry are also well represented, among them Priest Benshō, Tami no Kurohito, and Tori no Minori. The poets with the most poems included are Fujiwara no Umakai (six), Fujiwara no Maro (five), and Fujiwara no Fubito (five). Prominent in the anthology are poets belonging to the coterie of *kanshi* patron Prince Nagaya (684–729), leading to speculation that the compiler was likely someone in this circle.[72]

Nearly all of the poems are *gushi*, "old-style poetry," a genre structurally freer in linear form and prosodic conventions than the regulated verse forms. Only a small number of later poems in the collection by leading poets such as Fujiwara no Umakai and Isonokami no Otomaro approach the prosodic standards of *jinti shi*, "modern-style [regulated] verse," as written in China during the Tang period.[73] These poems display adherence to tonal prosodic rules and to requirements governing the use of parallelism and antithesis. Roughly two-thirds of the poems in *Kaifūsō* are octaves, one

---

(*The Pursuit of Loneliness: Chinese and Japanese Nature Poetry in Medieval Japan, ca. 1050–1150* [Stuttgart: Franz Steiner Verlag, 1995], p. 18). However, *kaifū* means literally "recalling or cherishing the styles [of old]," the final syllable, *sō*, in *Kaifūsō* meaning literary "gems" or "masterpieces," not just any poetry. Thus, we have chosen to translate the title of the anthology "Poetic Gems Cherishing the Styles of Old." For the original text, see NKBT, 69, p. 62.
71. Ōsone, *Nihon koten bungaku daijiten*, p. 207.
72. NKBT, 69, p. 11.
73. *Nihon koten bungaku daijiten*, p. 206; Ōsone and others, *Kanshi, kanbun, hyōron*, p. 7. Inoguchi Atsushi is able to identify only one good example of early Tang style regulated verse in the collection, this being *Kaifūsō* 115, a pentasyllabic octave by Isonokami no Otomaro. See Inoguchi Atsushi, comp. and annot., *Nihon kanshi*, vol. 1, Shinshaku kanbun taikei, 45 (Tokyo: Meiji Shoin, 1972), p. 8.

sixth quatrains, and a further sixth, extended verses, the longest having eighteen lines. All but seven are in pentasyllabic lines, the remainder being heptasyllabic. Notably, none is in the mixed-meter style that became popular in the ninth century.

Among the principal accomplishments demonstrated in this anthology are the technical mastery of the basic mechanics of Chinese versification (albeit not the regulated forms) and the establishment of lasting poetic conventions for poetic topoi, rhetoric, and tone, all of which were undergirded by a growing awareness of *kanshi* writing as a refined art. Indeed, the *Kaifūsō* poet well understood that *kanshi* composition was an important literary and social skill required of all courtiers, for whom higher education and the cultivation of artistic sensibilities were still firmly grounded in the precedents and tastes of Chinese tradition.

The poems in *Kaifūsō* remain largely within the thematic boundaries of Chinese court poetry. Many of them show the influence of the elegant late Six Dynasties tradition, with the sixth-century anthologies *Wen xuan* and *Yutai xinyong* (New Songs from the Jade Terrace) being important models. Aesthetically, the collection displays a restrained and subdued quality, the banquet poems generally devoid of excessive showiness and the lyrical verses seldom expressing passionate sentiments. Among the topics and conventions adopted from Chinese models we find paeans to imperial virtue (typically written at banquets), descriptions of the celestial beauty of palace scenery (for example, KFS 4, 21, 61), accounts of excursions (KFS 27, 118, 93), and celebrations of life in rural seclusion (KFS 9, 108). The influence of Buddhism is still relatively thin, with few verses touching on such themes as the evanescence of human life, which is common in mid- to late-Heian *kanshi*. The topos of romantic love, so central to court-period *waka*, is rarely in evidence, and social commentary is similarly uncommon.

Nature poetry figures prominently in *Kaifūsō*, with poems on spring being especially popular. The treatment of nature remains largely descriptive and impersonal rather than symbolic or lyrical in its intent, and the poet generally appears detached from the scene or else immersed inconspicuously therein, as seen, for example, in poem 15 by Emperor Monmu, "The Moon," translated below. This verse and several others of its type belong to the *eibutsu* (*yongwu*) genre, short descriptive "odes on objects," which became popular in China during the Southern Qi dynasty (479–502).[74] These describe individual objects, usually without lyrical or philosophical comment. Other *yongwu* subjects found in this collection include snow, a pine tree, and a beautiful woman.

---

74. On the *yongwu*, which Stephen Owen calls "one of the most stable and enduring of poetic subgenres [of *shi*]," see Owen's *The Poetry of the Early T'ang* (New Haven: Yale University Press, 1977), pp. 281–93.

Verses relating poets' private emotions or circumstances are relatively few, particularly among the earlier poems. Helen McCullough speculates that "lyricism of any kind posed an especially formidable challenge to the early *kanshi* author."[75] Indeed, propriety of form seemed to matter more than originality of content or depth of sentiment. Nonetheless, one can find occasional moments of appealing lyricism, as in the poem by Emperor Monmu (r. 697–707), "Expressing My Feelings" (KFS 16), translated below, in which Monmu expresses doubts about his fitness to rule the realm. Monmu's historical consciousness and sense of his own relative insignificance in the flow of time and human history are attitudes commonly seen in *kanshi* and reflect Chinese traditions. As James Liu writes, "Not only do we find in Chinese poetry a keen awareness of personal existence in time, but also a strong sense of history." Thus, in poems on historical themes, Chinese poets "[stress] the vanity of human endeavours by contrasting the glories of the past with the ruins of today."[76] Monmu's thoughtful, if arguably conventional, self-doubt and the lyricism of later *Kaifūsō* poets such as Fujiwara no Umakai, Fujiwara no Maro, and Isonokami no Otomaro, all of whom wrote on human failings such as greed and mediocrity, and their own lack of success at court, clearly demonstrate the appeal of the more personal poems in the collection.

Kaifūsō poetry makes frequent allusion to Chinese historical and literary works. These allusions underscore the fact that the Japanese intelligentsia were already well familiar with Chinese philosophical and literary traditions, even though the philosophical element in their poems is generally rather shallow. The typical *Kaifūsō* poem conveys an atmosphere of untroubled tranquility and a sense of well-being, this in contrast to the Buddhist-inspired pessimism coloring so much of later court literature. One can perceive a languid optimism and confidence, as well as a growing awareness of the importance of natural beauty in the pursuit of happiness. The first poem translated below, with its scene of a court banquet drawing to a close in a sublimely beautiful environment, the lords relaxing in their carriages ready to be taken home, epitomizes the spirit of *Kaifūsō* and indeed sets the tone for much of the court *kanshi* throughout the subsequent centuries of the Heian age.

75. McCullough, p. 94.
76. Liu, pp. 52–53.

✠ A Banquet at the Spring Gardens
Prince Ōtsu

I loosen my collar, gaze at the Marvelous Pond,
My eyes taking in the pleasures of the Golden Garden.
Clear and pure the mossy waters deep;
Dark and hazy mist over distant peaks.
The splashing of waves mingles with the music of the *koto*;
Chirping birds are heard with the sound of the wind.
The lords lie sprawled in their carriages, ready to go home:
How could Pengze's banquets even compare?

SOURCE: KFS 4, in Kojima Noriyuki, annot., *Kaifūsō, Bunka shūreishū, Honchō monzui*, Nihon koten bungaku taikei series (NKBT), 69 (Tokyo: Iwanami Shoten, 1964), p. 75; octave (pentasyllabic).
LINE 1: "Marvelous Pond" refers to a pond in the Japanese imperial palace gardens, the so-called "Golden Garden" in line two. It is an allusion to a pond in the imperial park of the Zhou dynasty kings and harks back to Ode 242 in *Shi jing* (The Book of Songs) titled "Ling t'ae" (Ling tai, Marvelous Tower), which has the lines: "The king was by the marvelous pond; / How full was it of fishes leaping about!" See James Legge, trans., *The She King or the Book of Poetry*, The Chinese Classics, vol. 4 (orig. pub. by Oxford University Press; reprint, Taipei: SMC Publishing, 1991), pp. 456–57.
LINE 2: "Golden Garden" may be an abbreviated reference to Golden Valley Garden (Jingu yuan), which reportedly belonged to the Jin dynasty bon vivant Shi Chong (249–300) and was the site of the first recorded poetry banquet in China, held in 296.
LINE 8: Pengze is the famous poet and imbiber Tao Yuanming (Tao Qian, 365–427), this sobriquet being the name of a district in modern Jiangxi province where Tao served briefly as a magistrate. He was China's first major eremitic poet and the quintessential model for reclusive verse in both China and Japan in later centuries.

✠ The Hunt
Prince Ōtsu

Dawn, we chose our ablest of warriors;
Dusk, we feast the multitudes of horsemen.
Dining on meat, everyone in high spirits;
Tipping our cups, all of us filled with cheer.
Crescent bows shining in the valley,
Cloud-like pennants flying before the peaks.
The sun has now gone down below the hills,
And yet the noble warriors tarry still.

SOURCE: KFS 5, in NKBT, 69, p. 78; octave (pentasyllabic).

❊ Expressing My Intentions
Prince Ōtsu

With flying brush, paper broad as the sky, I'll paint a crane in the clouds.
With the hills my loom, the frost my shuttle, I'll weave a brocade of leaves.
• • • • •
The time for the red sparrow, a letter in its beak, hasn't yet arrived.
The hidden dragon not yet employed, unable to sleep in peace.

SOURCE: KFS 6a, 6b, in NKBT, 69, p. 77; quatrain (heptasyllabic).
LINES 1 AND 2: Evidently, the prince wrote the first two lines, and an unidentified poet added lines three and four, either on the same occasion or later. In any event, the connection between the two couplets is not entirely clear (see NKBT, 69, p. 451). The poem is the earliest known example of *kanshi* verse-capping. On the surface these lines appear to be describing Ōtsu's poetic intentions; weaving a brocade of leaves probably means writing elegant poetry. But at a deeper level these sentiments may instead be a thinly-veiled expression of his political aspirations. The conception of this couplet is reminiscent of a poem titled "Lin tang huai you" (By a Forest Pond Recalling a Friend) by Wang Bo (649–76), which reads, "On a fragrant screen I paint the grasses of spring; / With a magic shuttle I weave the mist of dawn." However, one wonders whether Prince Ōtsu would have had access to the poetry of a Chinese poet who was almost his contemporary. It seems more likely that Ōtsu used an even earlier source.
LINE 3: The red sparrow is an auspicious omen, traditionally appearing with a message in its beak in times of enlightened rule by the emperor. This line appears to mean that the time for Ōtsu to seize power had not yet arrived. See the following poem and the biography of Prince Ōtsu in the Biography section for details about his unsuccessful attempt to take the throne in a succession dispute following the death of his father, Emperor Tenmu.
LINE 4: "Hidden dragon" is probably a metaphor for Ōtsu, who hoped to become emperor.

❊ Near the End
Prince Ōtsu

The golden crow gazes down on my house in the west;
Drumbeats hasten the end of this short life.
On the road to the Springs there are neither guests nor hosts.
To whose house this evening shall I head?

SOURCE: KFS 7, in NKBT, 69, p. 77; quatrain (pentasyllabic).
TITLE: This poem was presumably written after the prince had been arrested for complicity in a succession plot and had been condemned to death. He took his own life in the Tenth Month of 686. This style of death verse (with *rinjū*, "near the end," in the title) was common in the Six Dynasties tradition. See NKBT, 69, p. 77, n. 7.
LINE 1: Golden crow: a metaphor for the sun.
LINE 2: These are drums announcing nightfall.
LINE 3: The "Springs" are the Nine Springs, i.e., the underworld. The "guests" and "hosts" reference is saying that there are no places to stay on the way to the underworld.
LINE 4: Here, our translation follows another text in correcting the third character in line four, as noted in the collated textual variations found in NKBT, 69, p. 77.

COMMENT: A similar poem was later written by one Jiang Wei (fl. tenth century), titled "A Poem Written Just Before My Execution." Both Ōtsu's poem and that of Jiang Wei appear to be based upon a verse by Chen Shubao (553–604, r. 583–87), the last ruler of the short-lived Chen dynasty. Jiang's poem reads: "The drums of the government offices suddenly intrude. / The sun is about to sink in the west. / There are no inns in the Yellow Springs. / Where, then, this evening shall I lodge?" (Following the NKBT text, p. 451). Chen's verse reads as follows: "Drumbeats foretell what lies ahead for me. / The rays of the sun are setting in the west. / In the Yellow Springs there are no guests or hosts. / To whose house this evening shall I head?" (Following the text in Ōsone Shōsuke and others, comp., *Kanshi, kanbun, hyōron*, Kenkyū shiryō Nihon koten bungaku, vol. 11 of 13 vols. (Tokyo: Meiji Shoin, 1984), p. 12.)

❊ Enjoying Myself Among the Flowers and Bush Warblers
Priest Chizō

Very few folk with whom I can converse,
So leaning on my stick, I go in search of company.
This day in spring, a scent is in the air,
From a bamboo grove a sudden breeze appears.
Seeking friends, the warblers lend charm to the trees;
Filled with scent, the flowers make the thickets smile.
Although I am happy, wandering here and there,
I still feel ashamed that I'm poor at "insect-carving."

SOURCE: KFS 8, in NKBT, 69, pp. 79–80; octave (pentasyllabic).
LINE 8: "Insect-carving" is a common deprecatory term applied to literary.composition. While ostensibly belittling his own poetic talents, Chizō may also be disparaging versification in general as a trivial pastime.

❊ Expressing My Feelings on an Autumn Day
Priest Chizō

I'd like to find a spot that suits my nature,
So I've come to this place in search of "wisdom and virtue,"
Where the air is fresh, the mountains and rivers lovely,
Where strong winds blow, the scenery sublime.
Swallows' nests—summer has gone.
Wild geese islet—autumn sounds are heard.
So it is that the Worthies of the Bamboo Grove
Were never startled by honor or disgrace.

SOURCE: KFS 9, in NKBT, 69, p. 80; octave (pentasyllabic).
LINE 2: "Wisdom and virtue" effectively means rivers and hills (or mountains), following a passage in *Lun yu* (The Confucian Analects) where Confucius states, "Those who are wise love rivers, and those who are virtuous love mountains." See NKBT, 69, p. 80.

LINE 5: The nests are empty, as the swallows have migrated for the approaching winter.
LINE 7: "Worthies of the Bamboo Grove" is an allusion to a celebrated coterie of seven third-century literati-recluses who passed their days in a leisurely fashion, practicing alchemy, playing music, drinking wine, composing poetry, and indulging in philosophical discussion.
LINE 8: The departure of summer and onset of autumn, as seen in the third couplet, are a reminder of the constant cyclical movement of the universe, governing not only the seasons but also human affairs and fortunes. In this final couplet, the poet praises the Worthies for drawing a lesson from nature and maintaining equanimity no matter what comes their way, hinting that we could do well to follow their example.

▓ The Moon
Emperor Monmu [Aged twenty-five]

The moon a boat, moving down a misty shore;
Floating with cassia oars near a hazy beach.
Drifting above the tower, a dazzling white;
Submerged in my wine, as round as a wheel.
Slanting light fragmented beneath the water;
Autumn moon shines anew through leafless trees.
Solitary, a mirror among the stars,
Drifting back to the ford of the Milky Way.

SOURCE: KFS 15, in NKBT, 69, pp. 86–87; octave (pentasyllabic).
AUTHOR: The Prince's age appears here in the *Kaifūsō* text itself alongside the poet's name, a common feature seen elsewhere as well.
LINE 2: The modifier for "oars" here is actually the character for "maple." However, this word was glossed as both "maple" and "cassia" (*katsura*) in Heian-period dictionaries; the latter meaning was probably the one intended in this case. A huge cassia tree was said to grow on the moon, hence this image. The sliver of moon appears to drift through thin clouds, looking like a small skiff on the seas.

▓ Expressing My Feelings
Emperor Monmu [Aged twenty-five]

Although I am old enough to wear the crown,
My knowledge is such that I dare not rule the realm.
I ponder the problem, wondering day and night
How I can improve my blockish mind.
Unless I take antiquity as my guide,
How will I realize my ambitions as a ruler?
Yet I lack that "thrice-breaking" diligence;
Perhaps I'll simply copy a verse or two.

SOURCE: KFS 16, in NKBT, 69, pp. 87–88; octave (pentasyllabic).

LINE 2: "Rule the realm" is literally "let my robes fall" (*chui shang*), an expression originating from the *Zhou yi* (The Rites of Zhou), where the following line occurs: "The Yellow Emperor, Yao, and Shun let their robes fall and the world was governed."

LINE 7: "'Thrice-breaking' diligence" is an allusion to an ancient story which relates that Confucius so loved the *Yi jing* (The Book of Changes) that he thrice broke the binding on his copy as a result of reading it so many times. The emperor is declaring that he is far behind Confucius where dedication to study is concerned.

✖ Snow
Emperor Monmu [Aged twenty-five]

Rising gauzy clouds like sacks of pearls;
Petals of fresh snow, shimmering and bright.
In the forest, resembling willow down;
On the beams, it looks like dancing dust.
Replacing my lamp, lighting my books at night;
Blown by the wind, whirling about on the River Luo's banks.
Look at the plum blossoms in the garden—
The winter branches still bear signs of spring!

SOURCE: KFS 17, in NKBT, 69, p. 88; octave (pentasyllabic).
LINE 4: A well-known Han dynasty figure named You Gong was said to be such a fine singer he could make the dust on the beams rise and dance about when he sang.
LINE 5: This brings to mind the tale of Sun Kang, a poor but diligent scholar who at night studied by moonlight reflected by fallen snow, because he could not afford a lamp.
LINE 6: This is inspired by a line from Cao Zhi's (192–232) famous poem *Luo Shen fu* (Rhapsody on the Goddess of the River Luo), which reads: "Fluttering and blowing around—ah! Like snow whipped about by the rushing winds." According to tradition, Luo Shen (known also as Fufei) was the daughter of the god-emperor Fu Xi and is said to have drowned while crossing the River Luo.
LINES 7 AND 8: The snow clinging to the branches is "mistaken" for bunches of white blossoms. This instance of deliberate poetic confusion is a common conceit (called *mitate* in Japanese) found in both Chinese and Japanese poetry.

✖ A Poem Written in Response to an Imperial Order to Accompany the Imperial Procession
Middle Counselor Ōmiwa no Asomi Takechimaro, Junior Third Rank [Aged fifty]

Lying ill, my hair already white,
Feeling as if about to leave the world,
When to my surprise there came an imperial command
To accompany His Majesty on a spring visit to the Park.
From pine-treed cliffs gurgling falls descend;
By bamboo banks new flowers come into bloom.

I am just a simple rustic type,
Undeservedly asked to ride in the attendants' carriage.

SOURCE: KFS 18, in NKBT, 69, pp. 88–89; octave (pentasyllabic).
AUTHOR: Takechimaro wrote this poem the year of his death, in 706. *Asomi* (*ason* in Heian times), which appears in his name, was the second in a simplified system of *kabane* honorific court titles (*yakusa no kabane*) devised in 684 when the old clan title system, based on hereditary and occupational criteria and in use since around the late fifth century, was overhauled. Under this new scheme, the title *mahito* became the first of the *kabane*, *asomi* the second. The latter was reserved for certain influential Omi clans whose genealogical proximity to the imperial house was considered to be one degree more distant than those assigned the title *mahito*. The third through eighth *kabane* in descending order were: *sukune, imiki, michinoshi, omi, muraji,* and *inagi*. *Asomi* was appended to the surname, appearing before the given name in the case of persons holding the third rank or higher.
LINE 7: "Simple rustic type" alludes to a passage in Book XI, "The Men of Former Times," in *Lun yu* (The Confucian Analects), which Legge translates as follows: "The Master said, 'The men of former times, in the matters of ceremonies and music, were rustics . . . while the men of these latter times, in ceremonies and music, are accomplished gentlemen.'" See Legge, trans., *Confucius: Confucian Analects, The Great Learning and The Doctrine of the Mean* (orig. pub. Oxford: Clarendon Press, 1893; reprint, New York: Dover Publications, Inc., New York, 1971), p. 237.

❊ Strolling About, Gazing at the Scenery
Prince Inukami, Senior Fourth Rank Lower, Civil Affairs Ministry

For a while, having leisure time to fill,
We wander along the banks of Yao Pond.
By the Chui Tower warblers have started to sing.
In the cassia courtyard the first butterflies flit about.
Pairs of bobbing ducks swim by the banks.
A lone peeping egret holds a fish in its mouth.
Into cloud-etched cups we pour the foggy mist,
While men of talent recite splendid verse.
We linger among the rivers and the hills,
Giving ourselves to pleasure like the Seven Worthies.
Although we've enjoyed the woods and ponds to the full,
We have not exhausted the delights of this lovely spring.

SOURCE: KFS 21, in NKBT, 69, pp. 91–92; *koshi* in twelve lines (pentasyllabic).
LINE 2: In Chinese mythology, Yao (Jasper) Pond is an enchanted pool in the Kunlun mountains, where Xi Wang Mu (Queen Mother of the West), a goddess, was said to reside. According to legend, King Mu of the Zhou dynasty was invited to an elaborate banquet with Xi Wang Mu at Yao Pond. The poet is implying that the present group of courtiers is enjoying a privilege of a similar magnitude.
LINE 3: This tower, a building in the palace grounds where music was played, was named after one in the southeastern part of modern Kaifeng county, Henan province, built by King Hui of Liang during China's Warring States period (403–221 B.C.).

LINE 7: "Cloud-etched" may refer to decorations on the sides of these vessels. "Foggy mist" appears to be a poetic euphemism for wine, which may well have been drunk warm and hence gave off steam.
LINE 9: "The rivers and the hills" is literally "wisdom and virtue." See note to KFS 9, line two.
LINE 10: On the Seven Worthies, see KFS 9, above.

Thinking of Home While in China

Priest Benshō

At the sun's edge, I stare at the source of the sun.
Among the clouds, I gaze above the clouds.
Far have I journeyed to toil in this faraway land,
Ever lamenting the hardships of "Ever Tranquil."

SOURCE: KFS 27, in NKBT, 69, p. 97; quatrain (pentasyllabic).
TITLE: The poet studied in China for several years, from around 701.
LINE 1: "Source of the sun" (Nihon) is the word for Japan.
LINE 4: "Ever Tranquil" is a literal translation of the name Chang'an, the capital of China, where the poet was living.
COMMENT: In each line of this poem characters one and four are identical ("sun" in line one, "clouds" in two, "far" in three, and "ever" in four), creating word plays and lending an element of whimsy to this nostalgic verse.

Written on Imperial Command at the Ritual Purification Ceremony Held the Third Day of the Third Month

Sena no Kimi Yukifumi, Junior Fifth Rank Lower, Tutor to the Heir Apparent [Aged sixty-two]

The Emperor's compassion extends to every realm;
The Kingly Way enriches all living things.
Bamboo leaves throughout the purified garden;
Peach blossoms lightly float on the winding stream.
Beautiful clouds drift by in the sky above.
Luxuriant trees in bloom here in the park.
Aware of my dullness, I've tried my hand nonetheless.
But how could I ever match His Majesty's brilliance?

SOURCE: KFS 61, in NKBT, 69, p. 125; octave (pentasyllabic).
TITLE AND AUTHOR: The year the banquet was held is unknown. On the third day of the Third Month ("Double Third") the Japanese court held a ceremony known as Kyokusui no En, "Winding Stream Feast," also called Megurimizu no Toyo no Akari. This was an ancient practice of Chinese origin, dating back to the third century or perhaps earlier. The ceremony included a purification ritual where a cup of wine was cast adrift to float down a stream; meanwhile the participants were required to compose poems. If a poet succeeded in completing his verse by the time the cup reached his position on the bank, the wine was his to drink.

One famous instance of this practice occurred at a party held by the calligrapher Wang Xizhi (307–65), who, on the Double Third in 353, is said to have gathered together a group of forty-one scholars at the Orchid Pavilion (Lan ting, located in modern Shaoxing county, Zhejiang province). A reference to floating wine cups is also found in the *fu* "Xian ju fu" (Rhapsody on Living in Idleness) by Pan Yue (Pan Anren, 247–300). On the *kabane* clan title *kimi*, which is found in the poet's name, see the title note attached to KFS 18, above.

LINE 3: Bamboo leaves was a code word for *sake* (NKBT, 69, p. 125).

❈ Passing the Ruins of the Former Residence of Counselor Ōmiwa

Fujiwara no Asomi Maro, Junior Third Rank, Minister of War and Master of the Left and Right Capital Offices

One day he resigned his lofty post and departed,
Leaving admonitions to last a thousand years.
The pines and bamboo show the colors of spring,
But now his old home is bereft of his noble face.
No more clear nights of wine and *koto* music;
Gone from his tumbledown gate the carriages and horses.
All land belongs to His Majesty's realm.
Were *I* to go home what would become of me?

SOURCE: KFS 95, in NKBT, 69, p. 159; octave (pentasyllabic).
TITLE: "Counselor Ōmiwa": Ōmiwa no Takechimaro (657–706). See his poem, KFS 18, above.
LINES 1 AND 2: In 692, Takechimaro remonstrated with Empress Jitō (r. 686–97), urging her not to go to Ise during the busy harvest season, lest such a visit disrupt the peasants' labors. Unhappy that his advice was ignored, he resigned as middle counselor. In 702 Takechimaro made a comeback, serving first as governor of Nagato (modern Yamaguchi prefecture). The following year, he became master of the Left Capital Office, occupying this post until his death
LINE 5: The *koto* is a long, horizontal zither-like instrument with many strings, which are plucked and strummed. The instrument came into Japan from China during Nara times. The Chinese antecedent was the *qin*.
LINE 8: The poet seems to be wondering aloud what would happen if, like Takechimaro, he himself ever left the court and tried to seek employment on the outside. Various alternative versions of line eight exist. One text substitutes "you" for "I."

❈ Passing the Ruins of the Former Residence of Counselor Ōmiwa

Fujiwara no Asomi Maro

Who can say that the Way of the ruler is easy?
Yet it's always been hard for a subject to be righteous.
His remonstrances were in the end ignored;
He went back home, resigning from his post.
Wandering around at leisure, in Xi Kang's bamboo grove;
Sunk in melancholy thought, adorned with the orchids of Chu.
Once the palace gates had opened to him again,

He was as happy as a fish returned to water!

SOURCE: KFS 96, in NKBT, 69, p. 159; octave (pentasyllabic).
LINE 3: On these remonstrances, see the notes to the preceding poem.
LINE 5: Xi (Ji) Kang (223–62) was a famous poet, essayist, and thinker, one of the so-called "Seven Worthies of the Bamboo Grove." See KFS 9 for details on this coterie. Xi had a strong interest in Daoism and wrote a treatise titled "Yang sheng lun" (Disquisition on Nurturing Life). He was renowned for his unconventionality and contempt for government service and spent most of his twenties living in retirement on his estate outside of Luoyang.
LINE 6: "Adorned with the orchids of Chu" brings to mind the image of poet Qu Yuan (340?–278? B.C.) bedecking himself with flowers (among them, orchids) in his famous poem "Li sao" (Encountering Sorrow). Qu, a loyal official from the state of Chu, was unjustly criticized at court and banished to the south. "Li sao" details his wanderings and musings while in exile. For a translation, see Burton Watson, trans., *The Columbia Book of Chinese Poetry* (New York: Columbia University Press, 1984), p. 54. Watson points out that the autumn orchids symbolize "[Qu Yuan's] talents and superior moral qualities" (ibid.). Maro is likening Takechimaro to Qu: both were loyal officials and scholars who were unfairly deprived of their posts.

▧ Expressing My Feelings
Tajihi no Mahito Hironari, Middle Counselor, Junior Third Rank

While young, I lacked the will to study hard;
Now an adult, I have no literary skills.
At times I find myself at poetry gatherings
And end up feeling ashamed of my lack of talent.

SOURCE: KFS 101, in NKBT, 69, pp. 162–63; quatrain (pentasyllabic).
LINE 1: "The will to study hard" is literally "firefly-and-snow will," and alludes to two well-known stories, each about a poor but dedicated scholar who found a means to continue his studies at night without the benefit of a lamp. Che Yin gathered a bag of fireflies and used these as his source of light. The second individual, Sun Kang (see also poem KFS 17, above), studied at night by moonlight reflected off fallen snow.

▧ Secluded Dwelling
Tami no Kurohito, the Hermit

I ventured away from the noisy, dusty world,
Searching for an enchanted cassia grove.
In the cliffs and valleys no signs of the mundane world;
On the mountain roads some young men gathering wood.
The springs and rocks diverse wherever I go,
But wind and mist the same in every place.
If you want to know why mountain folk are happy,
It's the pure winds that blow through the pines.

SOURCE: KFS 108, in NKBT, 69, pp. 171–72; octave (pentasyllabic).
LINE 1: "Dusty world": a conventional Buddhist reference to the mundane human world.
LINE 2: "Enchanted cassia grove" simply means a scene of natural beauty in the wilderness.

◈ Five Poems, Untitled
Priest Dōyū

The one thing on my mind—ah!
    Is being free of cares.
This goal I would pursue—ah!
    Made hard by passions and desires.
Whether the road be easy or steep—ah!
    All depends on me.
The stalwart, once departed—ah!
    Never will return.

SOURCE: KFS 110, in NKBT, 69, pp. 174–75; quatrain (heptasyllabic).
TITLE: This is the only surviving poem of the set. Following this verse are two unnumbered (*bangai*) poems that some speculate belonged to the original set. Others, however, believe they were not originally connected to KFS 110, being added some time later by an unidentified poet. This poem and the first of the *bangai* poems, below, are closely modeled on "Si chou shi" (Four-fold Sorrow) by Zhang Heng (78–139). See NKBT, 69, pp. 174, 472. Each line in this and the next poem has a caesura after the third character, marked by the word *xi*, an exclamatory word equivalent to "ah!" or "oh!" most commonly seen in *Shi jing* (The Book of Songs).

◈ Untitled
Authorship unknown, possibly by Priest Dōyū

The one thing on my mind—ah!
    Is the Joyous Land.
There I long to go—ah!
    My dullness makes it hard.
In trying, I may grow old—ah!
    But why not keep on striving?
Days and months slip by—ah!
    Never to return.

SOURCE: KFS, unnumbered (*bangai*) verse 1, immediately following KFS 110, in NKBT, 69, p. 175; quatrain (heptasyllabic).
LINE 1: Joyous Land: the heaven of the Buddhist afterlife.

⌘ In the Mountains
Authorship unknown, possibly by Priest Dōyū

What is there to see now in these mountains?
Tired birds heading home as the sun goes down.
A thatched hut in the dampness and the wind.
Cassia moon shining down on the rocks and waters.
The fruit on the trees can sustain this aged body;
The old cotton robes I wear keep out the cold.
Here, I have no one to keep me company;
With stick in hand, I go walking in the hills.

SOURCE: KFS, unnumbered (*bangai*) 2, immediately following *bangai* 1, above, in NKBT, 69, p. 175; octave (pentasyllabic).
LINE 4: According to legend, a cassia tree grew on the moon.

⌘ For an Old Acquaintance
Isonokami no Asomi Otomaro, Middle Counselor and Minister of Central Affairs, Junior Third Rank

Ten thousand miles separating wind and dust.
Third Month of winter, orchids now all withered.
More and more my temples are flecked with frost;
Increasingly my eyebrows knit in the cold.
The drake is lost within the mist at dusk;
The goose flies through clouds, distressed at dawn.
Who knows when we will share our thoughts again?
Choking back my sorrow, I grieve alone.

SOURCE: KFS 117, in NKBT, 69, p. 179; octave (pentasyllabic).
TITLE: The "acquaintance" was most likely Kume no Wakame, the widow of courtier Fujiwara no Umakai, who died in the smallpox epidemic of 737. She had been sent off to Shimōsa as punishment for having illicit relations with the poet. See NKBT, 69, pp. 176 (note 7). For his part, Otomaro was exiled to Tosa province on the island of Shikoku (NKBT, 69, p. 506), remaining there 739–43. *Man'yōshū* contains five Japanese poems (nos. 1019–23) written by him during the Tosa years. After receiving a pardon, Otomaro successfully resumed his career, reaching the junior third rank in 748/2.

⌘ Thoughts of the Bedchamber on an Autumn Evening
Isonokami no Asomi Otomaro

Away in this village, I often dream at night.
I seem to be talking with you, my beautiful one.

In bed, our joy is how it used to be.
When I awake, I am sad and weep in vain.
Helplessly pondering, gazing at the moon,
Alone I sit, listening to the wind in the pines.
Mountains and rivers, steep and easy roads;
I toss and turn, recall times with you in bed.

SOURCE: KFS 118, in NKBT, 69, pp. 179–80; octave (pentasyllabic).
TITLE: Japanese and Chinese boudoir poems, while typically written by men, are usually composed in the persona of a woman.
LINE 1: The poet was living in exile in Tosa province at the time and is probably addressing the poem to Kume no Wakame. See preceding poem.

▨ Lamenting Old Age
Authorship unknown

An old man now with frosty temple hair,
Alone and poor, I've a right to feel self-pity.
On spring days, what need to kill the time?
. . . .
Laughing, I pick plum blossoms and sit awhile,
Then frolic about as though a young man still.
Mountains and rivers by nature have no owner;
Life and death likewise in Heaven's hands.
For the heart to possess the beauty of covered brocade,
One must be clad in cotton lined with leather.
A castle may be cut off by a moat,
Yet the cold moon shines endlessly upon it.

SOURCE: KFS, unnumbered (*bangai*) 3, immediately following KFS 120, in NKBT, 69, p. 182; *pailü* (pentasyllabic).
AUTHOR: The authorship and provenance of this poem are unknown. The poem may have been added to KFS later. See NKBT, 69, pp. 7–8.
LINE 4: This line is missing in the text.
LINES 9 AND 10: Line nine is more literally, "the beauty of brocade with a plain garment to cover it," this symbolizing modest behavior and the desire to be unostentatious. The line recalls a passage in *Zhong yong* (The Doctrine of the Mean), chapter 30, which reads, "It is said in the *Book of Poetry*, 'Over her embroidered robe she puts a plain single garment,' intimating a dislike to [*sic*] the display of the elegance of the former. Just so, it is the way of the superior man to prefer the concealment of his virtue, while it daily becomes more illustrious. . . ." See Legge, *Confucius: Confucian Analects, The Great Learning and The Doctrine of the Mean*, pp. 430–31. The beauty of brocade, the "embroidered robe" in Legge's translation, is an indirect reference to the virtue of modesty.
LINE 10: Leather-lined cotton robes were traditionally the dress of rustic hermit recluses.

RYŌUN SHINSHŪ (THE NEW CLOUD-TOPPING COLLECTION)

Ryōun shinshū is the first and the smallest of three imperially-sponsored anthologies of *kanshi* compiled during the early ninth century, a period often considered the golden age of classical *kanshi*. Better known simply as *Ryōunshū*, this collection dates from 814 and includes poems composed as far back as 782 and as late as the year of publication.[77] "Cloud-Topping" (*ryōun*) in the title means "superlative." Many of the verses are formal, thematically conventional compositions written on command at banquets held in Emperor Saga's court; not surprisingly, among these we find a fair number of formulaic offerings written to extol the emperor's virtue. The principal patron of Chinese literary composition, Saga was also considered the leading *kanshi* poet of his day, his works receiving high praise in the preface to the collection, being compared to "shining pearls in a river whose waters run clear" and said to be like "jewels lying hidden in the water's depths, the shoreline enriched."[78] Of all the poets with works in the three imperial anthologies compiled in the early ninth century, Saga has the largest number of compositions, with twenty-two of the ninety-one items in *Ryōunshū* and some eighteen percent of the total number of poems in these three collections.

The principal compiler of *Ryōunshū* was Ono no Minemori (777–830), a courtier and noted *kanshi* poet. Thirteen of his verses appear in the collection, making him the second best-represented poet, coequal with Kaya no Toyotoshi (751–815), an important editorial consultant in the project and a literary luminary in his day. Of the twenty-four poets whose works are found in the anthology, nearly all were members of the imperial family or the aristocracy. Many in the latter category were courtiers belonging to

---

77. See preface to the anthology contained in Kojima, *Kokufū ankoku jidai no bungaku*, vol. 2 (bk. 2), p. 1335.
78. Ibid.

Saga's literary salon, among them, Fujiwara no Fuyutsugu, Yoshimine no Yasuo, Shigeno no Sadanushi, and Ono no Minemori himself. Fourteen of the *Ryōun shinshū* poets also have poems in the second imperial anthology, *Bunka shūreishū*. The poems themselves are arranged by author in descending order of rank, the first two poets being the emperors Heizei and Saga. Poems by Buddhist priests are entirely absent, although there are a few compositions with Buddhist themes, such as RUS 74, by the compiler's father, Ono no Nagami, translated below.

The anthology begins with a preface by Minemori, which discusses the value of literature in governing the realm and lauds the political and literary accomplishments of Emperor Saga. As with *Kaifūsō*, the stated rationale for compiling the anthology is to prevent the further loss of important poetic compositions. With what may well just be *pro forma* modesty, Minemori admits to being reluctant to serve as compiler, declaring that he had wished to quit the project but was not permitted to do so. The preface also informs us that when Minemori and the other compilers needed advice about what poems to include, the final decision was left to Kaya no Toyotoshi, whom Minemori praises as one of the great geniuses of his age. We also learn that when Toyotoshi became too ill to come to court, Emperor Saga assumed this advisory role in his stead. Toyotoshi was evidently a close friend of Minemori's father, Ono no Nagami, which may explain his significant role in the compilation process and the large number of his poems that were included in the collection.

Ryōunshū verse possesses a genteel elegance and a lofty, but detached, even impersonal, tone. The poets frequently employ allusive indirection and such devices as the rhetorical conceit of "oblique" (*yipang*) logic, reflecting the influence of late Six Dynasties and early Tang "palace style" poetry. Many of these palace poems were composed by Saga and his courtiers during excursions and on recreational and festive occasions, such as the Double-Ninth autumn festival. While describing the magnificence of the natural surroundings, the main intention in these poems was to convey the contentment and serenity felt by the assembled company, distanced, if only temporarily, from the responsibilities of court life. The most accomplished poems in *Ryōunshū* are noticeably more lyrical than are those of its predecessor *Kaifūsō*, some showing the distinct influence of eremitic Six Dynasties poets like Tao Yuanming (365–427). Many display a desolation of the spirit and a darkening philosophical tone springing from professional disappointments and other such personal setbacks, a trend which becomes more prominent in subsequent anthologies from the Heian age.[79] Typical themes and topoi include separation from friends, growing old, living in seclusion,

---

79. The single exception is *Bunka shūreishū*, where such gloomy portraits are notably absent. See Ōsone and others, *Kanshi, kanbun, hyōron*, p. 14.

and frustrated ambitions. These compositions offer a sobering contrast to the more impersonal and somewhat overly sanguine palace poems written at imperial banquets and on excursions. One example exhibiting this more personal style is Kamitsukeno no Ehito's "A Poem Submitted with a Memorial to the Throne Immediately After Returning to the Countryside on a Spring Day" (RUS 55), in which Ehito laments the demise of his public career and the run-down condition of his country home, to which he has now retreated.

Although we find some new topics in this collection, such as illness, gift giving, and temple excursions, most are still within the thematic range of Six Dynasties models, as is true of the other two contemporary imperial anthologies. The imagery, rhetoric, and diction are also cast in the Six Dynasties mold, a typical example being Saga's poem "Written on a Summer Day Spent at Kankyoin with Fujiwara no Fuyutsugu, Left Major Captain in the Imperial Bodyguards" (RUS 10), which celebrates the pleasures of a summer excursion, including tea-drinking, poetry composition, music, and fishing.

The poems in *Ryōunshū* overall display a higher level of artistic and technical sophistication compared to *Kaifūsō*. Particularly noteworthy is the appearance of extemporaneous rhyme-matching poems usually written in response to, and in rhyming harmony with, poems composed on the same occasion, a typical example being Emperor's Saga's poem (RUS 4, untranslated), "Written at a Banquet Held for Courtiers on the Double-Ninth at the Shinsen'en: A Poem with the Rhyme-Words *Kong, Tong, Feng,* and *Tong*." Poems incorporating specific assigned rhyme words or ones that are written on prescribed topics also become evident in *Ryōunshū*.[80] Owing to the influence of the "modern" Tang forms, there is a marked increase in the number of heptasyllabic octaves, these constituting about four-fifths of the verses in the collection. From this point forward, heptasyllabic lines were to emerge as the predominant form. Donald Keene suggests that this development may reflect a growing confidence among poets as well as a heightened familiarity with mid-Tang poetic trends.[81]

Scholars generally agree that the poets in *Ryōunshū* and the next two imperial anthologies largely succeeded in conforming to the key rules of regulated verse, unlike their predecessors in *Kaifūsō*.[82] However, poets often had difficulty sustaining rigorous antithesis and parallelism, especially in the second of the middle two couplets of an octave. They also seem to struggle at times to bring their poems to a memorable conclusion with an observation that leaves a lingering impression: some of Emperor Saga's excursion poems, for example, finish with a less than convincing expression

---

80. *Kaifūsō* contains only one poem composed with a set of assigned rhyme words, poem 23.
81. Keene, p. 190, based on the findings of Kojima Noriyuki.
82. On the question of compliance with regulated verse rules, see the Introduction, pp. 16–20.

of nostalgia for the city he has left behind. Courtiers, for their part, were at least able to fall back on admiring, albeit trite-sounding, comments about the emperor and the realm in their closing couplets. Such sentiments are seen in Ono no Minemori's octave "Written on Imperial Command at the Shinsen'en Fishing Platform on a Summer Day" (RUS 57), which concludes with the lines, "Fish naturally look up in awe of His heartfelt beneficence, / All enjoying life among the pondweed."

One also observes the advent of mixed-meter poems. RUS 80, by Takaoka no Otokoe, "Attending the Flower Banquet at Shinsen'en and Composing a Piece on Imperial Command About Falling Flowers," translated below, ably and playfully demonstrates this linear irregularity, growing from a mere three-word line to five- and then seven-word lines (3-5-5-5-7-7-7-7). Finally, we note the presence of longer poems, some ten of which are found in this collection. Yet the longest is still only twenty-six lines, far shorter than certain works by the Chinese masters but an advance on the longest verse in *Kaifūsō*, which has just eighteen lines. Evidently, *kanshi* poets were becoming more proficient in their compositional skills and learning to cope with the technical demands that such lengthier narrative treatments entailed.

❊ Written on a Summer Day Spent at Kankyoin with Fujiwara no Fuyutsugu, Left Major Captain in the Imperial Bodyguards
Emperor Saga

Whenever I wish to escape the heat to Kankyoin we go.
Here we take up our fishing rods on a pavilion beside a pond.
Green willows by the curved bank, dark in the setting sun;
Sound of pines on the winding shore, cold this summer season.
Reciting poems, tirelessly we grind the fragrant tea;
Feeling inspired, the very time for listening to graceful strings.
We stare awhile at the pure spring, washing away our cares;
So easy to enjoy ourselves on such a peaceful day.

SOURCE: RUS 10, in Kojima, *Kokufū ankoku jidai no bungaku: Kōnin-, Tenchō-ki no bungaku o chūshin to shite* (*hohen* exp. ed.), vol. 2 (bk. 2), pp. 1418–23; octave (heptasyllabic).
TITLE: Fuyutsugu (775–826) was a courtier and patron of literature who served a succession of emperors and held many high offices, becoming minister of the left in 825. His daughter Nobuko married Emperor Ninmyō and gave birth to the future emperor Montoku. Fuyutsugu was particularly close to Emperor Saga (786–842), whose trust and favor he enjoyed.
Kankyoin (shortened in the poem to Kan'in) was Fuyutsugu's residence, which was located near Nishi no Tōin, to the south of Nijōdōri in modern Kyoto (ibid., pp. 1418–19). This verse may date from around the Fourth Month of 814, the year the anthology was compiled. See ibid., p. 1419.

LINE 5: Tea was first introduced to Japan from China in the early ninth century by the founder of the Tendai sect, Priest Saichō (767–822). Tea was planted on Mt. Hiei, and the first emperor to taste it was Saga, in 815, according to Ivan Morris, *World of the Shining Prince: Court Life in Ancient Japan* (Harmondsworth: Penguin Books, 1969; Peregrine ed., paperback; orig. pub. 1964, Oxford University Press), p. 160. However, the present poem, if written in 814 as is generally thought, would indicate that tea drinking among the high nobility dates from somewhat earlier.

Thinking About the Capital While Staying at the Kayō Lodge
Emperor Saga

Here at the Kayō Lodge I have sojourned for several nights.
The wind in the pines this moonlit night vexes the traveler's heart.
I can hear the cries of mountain monkeys, deepening the visitor's woe.
Who could help recalling the sight of the capital in spring?

SOURCE: RUS 11, in Kojima, *Kokufū ankoku jidai no bungaku*, vol. 2 (bk. 2), pp. 1424–27; quatrain (heptasyllabic).
TITLE: The Kayō Lodge was part of the Kayō Detached Imperial Palace and was situated in the countryside along the Yodokawa (the Yodo River). This lodge, known also as Yamazaki no Rikyū (the Yamazaki Imperial Retreat), is thought to have been located in the vicinity of Rikyū Hachimangū in modern Ōyamazaki-chō, near Kyoto (ibid., pp. 1424–25). In autumn, it was a favorite imperial hawking ground and boating spot. Kayō is the Japanese reading of Heyang, an area on the northern reaches of the Yellow River in China's Henan province.
COMMENT: This verse, like several before and after it, probably dates from the Second Month, ca. 811–13. See ibid.

The Pleasures of Daybreak at the Lodge on the River
Emperor Saga

Last night I slept at this lodge in a village near the river.
In the evening fishermen's songs from the shore could be heard in my room.
Humid air dampened my pillow as I lay asleep in bed;
The sound of the pines after I awoke somehow compelled me to listen.
On the horizon the dawn moon—exactly like a mirror;
Beyond my door the morning hills—a scene from a painted screen.
I realize that the rosy mist has made my pleasure complete—
Especially now that the plants on the banks are growing lushly green.

SOURCE: RUS 12, in Kojima, *Kokufū ankoku jidai no bungaku*, vol. 2 (bk. 2), pp. 1427–33; octave (heptasyllabic).
TITLE: The emperor was still sojourning at the Kayō Lodge, as in the preceding verse.

❈ Written Upon Presenting a Gift of Silk to Priest Kūkai
Emperor Saga

This tranquil priest has long dwelled among the cloudy peaks.
From afar, I can guess that deep in the hills the spring must still be cold.
The pines and cypresses are well aware how peaceful is your life.
The mist and haze don't know how long you've followed your simple diet.
In recent days, there's been no news from your temple in the hills.
In the capital now, the flowers and willows have all come out in bloom.
Enlightened one, please do not spurn the trifling gift I offer:
I give it to rescue our people from the troubles of this world.

SOURCE: RUS 24, in Kojima, *Kokufū ankoku jidai no bungaku*, vol. 2 (bk. 2), pp. 1486–91; octave (heptasyllabic).

TITLE: Kūkai, posthumously known as Kōbō Daishi, lived 774–835. An eminent Buddhist priest, *kanshi* poet, calligrapher, and literary scholar, he founded the esoteric Shingon (Ch. Zhenyan) sect, centered at Kongōbuji temple, which was built by Kūkai on Mt. Kōya in 816. He studied Zhenyan Buddhism in China during the years 804–6. Kūkai became abbot of Tōji, another important Shingon center, in 823. Kojima estimates that Saga composed this verse during the Third Month of 814 (ibid., p. 1487).

LINE 1: Kūkai was practicing religious austerities on Mt. Takao at the time. He lived there between 810 and 816 and then went to Mt. Koya.

LINE 8: Saga hopes that his gift will lead Kūkai to offer prayers for the Emperor's subjects.

COMMENT: Of interest is Kūkai's reply to this verse, written the same month and titled "A Poem Expressing Appreciation for the Emperor's Kind Gift of a Hundred Bolts of Silk and a Poem in Heptasyllabic Lines." It is found in the third *maki* of a posthumous collection of Kūkai's poems titled *Seireishū* (The Spirit and Mind Collection), assembled by his follower Shinzei. This is translated below, following the Kojima text in ibid., pp. 1491–92:

> This priest endures much hardship as he travels these cloud-covered hills.
> The wind and snow are pitiless; the nights of spring are cold.
> Five staffs in all I've held while reading the Buddha's law.
> Six years I've worn coarse garb and lived on simple food.
> You have always made sincere efforts, true as the sun and moon;
> Though dull, I'm aware of your generosity, reminiscent of the age of Yao.
> The Buddhas ardently support the First Son in the love he shows for his subjects;
> What need has he to worry about the suffering of the people?

❈ A Moonlit Night in Early Autumn
Yoshimine no Ason Yasuyo, Commander of the Left Military Guards and Governor of Tajima, Junior Fourth Rank Lower

Evening, the fifteenth day of autumn:
The night is long, nocturnal winds blow cold.
Dew hangs pale upon the spider webs;
The leaves on the trees not yet turning yellow.

SOURCE: RUS 50, in Kojima, *Kokufū ankoku jidai no bungaku*, vol. 2 (bk. 2), pp. 1610–12; quatrain (pentasyllabic).
AUTHOR: Yasuyo was one of the chief compilers of the *kanshi* anthology *Keikokushū*.

✖ A Poem Submitted with a Memorial to the Throne Immediately After Returning to the Countryside on a Spring Day

Kamitsukeno no Ehito, Vice-Governor of Inaba and Senior Secretary in the Council of State, Junior Fifth Rank Upper

I sought a stipend, ended up with nothing;
Returned to my fields, walked through the tumbledown gate.
The garden in ruins, just the walls of my home still stood.
The hedge had gone, only flowers remained.
Empty-handed and on the verge of starving,
I hung my head; the sun had just gone down.
Such is the suffering that comes our way in life.
Where will I find the beneficence of spring?

SOURCE: RUS 55, in Kojima, *Kokufū ankoku jidai no bungaku*, vol. 2 (bk. 2), pp. 1630–34; octave (pentasyllabic).
LINE 8: Here Ehito is wistfully alluding to the patronage and support of the emperor.

✖ Written on Imperial Command at the Shinsen'en Fishing Platform on a Summer Day

Ono no Ason Minemori, Director of the Palace Storehouse Bureau, Director of the Left Imperial Stables, and Governor of Mino, Junior Fifth Rank Upper

This fishing platform was only recently built.
Floating posts protrude from the water's depths.
Water close; we let out all our line.
Eaves low; our poles can touch the water.
The bank is noisy, sound of the cataract.
The shore dark, shade of tangerines and citrons.
Fish naturally look up in awe of His heartfelt beneficence,
All enjoying life among the pondweed.

SOURCE: RUS 57, in Kojima, *Kokufū ankoku jidai no bungaku*, vol. 2 (bk. 2), pp. 1646–49; octave (pentasyllabic).
TITLE: This poem is the second in a group of thirteen poems by Minemori in this anthology. Shinsen'en (or Shinzen'en) was an imperial park, the remains of which can be found in the garden of a temple (Shingon-shū Tōji sect) located across from the southern entrance to the Nijō Castle in modern Kyoto. It had a lake with a man-made island, a fishing pavilion, and

waterfalls. Shinsen'en originally extended from Nijō to Sanjō streets, north and south, and from Ōmiya on the east to Mibu Ōji on the west. However, most of the lake disappeared in the middle ages and the park itself was reduced to a smaller scale following the building of the Nijō Castle in the late sixteenth century. See Takemura Toshinori, *Kyō no shiseki meguri* (Kyoto: Kyoto Shinbunsha, 1987), pp. 84–85.

LINES 7 AND 8: The poet is using the fish to symbolize the emperor's subjects, who are portrayed here as being fortunate to enjoy his enlightened rule. The pondweed also functions as a symbol: just as it provides shelter and sustenance to the fish, so too does the Emperor provide succor to his subjects. Laudatory closures designed to glorify the emperor are commonplace in the final couplets of palace poetry. RUS 80, below, provides a similar example.

✖ Bidding Farewell to a Friend Who is Off to a Post and Presenting Him with a *Koto*
Ono no Ason Minemori

This plain *koto*, a token of our lasting friendship:
It's dusty and dirty, but surely you will not mind.
Think of that fine official in Shanfu town;
May you gain the Lord of Wucheng's great renown.
Fine possessions are not what you desire;
This paltry gift is commensurate with my means.
Whenever you view the moon away from home,
Play it to console yourself while apart from us all.

SOURCE: RUS 68, in Kojima, *Kokufū ankoku jidai no bungaku*, vol. 2 (bk. 2), pp. 1715-19; octave (pentasyllabic).
LINE 3: Shanfu was a city in the state of Lu during China's Spring and Autumn period (770–476 B.C.). The person alluded to here is Fu Zi, the mayor of Shanfu, an enlightened official and a disciple of Confucius. According to tradition, he played the *qin* constantly.
LINE 4: Wucheng was another city in Lu. The lord referred to here is Zi You, who likewise was the city's mayor. A well-regarded official, he too was one of Confucius's disciples.

✖ The Farmhouse
Ono no Ason Nagami, Lieutenant General of the Aboriginal Subjugation Force and Vice-Governor of Mutsu, Junior Fifth Rank Lower

I built a cottage that stands among three paths.
I water my garden to provide myself with food.
Coarse distiller's grain is fine for filling my stomach,
A rocky spring enough to delight my senses.
Pines cast shadows deep within the water;
The sound of bamboo moving in the wind.
I pay the trifling land tax due in peacetime,
Living alone in my lodge on this little hill.

SOURCE: RUS 73, in Kojima, *Kokufū ankoku jidai no bungaku*, vol. 2 (bk. 2), pp. 1735–41; octave (pentasyllabic).

AUTHOR: Historians conjecture that Ono no Nagami served in the military sometime during the Enryaku era (782–805), under the command of General Sakanoue no Tamuramaro (ibid., pp. 1734–35).

LINE 1: "Three paths" is an allusion to the walkways crossing the famous garden of the Former Han dynasty recluse Jiang Xu, where pines, chrysanthemums, and bamboo, all symbols of longevity, were planted. The expression became a conventional metaphor in Chinese and Japanese poetry for the garden or abode of a scholar-recluse. Tao Yuanming's poem titled "Gui qu lai ci" (On Returning Home) employs the phrase.

Visiting a Temple
Ono no Nagami

Long weary of the miseries of the bird cage,
I've come to find the crossing that leads to release.
I've calmed my heart, returned to the Six Pāramitās;
Changed my ways and look now to the Three Wheels.
The moon in the water is not the true moon of dawn;
The flowers in the sky from a springtime that is not real.
Now that I've started my journey to Enlightenment this morning,
How could I ever go astray in the mundane world?

SOURCE: RUS 74, in Kojima, *Kokufū ankoku jidai no bungaku*, vol. 2 (bk. 2), pp. 1741–45; octave (pentasyllabic).

LINE 1: "Bird cage": a metaphor for the entanglements and responsibilities of the mundane world. This line is similar to the penultimate line in the first of a series of poems by Tao Yuanming titled "Gui tian yuan ju" (On Returning to My Garden and Field), which reads, "Long have I dwelled within the bird cage."

LINE 3: The Six Pāramitās are the practices and capacities through which a Boddhisattva attains Buddhahood, namely: charity, observing precepts, perseverance, energy, meditation, and wisdom. See Hisao Inagaki, *A Dictionary of Japanese Buddhist Terms*, third ed. (Kyoto: Nagata Bunshodo, 1988), p. 253.

LINE 4: The "Three Wheels" (*sanrin*) here refers to the three karmic vehicles (*sangō*) in Buddhism, namely, the body, the mouth, and the mind, the proper exercise of which can enable all living things to be reborn in the Pure Land.

LINES 5 AND 6: The poet is alluding to the theory of universal emptiness; that is, the illusory nature or non-substantiality of all phenomena, as seen in Buddhist thought.

My Field and Garden in Early Spring
Ōmi no Mahito Fukuramaro, Supernumerary Governor of Hyūga, Junior Fifth Rank Lower

By my cold window, the blossoms of five plums.
In my empty kitchen, a single cask of wine.
The power of the emperor is lost on the likes of me;

How can one grasp the eternity of heaven and earth?
One paddy, sufficient to feed myself;
Five willow trees beyond my door.
Enough for a little pleasure in my poverty—
Why would I ever be covetous of wealth?

SOURCE: RUS 75, in Kojima, *Kokufū ankoku jidai no bungaku*, vol. 2 (bk. 2), pp. 1745–51; octave (pentasyllabic).

TITLE AND AUTHOR: The author notation indicates that Fukuramaro held the junior fifth rank lower at the time this poem was composed. We know that he attained this rank in 797, so this verse must have been composed between that year and the year of his next promotion to the junior fifth rank *upper*, which occurred in 806. See ibid., pp. 1745–46. Fukuramaro, who flourished ca. 800, was probably a descendant of Emperor Tenchi, one indication being that his *kabane* peerage title *mahito* was normally reserved for nobility.

This title is reminiscent of Tao Yuanming's series of poems titled "On Returning to My Garden and Field." Fukuramaro's poem overall is clearly inspired by Tao's poetry, which often extols the virtues and pleasures of a quiet, pastoral life of simplicity and seclusion, far from the city with its mundane concerns and pressures.

LINE 6: "Five willow trees" brings to mind Tao Yuanming's prose piece "The Biography of Master Five Willow Trees." This gentleman, so named because of the five willow trees planted around his house, is believed to have been Tao himself.

❈ Expressing My Aspirations
Ōmi no Mahito Fukuramaro

The solitary tree has long been twisted and gnarled.
Autumn, and it stands bereft of its leaves.
Day and night, beset by wind and frost.
How long will it have to wait for its day of glory?

SOURCE: RUS 76, in Kojima, *Kokufū ankoku jidai no bungaku*, vol. 2 (bk. 2), pp. 1751–53; quatrain (pentasyllabic).

COMMENT: The poet likens himself to a leafless, frost-laden tree to vent his dissatisfaction over the slow progress of his official career. "Glory" in line four refers both to the flourishing of vegetation and to human glory.

❈ Attending the Flower Banquet at Shinsen'en and Composing a Piece on Imperial Command About Falling Flowers
Takaoka no Sukune Otokoe (Otoe), Vice-Governor of Yamashiro, Second-Class Junior Fifth Rank Lower

Falling flowers drift,
Flying away, landing in the courtyard.
I used to believe they were blown down by the wind,
But now I am aware they are governed by the laws of change.

Coming and going, floating in the wine goblet of the Emperor.
First a constant shower, then ceasing, they dot His Majesty's clothes.
Even the mindless plants and trees have the greatest love for His person.
All the more we minor subjects, who've drunk from his cup of kindness!

SOURCE: RUS 80, in Kojima, *Kokufū ankoku jidai no bungaku*, vol. 2 (bk. 2), pp. 1765–70; *zatsugon*, octave in irregular meter.
TITLE: "Piece" is literally *hen* (Ch. *pian*). This poem is not in a regulated verse form but in a style that has irregular line length and is considered one of the miscellaneous, non-regulated verse forms or *zatsugon*. The number of characters in each line of this poem is: 3, 5, 5, 5, 7, 7, 7, 7. Irregular verse of this kind is first seen in the three official *kanshi* anthologies of the early ninth century. See the Introduction for further information.
The "second-class" rank system, *ge'i*, was first used when granting ranks to *gunji* (district magistrates) or men of provincial background. Later, it came to be employed when awarding ranks to families of lesser status.
The Flower Banquet (*kaen*) was held every spring from 812, for the purposes of enjoying the cherry blossoms, drinking wine, and composing verse.
LINES 3 AND 4: Here, the poet employs the common literary device of contrived misapprehension, paving the way for a sudden realization in line four. It has "just" dawned on him that the falling of the flowers belongs to larger cosmic process involving more than simply the wind. This event is part of the endless cycle of *yin* and *yang* that governs the entire universe.
LINE 7: The poet is fancifully suggesting that the blossoms are dropping because they long to be closer to the Emperor. They may be said to symbolize the Emperor's subjects.

Going Over Shinano Pass
Sakanoue no Imiki Imatsugu, Left Senior Recorder in the Council of State and Supernumerary Senior Secretary of Ise, Senior Sixth Rank Upper

Boulder on boulder, perilously steep;
Treacherous path, twisting, winding around.
I have lost my way in the snow in this far-off place.
My horse treads through low-hanging clouds.
The crags are cold—hard for flowers to bloom;
The valleys are deep—early it grows dark.
Where is my old home village to be found?
The traveler's mind grows ever more confused.

SOURCE: RUS 81, in Kojima, *Kokufū ankoku jidai no bungaku*, vol. 2 (bk. 2), pp. 1770–75; octave (pentasyllabic).
TITLE: Shinano Pass was near Fujimidai, in modern Nagano prefecture. See ibid., p. 1771.

✠ Written While Stopping at My Friend's Mountain Retreat on a Spring Day: I Drew the Rhyme-Word "Fly"

Kuwahara no Haraka (Haraaka), Major *So-i* Rank Lower,
Presented Scholar and Extranumerary Professor in Sagami Province

Several days have passed since spring began.
I hear the sound of warblers flying about.
Mist veils the willows of our host;
Flowers scent the clothing of the guests.
A country boy herding cattle passes by;
An old man from the hills heads home with firewood.
The old man of Hanyin was surely not alone:
Here, you too can free your mind of schemes.

SOURCE: RUS 89, in Kojima, *Kokufū ankoku jidai no bungaku*, vol. 2 (bk. 2), pp. 1819–24; octave (pentasyllabic).

TITLE AND AUTHOR: The *so-i* (*sho-i*) rank, which Haraka held, was the lowest of the court ranks, *so-i* being one level lower than eighth. Like ranks four through eight, each of which were subdivided into four levels—senior (*shō*) upper and lower and junior (*jū*) upper and lower—*so-i* too had four levels, major (*dai*) upper and lower and minor (*shō*) upper and lower.

Kuwahara no Haraka (789–825) assumed the position of scholar-professor in distant Sagami province probably sometime between 810 and 823 (ibid., pp. 1819–20).

This poem title indicates that Haraka, likely a participant in a poetry exercise or contest, had received a character for use as the rhyme-word of his poem. Usually the rhyme-word occurred at the end of the second line, with all even lines ending with a word in the same *inmoku* (rhyme category). It was a common practice among the elite at poetry gatherings to draw lots for a rhyme-word.

LINES 7 AND 8: There is an anecdote in *Zhuangzi* where Confucius's disciple Zi Gong, traveling in the area south of the Han River, encountered an elderly man who was irrigating his fields in an inefficient and time-consuming manner. Zi Gong told him of a more laborsaving method, but the old man showed complete disinterest, saying that adopting mechanical contrivances of any kind fostered the development of a designing and calculating mind. Chastened by this response, Zi Gong had no reply. The ideal of freeing the mind of schemes harks back to this story, for the poet is visiting a place where, at least in his imagination, the same primitive and rustic way of life still prevailed.

✠ Written While Drinking at a Friend's Mountain Retreat on an Autumn Day: I Drew the Rhyme-Word "Eaves"

Kuwahara no Haraka

I'd heard of this secluded mountain retreat;
Grabbing onto vines, I scrambled up for a look.
White clouds wafting upwards from our cups;
Yellow chrysanthemums sticky in our hands.
Close to the wilds—animals sit there, tame.
Near to the woods—birds watch us from the eaves.

We've climbed to these heights yet are still of the human world,
For we find ourselves both officials and recluses at once.

SOURCE: RUS 90, in Kojima, *Kokufū ankoku jidai no bungaku*, vol. 2 (bk. 2), p. 1825; octave (pentasyllabic).

LINE 4: The assembled gentlemen were likely celebrating the Double-Ninth autumn festival, held on the ninth day of the Ninth Month, when scholar-officials hiked up mountains and picnicked, their climbing symbolic of their desire to scale to the heights of success. They wrote poems while sitting among chrysanthemums, symbols of longevity, which they plucked and floated in their wine cups. The Double-Ninth was considered the best day for picking these flowers, in part because of the phonetic resemblance between the Chinese words for "nine" and "chrysanthemum."

LINE 8: This is to say they are recluses in spirit, even though they are in public service.

BUNKA SHŪREISHŪ (ANTHOLOGY OF SPLENDID LITERARY FLOWERINGS)

The best known of the three imperial anthologies compiled in the early ninth century, *Bunka shūreishū* was commissioned by Emperor Saga and probably completed in 818. The preface states that in the four years since the appearance of *Ryōunshū*, "more than one hundred pieces" had been composed,[83] presumably meaning poetic works considered worthy of preservation. A larger and more systematically organized collection, *Bunka shūreishū* comprises poems composed between 782 and 818. One Prince Nakao, whose lineage is uncertain, is credited with compiling the work. Conspicuously absent in the compiler's introduction is the conventional assertion regarding the political importance of literature in helping bring order to the realm, perhaps reflecting a more aesthetic orientation.

Bunka shūreishū contains 143 poems in three *maki* by twenty-eight poets, among whom Saga is the best represented with thirty-four compositions. Many of Saga's verses are followed by "response" poems by courtiers, among them Kose no Shikihito, with twenty to his credit,[84] Prince Nakao, with thirteen, and Kuwahara no Haraka with ten. Despite its closeness in time to *Ryōunshū*, several poets prominent in the latter are absent, Ono no Nagami and Kaya no Toyotoshi among them. Notable also is the inclusion of some five poems by one Wang Xiaolian, ambassador from the state of Parhae,[85] who visited the court with his secretary, Shi Renzhen, to whom poem 18 is attributed. Although court ladies rarely seem to have written *kanshi*, one female poet, Ōtomo Uji no Hime, is credited with one composition (poem 50) in this work.[86]

---

83. NKBT, 69, p. 193.
84. Note that by contrast, only one of his poems appears in *Ryōunshū*.
85. Parhae was a vassal kingdom of China in modern southeast Manchuria and northeast Korea, in existence 698–926.
86. Poem 55, by Kose no Shikihito, is a response to yet another verse by Ōtomo Uji no Hime, "My Feelings in the Boudoir One Autumn Night," which is not included in *Bunka shūreishū*.

As is perhaps obvious from the aristocratic backgrounds of the poets in this work, the themes and concerns are much the same as in the two earlier anthologies, with travel, interest in nature, and courtly social exchanges remaining the primary topoi. In contrast to *Kaifūsō*, whose compositions are grouped by author without consideration of theme, and those of *Ryōunshū*, which are similarly arranged by author in descending order of rank, the poetry in *Bunka shūreishū* is arranged according to subject category or genre, eleven in all, nine of which are borrowed from the Six Dynasties collection *Wen xuan*. Two additional categories not found in *Wen xuan* are also present: love and Buddhism, which account for twenty-one poems. Compared to the two previous anthologies, a heightened interest in Japan and things Japanese is apparent, as is an increase in poems by Buddhist priests, including the illustrious Priest Kūkai (774–835), founder of the Shingon sect. Notably absent in *Bunka shūreishū* are poems bewailing personal career misfortune of the sort seen in *Ryōunshū*, perhaps because the compilers preferred richly aesthetic, if somewhat impersonal, description over more subjective narrations of private misery.

The first of the three *maki* that make up *Bunka shūreishū* contains forty-one items, including fourteen excursion poems, four on banquets (many occurring in summer, when the capital-dwellers sought refuge from the heat), ten on parting, and thirteen *zōtō*, "poetic exchanges." The second volume comprises fifty-four poems in the categories of history, *jukkai* (expressions of feelings), *enjō* (love), *gafu* (ballad-style folk lyrics), *bonmon* (Buddhism), and *aishō* (laments). The third volume consists of forty-eight "miscellaneous verses," a classification for poems not belonging to any other category. This represents a larger proportion of such verse than is found in the two previous collections. Many of the miscellaneous poems belong to the *yongwu* genre and focus upon a variety of natural topics and phenomena, such as seagulls, butterflies, spring snow, and falling leaves. These tend to be stylized portraits of objects in nature rather than realistic descriptions.

The poems in *Bunka shūreishū* vary somewhat in length, although the octave is the preferred form overall, accounting for a little more than half of the poems. Twenty-two longer verses, many ranging between thirty and forty-four lines, are to be found in the miscellaneous and love sections. These longer compositions, for example, poems 51, 129, 130, and 139, are noteworthy in that several have an uneven number of lines as well as irregular meter in a few cases. There are some forty-four quatrains, the majority appearing in the miscellaneous section and being mostly in the heptasyllabic form, the preferred line length by this time.

The influence of late Six Dynasties court poetry is still prevalent, particularly among the excursion poems. *Bunka shūreishū* also has a deeper Buddhist tinge than the preceding anthologies, with poems about visits to

Buddhist temples and the spiritual solace derived from these pilgrimages nearly overshadowing poems about imperial pleasure expeditions. In mood and tone, these poems are dignified and calm rather than darkly despairing or pessimistic. The expressed desire of the poets to live in rural seclusion seems to stem more from a personal quest for spiritual serenity of a metaphysical nature than from any deep disillusionment with human society and official life.

Drifting in Our Boat on the Great Lake One Summer Day
Emperor Saga

To the Land of Water we have come in search of coolness;
On the Great Lake, floating aboard our boat.
A wind blows, whipping up the waves.
Among the clouds a boat with lowered sail.
Inlet fragrant, rich with tangerine scent;
Islets dark with the verdure of the reeds.
A group of women from a hamlet, picking lotus roots for food;
Some old men from a village catching fish.
The summer sun sinks behind the western mountains.
Shrill monkeys cry out from the northern hills.
The pleasures of drifting in our boat seem unending.
We cease our poling and turn our prow toward shore.

SOURCE: BKSRS 8, in NKBT, 69, pp. 203–4; *pailü* (pentasyllabic), in twelve lines.
LINE 1: Land of Water—a reference to Ōmi province, site of Lake Biwa, the "Great Lake" seen in the title.
COMMENT: This poem was probably written on 815/4/22, according to the official history *Ruijū kokushi* 31 (NKBT, 69, p. 203).

Enjoying the Coolness at the Saga'in Retreat: I Drew the Rhyme-Word "Return" and Wrote this Verse on Imperial Command
Kose no Shikihito

Tired of the heat, His Majesty has come to this place—
A pristine and quiet spot, far removed from the world.
Beside the pond, seeking coolness, standing in the bamboo shade;
Among the rocks, escaping the heat, sheltering under the pine canopy.
A thousand years of patchy moss thickly covers the steps;
A single cloud in the bright sunlight floats homeward past the peaks.
This mountain retreat, remote and secluded, is but a simple place,
From dawn to dusk, just the sound of water in the spring.

SOURCE: BKSRS 10, in NKBT, 69, p. 205; octave (heptasyllabic).

TITLE: Each poet participating in the group activity of writing Chinese poems drew lots for a rhyme-word and was required to use this word in his own composition to provide the basic rhyme. The rhyme-word "return" occurs at the end of line six in the original poem and we have rendered it as "floats homeward."

COMMENT: Kose no Shikihito probably composed this poem on the sixteenth day of the intercalary Fourth Month of 817.

Sending Off Fujiwara no Yoshino, Secretary of Mino: I Received the Word "Flower"
Crown Prince Ōtomo

Tonight in haste we say farewell, from one another part.
I never thought we'd separate, disperse like scattered flowers.
Lament not that a thousand miles of clouds will lie between us;
For men like ourselves each place is home, no matter where we go.

SOURCE: BKSRS 21, in NKBT, 69, p. 214; quatrain (heptasyllabic).

TITLE: Fujiwara no Yoshino (d. 846) was the grandson of the famous courtier Fujiwara no Maro (695–737) and the son of Tsunatsugu, head of the War Ministry. In addition to serving in the post mentioned here, Yoshino also served variously as junior assistant head of the Central Affairs Ministry, minor captain of the Imperial Bodyguards, and supernumerary middle counselor, retiring at the senior third rank.

COMMENT: This poem dates from 813. Crown Prince Ōtomo took the throne as Emperor Junna in 823.

Saying Farewell to My Literati Friends
Ono no Minemori

Since I became an official, ten years or so have passed.
Half my literati friends are dead; half are new acquaintances.
We have traveled the same road all along—for me, no "old" or "new."
What pains me is that soon I'll be ten thousand miles away.

SOURCE: BKSRS 22, in NKBT, 69, pp. 214–15; quatrain (heptasyllabic).

Bidding Farewell to Ōtomo, Secretary of Awa, in Early Spring
Ki no Suemori

Now that you have your orders, you'll be leaving for distant parts.
New Year is here, early spring, but still the wind is cold.
If you need to know that my spirit is there, keeping you company,
Watch for me in your dreams each night, at the inns where you shall stay.

SOURCE: BKSRS 28, in NKBT, 69, p. 219; quatrain (heptasyllabic).
TITLE: Ōtomo, unidentified, was heading for Awa province in what is today Bōsō Peninsula, across the bay from Tokyo.
LINE 2: The Japanese New Year traditionally began on the first day of the first lunar month, which was considered the first day of spring. This day varies from year to year by the western calendar, falling somewhere between January 20 and February 20.

❀ One autumn morning after hearing wild geese, I sent the following poem to Emissary Gao and his scribe Shi, who were visiting the court from Parhae

Sakanoue no Imao (Imatsugu?)

The great sea so difficult to cross.
Unable we are to send your boat on its way.
Oh, to be like the geese of Shaanxi and Gansu,
Crossing in spring, returning in the fall!

SOURCE: BKSRS 35, in NKBT, 69, pp. 224–25; quatrain (pentasyllabic).
TITLE AND AUTHOR: This verse was reportedly written during the Ninth Month of 814. Emissary Gao was Gao Yingshan; the scribe was Shi Renzhen (NKBT, 69, p. 224). Parhae (Ch. Bohai) was a large Tungusic state encompassing parts of northern Korea and southern Manchuria. It came into existence in 698, created from a portion of Koguryö (J. Kōrai), an early state in northern Korea that had escaped annexation by China. In 713 Parhae was officially recognized by China as a tributary state. Parhae and Japan had close relations, the former becoming a virtual vassal state of Japan as well, in hopes of gaining trade and protection. The kingdom fell in 926. Poet Sakanoue no Imao has not been identified. Imao may be a scribal error for Sakanoue no Imatsugu, author of BKSRS 36. See NKBT, 69, p. 514.
LINE 1: The "great sea" (*taikai*) is the Sea of Japan, extending between Korea and Japan.
LINE 3: Shaanxi and Gansu are provinces in northwest China.

❀ Written to Match a Verse Titled "Sick in Bed on the Day of the Double-Ninth Festival"

Ono no Minemori

The Sagely One has been indisposed for many days on end,
And now the Double-Ninth Festival has suddenly arrived.
The autumn chrysanthemums are unaware that the regal banquet's off:
Several of the yellow flowers bloom before the Palace.

SOURCE: BKSRS 49, in NKBT, 69, pp. 236–37; quatrain (heptasyllabic).
TITLE: The Double-Ninth Festival, also known as the Chrysanthemum Festival, was held on the ninth day of the Ninth Month, in autumn. See the notes to RUS 90, above.
LINE 1: The Sagely One is Emperor Saga, who fell ill on 816/9/4, just days before the Double-Ninth. Because of this, the festivities were canceled that year.
LINES 3 AND 4: The suggestion is that the flowers are blooming in vain, wasting their sweetness on the desert air, so to speak.

Late Autumn, Expressing My Feelings
Ōtomo Uji no Hime

The season of desolation is here, the year draws to a close.
Quiet and still by my chamber door, cold the autumn days.
Faraway geese in cloudy skies, their cries well suit the time;
In the trees by the eaves the chirping of late cicadas fades away.
Chrysanthemums by the pond, covered in dew, the remaining flowers cold.
Lotuses by the banks, laden with frost, the aged cups now withered.
Lonesome I feel, alone I lament over how the seasons rush by.
The fallen scattered leaves all around I cannot bear to see.

SOURCE: BKSRS 50, in NKBT, 69, pp. 237–38; octave (heptasyllabic).

Written on Imperial Command While Accompanying the Emperor to Bonshakuji
Crown Prince Ōtomo

His Majesty took a break from his duties, weary of the sweltering heat.
In the afternoon, he went to the temple to pay the Buddha a visit.
Four or five old priests emerged to greet the imperial carriage.
They'd long cast off all ties and cares, their minds perennially void.
Over treetops we crossed a swinging bridge, parting the clouds as we went.
Over steep steps leading up a cliff we brushed aside the mist.
As I looked up at the Buddha's face all worldly entanglements vanished.
I found myself wondering—maybe I've found my way to Condor Peak.

SOURCE: BKSRS 74, in NKBT, 69, p. 260; octave (heptasyllabic).
TITLE: Bonshakuji was a temple located on the eastern slopes of Mt. Hiei in the modern city of Ōtsu, east of Kyoto. It was built in 786, rebuilt in 1057, and then in subsequent years fell into disrepair.
LINE 2: This visit occurred in the Fourth Month of 815.
LINE 8: Condor Peak (Skt. Gṛdhrakūṭa-parvata), which the Japanese call Jūho or Ryōjusen, was the site of the Buddha's legendary retreat. Located in Magadha, India, it was said to resemble the head of a condor.

Written on Imperial Command While Accompanying the Emperor to Bonshakuji
Fujiwara no Fuyutsugu

We climbed up to Bonshakuji so His Majesty could ask about the Way.
Bonshakuji—a lonely place, so tranquil and remote.

Old priests sit in meditation, never going outdoors.
Young men follow the Buddhist path, never descending the mountain.
Quiet and deserted the shrine that stands beyond the misty clouds.
Lonesome and silent the meditation rooms among the bamboo and pines.
They've found the bridge to eternal Buddhahood for every sentient being.
The dust and noise of the mundane world have no place in their lives.

SOURCE: BKSRS 75, in NKBT, 69, pp. 260–61; octave (heptasyllabic).

⚿ Written to Match Priest Saichō's Poem "Thoughts While Lying Sick Abed"
Emperor Saga

I have heard that high upon that cloudy peak,
Lying there sick, you're close to grasping the Truth.
You have learned that all phenomena are an illusion;
Glimpsing the Void, you've come to hate your body.
Dark the cypresses, forlorn the meditation garden;
Bright the flowers, springtime at your temple.
Do not fret that the Buddha is slow in coming
To save all people who live in this world of dreams.

SOURCE: BKSRS 76, in NKBT, 69, pp. 261–62; octave (pentasyllabic).
LINE 2: That is, he has almost reached Buddhist enlightenment.
COMMENT: Saichō's poem was written around 812. See NKBT, 69, p. 261.

⚿ A Poem Written to Match Priest Saichō's "Thoughts While Lying Sick Abed"
Prince Nakao

An ancient temple in the forest to the north.
A noble priest, so pure from head to toe.
His mind on Tendai, clear as the moon seen through vines;
His thoughts away in the clouds of the Buddha's Mountain.
Quiet courtyard, plantains in all their beauty.
Deserted halls, a tolling temple bell.
He lies there ill, as if deep in meditation.
No one comes—just the cries of mountain birds.

SOURCE: BKSRS 77, in NKBT, 69, p. 262; octave (pentasyllabic).
LINES 3 AND 4: Buddha's Mountain is commonly a reference to Mt. Tiantai (J. Tendai), in Zhejiang province, China, where the Tiantai sect originated. However, in a Japanese context, the

poet more likely had in mind the center of the Tendai sect, which was established by Priest Saichō himself on Mt. Hiei at Enryakuji temple in the early ninth century.

🎌 Written to Match Priest Saichō's Poem "Thoughts While Lying Sick Abed"
Kose no Shikihito

Our teacher in the temple on the mountain
Lies abed in the clouds and mist, pleading poor health.
Monkeys and birds feel quite at home at the temple;
Divinities and gods watch over the *dharma* mats.
Flowers in the river valley bloom before the Buddha;
The moon above the peaks inclines toward the priest.
You are well aware that everything is an illusion:
Look at yourself and you'll find the cure at hand.

SOURCE: BKSRS 78, in NKBT, 69, p. 263; octave (pentasyllabic).
LINE 2: Shikihito seems to be cynically suggesting that Saichō's illness was illusory and that from a Buddhist point of view, he could overcome his frailties by strength of will alone. The phrase translated as "pleading poor health" could instead mean "pretending to be ill."

🎌 A Verse to Match the Poem "A Lament for Lady-in-Waiting Ono"
Fujiwara no Fuyutsugu

In her days of beauty, she served within the Palace's inner sanctum.
Hair greying, she left her post, to her hometown she returned.
The moonlight shining upon the river vanishes without a trace;
A lamp in the wind is unable to shed a ray of smoky light.
Palace ladies speak in praise of her purity and virtue;
Biographies of chaste women record her modesty and goodness.
His Majesty is deeply moved, aggrieved by her passing;
"If your spirit possesses consciousness, may you rest in peace."

SOURCE: BKSRS 83, in NKBT, 69, pp. 266–67; octave (heptasyllabic).
TITLE: The poem referred to here is Emperor Saga's lament for Ono no Ishiko, a much-respected lady-in-waiting at court who died at age seventy-one on 816/3/22. She held the senior third rank at the time of her death, having been promoted from junior third earlier in the year (NKBT, 69, p. 482, n. 83). Ishiko served the imperial consort.
LINE 2: Her home was in Nagaoka, near Kyoto.
LINE 6: The biographies in question would have formed part of the official court historical records. "Lie nü zhuan" (The Biographies of Chaste Women) constituted a traditional category in the official dynastic histories of China.

A Lament for Priest Genpin
Emperor Saga

From early in life this noble priest was without a fixed abode.
On a famous mountain he hid away, growing old in the wind and frost.
Following karma, transformed himself, long hating the world of dust.
Returning to the Path, he found enlightenment, then suddenly passed away.
His old retreat surrounded by pines, bushy and verdant still;
The new pagoda obscured by plants grows desolate from neglect.
Vacant the mat where he used to sit, only the light of the moon.
Who adds incense to his golden burner, now that he has gone?
In the Buddhist forest, we often see the breaking of branches and trunks;
The temple itself shall always remember the loss of its beams and posts.
Priests and laity all in mourning, the body-viewing now over.
Far into the distance they gaze in worship, facing toward the west.

SOURCE: BKSRS 85, in NKBT, 69, pp. 268–69; *pailü* (heptasyllabic), in twelve lines.
TITLE: This verse was written soon after Genpin's death on 818/6/17, probably at the time of his funeral. Genpin, whose surname by birth was Yuge, was well over eighty when he died. Early in his career, he was a priest at Kōfukuji temple in Kyoto. One source relates that he abhorred the rising influence of Priest Dōkyō and went into seclusion on Mt. Hōki (Hahaki), in the western part of modern Tottori prefecture, where he established the Amidadera temple. When Emperor Kanmu took ill in 805, Genpin returned to Kyoto, but later went back to Mt. Hōki to dwell in seclusion. He was awarded the illustrious title of Daihōshi Genpin Daisōzu (Grand Bishop Genpin) in 806, this being the second highest rank in the Buddhist hierarchy. Genpin later took up residence in the Tōsenji temple in Bitchū, enjoying the favor of Emperor Saga, who sent him letters and lavish gifts. For further details, see NKBT, 69, p. 483 and source materials from *Ruijū kokushi*, *maki* 186, cited therein.
LINE 2: The mountain was Hōki. See preceding note.
LINES 9 AND 10: The damage to trees in the forest is an allusion to the loss of Genpin. Similarly, "beams and posts" refers to important priests like Genpin himself.
LINE 12: That is, toward the Western Paradise of Pure Land Buddhism.

Written in Response to a Poem by Shigeno no Sadanushi, Secretary in the Central Affairs Ministry, Which Was Written to Match the Poem "Visiting the Site Where the Hermit Used to Live," by Taira no Satsuki, Clerk of Musashi
Emperor Saga

Forlorn and silent the place where the hermit lived.
His skeleton lies there, bleached by wind and frost.
Over the years, his books grew old and tattered.
His alchemy stove stands cold among misty vines.
Pine trees overhang his cliffside dwelling.
A rock served as his bed in the empty chamber.

Enlightenment reached, to heaven he ascended,
While here in the mud I am left to grieve alone.

SOURCE: BKSRS 93, in NKBT, 69, pp. 273–74; octave (pentasyllabic).
TITLE: Sadanushi's verse does not survive, but Satsuki's is included as BKSRS 95, below. The
identity of the hermit is unknown. It is not clear whether Saga personally visited the site de-
scribed in his poem.

✖ Written to Match a Poem by Taira no Satsuki, Clerk of Musashi, Titled "Visiting the Site Where the Hermit Used to Live"
Fujiwara no Fuyutsugu

Fleeing into seclusion, never to return;
Renouncing the flesh, turning his back on the world.
The moon shines down upon his mystical texts;
Aged monkeys lament beside his white bones.
The wind blows through, forlorn his gate in the pines;
The spring gushes forth, cold his house of stone.
White clouds everywhere, nothing to be seen.
Recalling the past, I sorrow here all alone.

SOURCE: BKSRS 94, in NKBT, 69, pp. 273–74; octave (pentasyllabic).

✖ Visiting the Site Where the Hermit Used to Live
Taira no Satsuki

I would like to ask the hermit who lived in seclusion:
How many years did you spend in that distant place?
Mystical texts lying idle and unread;
Alchemy stove that has long since ceased to smoke.
His form has vanished from underneath green pines,
Yet his reputation endures in those whitened bones.
Now, visiting the place where he used to live,
I find that tears are streaming down my face.

SOURCE: BKSRS 95, in NKBT, 69, pp. 274–75; octave (pentasyllabic).

❖ Moon at the Fifth Watch: A Verse to Match the Ten Kayō Poems
Yoshimine no Yasuyo

The traveler is lying awake, the fifth watch has arrived.
I happen to spy the solitary moon in the sky above the peaks.
As soon as I see that mirror so round, the gloom of travel lifts.
I am sure my wife at home in her room still has me in her thoughts.

SOURCE: BKSRS 102, in NKBT, 69, p. 280; quatrain (heptasyllabic).
TITLE: Emperor Saga wrote a series of ten poems about Kayō, where he had a country retreat.
Only four of these are contained in BKSRS, nos. 96–99. On Kayō, see RUS 11. The fifth watch
was the period from 3 A.M. to 5 A.M.

❖ Seagulls on the Water: A Verse to Match the Ten Kayō Poems
Prince Nakao

The traveler is standing on the north side of the river.
In the mist he sees a gull, squawking and shaking the water from its wings.
Tame by nature, the seagull has no fear of being caught,
Especially since His Majesty's virtue extends even to the birds!

SOURCE: BKSRS 104, in NKBT, 69, pp. 281–82; quatrain (heptasyllabic).
TITLE: This is the second of four matching poems by Prince Nakao, nos. 103–6, all of which
were inspired by Saga's Kayō poem series. See notes to the preceding poem.
LINE 1: The traveler is Emperor Saga. We observe an unusual lack of honorific language in this
line, although a verb appropriate for the emperor is used for "sees" in line two.
LINE 4: "Birds" is more literally, "those who fly and float."
COMMENT: In this poem and the next, the reputed tameness of seagulls functions as a vehicle
to exalt the virtue of the emperor. The fanciful implication in the last line is that even the birds
have been transformed by the power and benevolence of His Majesty, at whose approach they
do not fly away.

❖ Seagulls on the Water: A Verse to Match the Ten Kayō Poems
Asano no Katori

The Kayō Detached Imperial Retreat is built beside the river.
Without any effort, His Majesty can watch the flocks of gulls.
They know what people are thinking—tame, they do not fly away.
With the current, against the current, playing in the waves.

SOURCE: BKSRS 108, in NKBT, 69, pp. 283–84; quatrain (heptasyllabic).
TITLE: This is the second of two rhyme-matching poems, nos. 107 and 108, written to com-
plement Emperor Saga's Kayō verses. See notes to the preceding two poems.
LINE 1: On Saga's imperial retreat at Kayō, see the notes to RUS 11, above.

LINE 3: This line alludes to the reputed ability of seagulls to divine the intentions of human beings. Both *Zhuangzi* and *Liezi* contain anecdotes about a boy who had a special relationship with seagulls, which always flocked around him without fear. One day, the boy's father asked him to capture one of the birds. The boy assented but the next day discovered that the seagulls would no longer approach him.

✴ Dance of the Butterflies: A Verse to Match "Four Poems Written on a Spring Day" by Kose no Shikihito
Emperor Saga

Bunches of butterflies, here and there, flutter wildly in the air.
So many different colors and hues, among the flowers and trees.
By nature, they don't depend upon the music of strings and reeds.
Mindlessly they dance about, aloft on the breezes of spring.

SOURCE: BKSRS 110, in NKBT, 69, p. 285; quatrain (heptasyllabic).
TITLE: This is one of two matching poems by Saga written in response to Shikihito's "Four Poems Written on a Spring Day." The other is BKSRS 111, "Flying Swallows," not translated. Shikihito's four poems do not appear in this anthology and are presumed lost.

✴ Flying Swallows: A Verse to Match "Four Poems Written on a Spring Day" by Secretary Kose
Asano no Katori

Clad in robes of black and white, they enter the scented boudoirs.
In pairs they come, in pairs they go, never roosting alone.
High they ascend to their nests on the beams, where they live a life of ease,
Then low they fly for a little while, from the blinds across to the door.

SOURCE: BKSRS 112, in NKBT, 69, p. 286; quatrain (heptasyllabic).
TITLE: Secretary Kose: Kose no Shikihito.

✴ Hearing a Cock Crow at the Old Checkpoint
Emperor Saga

Beacon-fires no longer burn, the forts have been abandoned.
Nothing left but the cocks of dawn, crowing short and long.
Since the death of Meng Chang, an eternity has passed.
What traveler now makes crowing sounds, waking people up?

SOURCE: BKSRS 117, in NKBT, 69, pp. 289–90; quatrain (heptasyllabic).

TITLE: The checkpoint in question may have been near Yamazaki, not far from the old Kayō Imperial Retreat (NKBT, 69, p. 289).

LINES 3 AND 4: This is a reference to an historical anecdote about Meng Changjun (d. 279 B.C.), who served as minister of the Qin state during China's Warring States period. Under suspicion at court, Meng attempted to flee the state. A few steps ahead of his pursuers, he arrived just before dawn at a checkpoint, which did not open until cockcrow. One of Meng's retainers imitated the sound of a cock, which caused the gates to be opened, enabling the party to make good its escape.

※ A Poem to Match His Majesty's Verse "Hearing a Cock Crow at the Old Checkpoint"
Kuwahara no Haraka

Ever since the fighting ceased this checkpoint has fallen from use.
Only the sound of someone's rooster heralding the dawn.
Naturally endowed with the spirit of *yang*, it knows when daybreak comes;
This time, though, it has not been awakened by the likes of Meng Changjun!

SOURCE: BKSRS 118, in NKBT, 69, pp. 290–91; quatrain (heptasyllabic).

LINE 1: This fighting presumably refers to battles against the *emishi* "barbarians" of Ainu descent during the eighth century. There were many military fortifications in the provinces of Mutsu and Dewa in northern Japan, which served as bases of operations against the *emishi* resistance. Gradually the frontier was extended northward, but the hostilities did not end until around 800.

LINE 4: Meng Changjun—see notes to the preceding poem.

※ A Poem to Match His Majesty's Verse "On Passing Through the Old Checkpoint"
Miyabe no Muratsugu

The Emperor's plans are far-reaching; the same laws govern us all.
The road through the pass has long been open; empty the old forts now.
From time to time white horses arrive—no officers asking questions.
Travelers coming from east and west pass through day and night.

SOURCE: BKSRS 119, in NKBT, 69, pp. 290–91; quatrain (heptasyllabic).

TITLE: The emperor's verse referred to here is not found in this collection.

LINE 1: The second half of this line reads literally, "the carts and writing are the same." This is a reference to the policies of standardization implemented throughout the realm and is first seen in *Zhong yong* (The Doctrine of the Mean). In the original context this meant that throughout China all carts were required to have matching axle widths (to reduce rut formation on the roads), and all regions had to use the same characters in their writing.

COMMENT: This poem celebrates the supposed high degree of unity and national stability achieved in Japan by this time. Travelers were now able to journey at night as the barriers were not closed after dark. Moreover, people were no longer stopped for payment of road-taxes.

❋ At Reizei'in each of us wrote on a poetic topic: I was assigned "pines in the valley"
Emperor Saga

Luxuriant, bushy, the verdant pines that grow in the hidden valley.
Aged and vast, they've endured for years and have never once seen frost.
Always draped with *heira* vines, their countless branches heavy.
At times sealed in by clouds and mist, a canopy so broad.
High in the trees the wind soughs mournfully, cold even in summer.
Their ancient color the deepest green, dark in the setting sun.
It is not in the nature of these pines to scale to the top of the peaks;
They merely stand there, blown by the wind, playing notes *kyū* and *shō*.

SOURCE: BKSRS 123, in NKBT, 69, pp. 293–94; octave (heptasyllabic).
TITLE: Reizei'in (later called Satodairi) was one of Emperor Saga's detached retreats in the Heian capital, located on the west side of the Horikawa River, adjacent to the imperial palace.
LINE 3: *Heira*, spindle or dodder, was used to produce a thin, coarse fabric for making the garments worn by recluses and priests.
LINE 7: These trees may be a symbol for worthy officials who hide their light under a bushel, never ascending in the official hierarchy because their talents have remained undiscovered.
LINE 8: These notes were the first two tones in the pentatonic scale.

❋ At Reizei'in each of us wrote on a poetic topic: I was assigned "bright white waterfall" and composed this poem on imperial command
Kuwahara no Haraka

Layers of mountains pierce the sky, towering over the park.
Like cloth unrolled, a sheet of water tumbles from above.
Dashing with the force of cranes in a flock, startled and winging away,
A string of pearls strikes the water, flying up then dashed to bits.
The sun shines down upon the cliffs, but misty rain still falls;
No clouds are found above the rocks, yet thunder always roars.
Long have I known about these falls, but I see them now for myself;
Why should I bother to visit Mount Tiantai and give up eating grain?

SOURCE: BKSRS 124, in NKBT, 69, pp. 294–95; octave (heptasyllabic).
TITLE: In the original text, "bright white waterfall" is literally "water like bleached cloth." This expression derives from language in the prose-poem (*fu*) by Sun Zhuo (320–77) titled "Wandering on Mt. Tiantai," preserved in *Wen xuan*.
LINE 8: A line from the same *fu*, "Wandering on Mt. Tiantai," suggests that one would need to forgo eating grain and live on wild mushrooms if planning to visit Mt. Tiantai, since there was a prohibition against eating grain, meat, and fish at this holy site. Tiantai, in China's Zhejiang province, was famous for its spectacular waterfalls and was where the Buddhist sect bearing this name was centered.

On Hearing a *Koto* in a Mountain Pavilion
Yoshimine no Yasuyo

Mountain visitor, sound of a *koto*—where is it being played,
Now as the moon shines brightly down on this garden of usnea moss?
As soon as I heard the music played on that "flaming tail" nearby,
The rushing waters of the Three Gorges I could hear from where I sat.

SOURCE: BKSRS 142, in NKBT, 69, pp. 315-16; quatrain (heptasyllabic)
LINE 2: Usnea is a variety of Spanish moss.
LINE 3: "Flaming tail" was the name of a *qin* (J. *koto*) belonging to Cai Yong (133-192), who reputedly made it out of scorched paulownia wood rescued from a fire. This term later came to be used to designate finely crafted *qin* in general.
LINE 4: The Three Gorges refers to an area along the upper reaches of the Yangzi River in the vicinity of the border between Sichuan and Hubei provinces. It is famous for the rugged beauty of its mountains and rivers.

"Rushing waters" (*liu chuan*) harks back to the similar phrase *liu shui* used by ZhongZiqi to describe what was going on in his mind when listening to the music of his friend Bo Ya, the renowned *qin* player. Bo Ya was so moved by Zhong's love for his playing that he destroyed his instrument after his friend died and never played again, believing that no one else could fully appreciate his music. The two men lived during the Spring and Autumn period, and the above account occurs in *Lüshi chunchiu* (The Chronicles of Master Lü, edited by Lü Buwei, d. 235 B.C.). *Liu chuan* is also the name of a famous piece of *biwa* music from the Heian period, which the *biwa* master and courtier Fujiwara no Sadatoshi (807-867) learned from a Chinese musician.

KEIKOKUSHŪ (COLLECTION OF VERSE FOR BRINGING ORDER TO THE REALM)

The third of the three early Heian imperial *kanshi* collections, *Keikokushū* (completed in 827) contains both poem and prose selections, all composed between 707 and 827. The inclusion of prose compositions is an important feature, as none of the three anthologies that preceded this collection contained such material. Commissioned by Emperor Junna (r. 823–33) and compiled by Shigeno no Sadanushi (785–852), Yoshimune no Yasuyo (785–830), Sugawara no Kiyokimi (770–842), and others, the anthology represents the culmination of the glorious *kanshi* flowering that occurred during the reign of the *kanshi* patron *par excellence*, Emperor Saga (r. 809–23). In its scale, *Keikokushū* represented a bold new artistic initiative, endeavoring to reflect the entire tradition of *kanshi* and *kanbun* composition in Japan, from the reign of Empress Genmei (r. 707–15) down to 827, while also bringing together the largest corpus of poetry and prose in Chinese ever seen in Japan.[87]

According to the preface, the work originally consisted of 2 scrolls with 20 *maki*, these containing 17 prose-poems (*fu*), 917 poems, 51 poem prefaces, and 38 exam essays, by 178 individuals. Of the 20 *maki*, only 6 survive, preserving 227 poems (including *fu*) by 96 poets, of whom only 15 were active during the Nara period. The most prominent figure in the anthology is once again Emperor Saga, with 26 poems, followed by the courtier Shigeno no Sadanushi, with 25. A detailed tally of the surviving 6 *maki* is as follows: *maki* 1 (17 *fu*, the entire original corpus of *fu*); *maki* 10 (11 *yuefu* and 48 Buddhist poems); *maki* 11, 13, and 14 (each containing *zatsuei*, "miscellaneous poems," 151 poems in total); and lastly, *maki* 20, with 26 of the original 38 civil service exam essays.

---

87. Kojima Noriyuki, annot., *Kokufū ankoku jidai no bungaku*, vol. 2 (bk. 3), pt. I (Tokyo: Hanawa Shobō, 1985), p. 1949.

The title of this collection seems to suggest that the compilers hoped to bolster the moral authority of the work by ascribing to *kanshi* a key role in bringing order to the Japanese state, an objective mentioned in the *Kaifūsō* and *Ryōunshū* prefaces as well. Given that *Keikokushū* appeared in the wake of a major epidemic and a drought, which had a politically destabilizing effect upon the realm, the avowed didactic purpose expressed in the preface and in the choice of title may have been of special significance. Harking back to the Confucian notion of poetry's role in ordering the state may also have been an attempt to correct a perceived excess of aestheticism in the court of Saga's time and inspire a higher level of social responsibility and awareness among the elite. Nonetheless, the surviving poems in this collection are not generally conspicuous for their didacticism, with a few notable exceptions, one being poem 6, "A Prose-Poem to Match One by "Wa-," Junior Assistant Minister, on the Wagtail," by Prince Nakao, celebrating the universality of parental love in both the human and natural worlds. The *fu* in the first *maki* and some of the verse in *maki* 10 also often highlight Buddhist principles, including the inherent sadness of all existence and the congruence between the natural and human worlds, both with their unending cycles of birth and death, flourishing and decay. Here and elsewhere, the compilers chose to give a measure of prominence to the philosophical themes of impermanence and the cycles of nature and the seasons, especially autumn.

The 151 *zatsuei* are typically informal, often occasional, poems composed on a wide variety of freely-chosen (as opposed to assigned) topics. As in *Bunka shūreishū*, many of these *zatsuei* are "odes on objects," covering a variety of phenomena such as spring rain, snow, swallows, chrysanthemums, and the sky, as well as more down-to-earth and sometimes novel topics such as house dust, furniture, and food—even a shoulder of pork, the subject of poem 203 (translated below), which disarmingly begins: "Red the meat of the pork shoulder, white the fat congealed. / Upon a platter, it now awaits the hand of Ding the Cook."

Overall, much of the poetry in the collection possesses considerable literary and historical interest, as the translated selections should illustrate. Although *Keikokushū* has received relatively little attention from western and Japanese scholars, this anthology preserves some of the most appealing *kanshi* composed during the Heian period and clearly deserves closer study and greater appreciation.

� A Prose-Poem to Match One by "Wa–," Junior Assistant Minister, on the Wagtail

Prince Nakao

1   How diverse the manifestations of the Creator,
    Embracing countless species, giving them shape.
    There is a small bird that lives along the riverbanks,
    A creature endowed with spirit and soul,
5   Basking in the diffuse light of Alioth,
    Possessing the pure essence of Venus and Mercury.
    It spends its life by the water, doing as it pleases;
    Or on the plains, living a life of toil.
    When spring breezes gently blow,
10 And the scenery is at its best,
    The male and the female
    Mate and produce offspring.
    Along the banks in the green grass
    They seek refuge in the bushy foliage.
15 From without, their nests look dense, perched high up in the trees;
    From within, they seem open; the birds can easily see out.
    Hawks and eagles cannot espy them,
    Crows and kites cannot tell they are there.
    Unlike the swallow nests atop curtains, easily overturned;
20 So different from the garden wrens, living in such danger.
    She nurtures her white eggs under her wings,
    Then breaks the white jade to bring forth her chicks.
    Aware that her offspring can't yet feed themselves,
    She strives to nourish them, thinking not of herself.
25 Then on a good day, at a good time,
    With the weather clear and the clouds trailing low,
    She wags her tail, straightens her feathers,
    And leads the chicks away from the nest.
    Emerging from the thicket, they fly in confusion,
30 Then gather on the banks, all squawking.
    Some go south, some go north,
    Some to the east, others to the west.
    Facing their mother, dappled wings flapping,
    Yellow beaks open, demanding to be fed.
35 Oh, how young this flock of chicks!
    Looking just to their mother, completely dependent;
    Importuning piteously, wherever they are.
    Away from the safety of the nest, there's not a moment of ease.
    Mindful of how short their feathers still are,

40　The mother feels pity, for they cannot fly quickly.
　　Thus, when catching insects she is never greedy;
　　Finding kernels of grain, she doesn't eat them herself.
　　How is it that while these birds lack intelligence
　　The mother is capable of such limitless love?
45　And so, with the slanting sun on the peaks,
　　The garden now half-covered with shadows,
　　And the swallows starting to peer at the beams,
　　The red orioles roosting in the woods,
　　The mother wagtail's thoughts are on feeding her chicks.
50　Sadly calling in the evening glow,
　　Seeking much but finding little:
　　So many mouths but food is scarce.
　　The poor man caring for his mother
　　Will feel all the sadder for seeing these birds.
55　And the widow holding onto her children
　　Is bound to feel teary if she sees them.
　　When the birds set out, they wag their tails,
　　Calling as they fly around,
　　Reminding us of the older brother befriending the younger,
60　And the younger brother serving the older.
　　Whoever hears of the birds will heave a sudden sigh;
　　Anyone thinking about them will be deeply moved.
　　How natural their instincts—
　　Not something acquired through learning.
65　Who is to say they are different from humans?
　　Verily no different from beings with a soul!

SOURCE: KKS 6, in Kojima, *Kokufū ankoku jidai no bungaku*, vol. 2 (bk. 3), pt. I, pp. 2330-57; *fu* (prose-poem) in sixty-six lines.
TITLE: The abbreviated surname "Wa–" appears to be Wake, perhaps a reference to Wake no Nakayo, a poem by whom immediately follows. The original *fu* on the wagtail, which the present poem matches, has not survived. See ibid., p. 2330.
LINE 5: Alioth, the fifth star in the "handle" of the Big Dipper (Ursa Major).
LINE 8: Living "on the plains" alludes to Ode 164 in *Shi jing*, titled "Chang-te" (Changde, The Cherry Tree), which has the lines "There is the wagtail on the level height;— / When brothers are in urgent difficulties, / Friends, though they may be good / Will [only] heave long sighs." ("Level height" we more idiomatically render as "plains," as they are the same word, "*yuan*" in the Chinese. See Legge, trans., *The She King*, p. 251.
COMMENT: The *fu*, a descriptive narrative genre, most often translated as "prose-poem" or "rhapsody," is a major Chinese literary mode that became popular in the Han dynasty. It remained influential through the Six Dynasties and was subsequently introduced to Japan, where it was similarly popular throughout the Heian period.

Autumn Is a Time to Mourn: A Prose-Poem Written at Shinsen'en on the Day of the Double-Ninth Festival

Wake no Nakayo

Autumn is a time to mourn!
We mourn that time never stands still,
Lament how the cold air snatches away the heat,
And sorrow as strong winds strip the trees of their leaves.
With each falling leaf, we think more of old age.
The wife alone with her fulling blocks pines for her husband on the frontier.
Autumn is a time to mourn!
We mourn that all things wither and die.
Willows knit their brows in the imperial gardens;
Chrysanthemums bloom radiantly beside the old railings.
The black and white swallows have flown away, rest quiet in forest nests;
The patterned fish have gathered together, cold in the mossy water.
Crickets toil miserably at their late autumn spinning;
Migrating geese feel tired, for the journey they make is hard.
Indeed, we must have confidence in the progress of the seasons—
How truly diverse the phenomena of nature!

SOURCE: KKS 16, in Kojima, *Kokufū ankoku jidai no bungaku*, vol. 2 (bk. 3), pt. I, pp. 2492–2500; *fu* in sixteen lines.

TITLE: This is the eighth *fu* in a group of nine all with the same title, nos. 9–17 in this collection. On the Shinsen'en gardens, see the notes to RUS 57, above.

LINE 6: These blocks were used to pound pieces of cloth. The process of fulling entailed shrinking and thickening the cloth with moisture, heat, and pressure. The pounding of fulling blocks is a stock image in *kanshi* and Chinese poetry generally, designed to evoke the melancholy atmosphere of autumn and the loneliness of wives preparing winter clothing for their husbands at the frontier on military service. The noise of these blocks also figures in poems on the theme of the traveler's nostalgia for home. Perhaps the earliest Chinese reference to fulling is found in a poem titled "Fulling Clothes" by Xie Huilian (397–433), contained in *Wen xuan*.

LINE 9: That is, the willows are in decline and seem to look distressed as winter nears.

LINE 13: "Spinning" is a metaphor for the chirping of crickets, a sound that resembles the regular, mechanical clacking of a spinning wheel.

Song of the Plum Blossoms: Two Poems in the *In* Style

Ono no Minemori

(No. 1)

Out beyond the crystalline window a single plum tree stands.
To enjoy its scent, I removed a paving stone, planted the tree in its place.
As the spot is close to His gracious warmth the blossoms have opened early.
Through the imperial curtains wafts their fragrance on the wind.

SOURCE: KKS 27, in Kojima, *Kokufū ankoku jidai no bungaku*, vol. 2 (bk. 3), pt. II, pp. 2573–75; *in* ballad-style quatrain (heptasyllabic).

TITLE: This poem and the next are examples of the *in* ballad style, a variety of *yuefu*. *Maki* 10 of KKS preserves eleven such poems. Ninth-century Japanese *yuefu* are typically unsung pseudo-folk lyrics of varying length, often rustic or heroically martial in tone. Many other themes, some personal, are also commonly encountered. As a genre, Japanese *yuefu*, like those of the mid- to late-Tang dynasty, are not defined by a unique formal structure but were often written in the then-popular regulated verse forms, which included the octave and quatrain. Among the *yuefu* of Li Bo are poems on the themes of love and nostalgia for the past, while those of Du Fu often portray the plight of the common people. These subjects were also popular among Japanese court poets. By the late Tang, the distinction between *yuefu* and *shi* in China had become "insignificant" (William H. Nienhauser Jr., ed. and comp., *The Indiana Companion to Traditional Chinese Literature* [Bloomington: Indiana University Press, 1986], p. 963); similarly, it is often difficult to distinguish one from the other in Japanese *kanshi* of the ninth century.

LINE 3: "His": His Majesty, the emperor.

(No. 2)

All the plants are cold and have no color.
Only the plum blossoms showing signs of spring.
They'll add to the beauty of makeup freshly applied,
Showering their petals on the courtesans in their chambers.

SOURCE: KKS 28, in Kojima, *Kokufū ankoku jidai no bungaku*, vol. 2 (bk. 3), pt. II, p. 2576–77; *in* ballad-style quatrain (pentasyllabic).

❊ Watching the Old Priest Heading Back to the Hills
Retired Emperor Saga

The monk by nature is far removed from the affairs of the mundane world.
With robe and bowl he wanders alone, away into the mist.
He's bound to go to the end of the road, through the autumn hills,
For that is where he makes his home, deep among the clouds.

SOURCE: KKS 30, in Kojima, *Kokufū ankoku jidai no bungaku*, vol. 2 (bk. 3), pt. II, pp. 2582–84; quatrain (heptasyllabic).

TITLE AND AUTHOR: The identity of the old priest is unknown. Saga left the throne in 823 but continued to be active in the literary and political life of the court long after his retirement.

❊ Watching the Old Priest Heading Back to the Hills: Written on Imperial Command
Fujiwara no Fuyutsugu

To the Dark Void the old priest returns, through the fallen leaves.
Staff in hand and back bent, he walks for an hour or more.

He says to himself, "Once I'm home, I'll never leave again."
Better to rest among the clouds than ask to be given a castle!

SOURCE: KKS 31, in Kojima, *Kokufū ankoku jidai no bungaku*, vol. 2 (bk. 3), pt. II, pp. 2585–88; quatrain (heptasyllabic).
LINE 4: This line might be a continuation of the priest's thoughts in line three rather than the poet's own comment. Regarding the castle, Kojima offers as a possible explanation an anecdote from *Shi ji* (Records of the Grand Historian, compiled by Sima Qian [ca. 145–ca. 85 B.C.]), chapter 34, in which Duke Shao of Yan, hoping to attract talented men to his court, asked one Guo Wei for advice. Guo replied that the duke should start by employing him, whereupon the duke built Guo a castle and took him on as an advisor.

✠ A Five-Character Poem Written to Match a Poem by Hermit Harumichi Titled "Lying Ill in Bed on an Autumn Day at Kegonsanji"
Shigeno no Yoshinaga

Autumn draws to a close, and I am ill.
With staff in hand, I've come to this cloudy dwelling.
Distant the folk who walk the ancient path;
Scarce the birds on the way through the frosty forest.
Clouds go drifting by, their hearts unsettled.
My life too—floating and unreal.
Cries from a lone monkey fade away in the moonlight;
Sounds of the mountain as night begins to fall.
A conch is blown at the temple on the peak at dawn;
Stone chimes sound in the lingering wind from the valley.
So many days have I tarried at this temple,
Lying here lonely and forlorn in this hut of thatch.

SOURCE: KKS 36, in Kojima, *Kokufū ankoku jidai no bungaku*, vol. 2 (bk. 3), pt. II, pp. 2614–20; *pailü* (pentasyllabic), in twelve lines.
TITLE AND AUTHOR: A different version of the poem title appears in the table of contents for this volume of the anthology: "Written by the Rankless *Onshi* Shigeno no Ason no Yoshinaga to Match a Poem by Secretary Harumichi Titled 'Lying Ill in Bed on an Autumn Day at Kegonsanji.'" See ibid., p. 2530. An *onshi* was a courtier who was the son of a prince or aristocrat holding the fifth rank of higher and thus eligible by law to receive a so-called *on'i*, shadow rank, at age twenty-one. This shadow rank was typically between six and eight on the eight-rank scale and usually came with an appointment as a sentry in the Military Guards, or as a palace attendant in the Central Affairs Ministry. Why Yoshinaga was "rankless" at this time is unclear. Perhaps he was under twenty-one years of age and thus did not yet qualify for an appointment.

Korenaga [Koreyoshi] no Harumichi (?–?), a *kanshi* poet who later became a hermit, held various posts during the reign of Emperor Kōnin (770–81) and is known to have served as the junior secretary of Ōmi (most likely the secretarial post referred to in the alternate title) and as vice governor of Ise. Records also note his presence in 842 at a banquet for the emissary from the kingdom of Bohai. He enjoyed the favor of Emperor Saga, with whom he often exchanged *kanshi*. By 844, Harumichi had risen to the junior fifth rank, upper. See ibid., pp. 2607–8 and

Nihon koten bungaku daijiten, p. 488. Harumichi's forebears were from Kudara in Korea, but little else is known of his family background or the circumstances that led him to become a recluse. Poem 35, by Emperor Saga, has the same title as this one.

The temple Kegonsanji, known also as Kegonji, was probably located in the Kita-Saga area of Kyoto.

A Small Hall in the Zen Monastery
Nun Yamato

I've long wanted to come here and dwell in seclusion
And have always held this monastery in high regard.
I paid a visit to this place, coming by carriage;
Passed by here several times before.
Haze hangs in the air, darkening the trees on the mountain;
Mist catches the light, brightening the flowers in the wilds.
Nothing unfamiliar in this small Zen hall;
Pale moonlight shines into these rocky recesses.

SOURCE: KKS 49, in Kojima, *Kokufū ankoku jidai no bungaku*, vol. 2 (bk. 3), pt. II, pp. 2678–79; octave (pentasyllabic).

▨ In China, Looking at Priest Changfa's Small Manmade Hill
Priest Kūkai

Look at the bamboo, look at the flowers—just like spring back home!
But people's speech and the way birds sing—so novel, here in China.
Viewing the lovely scenery of the hillock in your garden,
I can tell that your mind is unsullied by the dust of the mundane world.

SOURCE: KKS 62, in Kojima, *Kokufū ankoku jidai no bungaku*, vol. 2 (bk. 3), pt. II, pp. 2755–58; quatrain (heptasyllabic).

▨ A Verse in Irregular Meter on the Appeal of Living in the Mountains
Priest Kūkai

1   I ask you, Master: Why did you go to that cold and distant realm?
    Those far-off peaks, so rugged and steep, can afford no peace of mind.
    Climbing up so difficult, climbing down so hard.
    Mountain spirits and forest demons make them their abode.

* * *

5   Haven't you seen, Sir, haven't you seen
    The red hue of the peach and plum blossoms in the imperial park?
    Dazzlingly bright, full of fragrance, all a single color.
    Some bloom in the rain, some are scattered by the wind,
    Fluttering here, fluttering there, then landing in the garden.
10 In spring ladies come in groups and pick them from the trees;
    In spring warblers gather in flocks, peck the flowers, then fly away.
    Haven't you seen, Sir, haven't you seen
    The Shinsen spring in the imperial palace?
    Bubbling up, then flowing along, fast as life and death,
15 Bubbling forth, then flowing away, how many thousands of times?
    Flowing, flowing, on it goes, down into the deep abyss,
    Into the deep abyss, swirling round and round.
    When, oh when, will these rushing waters finally cease their flow?
    Haven't you seen, Sir, haven't you seen
20 The countless people inhabiting the Nine Provinces and Eight Islands?
    From ancient times to the present day, no one has lived forever.
    Yao, Shun, Yu, Tang, and also Jie and Zhou,
    The Eight Descendants, Ten Able Ministers, and the Five Great Lords;
    Xi Shi and Mao Qiang; Mo Mu and those deformed;
25 Who among them could remain alive for ten thousand springs?
    The noble and the low alike, all of them dead and gone.
    Dead and gone, dead and gone, turning to ashes and dust.
    The chambers and halls of singing and dancing—foxes live there now.
    Like dreams and bubbles, a flash of lightning, we visitors to this world.
30 Don't you know, Sir, don't you know
    That we are thus? How can you live on?
    If you think about it day and night, you're bound to break your heart.
    You're the sun above the western hills, a man halfway to the grave;
    You're past the middle of your life, you're like a walking corpse!
35 Remaining there, staying on, won't do you any good.
    Be on your way, be on your way, you cannot stay where you are!
    So I say to you, masters of the Great Void,
    You, raised on the milk of the Buddha's knowledge: don't stay there,
        do not stay!
    I never tire of seeing the pines and rocks of the southern hills.
40 I never cease loving the pure waters that flow on the southern peak.
    Don't let false pride poison you with its vanity, profit, and fame.
    Perish not in the burning house of the Three Worlds of Transmigration,
    But take your Buddhist vows at once and enter Nirvana's realm.

SOURCE: KKS 63, in Kojima, *Kokufū ankoku jidai no bungaku*, vol. 2 (bk. 3), pt. II, pp. 2758–78; *zatsugon*, forty-three lines in length.

TITLE: This mountain was Mt. Kōya. Kūkai took up residence here in 816, after building the Kongōbuji temple, which served as the center of the esoteric Shingon sect. We may conjecture that this verse was written sometime between 816 and 827, the year *Keikokushū* was compiled. This poem also appears in *Seireishū*, a posthumous collection of Kūkai's verse. The opening objections (lines 1–4) to living on Mt. Kōya are meant to have been voiced by Yoshimine no Yasuyo (785–830), the fourteenth son of Emperor Kanmu (r. 781–806) and one of the chief compilers of this anthology.

LINE 20: The "Nine Provinces" refers to China, the "Eight Islands" to Japan.

LINE 22: Yao and Shun are semi-legendary emperors said to have lived during the twenty-fourth and twenty-third centuries B.C. According to tradition, Yu established the Xia dynasty (ca. 2100–ca. 1600 B.C.), and Tang was the founder of the Shang dynasty (ca. 1600–ca. 1028 B.C.). Jie and Zhou were the tyrannical last rulers of the Xia and Shang dynasties, respectively.

LINE 23: The "Eight Descendants" were the eight sagely retainers of the ancient Emperor Di Ku (known also as Gao Xin), who according to legend reigned during the twenty-fifth century B.C. The phrase "Ten Able Ministers" appears to derive from a passage in *Lun yu*, where reference is made to the ten talented ministers of King Wu of the Zhou dynasty (ca. 1027–256 B.C.). The "Five Great Lords" probably refers to a group of five important ministers who assisted Emperor Shun.

LINE 24: Xi Shi was a famous Chinese beauty who lived during the fifth century B.C. Mao Qiang, from the same period, was another remarkable beauty and a favorite concubine of the Prince of Yue. Mo Mu was the fourth concubine of the legendary Yellow Emperor; she was said to be ugly but enlightened and virtuous. Kūkai's point is that all famous people throughout history eventually die, regardless of their attributes and status.

LINE 33: "Sun above the western hills," i.e., the setting sun, here symbolizes the approaching twilight of one's life.

LINE 34: Yoshimine no Yasuyo, whom Kūkai is addressing, would have been at most forty-two at the time. We should remember, however, that the average life span was shorter in those days.

LINE 37: "Masters of the Great Void" is apparently Kūkai's term for meditators who grasp the unchanging nature of emptiness, as embodied in the character *a*, the first sound in the Sanskrit alphabet. In esoteric Buddhism, it is thought that this sound possesses mystic truth and that meditating thereon leads to Buddhahood. See Yoshito S. Hakeda, *Kūkai: Major Works* (New York: Columbia University Press, 1972), pp. 51–52, 219–20. We are indebted to an anonymous reader for advice on this point.

LINE 40: Southern peak—a reference to Mt. Kōya, where Kūkai was living as a priest.

LINE 42: The "Three Worlds" (J. *sangai*) is a Buddhist term representing the realms of desire, form, and non-form. In the temporal world, all beings live and transmigrate in an endless cycle of birth and death perpetuated by evil thoughts and deeds. The simile comparing the Three Worlds to a burning house derives from a passage in "The Parable of the Burning House," in *Myōhō renge kyō* (The Sutra of the Lotus of the Wonderful Dharma), a key text in the Tendai and Nichiren sects.

❋ Visiting a Mountain Temple on a Winter's Day
Kasa no Nakamori

A temple high in the sky above the clouds.
Empty walkways tilting over cliffs.
Waters pure, without a speck of dust.
Wind so still that the sutras are clearly heard.
The moss on the ancient rocks serves as a mat.
My room in the new quarters has a name of its own.

Beneath the trees all covered with bushy vines,
I listen alone to the sound of the evening bells.

SOURCE: KKS 73, in Kojima, *Kokufū ankoku jidai no bungaku*, vol. 2 (bk. 3), pt. II, pp. 2831–34; octave (pentasyllabic).

▓ Watching a Polo Game in Early Spring (We had the visitors from Parhae join in the fun)
Emperor Saga [Written during his reign]

Early morning, the haze has cleared on this beautiful day in spring.
The visiting envoys, seizing the chance, have gone to the courtyard in front.
Flailing sticks like crescent moons sweep high into the air;
A flying ball like a shooting star hurtles back to earth.
A shot to the left, the right intercepts; before the goal they scuffle.
Lines of performers stamp their feet, making a thunderous din.
Shouting loudly, pounding drums, urging their team to score.
But all who watch are soon chagrined, for the game is too easily won!

SOURCE: KKS 89, in Kojima, *Kokufū ankoku jidai no bungaku*, vol. 3, pt. I, pp. 3032–40; octave (heptasyllabic).
TITLE: Written on the sixteenth day of the First Month of 822, this poem describes a kind of ball game apparently introduced from China. A cross between hockey and polo, it was played partly on horseback and partly on foot to the accompaniment of music and dancing. The ball was moved around using a slim, curved stick, the objective being to get it into the other team's goal. Normally around forty players participated. The prize for winning this particular match is said to have been two hundred bolts of silk cloth (ibid., p. 3033).

▓ The Early Blooming Plum in the Tranquil Garden
Emperor Saga

In the garden there stood alone an early flowering plum.
In the First Month the winds were mild, so the tree came into bloom.
The purest white, it wasn't lonely in the secluded garden.
The tree's rich fragrance even found its way in through the windows.
Its withered branches slender and fine when first it felt that warmth.
Chilly petals, one by one, were shed on the ancient moss.
Such a pity those elegant ladies wantonly broke its branches;
Sad, too, that some rough old rustic moved the tree away!

SOURCE: KKS 101, in Kojima, *Kokufū ankoku jidai no bungaku*, vol. 3, pt. I, pp. 3096–3101; octave (heptasyllabic).
LINE 8: Rough old rustic: a palace gardener.

❖ Lying in Idleness During a Few Days Off Work
Yoshimine no Yasuyo

Days of leisure, cares all cast aside.
The Songs of Chu I read as spring winds blow.
By the peaceful eaves all kinds of birds are singing.
My gate is shut, outside visitors rare.
Shoots have started to sprout from bamboo clumps.
A heat haze shimmers beyond the willows.
Tranquil I lie, propped up high on pillows,
As blossoms fall from the trees out in the garden.

SOURCE: KKS 109, in Kojima, *Kokufū ankoku jidai no bungaku*, vol. 3, pt. I, pp. 3153–58; octave (pentasyllabic).
LINE 2: *The Songs of Chu* (*Chu ci*): a collection of poems written in China between the third century B.C. and the second century A.D. This is China's second earliest anthology of verse, following *Shi jing*.

❖ A Poem to Match One by Counselor Yoshimine Titled "Drinking at Leisure in the Autumn Hills"
Retired Emperor Saga

He fled the world and lives in the cloudy hills.
Late autumn, his cottage door is shut.
Unstrained wine he pours in the valley cookhouse;
Dried fish he broils in the rustic courtyard.
Wandering, chanting verse on what captures his fancy;
Talking, laughing, and then he plays the *koto*.
The company of high officials brings him joy,
Drunk together at dusk in the empty forest.

SOURCE: KKS 143, in Kojima, *Kokufū ankoku jidai no bungaku*, vol. 3, pt. II, pp. 3391–96; octave (pentasyllabic).
TITLE AND AUTHOR: Middle Counselor Yoshimine no Yasuyo was one of the compilers of KKS Kojima notes that when Yasuyo died in 830, some three years after the completion of the anthology, Emperor Saga wrote two elegiac poems dedicated to him, an indication of his respect and affection. See ibid., p. 3391.

� A Mixed-Meter Poem in the *In* Style on Fulling Cloth: Written to Match One by His Majesty (Composed while he was on the throne)
Kose no Shikihito

1   Female decorum dictates that a girl stay at home until she is ten.
Lessons in the Four Teachings she receives from her kindly mother.
From the time she starts to learn these rules she bears a heavy burden.
Needless to say, a woman's work is arduous indeed.
5   Spring, she raises silkworms, then she gathers up their silk;
Autumn, she weaves it into cloth to make clothes for the frosty season.
From this time on, the women must truly labor over their work;
Pretty maids in every household spur each other on.
The fulling now begins:
10   Early in the season of bitter cold the miseries of fulling begin.
The women must make their blocks resound, autumn's hammering din.
The paulownia that gave Shu Yu a fief now wielded in the moonlight.
No labor for them to produce a music fit for song and dance.
The pounding lasts throughout the night—as if they can't get enough.
15   A music as pleasing as tunes played on clay and bamboo flutes.
The ringing mingles with the clack of sash jades, lasting all night long.
A million mallets, a thousand blocks, with no two minds alike.
Those embittered by their lot feel especially melancholy.
Sun Wu's wife thought of her husband when wild geese flew above;
20   Dou Tao's wife wept alone, weaving a drake at her loom.
When a woman has finished her fulling, it is time to sew fine clothes.
Daybreak comes to her four-pillared room, fitful and bleak the wind.
She is tired out from using the scissors, cold her pretty hands;
Plying her needle she feels upset, unhappy her stitching looks rough.
25   She's unsure if her husband's measurements are what they were before,
So she follows the size of the clothes he wore before he went away.
Have you never ever seen them, the waters of the river Long?
Their roar is like the din of those women as they grimly full their cloth.

SOURCE: KKS 151, in Kojima, *Kokufū ankoku jidai no bungaku*, vol. 3, pt. II, pp. 3437–56; *zatsugon* in irregular meter, twenty-eight lines in length.
TITLE: The poem alluded to here, by Emperor Saga, apparently does not survive. Shikihito's poem, in mixed-meter, is largely composed of seven-word lines, with a sprinkling of threes and sixes. The *in* was a form of *yuefu*. See notes to KKS 27. On fulling cloth, see KKS 16.
LINE 1: This line has ten characters.
LINE 2: The Four Teachings are found in the *Hun yi* (Marriage) section of *Li ji* (The Book of Rites) and relate to correct virtues, proper speech, appropriate appearance, and expected responsibilities and accomplishments. These teaching were transmitted to a betrothed woman during the three months prior to her marriage.
LINE 9: This line is three characters long.

LINE 12: Shu Yu was the younger brother of Prince Cheng of the Zhou dynasty (ca. 1017–256 B.C.). Cheng pretended to enfief his brother Shu by giving him a leaf from a paulownia tree cut into the shape of the enfiefment insignia given to feudal princes. This symbolic act was apparently meant only as a joke, but Zhou Gong, the prince's counselor, told Cheng that his deed could not be treated as such and that Shu Yu would have to be enfiefed after all. Allusion to this anecdote has been made merely because the wood used to make the fulling mallets was also from the paulownia.

LINE 18: The women are discontented because their husbands have been taken away for military service in remote regions. They are fulling cloth to make their husbands winter clothes.

LINE 19: Sun Wu (206 B.C.–A.D. 8), a Han dynasty envoy, was held captive for nineteen years by the Xiongnu, a nomadic people living on the northern periphery of China. The reference to geese reflects a legendary aspect of the Sun Wu story: the Emperor supposedly shot a goose that had a letter tied to its leg bearing the news that Sun Wu was still alive.

LINE 20: Dou Tao was a provincial official who lived in the fourth century. His wife was named Su Ruolan. According to legend, when Dou was transferred to a remote post his wife missed him and thus embroidered on a piece of silk a long poetic palindrome she had composed, in 840 characters. Su Ruolan functions here as a symbol of the heartsick, doting wife longing for her absent husband. The drake is likewise a symbol of conjugal harmony.

LINE 27: This line is in six characters. The Long River is in northwest China. The reference may be intended to suggest a typical location where men were sent on military service in ancient times.

�֎ A Poem to Match One Titled "New Year's Eve"
Princess Uchiko

The reclusive one is idle, just letting the time slip by.
She muddles along and before she knows it, the end of the year is here.
The dawn candle is half-gone, the light of the stars has vanished.
Chilly flowers blooming alone in the snow's reflected light.
Sunny forest, warm mist, the chatter of chirping birds;
Shady valley, ice melting, lonesome sound of a brook.
Spring clothes from an old wooden box she tries on all night long.
When morning comes she'll surely see the first buds on the willows.

SOURCE: KKS 169, in Kojima, *Kokufū ankoku jidai no bungaku*, vol. 3, pt. II, pp. 3626–32; octave (heptasyllabic).

TITLE: The "New Year's Eve" poem is KKS 168, by Emperor Saga, Uchiko's father.

LINE 1: "The reclusive one" is the poet's reference to herself.

COMMENT: While we admire this poem, we find somewhat hyperbolic Konishi Jin'ichi's judgment that "the princess's shih is probably the finest composed in Japan in the first half of the ninth century." See Konishi, II, p. 158.

❈ Rain and Snow in the Quiet Courtyard
Crown Prince Masara [Aged seventeen]

Dark clouds gathering over myriad peaks.
White snow whirling in the palace grounds.
The moisture turns to ice on the paving stones.
Silent, the snow falls effortlessly from the sky.
The world turns white, the redness snatched away.
All the different things become as one.
I sit here alone, quietly gazing about;
Flurries of snow—I cannot make out the path.

SOURCE: KKS 174, in Kojima, *Kokufū ankoku jidai no bungaku*, vol. 3, pt. II, pp. 3653–54; octave (pentasyllabic), *zatsuei*.
AUTHOR: Prince Masara was the future Emperor Ninmyō (810–50; r. 833–50). Written in 826, this is his only KKS poem.
LINE 5: "Redness" suggests the colors of late autumn.

❈ Getting Drunk on a Winter's Day at the Farmhouse of a Friend
Iokibe no Nagauji

A homestead to the right of a long bank.
Fine fields spreading east and west.
I go through a quiet gate past some willows,
Reach the guesthouse, walking across a ditch.
Ice has formed, no ripples on the water;
Frost blows around, the canopy of foliage gone.
Nothing to do but enjoy the *koto* and wine;
Just the way it was in the Bamboo Grove!

SOURCE: KKS 183, in Kojima, *Kokufū ankoku jidai no bungaku*, vol. 3, pt. II, pp. 3702–8; octave (pentasyllabic).
LINE 8: On the "Bamboo Grove," see the notes to KFS 9, above.

❈ A Poem About Being Unable to Take the Examinations
Michi no Nagana

Delicate scaly ones battling waves, ashamed to be lacking in strength.
Feeble wings encountering winds, distressed at being driven back.
We note the tale of the boy from Handan learning a new way to walk.
On the road he crawled along, unable to get back home.

SOURCE: KKS 186, in Kojima, *Kokufū ankoku jidai no bungaku*, vol. 3, pt. III (Tokyo: Hanawa Shobō, 1998), pp. 3792–95; quatrain (heptasyllabic).

LINES 1 AND 2: The poet is likening his struggles as a scholar to those of a fish swimming against the waves and birds flying into winds.

LINES 3 AND 4: This is an allusion to a passage in the "Qiu shui" (Autumn Floods) section of *Zhuangzi*. A boy from Shouling went to Handan, the capital of the state of Zhao, to learn the style of walking followed by the inhabitants. In the process of learning this technique, he forgot how he used to walk, and when he returned to Shouling he had to crawl there. The parable illustrates the foolishness of slavish imitation and excessive striving.

COMMENT: Kojima provides evidence that the poet had been unable to take the civil service examination because of illness, probably beriberi, and suggests that the crawling is a reference to the poet's own crippled state. The poem may be hinting at both a weakened physical condition and at the same time the poet's insecurities about his scholastic abilities. See ibid., pp. 3792–93.

❊ A Poem Written for the Examinations on the Subject of the Number Three

Fun'ya no Mamuro

A time when Blue Bird lived upon the mountain,
When the red crow, an auspicious sign, appeared:
Tang of Yin repeatedly declined the throne.
Guan Zhong in the end was forced to resign.
Playing a melody, spring waters rapidly move;
Entering the lake, the Yangzi slowly flows.
Don't you know about friendships bringing profit and loss?
Long hanging down, those blinds of Master Dong.

SOURCE: KKS 189, in Kojima, *Kokufū ankoku jidai no bungaku*, vol. 3, pt. III, pp. 3808–15; octave (pentasyllabic).

TITLE: The stylistic convention employed in this poem required that each line include a reference to a famous event, situation, person, or place with which the number three was prominently associated. At the same time, the actual number could not be mentioned anywhere. Overall thematic coherence was not the goal; rather, the ability of the examinee to make an appropriate allusion in each line was the key, a high level of erudition and familiarity with Chinese civilization being required. Mamuro's poem appears to date from early in the Kōnin era (810–24). See ibid., p. 3809.

LINE 1: According to legend, the goddess Xi Wang Mu lived on a mountain in the western part of China and had three birds as her messengers. They had black eyes and red heads and were known as Da Li, Xiao Li, and Qing Niao ("Blue Bird").

LINE 2: A red crow with three legs supposedly inhabited the sun. The appearance of three-legged birds was considered an auspicious omen.

LINE 3: Tang was King Cheng Tang, the founder of the Yin (Shang) dynasty. After Jie, the tyrannical last emperor of the Xia dynasty, was deposed, the three thousand feudal lords gathered to select a new ruler. None of them felt worthy of the honor and looked to Tang to ascend the throne. Tang finally accepted after declining three times.

LINE 4: Guan Zhong was a famous statesman who masterminded the ascension of Duke Huan of Qi to the leadership of an alliance of feudal lords during the seventh century B.C. During his career Guan served three lords, each of whom ended up dismissing and banishing him.

LINE 5: This line appears to allude to the Three Gorges, on the upper reaches of the Yangzi.

LINE 6: The lake here is Taihu, which was fed by three tributaries of the Yangzi, these being the Jingjiang, Songjiang, and Zhejiang rivers. An alternative explanation, to which the KKS commentary also gives credence, has the lake being Dongting, in Hunan province, which is fed by the rivers Xiang, Yuan, and Yangzi.

LINE 7: This line refers to a passage from chapter 4 of book 16 in *Lun yu*, which reads: "Confucius said, 'There are three friendships which are advantageous, and three which are injurious. Friendship with the upright; friendship with the sincere; and friendship with the man of much observation:—these are advantageous. Friendship with the man of specious airs; friendship with the insinuatingly soft; and friendship with the glib-tongued:—these are injurious.'" See Legge, *Confucius: Confucian Analects, The Great Learning and The Doctrine of the Mean*, p. 311.

LINE 8: The famous Confucian scholar Dong Zhongshu (second century B.C.) was said to be so dedicated to his studies that he kept the blinds down in his room for three years to avoid being distracted by the view of the garden outside.

※ A Poem Written for the Examinations on the Subject of the Number Three

Ishikawa no Ochindo

Manqian's literary abilities were great.
Xiangru wrote his prose-poems slowly.
In seeking friends, advantages are to be had.
When exchanging views, these people become my teachers.
The crow's shadow is hanging over the sun.
Doleful cries of monkeys within the Gorges.
Soaring to the heavens, the bird long suffered distress.
Zhongshu's blinds long remained unrolled.

SOURCE: KKS 190, in Kojima, *Kokufū ankoku jidai no bungaku*, vol. 3, pt. III, pp. 3815–21; octave (pentasyllabic).

LINE 1: Manqian (154–93 B.C.) was the style-name of Dongfang Shuo, a famous wit and scholar who served as censor and imperial confidant in the Han court. Many legends came to surround this individual, one being that on three occasions he stole from the goddess Xi Wang Mu the peaches of immortality, said to ripen only once every 3000 years. As in the previous poem, the poet was obliged to allude indirectly to the number three in each line of the poem.

LINE 2: Xiangru is Sima Xiangru (179–117 B.C.), renowned as China's most famous and influential poet of the *fu* (prose-poem or rhapsody) genre. Two possible connections with the number three exist, the first being that there were three imaginary protagonists in his famous prose-poem "Tianzi youlie fu" (Rhapsody on the Emperor's Hunt). The second possibility, somewhat more tenuous, is as follows: the aforementioned prose-poem is made up of two parts, the "Zixu fu," written first, and the "Shanglin fu," added subsequently, after Sima became employed as a court poet by Emperor Wu. The composition process was thus spread over "several years" (possibly three), according to the official dynastic history *Han shu*.

LINE 3: This alludes to a passage in *Lun yu*, which identifies three types of friends who are beneficial and three types who are injurious. See notes to line seven in the previous poem.

LINE 4: See book 7 of *Lun yu*, where Confucius says that when walking in a group of three, one should learn from the other two persons, taking them as one's teachers, adopting their good points and avoiding their bad ones.

LINE 5: See the note to line two in the previous poem.
LINE 6: These are the Three Gorges, located on the upper reaches of the Yangzi River.
LINE 7: From a passage in chapter 40 of *Shi ji*, inspired by the biography of King Zhuang of Chu, which reads as follows: "It didn't fly for three years but when it did, it flew to the heavens. It hasn't sung for three years, but on doing so, it will startle everyone." See Kojima, ibid., pp. 3819–20 for the text of this passage.
LINE 8: This person is Dong Zhongshu. See the note to line eight in the previous poem.

A Poem Written for the Examinations on the Subject of Dust
Fujiwara no Sekio

On the purple roads the winds of evening blow.
The red dust rises up in clouds.
Dust on beds is put to flight by lightning.
Dust on beams disperses when people sing.
The teachings of Master Lao about hidden virtue;
The desire of Master Fan to maintain frugality.
Sweeping through forests, resembling thin mist.
Blowing over ponds, looking like light rain.
On the battle roads following firewood dragged along;
In the women's quarters darkening the mirrors.
No intention of forming a lofty mountain,
It merely flies about as if feeling startled.

SOURCE: KKS 193, in Kojima, *Kokufū ankoku jidai no bungaku*, vol. 3, pt. III, pp. 3839–50; *pailü* (pentasyllabic), in twelve lines.
LINE 1: "Purple roads" are those in the capital; purple is a color associated with the emperor.
LINE 5: This line alludes to a phrase in chapter four in *Laozi*, which reads: "to obscure the light [of one's knowledge and virtue] and mix with the dust [of the mundane world]."
LINE 6: Master Fan was Fan Dan (Fan Shiyun, d. 185), a high official in the Han court who reputedly lived in such poverty during his youth that the inside of his cooking pot was covered with dust from having been unused for so long.
LINE 9: This is an allusion to an event recorded in *Zuo zhuan* for the twentieth year of the reign of Xi Gong, which relates how a certain general tied firewood to the back of his military chariot and dragged it along to stir up dust, in order to trick the enemy into believing that a large army was passing.

An Irregular-Meter Verse About a Shoulder of Pork
Prince Nakao

Red the meat of the pork shoulder, white the fat congealed.
Upon a platter, it now awaits the hand of Ding the Cook.
The knife with bells is sharpened on a stone till the edge is a frosty white.
The seated guests stare at the meat, then eat, chewing on and on.

Once the salted plums appear, people scramble to feed.
Mouths sated and feeling relaxed, what else could they want?
That stouthearted warrior of the Han—surely you know of him.
His sword drawn, how could he say no to a cup of wine?

SOURCE: KKS 203, in Kojima, *Kokufū ankoku jidai no bungaku*, vol. 3, pt. III, pp. 3925–30; *zatsugon*, octave: seven words per line, except for line seven, which has eight.
LINE 2: Ding the Cook is a character in *Zhuangzi*, who was skilled with a carving knife.
LINES 7 AND 8: This alludes to a scene in the biography of the military commander Xiang Yu in *Shi ji*. The warrior was Fan Kuai, who, upon being offered a shoulder of pork by Xiang Yu, placed it upon his inverted shield and began carving it up with his sword. A little later, Xiang offered him wine. Line eight seems to provide the answer to the question posed in line six.

▧ Two Poems Matching Ones Titled "Song of the Fisherman"
Princess Uchiko

(No. 1)
White his hair—what sort of fellow this old man?
Though times are good he's not employed and fishes in the river.
Eating fragrant rice, wrapping his purple fish.
He seeks neither fame nor glory, leads a simple, honest life.

KKS 221, in Kojima, *Kokufū ankoku jidai no bungaku*, vol. 3, pt. III, pp. 4105–8; *zatsugon*, quatrain in irregular meter.
TITLE: These two poems were written to match a series of five by Emperor Saga (KKS 216–20).
LINE 3: This poem and the next have only six characters in the third line, a feature generally associated with the *etchō* mode. All other lines have seven. For information on this poetic subgenre, see HCMZ 22, et seq., below.

(No. 2)
The springtime river flows full and swift, blue waves clear and pure.
Here the solitary old fisherman washes the cords on his cap.
What village is he from? What might be his name?
On the riverbank quietly singing—a peaceful life he leads.

SOURCE: KKS 222, in Kojima, *Kokufū ankoku jidai no bungaku*, vol. 3, pt. III, pp. 4108–11; *zatsugon*, quatrain in irregular meter.
LINE 2: This is an official cap, indicating that the man once served the court. He may be preparing to return to official service.

HENJŌ HAKKI SEIREISHŪ (THE SPIRIT AND MIND COLLECTION: THE REVELATIONS OF PRIEST HENJŌ [KŪKAI])

Henjō hakki seireishū, "The Spirit and Mind Collection: The Revelations of Priest Henjō [Kūkai]," is generally known by the abbreviated title *Seireishū* (*Shōryōshū*). This anthology contains most of the surviving Chinese prose and poetic works of Priest Kūkai (774–835), a renowned Buddhist cleric and the founder of the Shingon sect. Kūkai is also considered one of Japan's three most accomplished calligraphers. Compiled between 827 and 835, *Seireishū* consists of pieces written by Kūkai ca. 804–834, preserving some of the most distinguished pieces of Chinese prose and poetry written in the Heian period. The final three *maki* were lost quite early, but in 1079 a priest named Saisen (1025–1115), from Ninnaji temple in Kyoto, reconstructed the items originally present in the missing volumes and republished the emended anthology, although some of the pieces are conjectured to be forgeries. These varied materials provide us with detailed insights into Kūkai's remarkable life and deepen our understanding of the inner workings of Heian court society and the Buddhist establishment.

The anthology includes a preface by the original compiler Priest Shinzei (800–860), a disciple of Kūkai, followed by some 113 poems and pieces of prose (of which 108 have been established as genuine Kūkai works), these divided among ten *maki* as follows: (1) *shi* and *fu*; (2) stele inscriptions; (3) poetry and prose written to accompany gifts; (4) memorials and further prose items; (5) official memoranda and letters to the court, written in China; (6–7) *negaibumi* or *ganmon* (petitions) and *dashinbun* (documents recording *dahṣiṇa*, "alms-giving"); (8) the same content as the preceding two *maki*, with the addition of *hyōbyaku* (formal announcements made at prayer and memorial services); (9) memorials and other documents addressed to the gods and Buddhas; and (10) letters, poems, and sample essays from the civil exams, as well as appraisals, eulogies, and panegyrics (*san*).

According to the preface, Kūkai preferred to compose spontaneously as the spirit moved him and never bothered to rewrite anything. Many of his works are in elegant parallel prose, but the letters contained in this anthology are in a more lucid, informal style. Kūkai's Buddhist writings, which represent the pinnacle of Heian Buddhist literature, possess rich literary value, displaying careful construction, a peerless mastery of rhetoric, and depth of philosophical content. Kūkai was also skillful in evoking the pleasures and austerities of Buddhist life through the eyes of the hermit living in bucolic isolation. The ten poems that we have translated from this collection constitute an unusual series titled "Nine Meditations on Death." They are all pentasyllabic and all except one are twelve lines long. Each describes a different stage of human decay and disintegration, offering a fascinating mixture of Buddhist and anatomical commentary unique in the Heian tradition.

▨ Nine Meditations on Death: Ten Poems

(No. 1) Recently Deceased

The time we have upon this earth is short.
The years we spend within the Springs are many.
Life passes quickly, ephemeral as gossamer;
No time at all before each one of us dies.
Quick as wind and clouds we leave the Storehouse of Desire;
Like a snuffed-out fire, the vessel of longing perishes.
Our allotted life span having reached its end,
Our names are entered on the Register of the Dead.
A long life is as fleeting as the mist,
No recreating Trāyastrimśa in this world.
No way for us to be redeemed from death—
I sigh aloud, sadness and pain in my heart.

SOURCE: For the source of this poem and the subsequent nine in the series, see the first note to poem 10, below.

TITLE AND AUTHOR: See the notes to the tenth poem below for an explanation of the seeming textual inconsistency between "nine meditations" and "ten poems." There appear to be ten poems or "meditations" in all, not nine. The attribution of this series to Kūkai has been a point of controversy, as the poems were apparently found scribbled anonymously on a wall in the southern corridor of the Kai Yuan temple in China. While some believe Kūkai did in fact write the series, one premodern source suggests the contrary. Still another scholar asserts that Kūkai copied poem 9 from another source, instead of actually composing it. See NKBT, 71, p. 539, n. 420.

LINE 2: "Springs" (an abbreviation of *kōsen*, "yellow springs," Old J. *yomotsukuni*) is a traditional allusion to the underworld.

LINE 5: "Storehouse of Desire" is a Buddhist metaphor for the human body.

LINE 10: Trāyastrimśa (J. Tōriten), the "heaven of the thirty-three [gods]," is one of the heavens of *yokkai*, the realm of desire, located at the top of Mt. Sumeru, according to Buddhist cosmology. It is a place where human life is said to last a thousand years, each month stretching out to last a year.

COMMENT: According to the research of James Hugh Sanford in "The Nine Faces of Death: Su Tung-po's *Kuzō-shi*" in *The Eastern Buddhist* 21 (n.s.), 2: 54–77, Kūkai's "nine meditations or thoughts" (J. *kusō*, Skt. *aśuubha-bhāvanā*) on the nine faces or aspects (*kuzō*) of death constitutes one of the earliest Japanese treatments of death and the decay of the human body. Its source evidently is found in earlier Buddhist meditational practices designed, in Sanford's words, "to aid the attainment of Nirvāṇa through a systematic contemplation of the vanity, impermanence, and foulness inherent in this world" (p. 57) and thus help free one from attachment to the human body. Sanford explains that these meditations are often conducted in a graveyard and "consider the living body and find it to be not a thing of beauty but rather a sack of blood, guts, and undigested food . . . ." He further notes, "In the same general vein . . . is the visualization of the nine stages of the process of death and corruption," the *loci classici* of which are the *Satipatthana-sutta* and the *Visuddhimagga* (ibid.). As Sanford also observes, these sutras outline in nine and ten gruesome stages, respectively, the putrification of the human body following death, presumably to serve as a commentary on the Buddhist truths of impermanence and the demise of all living things (p. 58). For additional details on these steps, which are similar to several in Kūkai's group (particularly those related to the stages of 'swollenness or bloat,' 'bones still linked' and 'scattered bones'), see Sanford, pp. 57–58. The precise source, if any, for Kūkai's enumeration is uncertain.

There is another later and better-known series of nine poems in Chinese on "the faces of death," which has been attributed, probably erroneously, to the illustrious Song dynasty poet Su Dongpo (Su Shi, 1036–1101). Sanford states that it now seems certain that this cycle of poems was of Japanese provenance and probably did not come together to create the surviving textual version until "perhaps as late as the Ashikaga [1392–1573] period." See Sanford, p. 59 on the problem of attribution and also pp. 63–75 for a translation of the Su Dongpo series, which contains the following elements: a preface; nine two-verse poems in Chinese, each verse containing four heptasyllabic lines; eighteen *waka* poems (two for each of the nine steps); and nine line illustrations of the process of bodily decay. We thank the anonymous reviewer who recommended that we investigate these later poems.

(No. 2) Puffiness and Bloat

A place where wolves and tigers fight for food,
Where the hills and mounds are vast, devoid of people.
Isolated, far from the human world;
The pure bright moon travels overhead.
Autumn leaves everywhere, mournfully rustling in the wind;
Miserably rising, scattering all around.
And then a corpse I happen to espy;
Naked, on a hillock of pines it lies,
With hair spread out, sleeping the eternal sleep.
The Four Stages of Being have run their cycle.
Dining once on flesh of bird and beast,
But now a feast for the animals in the wild.

(No. 3) Decay and Discoloration

No way to escape the Lictors of Hell;
The Pit of Death is deep and never ends.
The full moon in its brightness now obscured;
The precious mirror has turned a milky white.
Like a lamp extinguished by a whirling wind,
Like a branch that has been stripped of all its leaves.
As days go by, the corpse continues to rot.
A month and now the body has turned black.
White maggots wriggle in every hole,
While bluebottles fly above the bones.
One searches for what was lovable in the past—
Oh so tragic, such a cause for shame.

(No. 4) Decomposed and Scattered, Defiling the Earth

The Four Elements are truly to be loathed.
The Five Aggregates in principle cannot be trusted.
Once air and fire are gone, they never return;
Water and earth are bound to rot away.
Black and blue, a large and swollen mass:
Suppurating, bruised, a smell like rotting vetch.
The liquids oozing from the nine holes of the body
Create a dreadful stench all around.
Wild animals crouch beside the corpse;
Baleful birds caw as they pick at the flesh.
The body remains in the dust, there in the wilds.
Whither has its soul now returned?

LINE 1: The Four Elements: the material making up the human body, namely, earth, water, fire, and air.
LINE 2: The Five Aggregates: the five constituent elements of all existence: matter or form, perception, conception, volition, and consciousness.
LINE 3: "Air and fire": the sources of breath and warmth, respectively.

(No. 5) Disintegrating Remains

Mistaken views—a net so hard to flee;
Human existence not granted us for ever.
Life as fleeting as an arrow in flight,
The body insubstantial as mist at dawn.
A face once lovely now suppurates and bleeds.
A scented body now worthless, in decay.

The stench travels afar, borne on the wind.
The fat on the stomach melts away in the heat.
Brocaded garments ashamed of all the rot;
Her fancy pillow cannot see her now.
Mournful sighs that none will ever hear.
Brush tears aside and take a different road.

(No. 6) The Intact Skeleton

Fearful of shadows, unaware of being in the shade;
Like a butterfly, alive in the floating world.
Her life was short, went by like a lightning bolt.
Then she turned to dust beneath the pines.
A beauty of the capital while alive,
Yet now she is a pile of whitened bones.
The yellow swan does not cry out to her;
The green willow will never return to the fields.
Spring flowers are fragrant, but for naught;
The moon vainly illuminates the hills.
Alas! Lonely throughout eternity—
Alone to the end, never seeing the spring.

LINE 7: The yellow swan was an imaginary bird in Chinese lore said to restore the dead to life.
LINE 8: The exact meaning of this line as originally written is unclear. Suspecting that the third and fourth characters have been mistakenly reversed, we have provisionally emended the text.

(No. 7) White Bones Still Connected

A lonely, silent spot forsaken by man;
Quiet and desolate, far from where people gather.
I happen to see the remains of a rotting skeleton,
Suddenly, there upon the marshy ground.
Pines and cypresses offer abundant shade,
Wild seedlings sprout in the damp by the bones.
Forever being bleached by wind and clouds;
Moistened, too, by drops of frost and dew.
As days come and go the bones dry out.
As years pass, the bones grow ever whiter.
And even though the willows put down roots,
How could one ever summon Pianque back?

LINE 12: Qin Pianque (Pianchao, fifth century B.C.), was a renowned Chinese physician said to have been able to see inside the bodies of his patients and bring the dead back to life.

(No. 8) White Bones Scattered

Long vanished, gone like an empty dream;
This realm of dust is nothing but a bubble.
Sahā a place of misery to be loathed,
Jambudvīpa affords no restful sleep.
Skin and blood are unlike the nighttime moon.
The willowy bones will never flower again.
The nails and hair defile the growing plants.
Head and neck bones scattered east and west.
Fallen leaves half cover her remains.
The autumn chrysanthemums look so lovely now.
Streams of tears, I cannot hold them back.
I weep for her, my sorrow all in vain.

LINE 3: Sahā (J. *shaba*) is the human world, where people must endure suffering.
LINE 4: Jambudvīpa (J. *enbu* or *enbudai*) in Buddhist cosmology was a triangular island south of Mt. Sumeru inhabited by ordinary human beings.

(No. 9) The Body After Turning to Dust

Mountains and rivers last more than a thousand ages,
But a man and his deeds last less than a hundred years.
The skull and knee joints totally disappear.
The coffin, too, likewise turns to dust.
If corpse and soul are without a proper place,
How can the gods and spirits guard the grave?
Carved on the tombstone your insignificant name;
The dirt of the grave mound covers you in vain.
The bones over time turn to white and yellow earth.
The dark wind finally carries the dust to the hills.
All we have is the treasure of the Three Vehicles.
Without these teachings, the Eight Sufferings will ensue.

LINE 11: The Three Vehicles (*sanjō*) are the three traditional sources of the Buddhist teachings, namely, the Boddhisatvas, the *engaku* (Skt. *pratyekabuddha*) sages, and the disciples of the Buddha.
LINE 12: The Eight Sufferings refers to the physical pain and tribulations resulting from the following phenomena: birth, aging, illness, death, the loss of loved ones, meeting people one dislikes, failure to attain one's wishes, and the development of the mind and body.

(No. 10) Untitled

The Six States of Consciousness—where can they be found?
The Four Elements—and now just a name remains.
The cold moss covering the grave mound is green;
The summer grasses pierce the hill as they grow.
Within the bag, some grain may still be found.
Beneath the pines, the hair is still blue-black.
Bluish clouds gather above the mound,
As the pine trees sigh mournfully in the night.

SOURCE: SRS 111 (a series of ten poems), in Watanabe Shōkō and Miyasaka Yūshō, annot., *Sangō shiki, Seireishū*, NKBT, 71 (Tokyo: Iwanami Shoten, 1965), pp. 460–69; nos. 1–9, *pailü* (pentasyllabic), each in twelve lines; no. 10, octave (pentasyllabic).

TITLE: This last poem in the series appears in NKBT as the final eight lines of poem 9, but the annotators suggest that it may instead be a separate tenth poem, since it has a different rhyme scheme. If it is indeed a separate, additional poem, this would explain why the series title specifies ten verses rather than nine. See NKBT, 71, pp. 460, 468.

LINE 1: The Six States of Consciousness (J. *rokushiki*) are visual, auditory, olfactory, gustatory, tactile, and non-sensuous consciousness.

LINE 5: Presumably, the deceased was carrying this bag when she died. That the bag still contained grain seems to be an ironic comment on the inescapability of death, which can come even when one has adequate provisions.

DENSHI KASHŪ (THE SHIMADA POETRY COLLECTION)

This appealing anthology of poetry by the noted scholar Shimada no Tadaomi (828–92?) is one of the earliest extant private collections of *kanshi* by a single individual.[88] *Denshi kashū*, compiled around 892, contains 214 poems, all written between 843 and 891.[89] The poems are arranged in roughly chronological order, beginning with one written when the poet was sixteen. The text that has come down to us is composed of three *maki* in a single volume and appears to be a later version of a manuscript in ten *maki* titled *Den Tatsuon shū* (Master Shimada Tatsuon's Collection).[90] Most of the poems in the first *maki* date from 843–48, although the same *maki* contains some items composed during 865–66. The middle *maki* spans 881–83, with no chronological inconsistencies in the ordering of the poems. The third and final *maki* consists of works written between 882 and 891 as well as earlier poems dating from the years 871–74, together with an even earlier poem on Tadaomi's civil service examination experiences. As might be expected given the clear preference by this time for longer line length, most of Tadaomi's poems are heptasyllabic, with *lüshi* outnumbering *jueju* by a wide margin.

Tadaomi had a rather uneventful official career, with relatively few bureaucratic successes. He studied with Sugawara no Koreyoshi (812–80), father of the renowned *kanshi* poet and statesman Michizane (845–903).

---

88. Others include Priest Kūkai's *Seireishū*, completed some fifty years earlier, and a private anthology of verse and prose by Miyako no Yoshika (834–79), titled *Toshi bunshū* and compiled around 879 (only one incomplete volume is extant). Sugawara no Michizane's important collections, *Kanke bunsō* (900) and *Kanke kōshū* (903), should also be noted.
89. The commentary by Kojima Noriyuki and others in *Denshi kashū chū*, vol. 1 of 3 vols., Kenkyū sōsho, 98 (Osaka: Izumi Shoin, 1991), p. 210, clarifies that the two poems 50-a and 50-b, which some texts have considered to be a single composition, are actually two separate works. Our total poem count reflects this fact.
90. Tatsuon was Tadaomi's Chinese-style sobriquet.

Michizane himself later married one of Tadaomi's daughters, further cementing what was already a close relationship between the two families. After an unremarkable succession of capital and provincial appointments, Tadaomi reached the junior fifth rank upper in 872. Although Japanese reference works indicate that he advanced to *monjōshō* status sometime around 854, presumably having passed the civil service exam,[91] Robert Borgen believes that Tadaomi actually never sat the civil service test at the conclusion of his Academy studies. He suggests that instead, like most of his peers, Tadaomi entered the bureaucracy directly, without the benefit of the *shinshi* ("presented scholar") credential.[92] Tadaomi was thus obliged to start out at a low rank. This apparent failure to receive a recommendation as a candidate for the exams put him at a distinct disadvantage throughout his career. A contributing factor was the comparative obscurity of his family lineage, which appears to have handicapped him in his quest to receive the high posts in the bureaucracy he desired.[93] Indeed, the most responsible positions Tadaomi obtained were only those of junior assistant head of the War Ministry and director of the Bureau of Medicine, this latter appointment not granted until 891, around the time of his death. Dissatisfaction over his undistinguished career is, not surprisingly, a recurring topic in Tadaomi's poetry.

Perhaps the most noteworthy event in Tadaomi's professional life occurred in 883/4, when his prowess as a *kanshi* poet led to his being summoned back from his post as vice-governor of Mino province to help entertain some visitors from Parhae, with whom he also wrote and exchanged poems. Tadaomi held only the junior fifth rank upper at the time, but as Borgen relates, he received a promotion to director of the Bureau of Buddhism and Foreign Visitors (Genbaryō) in the Civil Affairs Ministry for the duration of this assignment, working alongside Michizane as a subordinate.[94] Earlier, in 859, Tadaomi was similarly recalled (from Echizen) to assist with entertaining visitors from Parhae with poetic exchanges.

The best of Tadaomi's poetry is marked by a sense of spontaneity and a distinctively native flavor evident in the mundane and seemingly insignificant phenomena that fill his verse. Tadaomi was not one to posture grandly or make a display of his artistic refinement, instead showing a preference for describing life's simple pleasures and the joys of seclusion, as seen, for

91. See, for example, Kondō Haruo, comp., *Nihon kanbungaku daijiten* (Tokyo: Meiji Shoin, 1985), p. 307. Under Ritsuryō law, a *monjōshō* or *shinshi* ("presented scholar") was an Academy student who had passed the third lowest of the four levels of the civil service examinations. See the first note to *Kanke bunsō* 1 for details.

92. Robert Borgen, *Sugawara no Michizane and the Early Japanese Court* (orig. Cambridge: Council on East Asian Studies, Harvard University, 1986; reprint, Honolulu: University of Hawaii Press, 1994), pp. 92–93. On the *shinshi* credential, see the preceding note.

93. Ibid.

94. Ibid., p. 232.

example, in DSKS 132, "Medicine," a quatrain that describes Tadaomi's garden and ends with an unexpected twist:

> I planted herbs, and as spring passes they've spread all over the ground.
> Luxuriant, they keep out the heat—their abundance fills my garden.
> People come to pick the plants, then draw back in surprise:
> From out of the bushy wolfberry vines, the barking of my dog!

We find a range of novel topics, including pine nuts and wild spinach soup, a paper kite, shoes, a dried shrimp, a snap-beetle, and pieces of ice. The unconventional subject matter seems to prefigure the earthy topoi and individualism of the Gozan (Five Mountains) *kanshi* tradition of Muromachi times. Overall, Tadaomi relies somewhat less than most poets of his day upon Chinese models and sources, his most successful poems dealing with down-to-earth topics from his immediate surroundings and written in plain, direct language. Few before him could match his ability to describe realistically, with true immediacy and authenticity, the realities of everyday life in Japan, including its mores and sensibilities. In short, Tadaomi's verse demonstrates how well *kanshi* had become assimilated into the Japanese cultural environment, serving now as an essential medium for the expression of personal feelings and concerns.

❈ Going to Master Shimada's Homestead on a Spring Day

Since getting drunk last autumn here, I have missed your mountain cuisine.
Now it is spring, and we wander about in an area near the road.
Losing ourselves on a blossomy trail, we hear a barking dog.
The travelers reach a grove of trees, summoned by a warbler's call.
Then dine once more on pine nuts—I never tire of the taste.
Sip again that wild spinach soup—a flavor I cannot describe.
Warm hospitality every time; you are always glad to see me.
Do not discard your four-rhyme poems; trade them for my rubbish!

SOURCE: DSKS 3, in Kojima Noriyuki and others, annot., *Denshi kashū chū*, vol. 1, pp. 13–18; octave (heptasyllabic).
TITLE: "Master Shimada" (Den Taifu) was probably Tadaomi's grandfather, Kiyota (779–855). See *Denshi kashū chū*, vol. 1, pp. 309–12.
LINE 7: The second half of this line reads literally, "You never show the whites of your eyes."
LINE 8: "Four-rhyme poems" refers to regulated verse, *lüshi*, in eight lines. "Rubbish" is Tadaomi's self-deprecatory reference to his own verse.

❈ A Poem Sent to My Neighbor's House to Beg for Paper

My heart is full of autumn thoughts, piling up like clouds.
Not having any paper, I'm distracted and upset.
I ask you not to be displeased with this request of mine.
My intention is to write some poems and send them over to you.

SOURCE: DSKS 5, in *Denshi kashū chū*, vol. 1, pp. 22–26; quatrain (heptasyllabic).

❈ Listening to Bush Warblers at a Mountain Temple

Soft and gentle the sound of their call, adding such charm to the spring.
Hearing them now at this mountain temple, my feelings for them deepen.
You should be back in the real world, warbling in the trees,
Rather than uselessly bothering the priests as they contemplate the Void.

SOURCE: DSKS 15, in *Denshi kashū chū*, vol. 1, pp. 48–50; quatrain (heptasyllabic).
LINE 4: "Contemplate the Void": meditating in order to reach enlightenment.

❈ [Title Missing]

Put chrysanthemums in water then sip—no practice older than this.
Then blow aside the flowers in your cup— nothing else compares.
Habitually drinking these brews, I know, increases our vital forces;
And taking them over time will make the body nimble and light.
Eating pine flowers to practice the Way is mostly just a sham;
Downing cypress seeds to achieve immortality seldom actually works.
Of all the medicines known to us, many are efficacious.
But one must try *chrysanthemums* to live as long as the ailanthus!

SOURCE: DSKS 17, in *Denshi kashū chū*, vol. 1, pp. 63–66; octave (heptasyllabic).
TITLE: A later editor added the "Title Missing" notation, which we have retained.
LINES 1 AND 2: It was the custom on the day of the Double-Ninth Festival to drink wine or water with chrysanthemums floating therein, to promote longevity.
LINE 5: "Pine flowers" (*shōka* or *matsu no hana*)— the common designation for the short-lived male pollen strobili of the pine, sometimes called the "pollen cone." In common with other members of the class *Gymnospermae*, pine trees have no flower or fruit. Pine pollen is edible and highly nutritious.
LINE 8: Ailanthus is a genus of tree that includes the toon and the tree of heaven. Native to warmer parts of Asia and Australia, the ailanthus is mentioned in *Zhuangzi*, in the "Xiaoyao you" (Free and Easy Wandering) chapter, as a long-lived tree whose "spring lasted 8000 years." See *Denshi kashū chū*, vol. 1, p. 66.

✻ A Poem Written to Match One Received from the Presented Scholar "Taka–" on the Subject of the New Year

Earlier I gave you my humble verse, but you did not read it through.
Now you have kindly looked at it, adding to my joy.
But even if wrapped in endless sheets, a stone won't be seen as a jewel,
A lead sword, good for using just once, cannot be seen as sharp.
A book of verse should simply aim to shed light on the times of the Sages.
One's poems may be numerous, but it does not mean they're great.
Although I've received a verse from you, whatever can I do?
My New Year's words, with title added, I'll offer to the gods.

SOURCE: DSKS 21, in *Denshi kashū chū*, vol. 1, pp. 85–87; octave (heptasyllabic).
TITLE: The commentary notes that the abbreviated surname "Taka–" is likely "Takashina" and possibly an allusion to one Takashina no Yoshinori. See ibid., p. 85.

✻ Thanking My Friend "–no" for His Kind Gifts of a Lacquered Book Bag, Shoes, and Other Things

The bag looks so unusual and novel—it gave me quite a surprise.
The shoes feel secure and comfortable—I am now so light on my feet.
Through dark ice, glossy and shiny, the spidery graphs can be seen;
Black waves rolling in, shaped like a goose's beak.
The poems and writings piled on my desk will be nicely hidden from sight;
On the road, in the mud and rain, my progress won't be slowed.
Looking at your kindly gifts, I know that our friendship is fast.
As I use them in my daily life, will I ever forget your kindness?

SOURCE: DSKS 24, in *Denshi kashū chū*, vol. 1, pp. 97–101; octave (heptasyllabic).
TITLE: The syllable "–no" is an abridged form of a surname such as Shigeno, Sugano, or Ono, but the exact identity of this individual is unknown. See ibid., pp. 92–93, 97. This shortened name also occurs in poem 23 (untranslated).
LINE 3: Spidery graphs, literally "insect characters," may refer to old-fashioned seal characters adorning the bag.
LINE 4: Tadaomi is describing the upwardly curving tips of the lacquered shoes given to him along with the bag.
LINE 7: The original language in the second half of the line alludes to a famous saying on friendship, which likens the inseparability of friends to lacquer and glue that have been mixed together.

A Poem on the First Snow

My first glimpse of the white snow—specks dotting my robe.
It doesn't yet lie deep on the ground, walking isn't hard.
Amazing! Ma Gu must be turning her clothes inside out.
We should also note that Tian Lao is plucking his hoary hairs.
In the icy cold, the snowflakes scatter before my quiet gaze.
Sun comes up, winds arise, blowing restless snowy drifts.
No point in saying my white hairs are as few as the flakes of snow,
For jade dust piles up over time to form a great jade mountain.

SOURCE: DSKS 26, in *Denshi kashū chū*, vol. 1, pp. 105–9; octave (heptasyllabic).
LINE 3: Ma Gu was a Chinese immortal famous for her long, claw-like nails, which she used to scratch her back. Tadaomi is likening the snow to flecks of skin that have come loose owing to her scratching and are now flying around as she turns her robes inside out.
LINE 4: Tian Lao: an ancient immortal in Chinese mythology who served the Yellow Emperor.

The Night Winds Are Cold

I urge you not to fear the noise made by the wind at night.
That chilly light mostly comes from places far away.
The Emperor's kindness fills the realm, my brazier's filled with fire.
In the winter cold, I am never afraid my clothes might be too thin.

SOURCE: DSKS 27, in *Denshi kashū chū*, vol. 1, pp. 110–12; quatrain (heptasyllabic).
COMMENT: Tadaomi seems to be saying that harsh winds and the cold winter light arise from foreign lands and should not be given undue attention. Japan, on the other hand, is "warmed" by the emperor's virtue, making winter bearable.

Meditating After Illness: An Impromptu Recitation of Things on My Mind

Whether I lived or died was of no concern to me.
When has my weak and wasted condition ever been a bother?
What did I care if my legs were feeble, and I found it hard to walk?
Luckily, I was able to focus my mind and keep it from wandering away.
The principles of right and wrong I could grasp while all alone;
Kindly feelings and cool disregard I could still discern while ill.
Heaven has made this heart of mine like an empty boat;
The routine trials of daily life no longer stir my emotions.

SOURCE: DSKS 32, in *Denshi kashū chū*, vol. 1, pp. 127–30; octave (heptasyllabic).

LINE 7: "Empty boat": an ideal Daoist spiritual state characterized by a mind free of preconceptions and desires. This reference derives from lines in the "Yu kou" (Opposing Rebels) chapter of *Zhuangzi*, which read: "Those who are cunning, labor, and those who are knowledgeable, worry. Those without ability seek nothing; sated, they wander around freely, floating like an unmoored boat, empty and drifting about."

✠ On a Day Off in Spring, Visiting a Friend and Fellow Student

We always wish to deepen the friendships we have with other folk.
What should we do to emulate the bond between Bo and Zhong?
The Confucianists are questioning whether poetry serves a purpose.
> [Of late, it has been widely bandied about that poetry is of no use.]
Recent laws prohibit us from drinking wine to excess.
> [There is a law that proscribes drinking in groups.]
The ups and downs of official life cause many to stumble and fall.
It's gloomy and dull beneath the blossoms, but I pay the matter no heed.
Now that I've come in earnestness to pay a visit to you,
As your fellow student, I pledge our friendship shall be as strong as iron.

SOURCE: DSKS 44, in *Denshi kashū chū*, vol. 1, pp. 183–87; octave (heptasyllabic).

LINE 2: Literally, "What should we do to emulate *the one who understood the music*?" The latter phrase, Ch. *zhiyin* (J. *chion*), means a kindred spirit or close friend and alludes to a famous anecdote about Zhong Ziqi and Bo Ya, two friends who lived during the Spring and Autumn period (722–486 B.C.). Bo Ya was a skilled *qin* player, and Zhong loved his music. Bo Ya was said to have been so moved by Zhong's appreciation of his playing that he destroyed his instrument after his friend died and never played again, believing that no one else was capable of fully appreciating his music. The above account can be read in *Lüshi chunqiu* (The Chronicles of Master Lü, edited by Lü Buwei, d. 235 B.C.).

LINE 3: As background, we need to note the so-called Ōtenmon incident (or purge) of 866/9. In the intercalary Third Month of that year, a fire had destroyed the Ōtenmon Gate at the imperial palace in Kyoto, and the courtier Tomo no Yoshio, then *dainagon* (major counselor), together with his son Nakatsune, were accused of arson (the question of their guilt or innocence has not been resolved—see Borgen, p. 63). Thirteen in all were punished; of these, Yoshio and seven others were sent into exile by the ruthless regent Fujiwara no Yoshifusa, who chose to make the most of the incident for his own benefit. Because these disgraced gentlemen belonged to the *kanshi* literary salons at court, many began to cast doubt upon the wisdom of utilizing Chinese literature and learning in the service of the state (ibid.). It is this climate of criticism to which Tadaomi makes reference in this line. This incident may have marked the beginning of the loosening of ties with China, which culminated in the termination of official missions to that country in 894.

LINE 4: A law enacted on 866/1/23 (before this poem was written) stated that since drinking parties outside the court had led to various excesses, including drunken brawls and other misbehavior, the consumption of alcohol was forbidden to everyone except the emperor and members of the higher aristocracy. Exceptions were made for religious ceremonies and when wine was required for "medicinal purposes." Scholar-officials also had to seek permission to associate with each other socially on holidays. It is questionable to what extent these drinking laws were enforced, although, for what it is worth, Michizane writes in his introduction to KKBS 49 (composed in 893) that the proscription against alcohol was always observed. See NKBT, 72, p. 142.

LINE 5: One wonders if Tadaomi was recalling the unfortunate circumstances of his friend and fellow scholar-official Ki no Natsui, who was exiled to Tosa province in 866/9/22 after being accused of complicity in the burning of the Ōtenmon Gate. On Tadaomi's friendship with Natsui, whose upright character he deeply admired, see Kinpira, pp. 232-34.

LINE 6: The translation of this line is tentative. Social events held beneath the cherry trees seemed dull perhaps because there was no wine to drink, owing to the prohibition mentioned above. At the same time, the poet seems to be saying that he is not bothered by the absence of alcohol, for what matters most is the cultivation of friendship.

COMMENT: There is some question as to when this poem was composed. In one instance, Kojima Noriyuki states that it was written just before the Ōtenmon incident, in 866 (*Denshi kashū chū*, vol. 1, p. 185), but his chronological table on p. 290 gives the date as 868.

�֎ Demanding Wine as We Lament the Passing of Spring

With each new day that comes along another disappears:
No sooner has the spring arrived we lament it's almost gone.
When flowers bloom at the houses in town, people throng to enter.
But there's no wine on the kiosk mats, so they never stay for long.
In the world of men, time is like the turning hub on a wheel;
In human society, honor and glory are like words written on water.
I long to shed the delusory thoughts that bind me to the world,
So if I demand the wine of the Immortals, please don't look askance.

SOURCE: DSKS 45, in *Denshi kashū chū*, vol. 1, pp. 188–92; octave (heptasyllabic).
LINE 4: Drinking wine at most social functions was proscribed at this time. See notes to the preceding poem for details.
LINE 6: "Words written on water" is a metaphor for transience.

✖ A Poem Shown to My Colleagues, Written After Seeing a Paper Kite Stuck on the Wall by the Chamberlains' Office

Aloft in the wind it tested its wings—the new paper kite.
How did it manage to end up stuck upon the earthen wall?
Though I'm well aware that our destinies rest in our own hands,
It's a pity that whether it flies or falls depends on what others do.
This kite is like a crane that stands mired in a marshy swamp—
Quite unlike the warbler in spring that shifts to a lofty tree.
Rising into the azure skies would seem its proper destiny.
So I beg you, sirs, don't keep shortening the silk string on *this* kite.

SOURCE: DSKS 48, in *Denshi kashū chū*, vol. 1, pp. 200–204; octave (heptasyllabic).
TITLE: The Chamberlain's Office (Kurōdodokoro) was established by Emperor Saga in the early ninth century. Three of its positions (for men of the fifth rank) were considered sinecures with no official duties, while other chamberlains were charged with performing administrative, ceremonial, and document-drafting functions on behalf of the emperor and those around him.

LINE 6: This line alludes to a portion of Ode 165 in *Shi jing*, titled Fa Mu, "Felling Trees," which reads as follows: "On the trees go the blows *chang-chang*; / And the birds cry out *ying-ying*. / One issues from the dark valley, / And removes to the lofty tree." (Legge, *The She King*, p. 253). The bush warbler comes out of the lowland valleys in spring and settles in the hills.

LINE 7: The poet is hinting here that both he and the paper kite have aspirations and the capacity to "rise in life." At this time, Tadaomi was forty-two, holding the junior fifth lower rank and apparently anxious to gain promotion. This was not to happen for another decade when, in 879/12, he was granted the junior fifth upper, the highest rank he ever received.

LINE 8: Tadaomi is making a word play on "silk string" (J. *shinrin*), a synecdochical term meaning "imperial edict." On one level, he is saying that he hopes the chamberlains will give the kite enough string so that it can soar. On another, Tadaomi is asking them to desist from shortening the imperial directives, which is to say, omitting favorable references to him in the imperial documents they draft. See *Denshi kashū chū*, vol. 1, pp. 203–4.

�֍ Feeling Pity for the Cherry Blossoms

Hitherto it was just a withered tree.
Then morning came, and it was half-covered in pink.
Our national fragrance—we know it is something special.
Those ordinary trees—we can see they are not the same.
People who break off sprigs should be locked in chains.
Birds that peck them ought to be put in cages.
I am bothered to see the blossoms fall so soon.
Would that we could bribe the winds of spring!

SOURCE: DSKS 54, in *Denshi kashū chū*, vol. 1, pp. 228–32; octave (pentasyllabic).

✖ The Shrimp: A *Zekku* in Thirty Characters

Out of the water, shriveled up and dry.
Arched back and long whiskers, we call you "Old Man of the Sea."
Rather like a court minister, clad in your crimson robes,
Yet reduced in appearance and so unlucky—unfit for auspicious times.

SOURCE: DSKS 57, in *Denshi kashū chū*, vol. 1, pp. 240–42; quatrain in irregular meter; *zatsugon*.

TITLE: A *zekku* is a four-line poem, normally in five- or seven-character lines. The lines in this poem have five, seven, nine, and nine characters, respectively.

LINE 2: "Shrimp" in Japanese is literally "old man of the sea." The shrimp's pathetic appearance may remind Tadaomi of himself and his own lucklessness.

❖ Climbing the Mountain of Tendai

My shins wrapped in arm-guards, staff in hand, sweat never drying.
At last I've climbed to the top of the mountain, reaching the very summit.
Lamentable that those noble lords have never been to this spot.
But now that I'm here, I truly feel I am better than them all!

SOURCE: DSKS 65, in *Denshi kashū chū*, vol. 1, pp. 262–64; quatrain (heptasyllabic).
TITLE: The mountain where the Tendai sect is centered is Mt. Hiei, to the northeast of Kyoto.
LINE 1: Arm-guards obviously were strapped to the arm, not the shin—a scribal error?

❖ On Seeing a Spider Spin a Web

The spider spins himself a web as the sun descends at dusk.
The net's mesh—how can he weave it from just single thread?
I wouldn't have thought you had the skill to produce such an orderly web.
Woven without a shuttle or loom—who could make such silk?
In the autumn cold, adorned with dewdrops, a string of hanging pearls.
A wind comes up and petals adhere, a figured-silk curtain swaying.
Every side so densely woven nothing ever slips through.
Those words of bidding by Tang of Yin might be fitting here.

SOURCE: DSKS 67, in *Denshi kashū chū*, vol. 1, pp. 267–70; octave (heptasyllabic).
LINE 8: This line alludes to a famous anecdote in the biography of Tang, the eighteenth century
B.C. founder of the Shang (Yin) dynasty, contained in *Shi ji*. During his military campaign
against the last emperor of the Xia dynasty, Tang came across a four-sided net strung up in the
wilderness. He slashed the net open on three sides to allow the animals trapped therein to es-
cape, declaring that they were free to leave but could stay and remain as his subjects if they so
desired. These are the "words of bidding" alluded to here. This incident greatly impressed the
other lords, convincing them that Tang's righteousness extended even to the birds and beasts.

❖ Late Spring

Warblers twitter noisily; I am tired of their late season song.
The flowers look drab, and I've never liked the sight of those aged branches.
Springtime has left me feeling dispirited and cold.
I seldom raise my blinds these days and mostly keep them down.

SOURCE: DSKS 71, in Kojima Noriyuki and others, annot., *Denshi kashū chū*, Kenkyū sōsho,
113, vol. 2 of 3 vols. (Osaka: Izumi Shoin, 1992), pp. 4–6; quatrain (heptasyllabic).
LINES 1 AND 2: The warbler is portrayed not as the conventional auspicious symbol of spring
but more subjectively as the cause of Tadaomi's ennui. Similarly, the gnarled cherry trees
perhaps remind him of his own decrepitude rather than the gentle dignity and beauty of the
flowers.

✠ Cooling Off on a Summer Day

Summer day, quietly resting, here in my bamboo pergola.
When it is hot, I love wearing robes of plantain cloth.
I've brought along three bits of ice and hold them in my mouth.
I have no use for those fancy gates—my cart is fully loaded!

SOURCE: DSKS 72, in *Denshi kashū chū*, vol. 2, pp. 6–7; quatrain (heptasyllabic).
LINE 4: Fancy gates: the homes of the wealthy and influential. "My cart is fully loaded" is an expression of contentment and satisfaction.

✠ Quietly Relaxing

My heart's at ease, no need to play the *koto* on and on.
I do have eyes, but why continue staring at the forest?
Lying peacefully, mind at rest, both my eyes are closed.
When in the mood, I sometimes hum with the wind in the bamboo.

SOURCE: DSKS 73, in *Denshi kashū chū*, vol. 2, pp. 8–10; quatrain (heptasyllabic).

✠ Going to Ryūmonji in the Rain During the Eighth Month of the Fifth Year of Genkei (881)

In the autumn rain, the sound of the falls grows louder as I listen.
Clouds gathering, mountains dark, but we must present our lamp.
  [At this time, we were going to the temple to make a gift of a lamp.]
We travelers should not feel upset if people and horses get wet.
If there were no rain at the Dragon's Gate, we could not climb up to see it.

SOURCE: DSKS 75, in *Denshi kashū chū*, vol. 2, pp. 14–16; quatrain (heptasyllabic).
TITLE: Ryūmonji, Dragon's Gate Temple, was located in Nara prefecture, on the northern bank of the Yoshino River in Yoshino district, near the Ryūmon Falls. These falls were named after China's famous Longmen (Dragon's Gate) Falls, which are near Luoyang.
LINE 4: This line alludes to a story in the biography of Li Ying in *Hou Han shu* (The History of the Latter Han Dynasty), which describes climbing up the Longmen Falls after heavy rain. The water was flowing swiftly, forming a solid sheet of water and giving the appearance that it could almost be climbed. A *kanshi* by Sugawara no Michizane, KKBS 374, also alludes to the Longmen phenomenon.

❋ A Poem About Myself

I never tire of composing verse, will do so till I die.
From the moment I first tried my hand I knew it was in my blood.
To commemorate the new reign period, I have written three hundred poems;
[In the spring of the first year of Jōgan (859), I presented 360 poems to meet my annual
tax responsibilities.]
In praise of great officials, I penned half a thousand verses.
[In the autumn of the third year of Saikō (856), I composed 416 historical poems.]
The pursuit of scholarship does not always lead to finding fortune.
The poems I write by habit each day are never perfect works.
I am not at all like that person who was fated to "fly and eat meat,"
So what would ever make me discard my ink slab and my brush?

SOURCE: DSKS 78, in *Denshi kashū chū*, vol. 2, pp. 26–33; octave (heptasyllabic).
LINE 3: The reigning emperor was Seiwa (r. 858–76). Using one's poetry as a substitute for tax
payment might have been a fanciful idea; on the other hand, similar language is seen in poem
120 in *Kanke bunsō*, where Sugawara no Michizane seems to be saying that his production of
verse was in lieu of payments in kind. The notion of writing 360 verses—presumably one per
day over a year—is seen also in the preface to Ki no Tsurayuki's *Shinsen waka*, a collection of
360 poems. Apparently, the earliest precedent for this practice of compiling collections 360
poems in length is seen in the Heian collection *Sone Yoshitada shū*. See *Denshi kashū chū*, vol.
2, pp. 28–29.
LINE 7: This is a reference to Ban Chao (32–102), the twin brother of the historian Ban Gu
(32–92). Unable to distinguish himself as a scholar, he went to a physiognomist, who advised
him that he would "fly and eat meat," because he possessed a "swallow's beak and a tiger's
neck." That is to say, he would likely distinguish himself as a military leader. Ban indeed
became a famous general, active over a thirty-year period in various campaigns in Central Asia.
Here, the poet is simply saying that he himself would never have succeeded as a warrior.

❋ On My Residence in the Eastern Suburbs

Let's not talk of my poor, cramped house in the suburbs east of town.
My life is peaceful; it's fitting that I should like this shabby village.
My post, I'm afraid, pays a meager salary, so I lack a fancy house.
Guests to my shame come not to my gate, for my wine cask's always empty.
In my garden of two or three *mou*, primary and secondary herbs.
In my study, the five thousand words of the Way and Power Classic.
I've fled the world to the eastern suburbs, and though the place is the same,
It is not as if I have left my lord, in the manner of Master Wang.

SOURCE: DSKS 79, in *Denshi kashū chū*, vol. 2, pp. 33–37; octave (heptasyllabic).
LINE 5: The land measurement *mou* (J. *ho*) varied somewhat over time but was roughly a sev-
enth of an acre. "Primary and secondary" is, more literally, "ruler and minister," these terms
designating the first two of three categories of medicinal herbs cataloged in the ancient classic
Shen Nong ben cao jing (The Herbal Canon of Shen Nong [the legendary God of Agriculture]).

There were 120 varieties in the top two categories of essential herbs, and 125 in the third category comprising the so-called "assistant" herbs (*Denshi kashū chū*, vol. 2, p. 35).

LINE 6: The Way and Power Classic is *Dao de jing*, the primary text of Daoism.

LINE 7: "Though the place is the same" simply means that both the poet and Master Wang (seen in the next line) settled in the eastern suburbs of their respective cities.

LINE 8: Master Wang: Wang Jungong, who is mentioned in the *Hou Han shu*, chapter 73, as leaving his official post to lead a life of obscurity in the eastern suburbs of the capital, where he worked as a cattle dealer. See *Denshi kashū chū*, vol. 2, p. 36.

�֎ No Vexing Encumbrances

No vexing encumbrances burden me, nor have I any cares.
Why would I strive to seek a life of grand extravagance?
I live my days just as I please, content with simple food.
My office fits my station in life, I'm glad for a post with leisure.
A fish released to frolic in the sea finds the shoreline waters vast;
A bird soaring into the skies finds the blue expanses high.
How is my life any different from the life of Bo Juyi?
I'm content to be where the sun comes up and immortal peach trees grow.

SOURCE: DSKS 80, in *Denshi kashū chū*, vol. 2, pp. 37–41; octave (heptasyllabic).

LINE 1: Vexing encumbrances, J. *keirui*, usually means family ties.

LINE 7: Bo Juyi (772–846): the most celebrated of the Chinese poets in Heian Japan.

LINE 8: "Where the sun comes up"—a reference to Japan. The immortal peach trees, *bantō*, a symbol of longevity, were said to bloom once every 3000 years.

✖ Looking in the Mirror

Are they the same or different? The point is surely moot.
The man in the mirror and the one in front are indeed two separate people.
I sit alone in this quiet pavilion, no one to keep me company.
Whenever I need to find a friend, I always open my mirror.

SOURCE: DSKS 81, in *Denshi kashū chū*, vol. 2, pp. 41–43; quatrain (heptasyllabic).

✖ Losing My Hair

I watch as I wash and comb my hair and see it falling out.
Old age and youth so unalike—no comparison at all.
Never say that as days go by our hair is growing thinner,
For the hair on the heads of our sons and grandsons is growing ever thicker!

SOURCE: DSKS 85, in *Denshi kashū chū*, vol. 2, pp. 53–55; quatrain (heptasyllabic).

LINES 3 AND 4: Tadaomi is comforting himself with the fanciful observation that there is no "net loss" of hair within his family, even though his own hair is thinning.

⚑ Exhorting Myself to Live in Quiet Retirement

A life span of a hundred years—who ever lives so long?
Although we manage to stay alive, time rapidly marches on.
When ill and weak, we cannot avoid living quietly in seclusion;
But to dwell in seclusion when one is well—now *that* is true retirement.

SOURCE: DSKS 86, in *Denshi kashū chū*, vol. 2, pp. 56–58; quatrain (heptasyllabic).

⚑ Medicine

I planted herbs, and as spring passes they've spread all over the ground.
Luxuriant, they keep out the heat—their abundance fills my garden.
People come to pick the plants, then draw back in surprise:
From out of the bushy wolfberry vines, the barking of my dog!

SOURCE: DSKS 132, in Kojima Noriyuki and others, annot., *Denshi kashū chū*, Kenkyū sōsho, 146, vol. 3 of 3 vols. (Osaka: Izumi Shoin, 1994), pp. 8–11; quatrain (heptasyllabic).
LINE 4: Wolfberry vine, *Lycium chinensis*, is also called the Chinese matrimony vine or medlar Its fruit was used to make a medicinal tonic.

⚑ Relating My Thoughts Upon Seeing a Snap-Beetle and Presenting Them to Master Sō

Kowtowing when it bumps into things; known as the kowtow bug.
Whenever it wants to avoid harm, it protects itself this way.
The bug in a trice glances up and down—you know he feels upset.
Then if you hit him several times his blood will start to run.
Looking like someone asking to surrender, finally confessing his crime;
Seemingly begging to be spared, submitting himself to capture.
This tiny insect has grasped the principle of clinging onto life;
And yet *this* fellow, six feet tall, hasn't any freedom at all.

SOURCE: DSKS 192, in *Denshi kashū chū*, vol. 3, pp. 321–26; octave (heptasyllabic).
TITLE: The snap-beetle is a small insect about a centimeter long, known variously in Japan as the *kome-tsukimushi* (rice-pounding bug) and the *nukatsuki-mushi* (head-knocking bug). It is able to flip itself over when placed on its back, and when held down will knock its head on the ground repeatedly with movements resembling the actions of a person pounding rice or bowing obsequiously. Master Sō is unidentified.

KANKE BUNSŌ (THE SUGAWARA LITERARY DRAFTS) AND KANKE KŌSHŪ (THE SECOND SUGAWARA COLLECTION)

Kanke bunsō is one of the largest extant collections of Chinese poetry and prose ever produced in Japan, containing some 159 prose pieces and 468 chronologically arranged poems by Sugawara no Michizane (845–903). A high-ranking scholar and official of legendary renown and the most prolific of all the Heian *kanshi* poets, Michizane presented this work to Emperor Daigo in the year 900. Three years later, he entrusted a collection of his later *kanshi, Kanke kōshū* (also known by the title *Saifu shinshi* [New Poems from the Western Headquarters]), to his friend and fellow literatus Ki no Haseo. This collection contained only forty-six poems, all of which were written during his period of exile in northern Kyushu, in Dazaifu (Saifu, see below).

Michizane had become the object of jealousy and suspicion at court late in his career, owing to the political power and influence he had amassed during the reign of Emperor Uda (r. 887–97). In 901, having been accused of treason and excessive ambition, he was sent into exile, where he died two years later in miserable circumstances. A rash of natural calamities following his death were attributed to his vengeful spirit, and as an act of propitiation Michizane was posthumously pardoned in 923. His court post was restored to him, and he was granted promotion to the senior second rank. For more than a millennium, Michizane has been enshrined across Japan as Tenjinsama (Tenman Tenjin), the patron god of scholarship and calligraphy.

In its original form, *Kanke bunsō* was one part of a larger twenty-eight *maki* collection of Chinese prose and poetry titled *Kanke sandaishū* (Collected Works of Three Generations of the Sugawara Family). This work contained not only Michizane's own writings, in twelve *maki*, but also ten *maki* of works by his father Koreyoshi (812-880), titled *Kan-sōkō shū* (The

121

Collection of Consultant Sugawara) and six devoted to the writings of Michizane's grandfather, Kiyokimi (770–842), an anthology known by the title *Kankeshū* (The Sugawara Collection). In time, Michizane's portion of the anthology became separated from the original collection, which was subsequently lost. The oldest surviving manuscript of *Kanke bunsō, Fujii Ransai kyūzō-bon*, bears the date 1656 and, like all other extant handwritten manuscripts, is apparently based upon a much earlier text known to have been copied in 1124 by Fujiwara no Hirokane (?–?). Hirokane's text was presented seven years later to the Kitano Jinja, a Shinto shrine dedicated to Michizane.[95] The earliest extant Sugawara poem, titled "Looking at Plum Blossoms on a Moonlit Night," KKBS 3 (translated below), was composed when the poet was about eleven, apparently as a composition exercise assigned by his teacher, Shimada no Tadaomi.

Michizane's most prolific period was his unhappy stint as governor of Sanuki, where he served from 886 to 890. One hundred and fifty of the poems in *Kanke bunsō*—nearly a third—were composed during these years in Sanuki and are mostly melancholy lyrical verses, displaying a plain rhetorical style. The 890s, during which time Michizane was back in the capital gaining ascendancy at court, saw the composition of a further 153 of the poems in the collection. Generally more formal and rhetorically ornate, about half of these items were written on court occasions and on imperial command. These are stylistically typical of Michizane's court-based poetry overall—skillfully wrought, with frequent Chinese allusions, but often lacking personal sentiment. Borgen attributes the relative paucity of private, lyrical verse written during these years to an insufficiency of leisure time for such pursuits and the need for discretion in Michizane's choice of poetic subject owing to his high position at court.[96] It seems also likely that the poet's sense of well-being and satisfaction during these glory years meant that he no longer needed to unburden himself in verse.

As with the poetry of Michizane's mentor, Shimada no Tadaomi, the influence of Bo Juyi is discernable in Michizane's verse, not only in the personalism of many of his poems but also in his occasional displays of moral and political skepticism and concern for the plight of the poor. Such concern is seen, for example, in the poems containing dialog with a poor peddler of reed hampers, poems 228–31, translated below. Michizane's poetry also offers early examples of the bittersweet lyrical tone Japanese critics since the mid-Edo period have referred to as *mono no aware*, the "pathos (*aware*) of things."[97] "A Literary Gathering on the Sixth Day of the

---

95. Kawaguchi Hisao, annot., *Kanke bunsō, Kanke kōshū*, NKBT, 72 (Tokyo: Iwanami Shoten, 1966), pp. 65–66.

96. Borgen, p. 225.

97. *Mono no aware* as a cathartic emotional quality (one identified with the very 'goodness' of lyrical expression) has been associated in particular with the literary theories of the National

Seventh Month" (poem 37) illustrates this complex mixture of emotions arising from the poet's melancholy recognition of the impermanence of all natural beauty and indeed life itself:

Autumn's here, the sixth day now, but not yet fully autumn.
Pale dew, glistening like pearls; the moon in the shape of a hook.
Thinking how the years rush by my heart is especially sad.
Without poetry and wine to depend upon, I'd never dispel my cares.

Through Michizane's remarkable corpus, we gain a rich and detailed picture of his inner life, a portrait perhaps more complex than that of any other poet of the court period. Michizane appears by turns maudlin and self-pitying, often fearful of enemies, both real and imagined, and given to moments of self-doubt. He is not above self-ridicule, occasionally writing of his own eccentricities and in one poem calling himself a "worthless, third-rate scholar" (poem 179, not translated). However, while seldom given to levity, Michizane also has a more sanguine side, which sees him enjoying the company of friends and his children, upon whom he doted, and taking pleasure in exercising his skills as a poet. When safely at home in the familiar environment of the capital, Michizane draws satisfaction from the domesticated beauty of the urban landscape, especially his own garden. And yet these lighter moments seem overshadowed by the misfortunes Michizane endured, which made him susceptible to insomnia and melancholia. Indeed, his most memorable poems are those that detail his tribulations in Sanuki and Dazaifu, where his sense of dislocation and deprivation seemed to function catalytically to stimulate his creative muse. Michizane's awareness of lost vitality and health was coupled with nagging doubts about the real value of his past service to the court and an acute sense of the ephemerality of bureaucratic success. During his exile in Dazaifu, he is seen to descend into a deep despondency, this reflected in poem 478, "I Never Leave My House," which begins, "Since being demoted and sent away, I've lived in this brushwood hovel. / Terrified and fearing for my life, I sit here cowering and crouched."

Michizane clearly had a stormier life than many of his peers, and his life experiences, combined with his poetic virtuosity and sensitive artistic

Learning (*kokugaku*) scholar Motoori Norinaga (1730–1801). However, as Mark Meli has pointed out in his recent article on *aware* as a term in literary criticism, this word was used even as far back as the mid-Heian period to signify the "gentle, pitiful, or sorrowful emotions" of a piece typically judged to be "artistically superior." It was also used more generally to denote a composition that was somehow emotionally moving (and thus praiseworthy as art) or even "movingly charming' (without necessarily being sad or sorrowful). See Meli, "'*Aware*' as a Critical Term in Classical Japanese Poetics," in *Nichibunken Japan Review*, no. 13 (2001), pp. 72–73.

temperament, coalesced to produce a varied and compelling poetic corpus seldom matched by any other *kanshi* poet. His verse in its totality thus offers a self-portrait of remarkable depth and poignancy that has moved generations of readers across the centuries, securing Michizane a well-deserved place as a first-echelon *kanshi* poet and one of the most distinguished figures in Japanese literature.

Looking at Plum Blossoms on a Moonlit Night

Written when I was eleven. My father ordered the Presented Scholar Shimada, to test me, and I wrote my first poem. I have placed it here at the beginning of this collection.

The light of the moon is like bright snow;
The plum blossoms like glittering stars.
How lovely! The moon has shifted
Into the garden, where the dewy blossoms are fragrant.

SOURCE: KKBS 1, in Kawaguchi Hisao, annot., *Kanke bunsō, Kanke kōshū*, NKBT, 72 (Tokyo: Iwanami Shoten, 1966), p. 105; quatrain (pentasyllabic).

TITLE: Shimada is Shimada no Tadaomi, the author of the previous collection of verse in the present anthology. Tadaomi was a student of Michizane's father Koreyoshi and was Michizane's personal tutor during his childhood.

Under Ritsuryō law, a presented scholar (J. *shinshi or shinji*) was an Academy student who had passed the third of four civil service examinations, collectively called *kakyo*. The *shinshi* exam consisted of two essay questions on government and a memory test on the *Wen xuan* and *Er ya* texts (Borgen, p. 75). During the Heian period, the term *shinshi* appears to have been used interchangeably with *monjōshō* (or *monjō no shō*), denoting both a student of literature and the humanities in the Academy and someone who had passed the qualifying exams for the civil service.

Conducted by the Ministry of Ceremonial, the four civil service examinations, each providing its own separate qualification, were as follows, listed in descending order of prestige: *shūsai* (Exceptional Talent), *myōgyō* (Classics), *shinshi* (Presented Scholar), and *myōbō* (Law). See Borgen, pp. 75–76. George Sansom notes a fifth additional degree, *san*, in mathematics. Most candidates attempted to obtain the highest degree, *shūsai*, but success was a fairly rare event: only sixty-five persons achieved this status between 704 and 937. See George Sansom, *A History of Japan Until 1334* (Stanford: Stanford University Press, 1958), p. 475. Before taking an examination, a candidate had to be recommended by the Academy. Those few selected each year were designated *monjō tokugōshō* (Candidates Qualifying in Literature). They received stipends and before attempting the *shūsai* examination were expected to study for about seven years. The exams consisted mostly of essay tests (*taisaku*) and from the ninth century largely focused on the composition and analysis of *shi* and *fu* poetry.

Passing one of the civil service examinations meant eligibility for employment in a government post. However, because of the hereditary nature of bureaucratic entitlement in the Japanese court, some Academy students received civil service positions without sitting tests, while others could take the *taisaku* examinations without ever being selected for *monjō tokugōshō* candidacy.

❖ Finding Pleasure in Solitude at Year's End (Composed at the age of fourteen)

The end of the year has now arrived—it certainly makes me sigh.
I'm happy in the knowledge that spring cannot be far away.
That wintery light will soon be gone—wherever will it go?
The warmth that shortly will arrive—in whose house dwells it now?
Ice has sealed the water's surface, no sound of any waves.
Snow dots the tops of the woodland trees; they seem to be in bloom.
A pity I did not realize that I should have studied hard;
Instead I've let the years slip by at the window of my study.

SOURCE: KKBS 2, in NKBT, 72, pp. 105–6; octave (heptasyllabic).

❖ Guttering Candle

This single guttering candle has kept on burning all night long.
Drop by drop its wax drips down, like the tears inside my heart.
The remaining light is growing faint, so I raise it to keep it alight.
I hastily lower the reed blinds, in case a breeze should blow.

SOURCE: KKBS 60, in NKBT, 72, p. 151; octave (heptasyllabic).
COMMENT: This was composed around 870, when Michizane was twenty-six.

❖ An Account of My Thoughts: To Abe, My Talented Colleague

Fan Ye's *Hou Han shu* on my back—all one hundred chapters.
Beyond the gates of the Academy the sun is just appearing.
If not for the sake of gaining fame and earning a salaried post,
Why would I care that there's only a couple of weeks left in the year?
[POET'S NOTE: Abe, I am upset that now, at year's end, you have decided for the time being not to go ahead with your exams.]

SOURCE: KKBS 61, in NKBT, 72, p. 151; quatrain (heptasyllabic).
TITLE: Abe (unidentified), a student at the Academy, apparently died young—see KKBS 72, below. This poem and the next were written in 871, when Michizane was twenty-seven.
LINE 1: *Hou Han shu* (History of the Latter Han Dynasty), compiled by Fan Ye (d. 445), was a major required text for students preparing for the civil service examinations.

✕ Drinking with My Schoolmates

This room of mine is barely ten feet square.
We've all had wine, several cups apiece.
It's growing late, I cannot make you stay.
So off you go then, come again sometime!
[POET'S NOTE: My fellow scholars left early, so I wrote this poem.]

SOURCE: KKBS 62, in NKBT, 72, p. 152; quatrain (pentasyllabic).
LINE 3: The NKBT commentator suggests that Michizane's friends were reluctant to stay late because they were busy studying for the exams. See ibid.

✕ Grieving over My Talented Colleague Abe

Who'd have thought the ways of the world would be so hard to predict?
Looking up at heaven I wail—how can I bear this grief?
All our lives we learned from each other; now it's over and done.
On your behalf I invoke Amida, facing toward the west.

SOURCE: KKBS 72, in NKBT, 72, p. 159; quatrain (heptasyllabic).
TITLE: On Michizane's colleague Abe, see poem 61, above.
LINE 4: The poet is chanting the invocation "Namu Amida Butsu," a prayer to the Amitabha Buddha. It was recited to facilitate the deceased's rebirth in Paradise.
COMMENT: This poem and the next two date from 876, when Michizane was thirty-two.

✕ Going Through the Snow to the Early Morning Session at My Office

The wind brings the sound of palace bells heralding the dawn.
Hurrying down the road I go, as snowflakes dance around.
For my body's needs, I wear a coat of leather three feet long.
To please my palate and warm myself, I have drunk two measures of wine.
Puzzled, I ask my cold-looking servant if there's cotton fluff on his clothes.
Alarmed, I watch my tired horse plowing through cloudy drifts.
Here at my office I never have a moment of repose.
I blow on my hands a thousand times as documents I draft.

SOURCE: KKBS 73, in NKBT, 72, pp. 159–60; octave (heptasyllabic).
TITLE: Michizane was junior assistant head of the Popular Affairs Ministry at the time.

❖ The Morning Session at My Office

My lamp behind me, sash tied on, for the start of the morning session.
Tirelessly I whip my lame donkey as down the road I go.
Drums announce the break of day—how far travels the sound?
South to the Ministry of Ceremonial, north to Central Affairs.

SOURCE: KKBS 74, in NKBT, 72, p. 160; octave (heptasyllabic).
LINE 2: Although the graph for "donkey" (J. *ro*) appears here, it may be intended to mean "horse" instead, since this character is sometimes glossed as [*m*]*uma*, meaning horse.
LINE 4: The Ministry of Ceremonial was located at the southern extremity of the palace, the Central Affairs Ministry to its north, near the center of the compound. The Minbushō (Popular Affairs Ministry), where Michizane worked, was between the two ministries.

❖ Journeying Through the Mountains in Autumn: A Poem with Twenty Rhymes (At the time I was on my way to make an offering at the shrine in Esshū)

1   On and on, the mountains never end.
    Lost in thought, uneasiness fills my heart.
    My reckoning tells me it is late autumn now,
    Dawn on the fifth day since our leaving home.
5   From what valley do those white clouds appear?
    On how many cliffs do those red trees grow?
    Whenever the freezing air descends upon us
    I feel the helpless anxiety of the traveler.
    I straighten my clothes, eat breakfast on my cold grass bed;
10 Urge the men to hitch the carriages, put the dawn lamps in place.
    We wind our way through the twisting, climbing road.
    A hanging bridge slants upward into the sky.
    The terrain dangerous, rocks always tumbling down.
    The heavens near, for a while we can touch the sky.
15 Though our bodies show no sign of being transformed,
    It's just as if we have left the world behind.
    The tired horses neigh beside a waterfall.
    The old servants have trouble with the guide rope on the trail.
    A priest with a metal staff points out the way.
20 Folk gathering firewood we meet along the path.
    Looking down, I spy a village below.
    Raising my hands, I decline its earthly distractions.
    Endless houses, like checkers on a board.
    Lake Biwa like a long and spreading sash.
25 Spindle and dodder for new clothes to be made;

Seeds of the elm, old money now all gone.
To quench our thirst we drink from a flowing spring.
To warm ourselves we burn the fallen leaves.
Cloaked in foggy mist, we feel disheartened.
30 Chilled to the marrow in the bleak and bitter cold.
I'm not in search of Daoist flying-pills,
Nor do I seek new students to recruit.
I am headed for the shrine to worship the gods,
To make an offering to avert disaster and evil.
35 Long days, the time just slips away.
The time of year when nature starts to wither.
A wind sweeps through, will likely blow till dawn.
The moon escorts us all throughout the night.
I ask how much of the journey yet remains,
40 And learn we still have very far to go.

SOURCE: KKBS 75, in NKBT, 72, pp. 161–63; *pailü* (pentasyllabic), in forty lines.
TITLE: Michizane was dispatched in 876 to Tsuruga no Tsu, a port in Echizen province (modern Fukui prefecture) to pray for rain at Kehi Shrine, as Japan was plagued by drought at the time (Borgen, p. 122). As Borgen observes, the shrine was only about fifty miles from the capital. Even granted that there may have been some exaggeration on Michizane's part concerning the level of "danger and excitement" he felt during the journey, it was nonetheless a dangerous trek over mountainous terrain, one requiring more than five days' travel on roads that were not very well developed (ibid., pp. 122-23). "Esshū," mentioned here in the title, embraced the old provinces of Echizen, Echigo, and Etchū.
LINE 22: The NKBT commentator suggests that Michizane and his party passed through the town but declined to stop and be entertained (ibid., p. 162).
LINE 24: "Lake Biwa" is *kōko* in the original, literally "rivers and lakes." However, *kō* is the second character in the old name for Shiga province, Ōmi (also called Eshū), where Lake Biwa is located. Thus, *kōko* probably means "the lake of Ōmi," i.e., Lake Biwa.
LINE 25: Spindle and dodder vines (*heira*) furnished the fibers used to weave the garments traditionally worn by recluses and priests.
LINE 26: During the Qin dynasty in China, a coin shaped like an elm seed was in circulation.
LINE 31: A pure white medicinal powder taken as a pill, which gave the user a feeling of lightness and euphoria, as if flying.
LINE 34: Instances of emissaries being dispatched from the court to make offerings at this shrine are noted in the Engi Code (ibid., p. 163).

A Moonlit Night at the Seaside (At the time I was in Esshū, praying to the Gods)

The autumn wind blows by the sea where I stay among flowering reeds.
All the more moving my view of the ocean, so desolate and vast.
Our voices as we laugh and talk are sure to make waves arise.
Composing aloud a verse, I write the words in the sand with my finger.
The short grass buried by the incoming tide as we amble along the beach.

There we sit until late at night, the moon casting slanted beams.
If I were allowed to come and go, enjoying this spot as I please,
Esshū could buy the services of this Confucian scholar!

SOURCE: KKBS 76, in NKBT, 72, pp. 163–64; octave (heptasyllabic).
TITLE: Michizane had arrived at his destination in Tsuruga (see previous poem).

✪ Gazing in the Evening Toward the Garden Pond

Spanish moss upon the ground—a pillow on the riverbank.
The moon shines, spring winds come at just the expected time.
Through a straggly hedge of orange trees I stare into the distance;
By the sandy embankment that winds and turns, I slowly amble along.
"The lord of the waves" I encounter when I dangle my fishing line.
"The nation's elders" I get to know when I plant medicinal herbs.
But now my thoughts are like broken strands of silk floss on a loom;
As my life goes on, who will notice the threads upon my temples?

SOURCE: KKBS 178, in NKBT, 72, pp. 242–43; octave (heptasyllabic).
LINES 5 AND 6: "Lord of the waves," *hashin* in the original language, is an expression from the "Wai wu" (External Things) chapter in *Zhuangzi*, and refers to fish. The commentator takes it to mean "emperor" (in contrast to "elders" in the next line), although we can find no textual precedent for this notion. See ibid., p. 243. *Kokurō*, in line six, literally "nation's elders," also means "licorice." Michizane in this couplet is commenting sardonically on his sense of isolation from important people at court, fish and licorice being the extent of his "important connections" of late.
LINE 7: Michizane may be saying that his sentiments have failed to reach the ears of others and are thus "broken" or "cut off." See ibid.
COMMENT: Michizane composed this poem in 885, when he was forty-one. In recent years, he had experienced various setbacks and had made enemies at court. First, in 880, his students had accused him of grading an exam unfairly. Then in 882, he was falsely accused of writing an anonymous poem attacking Minister Fujiwara no Fuyuo. Michizane's misfortune was to continue, for in 883 his young son Amaro died. In 886/1, soon after writing the present verse, Michizane was transferred to a faraway post in Sanuki province, Shikoku, where he spent four difficult years. See the notes to KKKS 478 and our biography of Michizane for further details.

✪ At a farewell banquet held on my behalf by the left middle controller, everyone wrote poems on the theme "giving a gift of words," each person being assigned a rhyme-word (I drew the word "time")

Appointed governor of Sanuki province—naturally I am sad,
All the sadder for seeing the words that you've presented to me.
What words did I find most precious of all in the poem that you wrote?
"Your father used to be my teacher"—this is what I'd say.

SOURCE: KKBS 185, in NKBT, 72, pp. 248–49; quatrain (heptasyllabic).
TITLE: Michizane's verse appears to be in response to a farewell verse written for him by his host, Middle Controller Fujiwara no Sukeyo (?–898). It was early in 886 and Michizane was about to depart for Sanuki to serve as governor. Sukeyo had been a student of Michizane's father. He served as chief of household for Fujiwara no Mototsune (836–91), whose favor he enjoyed. On Mototsune, see notes to the next poem.

Written at a Farewell Banquet Held on My Behalf in the Eastern Salon of the Chancellor (I drew the rhyme-word "flower")

As an official or as a scholar, I shall do my duty by the nation.
Hundreds of others stand on their own because of His Majesty's grace.
Now as I leave the Eastern Salon, what is my one regret?
That next spring I will not see the flowers bloom in the capital.

SOURCE: KKBS 186, in NKBT, 72, p. 249; quatrain (heptasyllabic).
TITLE: "Eastern Salon" (Tōkaku) was the name of Fujiwara no Mototsune's literary salon. Mototsune was the chancellor (*daijō daijin*) at the time. The leading political figure of his day, he used his position to create vacancies at court for his own relatives and close associates, removing others from their posts. Michizane became a casualty because he lacked sufficient political influence, in part because of his relatively undistinguished lineage. It is probable that his less than total loyalty to the powerful Mototsune was also a factor in his being sent away from the court (Borgen, pp. 155–56). In any event, Michizane was relieved of his court posts as junior assistant head of the Ministry of Ceremonial and professor at the Academy and was sent to serve as governor of Sanuki province. This appointment, which Michizane saw as tantamount to exile, upset him deeply, but he attempted to maintain a brave face in the presence of his colleagues and superiors, as this poem shows.

At a banquet held at the Northern Hall, each of us was assigned a word (I drew the rhyme-word "shift")

I'll have my fill of wind and mist in Nankai where I am headed.
What vexes me is that people will say that I'm going into exile.
I cannot forget that provincial service was not my forebears' vocation.
Anxiously I pace around, by the door to the Great Sage Temple.

SOURCE: KKBS 187, in NKBT, 72, pp. 249–50; quatrain (heptasyllabic).
TITLE: The Northern Hall was one of the four main buildings in the Daigakuryō or Academy, where young men of the fifth rank and higher were educated, preparing them for careers as officials. This was probably the same place as the Monjōin, which had lecture rooms and a student dormitory. See ibid., p. 681. The Academy was maintained by the Shikibushō (Ministry of Ceremonial) and located near the Shinsen'en gardens, not far from Nijō Castle in modern Nakagyō-ku.

This poem, like the preceding two, was written early in 886, when Michizane was about to leave for his post in Sanuki. Ironically, in this group poetry exercise Michizane drew the rhyme character *sen*, meaning "to shift," the second character of the expression *sasen su*, to be degraded in rank or given an inferior post. Was this simply an awkward coincidence? In our translation, this character is reflected in the phrase "going into exile," in line two.

LINE 1: Nankai refers here to the Nankaidō, "South Seas Circuit," one of seven groups of provinces. This circuit consisted of Kii, Awaji, Awa, Sanuki, Iyo, and Tosa, the latter four constituting the island of Shikoku.

LINE 3: This line does not reflect reality: although Michizane's father, Koreyoshi, never served in the provinces, his grandfather, Kiyokimi, served as vice-governor of Owari between 806 and 812. Kiyokimi was sent again to the provinces as supernumerary governor of Harima in 824.

LINE 4: This temple was dedicated to Confucius and housed an image of him.

Recited on a Night in Early Autumn

Autumn's early cool is here, I can tell I'm growing more homesick:
The hem of my robe ends up soaked each night before I even know it.
Even though I'm approaching fifty, my mind has not gone soft.
When not performing official duties I keep my thoughts to myself.
Letters from home have long stopped coming; writing verse chokes me up.
Affairs of the world make me wary; I rely on dreams as my guide.
Do not say that here at this place I lack for intimate friends:
Fresh breezes and the radiant moon enter my hut through the blinds.

SOURCE: KKBS 192, in NKBT, 72, pp. 252–53; octave (heptasyllabic).
LINE 2: His robe is soaked by the autumn dew and the tears he has shed.
COMMENT: This and several other verses that follow were written during Michizane's period as governor of Sanuki.

Moon in Autumn

A thousand drunken days can drive away a thousand cares.
Spring's hundred flowers can relieve a hundred worries.
If no one ever set his eyes upon the mid-autumn moon,
Then no one would ever feel his heart being torn apart by sorrow.

SOURCE: KKBS 195, in NKBT, 72, p. 256; quatrain (heptasyllabic).
COMMENT: Michizane wrote this poem in 886.

A Quiet Room Lit by a Lamp in the Cold: Written When I Was at an Inn with My Children on the Night of *Kōshin*

Every night the traveler is on guard, watching for the "three insects,"
Especially tonight when I plan not to sleep, staring at this cheerless lamp.
Though I force myself to show resolve and have somehow kept on going,
Time and again I fight back tears, feeling sorry for myself.

This hut of mine has a low roof, and starlight pierces the walls;
The mountains are close, and the snow seems to illuminate the screens.
During the fourth and fifth watches I've had nothing at all to do,
But smile and watch my little children reciting and learning their verse.

SOURCE: KKBS 211, in NKBT, 72, p. 266; octave (heptasyllabic).
TITLE: Michizane brought two of his children to Sanuki—some accounts say his youngest son Takami (876–913) and one of his daughters (ibid.). Michizane reportedly had as many as twenty-three children, according to Borgen, p. 145. *Sonpi bunmyaku* (vol. 4, pp. 59–61) lists a total of eleven boys and three girls, but there may have been others, by lesser wives. Michizane's principal wife was Nobukiko, Shimada no Tadaomi's daughter (Borgen, p. 144).
The Japanese believed that if one fell asleep on the night of the fifty-seventh day (called *kōshin* or *konoesaru*) of the sixty-day cycle, three insect-like creatures (*sanshichū*) said to reside in the head, the stomach, and the feet would emerge and ascend to heaven to inform the Heavenly Emperor of the sleeper's secret transgressions. People thus stayed awake on this night to prevent such an event from occurring. In Japan, the Buddhist deities Taishakuten and Shōmen Kongō, and the Shinto god Sarutahiko, were worshiped to avert trouble on this day.
LINES 1 AND 2: The poet has chronic insomnia, so it seems he is guarding against the "three insects" every night, not just on *kōshin*.
LINE 5: Starlight shining in through cracks or holes in the walls is suggestive of poverty.
LINE 7: The period from 1 A.M. to 5 A.M.

❋ Quietly Viewing the Scenery in Early Spring

Early I rise and sit; like dead ashes, my mind.
In the murky darkness, my spirit is in a dream.
The mountains have disappeared among the clouds.
The rain has ceased; the sound of rushing water.
Though I'd have to say that spring's already here,
Clearly the sun is not yet pleasant and warm.
I look around—there is nothing to be seen,
Just an old angler in the village by the sea.

SOURCE: KKBS 215, in NKBT, 72, pp. 268–69; octave (pentasyllabic).
LINE 1: The reference to dead ashes derives from the "Qi wu lun" (Discussion on Making All Things Equal) chapter in *Zhuangzi* and means having one's mind vacant, as if meditating.
COMMENT: This poem was written in 887.

❋ My Thoughts on the Twentieth of the First Month (A day on which a banquet is being held in the Palace)

Cold all over from head to toe, my nighttime tears profuse.
The spring breezes are blowing now, but they care not a whit for me.
I look about me left and right, nothing but fishermen's huts.
Angler's songs, high and low, are all that I can hear.

I remember the flocks of tame warblers perched on medicine trees;
It grieves me to serve as governor here, separated by the waves.
My children urge me to have some wine, give me three measures to drink:
To kill the time, forget my cares, there is nothing better than this.

SOURCE: KKBS 216, in NKBT, 72, p. 269; octave (heptasyllabic).
TITLE: As the annotation inserted by the poet indicates, a court banquet was held annually on this day in the Jijūden, a palace hall reserved for such festivities. Ten literati would recite Chinese verse, and dancing girls performed to musical accompaniment. See ibid., p. 684.
LINE 5: These trees, *yakujū*, possessed medicinal properties. One such tree was the camphor, J. *kusunoki*.

Sending a Portion of Good Herbal Medicine to the Clerk Named "Kura–"

Wanting to nurture you in your grey old age,
I've sent you some of my rehmannia decoction.
If you add it to the liquid in your cup,
You're sure to become a wine-drinking immortal!

SOURCE: KKBS 227, in NKBT, 72, pp. 280–81; quatrain (pentasyllabic).
TITLE: The full name of the clerk is unknown; only the first character of his surname is given here, a common practice in Heian *kanshi* poem titles.
LINE 2: Rehmannia is a variety of foxglove, the source of the heart stimulant digitalis.
LINE 3: "Liquid in your cup" is probably a poetic term for wine.

An Inquiry Addressed to Old Mister Reed Hamper

Let me put a question to you, snowy-haired old man:
"Reed Hamper" is the name you go by—why might this be so?
Tell me how old you are and where you make your home.
Also explain the reason why you are hunchbacked and lame.

SOURCE: KKBS 228, in NKBT, 72, p. 281; quatrain (heptasyllabic).
COMMENT: The "Reed-Hamper" poems (KKBS 228–31) were written during the Sanuki years.

Answering on Behalf of the Old Man

"Reed Hamper" is what I'm called because of the craft I practice.
I'm sixty and in my dotage now; my home is east of the hills.
Septic boils swelled and festered, the sores are what made me lame.
I don't recall what year it was, but I was just a child.

SOURCE: KKBS 229, in NKBT, 72, pp. 281–82; quatrain (heptasyllabic).

⚑ Further Questions

Come closer! I want to ask you more about your misery and pain.
The reason you are ailing is that now you are old and withered.
You sell your baskets in the villages—for little money, no doubt.
Surely since birth you've been unable to escape from hunger and the cold.

SOURCE: KKBS 230, in NKBT, 72, p. 282; quatrain (heptasyllabic).

⚑ Further Answers

Two daughters, three sons, and one old wife as well.
Going in and out of our thatched hut, crying aloud as one.
Today I feel much more at peace, blessed by your kind concern.
So saying, he wandered home with his stick, bearing a peck of rice.

SOURCE: KKBS 231, in NKBT, 72, pp. 282–83; quatrain (heptasyllabic).
LINE 4: Japanese law at this time required villages to care for the old, the sick, and the needy (ibid., p. 282). The old man may have received the rice as a charitable donation.

⚑ Three Poems on the Theme of Wandering About by Myself on a Spring Day

(No. 1)
Released for a day from my office duties to enjoy what is left of spring.
At the water's edge where flowers grow I linger by myself.
All I do is gaze afar, facing toward northeast;
Meanwhile my colleagues point and stare at the idiotic man!

SOURCE: KKBS 247, in NKBT, 72, pp. 299–300; quatrain (heptasyllabic).
LINE 3: That is, in the direction of Heian, where Michizane longed to return. The year was 888, and he was still in Sanuki.

(No. 2)
Flowers withered, birds all gone, a chilly springtime scene.
Driven by the urge to versify, I go out and try my hand.
Evening comes but I don't go home, I stand there loudly chanting.
The local folk say, "There's a scholar who has gone and lost his mind!"

SOURCE: KKBS 248, in NKBT, 72, p. 300; quatrain (heptasyllabic).

(No. 3)

The days are long, and now I find I cannot get much sleep.
Out I go, round up the children; together we do some study.
We happen to meet a thoughtful old man, out there dangling a hook.
All of us talk about our hopes, but no one mentions fish.

SOURCE: KKBS 249, in NKBT, 72, p. 300; quatrain (heptasyllabic).

❈ Looking in the Mirror

1   A man who has reached the age of forty-four,
     I've not yet started showing signs of age.
     There's nothing in my heart I try to avoid,
     So I look in the mirror, expecting to feel pleased with myself.
5   Half of my face can readily be seen,
     Then suddenly I knit my eyebrows in a frown.
     Whatever is the cause of this distress?
     I find that I have grown some new white hairs.
     Believing the mirror is coated with a film,
10 I wipe the dust away, again and again.
     Away it goes—I can trust its image once more,
     And know its reliability is not lost.
     The fires of ambition in my breast have not burned out,
     So I suck in my silvery whiskers, but in vain.
15 My mind is how it was when I was young,
     But the springtime of my past has long since gone.
     My senior fifth rank may indeed be high.
     My two thousand picul salary may be large.
     But opening the mirror box has brought regrets—
20 I have needlessly demoralized myself.

SOURCE: KKBS 254, in NKBT, 72, pp. 303–4; pailü (pentasyllabic), in twenty lines.
LINE 17: Michizane received this rank on 887/11/17.
LINE 18: A picul (Ch. dan) was equivalent to about 133 pounds. This was the typical salary, paid in grain, given to provincial governors during the Han dynasty (ibid., p. 304). Michizane is speaking figuratively.

❊ Planting Chrysanthemum Seedlings in Front of the Government Offices

When young, I loved chrysanthemums; now old, I love them more.
In front of the government offices, in several sloping fields,
I planted some yellow ones last year and sowed some wild seeds, too.
I asked a priest this spring to give me several that were white.
When they withered, I moved them under some shade trees in the garden.
When after rain they became too wet, I rushed to pile sand around them.
How fortunate if none of the flowers is harmed by the autumn winds;
I wonder how they'll compare to those on the banks of the river Li.

SOURCE: KKBS 288, in NKBT, 72, pp. 335–36; octave (heptasyllabic).
COMMENT: Michizane wrote this poem in Sanuki, in 889.
LINE 8: This river is in Henan province, in modern Nanyang prefecture, an area famous in earlier times for its large chrysanthemums.

❊ Beside the River, Tasting Wine

I'd heard that unstrained wine is just the thing for banishing cares.
While on a visit to the riverside I tried some I was offered.
First I had three measures—amazed by the heat in my hands.
Then I drank another cup and felt my brows relax.
We laughed and joked in the frigid air—it is hard to get drunk in autumn.
Poured cup after cup, relaxed and calm; dusk and we lingered on.
Leaning forward, I strained to catch the ramblings of the others,
Lying spread out, drunk by the river as the emerald waters flowed past.

SOURCE: KKBS 299, in NKBT, 72, pp. 344–45; octave (heptasyllabic).

❊ Seeing Plantains While on the Road

Rain has fallen; the plantains cannot stand up to the autumn.
Lost in thought as on I go, my mind is far away.
Everything in the universe—empty just like this.
Reflecting thus, I stay my whip, shedding tears on the head of my horse.

SOURCE: KKBS 300, in NKBT, 72, p. 345; quatrain (heptasyllabic).
COMMENT: The destruction of the plantains has reminded Michizane of the transience of life.

Old Pines in the Wind

I hear the wind, blowing at dawn, among the ancient pines.
A clear, dry, rustling sound, like coral being shattered.
Here in bed, I find I can't sleep quietly in peace.
That shivery sound chills me to the marrow—hateful, is it not?

SOURCE: KKBS 312, in NKBT, 72, p. 352; quatrain (heptasyllabic).

Torch in the Country Village

It's not a lamp, it's not a candle, nor a firefly.
In the desolate village, I am startled to see a tiny star of light.
I learn there is an old man who is seriously ill.
In the depths of night a pine torch lights the door to his humble hut.

SOURCE: KKBS 314, in NKBT, 72, pp. 352–53; quatrain (heptasyllabic).
LINE 4: We may surmise that a doctor had been called to treat the old man, thus, the presence of this pine torch.

Lying Idle on Account of Illness: Relating My Feelings to a Scholar at the Academy

There I brooded by the sea—for years I muddled along.
It pains me to think that I labored in vain just to end up chronically ill.
I had moxa treatment for my legs, left my post in unbearable pain.
With boils on my head that would not heal, I met you, my old friend.
My servants sorrow to see me looking like a fish alive in a kettle;
Guests smile on leaving this place where sparrows can be snared at the door.
But my body hasn't grown weak and frail, and my mind is still robust.
If my medical care should prove effective, what will happen next?

SOURCE: KKBS 325, in NKBT, 72, pp. 358–59; quatrain (heptasyllabic).
TITLE: "Scholar," *daigakushi* in the title, is probably a contraction of *daigaku hakase* (Academy professor). This person is believed to be Yoshibuchi no Chikanari (?–?), a scholar and historian. Chikanari was appointed professor of literature at the Academy in 886 and was invited to serve as a Chinese tutor to Emperor Uda in 890. Chikanari also held a provincial appointment, serving as vice-governor of Iyo. The two men had previously exchanged poems in the winter of 889, the year before Michizane wrote this verse. See ibid., pp. 698–99, note 325.
LINE 1: This refers to the poet's unhappy years in Sanuki province. When the poem was written, in 890, Michizane had recently left Sanuki and returned to the capital, where he lived in a state of limbo, recovering from his ailments and awaiting his next appointment. He received a new post in the Third Month of the following year (ibid., p. 87).

LINE 5: "Like a fish alive in a kettle" means to be fearful and in imminent danger. Michizane had made trouble for himself by hastily leaving his Sanuki governorship at the end of his term before the official changeover of administrations had occurred and the proper papers had been filed (Borgen, p. 199). Michizane was unemployed for a year after leaving Sanuki and sat idle at home, apprehensive about the impending evaluation of his term as governor. A second interpretation, one perhaps more in keeping with the sixth line, is that the poet is too poor to afford firewood to cook his food. This latter interpretation would yield the following translation of the line: "My servants sorrow to see me with my fish still alive in the kettle."

LINE 6: "Sparrows can be snared at the door": a common expression used to describe a forsaken and impoverished home.

� Expressing My Thoughts: Written During a Leave from Work

1   I made a request for five days' leave from work,
    Have ceased my morning duties for a spell.
    During this break, where is it that I'm staying?
    In my house, here at Senpūbō.
5   The gate remains shut; no one ever comes.
    The bridge is broken; horses cannot cross.
    I rise early and then I summon the boys
    To go and prop up the remaining chrysanthemums.
    I bid my old servant once the sun is high
10   To go and sweep the sand out in the courtyard.
    At dusk I stroll beside the eastern hedge,
    Thinning out the bamboo leaning over.
    At night I take account of all my books—
    Almost enough to fill up five whole carts.
15   Those I need I put aside as I find them;
    Those out of place I put back where they belong.
    A chilly sound—leaves falling on the steps;
    The dawn air—hoarfrost on the stone stairs.
    The cocks crow as I lie head cradled on my arm.
20   I sigh and contemplate loved ones far away:
    All my daughters have left and now are married.
    My grandson has gone, accompanying his father.
    The work I am doing never seems to end.
    How long the road that keeps us far apart!
25   I sigh and feel my stomach twist and turn;
    I sigh again and my tears fall in torrents.
    Sunrise in the east, but I haven't been to bed.
    Feeling dejected, I drink a cup of tea.
    Heaven cares not that I'm supposed to be at rest;
30   But here at home so much I have to do.
    Everything is caused by karma, from far back in the past.

We come, we go, our lives replete with sorrow.

SOURCE: KKBS 360, in NKBT, 72, pp. 389–91; *pailü* (pentasyllabic), in thirty-two lines.
LINE 4: Senpūbō, the family home, was near Gojō in Kyoto. To the west there was a tributary of the Horikawa river, thus the mention of the bridge in line six. See ibid., p. 390.
LINE 16: The commentator links this book-sorting activity with a commission given to Michizane by Emperor Uda to compile *Ruijū kokushi* (Classified History of the Nation, 200 *maki*), a compendium of knowledge gathered from the first five of the Six Histories (*Rikkokushi*). This work, thematically and chronologically arranged, appeared in 892/5. See NKBT, 72, pp. 390–91. That same month, Michizane was ordered to begin compiling another history, *Sandai jitsuroku* (Veritable Records of the Three Reigns, completed 901), which was the last of the Six Histories and covered the period between 858 and 886. See ibid., p. 88.
LINE 22: This grandson was Minamoto no Hideaki, son of Prince Tokiyo, born in 889/7.
COMMENT: This poem was written in 892.

❊ A Poem About Myself

Three or four months have passed since leaving home.
A hundred, a thousand streams of tears I've cried.
Everything now seems exactly like a dream.
Time and again, I gaze up at the heavens.

SOURCE: KKKS 476, in NKBT, 72, p. 477; quatrain (pentasyllabic).
LINE 4: See KKKS 478, immediately below, for information on the context of this poem.

❊ I Never Leave My House

Since being demoted and sent away, I've lived in this brushwood hovel.
Terrified and fearing for my life, I sit here cowering and crouched.
All I see of the government buildings is the color of their tiles.
My only contact with the Kannon Temple is hearing its tolling bell.
My spirit has left me—gone and joined that lone cloud in the sky.
But the world outside goes on its way, I keep company with the moon.
Though no restrictions are placed upon me, here where I reside,
Why would I stray beyond my door, even a single inch?

SOURCE: KKKS 478, in NKBT, 72, pp. 481–82; octave (heptasyllabic).
LINE 1: Michizane was by now in exile in Dazaifu. As minister of the right, he had become an object of jealousy and enmity among high officials at court, who, although generally of superior birth, were now below him in the hierarchy. Michizane had tried unsuccessfully to decline the post on three occasions, knowing that he had effectively risen above his proper station given his relatively unexceptional pedigree. The following year, he also asked to be relieved of his position as captain in the Right Imperial Bodyguards. In 901/1, an edict came down calling for Michizane's removal from office, on the grounds of his alleged ambitiousness, disloyalty, and supposed attempts to manipulate the former Emperor Uda. Michizane was exiled to

Dazaifu as supernumerary governor-general within days of being purged and was escorted from the capital under guard on 901/2/1. See Borgen, pp. 270–79, and our biography of Michizane, below.

❊ Hearing the Migrating Geese

Myself, I am a man in exile; you are visitors here.
All of us forlorn and lonely, lost souls tossed about.
I lie in bed and think about the time when I'll return:
What year, I wonder, will it will be? For you, it will be next spring.

SOURCE: KKKS 480, in NKBT, 72, p. 483; quatrain (heptasyllabic).
COMMENT: This poem was written in the autumn of 901.

❊ Autumn Evening

Sallow and haggard my countenance, hair the color of frost.
How much the more so now that I am a thousand miles away.
Once I wore the hatpin and sash—fetters of honor and glory.
Now in this hut in the wilds I dwell, a captive in disgrace.
Although the moon is as bright as a mirror, it sheds no light on this wrong;
Although the wind blows as sharp as a knife, it cannot dispel my gloom.
Everything I see and hear seems miserable and bleak.
The autumn season has now become an autumn for me alone.

SOURCE: KKKS 485, NKBT, 72, pp. 499–500; octave (heptasyllabic).
LINE 5: "This wrong" refers to the charges leveled against him by jealous detractors at court, which led to his banishment to Dazaifu.
LINE 8: Michizane seems to be saying that all of the unhappiness traditionally felt by poets in autumn is now being borne by him alone.
COMMENT: This poem was written on 901/9/15.

❊ An Impromptu Composition

Illness follows hard on the heels of old age and decline.
Misery descends upon me, making the most of my exile.
Nowhere to run and hide, away from all these villains.
Nothing to do but offer a prayer to Kannon, Goddess of Mercy.

SOURCE: KKKS 513, in NKBT, 72, p. 523; quatrain (pentasyllabic).
COMMENT: Probably written toward the end of 902, this poem shows Michizane despondent and in failing health. He died about two months later, on 903/2/25, at the age of fifty-nine. Borgen gives the possible cause of death as beriberi or maybe stomach cancer (Borgen, p. 304)

FUSŌSHŪ (ANTHOLOGY OF POETRY FROM OUR LAND)

This little-known anthology, which preserves some of the most intriguing and challenging *kanshi* of the period, was compiled during the years 995–98 by Ki no Tadana (957–99) and presented to Emperor Ichijō on 1006/8/6 by the prominent statesman Fujiwara no Michinaga (966–1027). According to an entry in Michinaga's diary, Tadana's widow had entrusted him with the collection in 1000. Ki no Tadana was a leading literatus during the reign of Emperor Ichijō (986–1011), and although his own one-volume literary collection, *Ki no Tadana shū* (The Ki no Tadana Collection), no longer survives, *Honchō monzui* has thirteen pieces attributed to him, including *fu* (prose-poems), prose introductions to anthologies of poetry, and various Academy exam essays. Some of Tadana's *kanshi* are also preserved in such collections as *Wakan rōeishū*, *Shijū kudaishō* (Collected Poems with *Kudai* [Allusive Titles]), and *Sakumon daitai* (Basics of Composition, compiled by Fujiwara no Munetada, 1062–1141), a compilation of essays on the mechanics of Chinese *kanbun* and *kanshi* composition.

Only *maki* 7 and 9 of *Fusōshū* survive, although there were 16 in the original collection (some sources indicate 12 *maki*), comprising poems by 76 poets in all. The two surviving *maki* contain 104 pieces by 24 leading Heian poets, among them, Ōe no Koretoki, Ki no Haseo, Miyako no Yoshika, Sugawara no Michizane, Miyoshi no Kiyoyuki, Tachibana no Aritsura, and Minamoto no Fusaakira. The extant poems were composed over an eighty-year period, most dating from the first half of the tenth century. The non-extant original text evidently spanned 170 years, beginning around the reign of Emperor Ninmyō (r. 833–50) and continuing down to about 984. The text of *Fusōshū* is thought to have become corrupted early in its history; *Meigō ōrai* (The Letters of Fujiwara no Akihira [989–1066]), mentions the high incidence of textual errors even at this early stage in the anthology's history.

142

Judging from the scale of the collection and the fact that it was compiled during Tadana's service as senior private secretary (*dainaiki*) in the Central Affairs Ministry and presented to the Emperor, scholars have concluded that *Fusōshū* was likely intended as a sequel to the three early Heian *kanshi* imperial anthologies, as well as to a fourth, now-lost collection known only from its title, *Nikkanshū* (Collection of Daily Sights [translation tentative]). That *Fusōshū* has received little attention even in Japan and has never been translated until now is probably due in part to the absence of a reliable text. Until fairly recently, the *Gunshō ruijū* edition, which contains numerous typographical and scribal errors, had been the only available printed version. Since 1989, Tasaka Junko has been publishing periodically small portions of the text, together with annotations. To date, three installments, amounting to about two dozen poems, have appeared: "*Fusōshū* zenchūshaku" (I–III), published in *Sōgō Kenkyūjo hō* (The Bulletin of the Central Research Institute), Fukuoka University. We have consulted these in the preparation of our translations, which follow. Tasaka has also produced a collated text titled *Fusōshū: kōhon to sakuin*, based on eight major manuscripts. This important achievement should greatly assist future scholarship on the collection.

Octaves in seven-character lines account for about four-fifths of the extant poems, an indication of the continuing preference for this form. There are by contrast only a small number of *zekku*, all of them heptasyllabic, and no *yuefu*. *Maki* 7 is made up of gift poems, recollections, and laments, while *maki* 9 mainly features banquet poems. *Fusōshū* may have been structured thematically along the lines of *Yiwen leiju*, a seventh-century Chinese classified encyclopedia.[98]

Many of *Fusōshū*'s poems display a hopelessness and sense of detachment from other human beings and their concerns. The poetic images are memorably forlorn and unsettling at times: a lone tomb in the wilderness shaped like a horse's mane, empty valleys echoing with the sound of chilly gurgling waters, and so on. The imperfect state of some of the texts and the absence of commentaries or notes providing proper context add to what is already a vague mysteriousness that seems to pervade this work. We hope that our translations succeed in conveying to the reader some of the curiously appealing sadness seen in many of these poems.

---

98. *Nihon koten bungaku daijiten*, p. 1099.

❊ A Poem Written in the Summer of the Fourth Year of Tengen (981) to Match One Titled "A Poem on the Death of a Child"

The Prince and Minister of Central Affairs [Minamoto no Kaneakira?]

No flowers or any willow catkins, warblers also few.
Lazily sleeping, rising late—who cares when the sun goes down?
The lotus roots in the pond four times have put forth lovely leaves.
Often I hear the crows in the forest, leading their chicks in song.
Stroking the trunk of the parasol tree cannot comfort the smaller branches;
The cultivation of bamboo shoots is hard on the mother culm.
Whenever I recall the past, I am wracked by pain once more.
So spurred on by my fellow poets, I have written several poems.

SOURCE: FSS 4, in Kawamata Keiichi, ed., [*Shinkō*] *Gunsho ruijū* 126, vol. 6 (Tokyo: Naigai Shoseki Kabushiki Kaisha), 1931, p. 188; Tasaka Junko, ed., "*Fusōshū* zenchūshaku" (I), in *Sōgō Kenkyūjo hō*, no. 119 (March 1989): 44–46; octave (heptasyllabic).

AUTHOR: The identity of this poet is uncertain. There were actually two persons who held the title Chūsho Ō ("Prince and Minister of Central Affairs"), the first being Minamoto no Kaneakira (914–87), more precisely known as Saki no Chūsho Ō, "The *Former* Prince and Minister of Central Affairs." The other was Prince Tomohira (964–1009), known as Nochi no Chūshō Ō, "The *Latter* Prince and Minister of Central Affairs." Both men were alive in 981 when this poem was composed, and both were competent *kanshi* poets. That year Kaneakira would have been sixty-seven; Tomohira, the less likely choice, was only seventeen. See Tasaka's explanation in ibid., p. 45. On Kaneakira's career, see our biography, below.

LINES 3 AND 4: The poet is recalling the number of years gone by since the death of his (or someone else's) child.

LINE 5: This probably means that comforting the parents cannot bring back the dead child. The parasol tree (*Sterculia platanifolia*, J. *aogiri*, Ch. *wutong*) is traditionally considered the national tree of China and, according to legend, the only tree upon which a phoenix would alight.

LINE 6: The mother culm hates to see her "children" raised for human consumption.

❊ Evening . . . we were preparing to head back to the capital. They had just loosened the ropes of the boat when . . . someone happened to present me with a poem, so we turned the boat around, stopped, and I wrote a matching-rhyme poem on the spot

Consultant Miyoshi [no Kiyoyuki]

A lone tomb shaped like a horse's mane stands on the ancient plain.
The traditions of the village elders hold that a venerable one lies there.
On an overgrown and frosty track mugwort fluff blows about;
As dusk draws near, a mournful wind scatters the fallen leaves.
Autumn brambles covered in thorns, not a soul in sight.
Chilly pines with ancient branches, new growth on the trees.
This desolate morning as I headed for home, my efforts all in vain.
I wept, for the teachings he handed down are no longer to be found.

SOURCE: FSS 6, in [Shinkō] Gunsho ruijū 126, vol. 6, p. 188; Tasaka, "Fusōshū zenchūshaku" (I), pp. 48–50; octave (heptasyllabic).

TITLE AND AUTHOR: The first ellipsis in the title is due to a gap of some ten characters; the second, a gap of three characters. We have corrected one word at the end of the title: raiin appears to be an error for hon'in (the rhyme of the original poem). Miyoshi no Kiyoyuki (847–918) was apparently returning to Heian after finishing his term as vice-governor of Bitchū, ca. 897. See ibid., p. 49.

LINE 1: The phrase "shaped like a horse's mane" refers to a kind of burial mound, presumably one with steeply sloped sides like a horse's neck. The commentary provides two possible locations for this mound, both in Kibinohara, Okayama prefecture. Both date from the mid-fifth century. It is not known who was buried in these places.

✙ Written for My Honored Teacher While I Was Ill
Yoshimune

A bag, a bamboo medicine chest, an old desk for my books.
Seated or reclining, I cosset myself, ever watchful of my health.
This illness has made me weary and thin, lasting many days.
Since reaching the age of "standing firm," three years now have passed.
In reputation, I may have fallen behind the other students,
But what grieves me most is the thought of dying before my aged mother.
If Boniu had been able to respond to the questions Confucius asked,
He would have said, "It may be Fate, but I still depend on your kindness."

SOURCE: FSS 7, in [Shinkō] Gunsho ruijū 126, vol. 6, p. 188; Tasaka, "Fusōshū zenchūshaku" (I), pp. 50–51; octave (heptasyllabic).

TITLE AND AUTHOR: The identities of this teacher and the poet himself are unknown. Shimada no Yoshimune and Katsurai no Yoshimune are two possibilities (ibid).

LINE 4: "Standing firm" (J. seiritsu) harks back to a passage in Lun yu, where Confucius said, "At thirty, I stood firm, at forty I had no doubts," as cited in James Legge, trans., Confucius: Confucian Analects, The Great Learning, and The Doctrine of the Mean, p. 146. We may infer, therefore, that the poet was at this time around thirty-three.

LINES 7 AND 8: These lines are derived from a passage in Lun yu, where Confucius was visiting his disciple Ran Geng, also known as Boniu, who was grievously ill. Confucius was deeply distressed to see Boniu at death's door but conceded that if he were to die it would be due to Fate and the will of Heaven. See ibid., p. 188. Yoshimune appears to be beseeching his teacher not to abandon or neglect him in his hour of need, a theme also present in FSS 9, below.

✙ The Hardships of Illness
Yoshimune

The road of life has a thousand perils, plaguing me all my days.
Critically ill, beyond all hope, I've begun to lose interest in things.
My aged parents, seventy years old, weep beside my bed;
My son of six stands next to me, crying and lamenting.

This humble dwelling is not the place where I'd choose to end my days.
[I say this because it is just a temporary residence.]
Nothing left in my . . . bamboo trunk, only borrowed books.
I look around me, no one here to whom I can entrust these texts.
I have no idea what will happen after I am gone.

SOURCE: FSS 8, in [*Shinkō*] *Gunsho ruijū* 126, vol. 6, p. 188; Tasaka, "*Fusōshū* zenchūshaku" (I), pp. 51–52; octave (heptasyllabic).
LINE 6: The first character in the original line is missing; it may modify "bamboo trunk."

✠ Written for Fujiwara, Middle Captain of the Left Imperial Bodyguards, While I Was Ill
Yoshimune

Since we parted company I have frittered my time away.
I've shut my gate and sorrow alone, feeling sick at heart.
Ten years in the black dragon's lair, but always empty-handed,
Only to find myself today in this snail-shell of a hovel.
Friends come asking about how I feel but not about my hunger;
Famous doctors have done their best, but they cannot cure my poverty.
Your kindness and benevolence, Captain—complete and all-embracing.
It is still my hope to spend the spring in this place of hibernation.

SOURCE: FSS 9, in [*Shinkō*] *Gunsho ruijū* 126, vol. 6, p. 188; Tasaka, "*Fusōshū* zenchūshaku" (I), pp. 52–53; octave (heptasyllabic).
TITLE: This person was apparently Fujiwara no Arisane (848–914). See Honma Yōichi, annot., *Nihon kanshi* (Tokyo: Izumi Shoin, 1996), p. 150.
LINE 3: In Chinese mythology, this dragon lived in a deep abyss and held a pearl in its jaws. Being in the lair seeking the pearl symbolized the quest for success in public life.

✠ Lying Ill in Bed on an Autumn Night
Miyako no Yoshika

Ill in bed, so lonely and forlorn;
Quiet solitude, far from worldly affairs.
Before the steps, no prints from any shoes.
Beyond the gate, the visitor's path overgrown.
I suddenly sigh—the woes of this transient life!
Yet I recognize I am like all other beings.
Appearances, I believe, cannot be real;
My spirit, I fear, has left and gone away.
The night is long; bitter cold the wind.
Slanting moonlight deep within my house.

Melancholy, I cannot fall asleep.
I hear the roosters crowing, short and long.

SOURCE: FSS 10, in [*Shinkō*] *Gunsho ruijū* 126, vol. 6, p. 188; Tasaka, "*Fusōshū* zenchūshaku"
(I), pp. 53–55; *pailü* (pentasyllabic), in twelve lines.

▓ Five Laments with Preface
Minamoto no Shitagō

I have five reasons for lamenting. I wish I could rise above them but cannot.
As the saying goes, "The heart moves within and manifests itself in words.
When words are inadequate, we sigh and lament."

In the summer of the eighth year of Enchō [930] I lost my father, who
died in the western part of the capital. This is my first reason for lamenting.

In the autumn of the fifth year of Shōhei [935] I said goodbye to my
mother, north of Kōryūji temple. This is the second reason.

I have an older brother who is alive and another who is dead. The
brother who is deceased was my father's eldest son. When he was young,
he climbed Mt. Tiantai and lived there for many years as a mendicant monk.
His reputation for having reached advanced enlightenment was known all
over the mountain; even the white clouds could not have obscured his name
after he died. His chanting filled the valleys, and the green pines still trans-
mit the sound to our ears. Everyone bitterly mourned his passing, especially
me. This is my third reason for lamenting.

My other brother is the middle son, and he resides by the lake in Ōmi
province. A fisherman, who lives in a hut open on both sides, he looks out
over misty waves that extend forever. In a letter I sent him, I talked about
the capital, which must have seemed far away. How will he ever establish
himself, build a reputation, and bring glory to the memory of our parents for
posterity? This is my fourth reason for lamenting.

I am my father's youngest son, and I received more kindness and love
than did my brothers. I was never taught to sing "The Song of Warm
Spring" but was instead admonished to make use of "The Three Periods of
Leisure" on cold nights. Although I studied with a teacher from an early age,
I've ended up a mediocrity. Now I fear that everything my father said he
wished for me has come to naught. This is my fifth reason for lamenting.

The autumn wind blows mournfully all around me. The trees at the
graves of my parents have grown old. The dawn dew weeps with me, and
the plants beside the path have withered. All of this makes me sigh deeply. I
shall now recite the poems without further delay. They are as follows:

PREFACE: The saying referred to in lines two and three is from the Great Preface to *Shi jing*, which reads: "The feelings move within and manifest themselves in words. When words are inadequate, we resort to sighs and exclamations." See Legge, trans., *The She King*, p. 34.

Kōryūji is located in Uzumasa in the ward of Ukyō-ku, Kyoto. Its exact significance to the poet is unclear, but his mother may have lived at this temple as a nun or else been buried in the vicinity.

Mt. Tiantai is a conventional reference to its Japanese counterpart, Mt. Hiei, northeast of Kyoto, where the Tendai sect was based. The lake in Ōmi province is Lake Biwa, in Shiga prefecture.

By mentioning that he had not been taught to sing "The Song of Warm Spring [and White Snow]," Shitagō is perhaps suggesting that his father only had the time to give him a basic education. This song was an ancient piece of music from the state of Chu, considered extremely lofty and refined. It is alluded to in Chinese and Japanese literature as a composition that only a small minority of talented persons was able to master. Thus, Shitagō may instead be implying that his father did not consider him talented enough to learn anything so sophisticated

"The Three Periods of Leisure" refers to blocks of free time occurring during prolonged rain, winter, and the nighttime hours, which were supposed to be used for study.

These five poems were written around 940–41. The poet was about thirty at the time.

(No. 1)

Since losing sight of his stern face ten years now have passed.

And yet I have no relatives with whom I can mourn and grieve.

I have long dwelt alone in poverty, behind my mugwort gate.

He delivered many admonitions while giving me my lessons,

Nonetheless, "The Song of White Snow" he never taught me to sing.

Gazing heavenwards, I find it hard to repay him for his virtue.

To make a name and be thoroughly filial are ingrained within my heart.

To this end, I must somehow go and worship at his grave.

SOURCE: FSS 11, in [*Shinkō*] *Gunsho ruijū* 126, vol. 6, p. 189; Tasaka Junko, ed., "*Fusōshū* zenchūshaku" (II), *Sōgō Kenkyūjo hō* 120 (February 1990), pp. 159–60, 163; octave (heptasyllabic).

LINE 1: The poet is writing about his father, who died in 930.

LINE 5: "The Song of White Snow" is a reference to "The Song of Warm Spring [and White Snow]," mentioned above in the poem preface.

(No. 2)

I cannot manage without my mother, not even for a minute.

How sad we had to part so soon; I grow old in this rustic hut.

How shall I find that distant spot, off where the river roars?

To find her lonely overgrown grave is all I wish to do.

Long ago, when I was young, I wanted to bring her oranges.

The pain was severe, yet I cherish still the kindness of her whippings.

The chilly winds of autumn are blowing through this room.

Would I have come to warm this seat for the sake of anyone else?

SOURCE: FSS 12, in [*Shinkō*] *Gunsho ruijū* 126, vol. 6, p. 189; Tasaka, "*Fusōshū* zenchūshaku" (II), pp. 163–64; octave (heptasyllabic).

LINE 5: Bringing oranges is an allusion to an anecdote in the biography of Lu Ji in *Sanguo zhi* (The Records of the Three Kingdoms [220–65]). When Lu Ji was six, he met the famous local leader Yuan Shu, who was so impressed with the boy that he gave him an orange. Lu put part of it inside his robe, and when he was leaving Yuan Shu, the remains of the orange fell out of his clothing as he was prostrating himself. Yuan Shu asked Lu if he thought it was polite to take food away like this, whereupon the boy explained that he wanted to bring the rest of the orange home for his mother. This anecdote exemplifies the spirit of filial piety.

LINE 6: In other words, Shitagō is grateful for the stern but fair discipline with which she raised him.

LINES 7 AND 8: The poet may be sitting in prayer at a temple, perhaps Kōryūji, in the vicinity of which his mother appears to have been buried.

(No. 3)

Atop Mt. Tiantai, all too soon he departed from this world.
Hearing so much about his fame, I'm often moved to tears.
Afternoon, and the pine tree flowers are drying out in the sun.
Leaves of the *heira*, vine of the Three Robes, frigid in the wind.
Perfectly imparting sagely wisdom came easily just to him.
Clad in rags, with a road to salvation that was not hard to follow.
Who would have thought he'd disappear with the fragrant incense smoke?
Bound in sorrow, my heart will forever be off in the distant clouds.

SOURCE: FSS 13, in [*Shinkō*] *Gunsho ruijū* 126, vol. 6, p. 189; Tasaka, "*Fusōshū* zenchūshaku" (II), pp. 164–65; octave (heptasyllabic).

LINE 4: "Three Robes" (*san'e* or *sanne*) refers to the various garments making up the wardrobe of priests and nuns: these were a formal robe, worn when begging or visiting the palace, another robe worn at services and lectures, and a third used for daily wear. *Heira* was a thin, coarse fabric spun from the fibers of spindle and dodder vines and was associated with the humble garb of the priesthood.

(No. 4)

My elder brother cast me aside, went away without me.
He lives apart, off in the northeast corner of Ōmi province.
Sinking low, no thought of returning—what is filial in this?
Drifting about, he found a place—how long has he lived by the lake?
At dawn he takes his solitary boat, heads off into the waves,
His mind made up by a mouthful of bass, blown by the autumn wind.
Letters from him have stopped arriving ever since last year.
When will I, his flesh and blood, be able to ask how he fares?

SOURCE: FSS 14, in [*Shinkō*] *Gunsho ruijū* 126, vol. 6, p. 189; Tasaka, "*Fusōshū* zenchūshaku" (II), pp. 165–66; octave (heptasyllabic).

LINE 6: This line alludes to a story about a third-century poet named Zhang Han, who is said to have resigned his high office one autumn (traditionally a time for homesickness) so that he could return to his home district, because he missed the local food, especially the sea bass. See *Jin shu* (History of Jin), biography 62, for the story. Just as Zhang Han declined to go back to his post, Shitagō's brother refuses to forsake his rustic lakeside existence.

(No. 5)

The leaves rustle mournfully; insects chirping, chirping.

I've finally learned that my gloom deepens as autumn marches on.

To steal some light (for I am not yet weary) I have pierced the eastern wall;

Though shadows shift, how could I mind being near the other students?

As I lie on my pillow, tears stream down, on this frosty night.

Here by the window, cold as a river this sorrowing heart of mine.

A joyless heart, an aching nose—who could ever imagine?

All alone, I chant aloud these five poems of lament.

SOURCE: FSS 15, in [*Shinkō*] *Gunsho ruijū* 126, vol. 6, p. 189; Tasaka, "*Fusōshū* zenchūshaku" (II), pp. 166–68; octave (heptasyllabic).

LINE 3: This line derives from an anecdote in chapter 2 of *Xijing zazhi* (Miscellaneous Records from the Western Capital) relating the story of Kuang Heng (first century B.C.), a minister who in his early years was so poor that he had no lamp. He thus made a hole in the wall between his own room and that of his neighbor to let the lamplight in, successfully carrying on his studies in the borrowed light.

LINE 4: "Shadows shift," that is, time passes. In order to live up to his late father's wish that he become a successful scholar, the poet (aged thirty at this time) is willing to keep on studying without complaint.

✱ **A group of friends drinking at a rustic pavilion on an autumn day, we composed verses on the topic "seeking a mountain and being at one with the hermits"**
Ki no Haseo

A leisurely day spent rambling about, all worldly schemes forgotten.

Seeking a place of deep seclusion, we came to a mountain hut.

While we talked, the dusk rain fell on the canopy of pines.
    [We encountered rain during this time.]

We vainly embraced the autumn wind as it tugged at our coarse thin clothes.

A stream followed its ancient course, winding below the floor;

Clouds floated by on prevailing winds, vanished from between the beams.

We milled around, preparing to part, regretting we had to leave.

No need for us in peaceful times to flee to the joys of seclusion.

SOURCE: FSS 16, in [*Shinkō*] *Gunsho ruijū* 126, vol. 6, p. 189; Tasaka, ed., "*Fusōshū* zenchūshaku" (II), pp. 168–69; octave (heptasyllabic).

LINE 4: "[Vainly] embraced the autumn wind": they may have been hugging themselves to stay warm.

LINE 6: We have tentatively supplied the word "wind" in the phrase "prevailing winds," which contains a missing character. "Between the beams" suggests that the clouds were being observed from within a semi-open wooden structure, the pavilion mentioned in the title.

LINE 8: In China, during times of political unrest, scholar-officials often sought safety in rural reclusion. The men in this poem, by contrast, are content with merely playing at being recluses for the day.

❀ Long-Cherished Thoughts on Retirement; Respectfully Presented to His Excellency
Miyako no Yoshika

Lacking talent, I am often ashamed that my work all seems so hard.
So I might as well hang up my cap, go off to a mountain retreat.
Nights, the cranes will awake me from sleep; chilly moon in the pines.
Dawn, the flying squirrels darting about; cold mist in the gorge.
Clouds hiding my valley home, heightening the sense of seclusion;
Water keeping me apart from the world, nature in wild abundance.
I have blundered for years on the path of learning—time just thrown away.
For now I'll plant a bamboo hedge to grow stalks for fishing poles.

SOURCE: FSS 17, in [Shinkō] Gunsho ruijū 126, vol. 6, p. 189; Tasaka, "Fusōshū zenchūshaku" (II), pp. 169–70; octave (heptasyllabic).
TITLE: The identity of the person to whom this is addressed is unknown.
LINE 2: "Hang up my cap": retire from bureaucratic service.

❀ Living Among Wood-Gathering Hermits in the Mountains
Kiyohara no Nakayama

Long I have dwelt in this faraway hut, distant from the world.
Woodcutters, rustic types—some I have come to know.
Following the winding valley afar, till my ax handle turns to dust;
Lying above the pure flowing water, resting on my side.
Carrying firewood through the gorge, escorted by the solitary moon;
Cutting medicinal herbs in the grottos, followed by a wisp of cloud.
Though living in the mountains carries the taint of lacking sufficient talent,
Who among those inhabiting this world has ever wanted to leave?

SOURCE: FSS 19, in [Shinkō] Gunsho ruijū 126, vol. 6, p. 189; Tasaka Junko, ed., "Fusōshū zenchūshaku" (III), in Sōgō Kenkyūjo hō, no. 152 (September 1993): 15–17; octave (heptasyllabic).
LINE 3: "Till my ax handle turns to dust" is an allusion to a famous legend concerning one Wang Zhi, a fourth-century woodcutter who discovered two immortals playing Chinese chess in a cave. He put down his ax and watched them play. Later, he found that the ax handle had rotted away, because many centuries had passed without his realizing it.

❀ No Recluses in the Mountains
Ki no Haseo

The recluses have all returned to virtue—at last they can hide no more.
They've cast aside their mugwort hairpins, left their thatched abodes.

The empty valleys echo with the sound of chilly gurgling waters;
The ancient mountains have no owners, lonely the evening clouds.
In the countryside, no one to see the lush blossoms in the haze.
The Crimson Gates have now been furnished with wings to lend support.
If Chao and Xu had been able to live to see this day arrive,
Would they have chosen to end their days as the sages of Yingyang?

SOURCE: FSS 21, in [*Shinkō*] *Gunsho ruijū* 126, vol. 6, p. 190; Tasaka, "*Fusōshū* zenchūshaku" (III), pp. 22–24; octave (heptasyllabic).
TITLE: Poem 20 has the same title, and Haseo's verse was likely written on the same occasion, a palace archery match held on 902/10/6 (ibid., p. 24). Haseo was consultant (*sangi*) and left major controller at the time.
LINE 1: "Returned to virtue" presumably means they have come out of retirement and returned to serve at the court.
LINE 2: Mugwort (J. *yomogi*): a common emblem of the rustic, impoverished life.
LINE 6: "Crimson Gates" is an allusion to the imperial palace; the "wings" are the recluses who have returned to official service to assist the emperor.
LINES 7 AND 8: Yingyang means the north side of the Ying River (Yingshui or Yingchuan), which originates in Henan. According to tradition, during the age of the semi-legendary Emperor Yao, in the third millennium B.C., there lived on the northern bank of the Ying two farmers, Chaofu and Xu You, a pair of dyed-in-the-wool sage-hermits. Chaofu means "Nest Man." His actual name is not known, and he is said to have taken up residence on a treetop in his old age. Legend has it that each of these men was offered the throne but vigorously declined it. Xu You even went so far as to wash his ears in the Ying to remove the defilement of Yao's suggestion that he serve. Chao in turn took offense at Xu You's washing his ears, saying he had polluted the river.

�֍ Written on a Wall for an Unnamed Retired Gentleman of the Southern Mountains
Sugawara no Michizane

Secret the name of this gentleman and the village whence he came.
Old and decrepit though he be, his mind is sharp and clear.
No wife inside his valley hut; the pines his old-age companions.
No taxes he pays on his mountain fields, millet growing wild.
Like a bubble he floats about, chants as he follows the Way.
In the vaporous mists his ears are cold as he reads the scriptures aloud.
Look at how he lives his life and his peaceful state of mind—
His single room seems worth much more than our one hundred castles.

SOURCE: FSS 23, in [*Shinkō*] *Gunsho ruijū* 126, vol. 6, p. 190; Tasaka, "*Fusōshū* zenchūshaku" (III), pp. 26–28; octave (heptasyllabic).
LINE 8: One hundred castles: the palaces and fine buildings in Heian.

✠ Expressing My Feelings While in the Mountains
Ōe no Koretoki

... I have no friends, and in my house no wife.
Lacking the means to build a career, I have said goodbye to the world.
In the viny depths of the dawn gorge the monkeys are crying out;
In the dusky grove where blossoms scatter, the birds are starting to call.
By the five lakes, I sell my herbs, following the clouds along;
By the three paths, my *koto* aslant, I wait for the moon to appear.
My mind calm as I lie on my pillow, all dreams of returning ceased.
How would it be to grow old and grey, here in this green ravine?

SOURCE: FSS 26, in [*Shinkō*] *Gunsho ruijū* 126, vol. 6, p. 190; octave (heptasyllabic).
LINE 1: The first character in this line is missing.
LINE 2: The poet's career status at this time is unclear, but it is known that he later held the junior third rank and was appointed to such important positions as director of the Academy (935) and middle counselor (960) during his lifetime.
LINE 5: "Five lakes," while originally referring to the five most famous lakes in China, came to mean "everywhere."
LINE 6: On the so-called three paths, see RUS 73, above.

✠ A Poem from a Set of Verses Presented Jointly with Fujiwara, Captain in the Imperial Bodyguards, During a Stay at a Mountain Dwelling
Fujiwara no Morokage

In this hidden place among the clouds, I divined a spot for a house.
Bracing winds blow pure and cool, the atmosphere serene.
Waters lapping upon the stones play the music of flutes and strings;
Mountains pressing against the windows create a painted screen.
Walking along I see trees I planted, garden bushy and dark;
Wherever I tread, I sink deep into patches of moss that dot the path.
Such splendid scenery, yet I'm loath to sightsee far and wide,
For I fear I'll love the tranquility so much I won't be able to return!

SOURCE: FSS 27, in [*Shinkō*] *Gunsho ruijū* 126, vol. 6, p. 190; octave (heptasyllabic).
TITLE AND AUTHOR: Neither Captain Fujiwara nor the poet Morokage can be identified.
LINE 8: That is, he will not want to return to the capital.

HONCHŌ REISŌ (POETIC MASTERPIECES FROM OUR COURT)

Honchō reisō was compiled by the courtier Takashina no Moriyoshi (?–?), who lived at least until 1014. Moriyoshi was the son of Naritada (923–98), who served as senior assistant head of the Ministry of Ceremonial and held the junior second rank. Moriyoshi's cousin Fujiwara no Sadako (Teishi, 976–1000), later became the consort of Emperor Ichijō (r. 986–1011), which aided the progress of Moriyoshi's official career. Moriyoshi held the posts of secretary of Iyo province and left minor controller, later rising to senior assistant head of the Popular Affairs Ministry. His highest rank was junior fourth rank lower. Moriyoshi's career appears to have languished after a family dispute with the statesman and *Honchō reisō* poet Fujiwara no Michinaga (966–1027), Emperor Ichijō's father-in-law and uncle. From a family of distinguished scholars, Moriyoshi himself was a student of Buddhism and also a poet, albeit not a particularly distinguished one, with five of his *kanshi* preserved in *Honchō reisō*. Two prose pieces by him are found in *Honchō monzui*. In 964, Moriyoshi established Kangakkai (The Promotion of Learning Society) and helped revive the group around 1005.

Honchō reisō, a private undertaking, was probably completed in 1010 and presented to the court the same year, although some scholars place the date of its compilation a few years earlier.[99] Notably, the anthology is roughly contemporaneous with *The Tale of Genji* and provides an important socio-literary link to that work. The collection was highly esteemed at court and was still being copied and circulated among the high aristocracy in the late eleventh and early twelfth centuries.[100] *Honchō reisō* contains *kanshi* written between 990 and 1010 and was evidently envisioned as a sequel to

99. *Nihon koten bungaku daijiten*, p. 1167.
100. In 1093, for example, an imperial consort was given a copy as a gift, and in 1137, Minister of the Right Fujiwara no Munetada (1062–1141) copied *Honchō reisō* together with *Fusōshū* as part of a larger, non-extant twenty-volume anthology titled *Inkashū* (A Collection of Rhyming Flowers). See ibid.

Fusōshū. It survives as two incomplete *maki,* these comprising 13 poem prefaces and some 154 poems, virtually all octaves in seven-character lines. Works by 29 poets, many of whom were in Michinaga's inner court circle, are present in the extant edition, although the original anthology appears to have had poems by 34 individuals. Most prominently represented in the present text are: Ōe no Mochitoki (955–1010), with 19 poems; Prince Tomohira (964–1009), with 18; Fujiwara no Korechika (974–1010), 15; Fujiwara no Tametoki (fl. ca. 1000), 13; Fujiwara no Kintō (966–1041), 11; and Fujiwara no Arikuni (943–1011), 10.

The poems in *maki* 1 seem to have been organized thematically around the four seasons: spring (with the beginning poems missing), summer (complete), autumn (end portion missing), and winter (missing entirely). *Maki* 2 is also thematically arranged, with the following categories: landscapes, Buddhism, the gods, mountain retreats, imperial virtue, laws, books and praise of study, worthies, poems in praise of virtue, poetry (*shi*),[101] drinking, poetic exchanges, farewell poems, nostalgia for the past, and expressing one's feelings.

The appeal of this anthology lies less in the realm of literary originality and style than in the varied insights the poetry provides into the private worlds—the simple pleasures and preoccupations—of some of the most famous statesmen and public figures of the time, most notably Fujiwara no Michinaga and his son-in-law Emperor Ichijō. For example, in poem 47, we find Michinaga reflecting on the pleasures of sitting in the summer breezes, his robes flapping in the wind, while in poem 65 he is drawing solace from the contemplation of a beautiful temple:

. . . .

Deep in the valley the sound of a waterfall flowing through the rocks.
Praying to Buddha, I feel sympathy for the aging frosty leaves.
Accompanied by priests, I head off into the dusky autumn hills.
Endless cycles of birth and death enmesh us in worldly passions.
Beholding the Great Compassionate One, how could I now feel
   sorrow?

In poem 104, Emperor Ichijō reflects on the burden of ruling the realm and voices his feelings of inadequacy for this task. Although *Honchō reisō* poets seldom reveal much of their deeper psychological selves, Emperor Ichijō is memorable precisely because he appears so unguarded, willing to

---

101. Although one would expect poetics or famous past poems to be the subject or theme of a section so named, in fact five of its six poems were written on the assigned topic, "reflections on not yet tiring of the wind and moon," at a poetry composition event held at Fujiwara no Michinaga's residence in the Fifth Month of 1005.

humble himself in a manner that seems to go beyond mere *pro forma* modesty. While the personal revelations of certain poets provide us with a degree of human and biographical interest, the majority of the poems are pleasant but impersonal public verse embodying the highly refined and elegant language and imagery associated with Six Dynasties court poetry. A typical example is poem 12, composed by Michinaga on the topic of fallen petals dancing above the water:

. . . .
Above the flow, charming as jeweled hairpins in disarray;
Along the banks, looking as airy as sleeves of light silk gauze.
Easily mistaken for powdered dancers as they whirl by the bay at dusk;
Hard to tell from court musicians as they drift across the waves.
Today we rejoice that the ways of old prevail here once again:
His Majesty favors us with a visit, returning to the district of Pei.

Two of the more thematically interesting court poems are by Minamoto no Tamenori (poems 97–98), praising the court for introducing measures to reduce palace expenditures and the tax burden upon the common people. Writes Tamenori, "Your Majesty's splendid edict states that expenditures should be cut, / And that delicacies served by the palace kitchen must not be in excess" (poem 97). Again in poem 98: "Officers and ministers shall no more exact taxation from the poor; / The imperial household shall take no revenue from fields lying fallow." Apart from several poems in *Denshi kashū* that deal with problems arising from the prohibition of alcohol (see, for example, DSKS 44), there are relatively few *kanshi* (or *waka*, for that matter) from this period that touch upon social or economic problems in the manner of Tamenori's verses. It is perhaps these poems on mundane subjects that leave the strongest impression upon the reader, bringing to life issues and concerns of the times to a degree rarely seen in Heian verse.

On a Boat Strewn with Fallen Blossoms from the Forest Trees (Using the character "wind" as the rhyme word)
Minister of the Left Fujiwara no Michinaga

In the forest, flowers are falling, branches growing bare.
I see them spread in vast profusion, blanketing the boat with pink.
Night, we moor by peach-blossom banks, rosy raindrops whirl;
Spring, heading out from willow dikes, sent off by a willow-down breeze.
Fan Li moored his boat by the shore, lost in a mist-veiled spot;
Zi You set off on a journey as the snow was blowing around.

Absorbed in all the opulent beauty, we halt our oars for a spell:
Interest piqued, I shall live out my days as an old reciter of verse.

SOURCE: HCRS 5, in Kawaguchi Hisao and others, annot., *Honchō reisō kanchū* (Tokyo: Benseisha, 1993), pp. 14–15; octave (heptasyllabic).
TITLE: This verse is one of several on the same theme written at a gathering held at Michinaga's residence on 1007/3/20. Michinaga held the senior second rank at this time.
LINE 5: Fan Li (ca. fifth century B.C.) served as minister in the state of Yue. He later also served the states of Qi and Tao, amassing a fortune and gaining lasting fame. The allusion to the anecdote about Fan Li and his boat has its source in *Shi ji*, where Fan speaks of wanting to spend time floating in a boat on the lakes and rivers, having accomplished his goals in life.
LINE 6: Zi You is Wang Huizhi (d. 388), a gentleman who lived surrounded by bamboo and was known for being unable to pass a single day without looking at it. According to one anecdote, on a snowy moonlit night after drinking alone, he set out in his boat to visit a friend named Dai Kui, only to turn around and return home after reaching the man's door, because his enthusiasm for seeing him had in the meantime subsided.

🏵 **A poem in seven-character lines written on imperial command in late spring at a banquet in the Higashi Sanjō Residence of the minister of the left; we all wrote poems on the theme "fallen petals dancing above the water"**
Fujiwara no Michinaga

Petals fall as cool spring breezes blow across the pond;
Dancing along, over the water, to the sound of warblers singing.
Above the flow, charming as jeweled hairpins in disarray;
Along the banks, looking as airy as sleeves of light silk gauze.
Easily mistaken for powdered dancers as they whirl by the bay at dusk;
Hard to tell from court musicians as they drift across the waves.
Today we rejoice that the ways of old prevail here once again:
His Majesty favors us with a visit, returning to the district of Pei.

SOURCE: HCRS 12, in *Honchō reisō kanchū*, pp. 34–36; octave (heptasyllabic).
TITLE: This poem was composed at a party hosted by Michinaga at his Higashi Sanjō residence on 1006/3/4 and is the second in a series of poems (HCMDS 11–21) all with the same title. The Higashi Sanjō residence, complete with its large gardens, was passed down through generations of the Northern Fujiwara branch, which descended from the first regent Yoshifusa (804–72). Located near modern Kamimatsuya-chō, it was destroyed by fire in 1177. The emperor alluded to here is Ichijō (980–1011; r. 986–1011).
LINE 8: Pei, in modern Jiangsu province, was the home district of Liu Bang (247–185 B.C.), founder of the Han dynasty. Liu began his career here, starting out as an obscure village headsman. After many years of battles, reversals, and conquests, he returned to Pei in triumph. Emperor Ichijō, who was around age twenty-six when this poem was written, had similarly returned to visit the site of his birth, Michinaga's residence, in Heian. In 999, Emperor Ichijō, whose mother was Michinaga's elder sister, Senshi (962–1001, the consort of Emperor En'yū), married his cousin Fujiwara no Akiko (Shōshi, 988–1074), one of Michinaga's daughters and

the mistress of Lady Murasaki, author of *The Tale of Genji*. Ichijō was thus Michinaga's nephew and his son-in-law.

⬚ The First Cicadas Have Just Begun to Chirp (Using the character "heart" as the rhyme word)
Emperor Ichijō

The Fifth Month has now arrived; emotions overcome us.
The first cicadas have just announced their presence with a song.
That languid drone—who would bother to listen yet again?
But when it ends we long in vain to hear their sound once more.
Surprised, we try to spy them among the willows on the banks.
Where might they be? Gone from the palace's windswept locust trees.
At times like this, we should not say that Heaven is lacking in skill:
The palace groves at summer's height will be filled with cicadas again!

SOURCE: HCRS 42, in *Honchō reisō kanchū*, pp. 87–89; octave (heptasyllabic).
COMMENT: This poem was composed 1003/5/6.

⬚ From All Around Pleasant Breezes Arise (Using the character "cool" as the rhyme word)
Minister of the Left Fujiwara no Michinaga

The pleasant breezes blowing through bring comfort to my heart.
Left and right, they ruffle my robe, help me forget that it's summer.
At my waist where I carry my sword, a clacking like bamboo in the wind;
To my carved seat inside the gazebo, the breeze brings the scent of lotuses.
The blinds and curtains all are raised, the hems of my robe now flutter.
In a thin silk gown I quietly sit, my head refreshingly cool.
How delightful that here by the pond it's not oppressively hot!
White waters rippling in the moonlight, covered with icy frost.

SOURCE: HCRS 47, in *Honchō reisō kanchū*, pp. 97–98; octave (heptasyllabic).
LINE 3: Michinaga is presumably referring to gusts of wind catching the scabbard of his sword and making it rattle.
LINE 4: The commentator in *Honchō reisō kanchū* suggests that Michinaga's seat is in an *azu-maya*, a thatched outdoor pavilion without walls.
LINE 8: Icy frost: the pale moonlight on the water.
COMMENT: This verse was apparently composed in the Fifth Month of 1010, while Michinaga was at his family's Higashi Sanjō residence attending lectures on the *Lotus Sutra*. See ibid., p. 98.

❋ From All Around Pleasant Breezes Arise
Tachibana no Tameyoshi

Since coming to the tower beside the water to flee the summer heat,
Little I've done except just sit, in the cool and pleasant breezes.
Nights, they enter the western window, scattering the papers on my desk;
Mornings, they blow through the eastern door, sweeping through my office.
The wind dries the trickles of sweat that flow inside my sleeves,
Then suddenly catches the three-foot sword I'm wearing at my waist.
What need was there in former times to go drinking north of the River?
Here beside the pond today let me offer you the last of the wine.

SOURCE: HCRS 48, in *Honchō reisō kanchū*, pp. 99–100; octave (heptasyllabic).
LINE 6: The sword is literally "three feet of frost," a phrase derived from the *Shi ji* biography of
Gao Zu (Liu Bang), founder of the Han dynasty.
LINE 7: An allusion to an anecdote from *Dian lun* (Treatise on the Classics), written by Cao Pi
(188–227, later Emperor Wen of Wei, r. 220–27) in which Liu Song, together with Yuan Shao
and his sons, drank wine on the northern side of the Yellow River to cool themselves. See
Honchō reisō kanchū, p. 100.

❋ Paying a Visit in Late Autumn to the Area Above Kiyomizu
Minister of the Left Fujiwara no Michinaga

Deep in the folds of Higashiyama, Kiyomizu temple.
Here in this quiet hall of thatch, I've left the world for a while.
Through the clouds the tolling of a bell arrives on the mountain mists;
Deep in the valley the sound of a waterfall flowing through the rocks.
Praying to the Buddha, I feel sympathy for the aging frosty leaves.
Accompanied by priests, I head off into the dusky autumn hills.
Endless cycles of birth and death enmesh us in worldly passions.
Beholding the Great Compassionate One, how could I now feel sorrow?

SOURCE: HCRS 65, in *Honchō reisō kanchū*, pp. 143–45; octave (heptasyllabic).
LINE 1: Higashiyama is a hilly region traditionally said to have thirty-six peaks, extending
north to south along the eastern side of Kyoto. It is famous for its scenic views and temples.
COMMENT: This poem is said to have been written 1010/9/30, at a literary gathering held at one
of Michinaga's residences (ibid., p. 145).

❋ Living in Retirement with No Outside Affairs to Manage
Minamoto no Michinari

Retired now, I've cast aside my hat-pin and tasseled cap.
What is more, I have no further outside tasks to perform.

Fellow poets of a similar mind I treat as honored guests,
While people in carriages pass my gate, chasing after power.
Lazy by nature, all I do is gaze at the flowers in the hedge.
Having left my post, I am startled no more by the government office drums.
Freedom is what suits me best; I have chosen a tranquil spot.
Thinking back, I laugh at how I once sought empty fame.

SOURCE: HCRS 93, in *Honchō reisō kanchū*, pp. 230–32; octave (heptasyllabic).
LINE 1: Hat-pin and tasseled cap: the headgear of the court official.
LINE 3: "Treat as honored guests" is literally "offer the hanging seat." The poet is alluding to a passage in the *Hou Han shu* biography of Chen Fan, who apparently never received guests except for one Xu Zhi, for whom he provided a special seat which he hung up after the man left.
LINE 6: These drums announced the opening of the government offices in the morning.

❖ My Home Is Silent, No Visitors Come
Fujiwara no Tametoki

All is silent in this ancient house where mugwort grows in profusion.
No one comes to visit me; I have no affairs to manage.
Once Di Gong left his post as judge, the dust by his gate stayed settled.
Master Yuan, content with poverty, was never touched by snow.
Weeds encroach upon my doorsill, pale the autumn dew.
Moss is growing on my door, red the setting sun.
I've long forgotten the courtesies shown to guests when they come and go.
Here in the capital I dwell apart—an old man, quiet and content.

SOURCE: HCRS 94, in *Honchō reisō kanchū*, pp. 232–34; octave (heptasyllabic).
LINE 1: Mugwort, a wild plant, is an emblem of rustic seclusion and sometimes neglect.
LINE 3: Di Gong was a judge who lived during the Han dynasty and served the emperor Wen Di. People frequently visited him, seeking to curry favor, but after losing his position he lost popularity. When Di subsequently regained his post, people began seeking him out again, prompting him to put a notice on his door expressing cynicism about the fickleness of human nature.
LINE 4: Master Yuan is probably a reference to the second-century recluse Yuan Hong, who, legend has it, sequestered himself in a mud hovel for eighteen years.

❖ Here in Retirement the Days and Months Seem Long
Ōe no Koretoki

An atmosphere of leisured calm pervades the Buddhist temple;
At times like these the days and months just naturally seem long.
My mind drifts on in this secluded room—no day ever seems short.
Living quietly in this neighborhood—plenty of time on my hands.

160

Spring rains at dawn erase all tracks, just as at Tao Qian's gate;
Autumn nights are as frosty and cold as the faded Lady Yan's chamber.
A man good for nothing at all, I dwell in my brushwood hut.
Leisured or busy, happy or sad—all are as one to me.

SOURCE: HCRS 95, in *Honchō reisō kanchū*, pp. 234–36; octave (heptasyllabic).
LINE 5: Tao Qian (Tao Yuanming): a famous Chinese poet who retired early to the countryside, where he spent his final years in rustic simplicity. See RUS 75, above. Presumably, the path to Koretoki's gate and the traces of footsteps had disappeared because few people came to visit.
LINE 6: Lady Yan is probably a reference to a favorite consort of Duke Wen of Zheng, who lived during the Spring and Autumn period (722–468 B.C.).

A Poem in Support of an Edict Ordering that Expenditures Be Cut by a Quarter; On Reducing Expenses for Imperial Clothing and Daily Victuals
Minamoto no Tamenori

Great the merit of our enlightened ruler, succoring the land.
Throughout your reign, with thrift and respect, serving the weary masses.
Your Majesty's splendid edict states that expenditures should be cut,
And that delicacies served by the palace kitchen must not be in excess.
In the time of Yao, the rivers flooded—great the misfortune and grief.
In the age of Tang, heat and drought drove people from their farms.
Imperial dynasties can hardly escape their Heaven-allotted span.
What need is there to blame yourself and long for those halcyon days?

SOURCE: HCRS 97, in *Honchō reisō kanchū*, pp. 239–41; octave (heptasyllabic).
TITLE: On 995/7/23, an edict was issued calling for a reduction of official expenditures by a quarter. Similar measures for economic retrenchment had been implemented even earlier, in 987 and 988. The emperor was Ichijō throughout this period.
LINE 5: Yao (putative r. 2356 B.C.–?) was one of China's semi-legendary emperors. During his reign vast floods occurred, which took many years to bring under control.
LINE 6: Emperor Tang was the founder of the Shang dynasty, reigning ca. 1766–1753 B.C. The first seven years of his reign saw drought and famine.
LINES 7 AND 8: The poet appears to be saying that great disasters occurred even during the reigns of the noblest of kings, so the Emperor should not feel personally responsible for any misfortunes that occur.

On Reducing the Taxation and Corvée Labor Exacted from the Provinces
Minamoto no Tamenori

His Majesty's kindness flows to every corner of the realm.
Is it so unlike long ago, when they sang and beat the ground?

The purple-seal decree was issued, then benevolent breezes blew;
The yellow-paper edict was proclaimed, and kind dew blessed the land.
Officers and ministers shall no more exact taxation from the poor;
The imperial household shall take no revenue from fields lying fallow.
In the furthest parts of the emperor's palace, I wonder if they know
That in every house the people cover their faces and weep for joy.

SOURCE: HCRS 98, in *Honchō reisō kanchū*, pp. 241–43; octave (heptasyllabic).
TITLE: This poem was probably written during one of the retrenchment efforts explained in the notes to the preceding poem (ibid., p. 243).
LINE 2: "When they sang and beat the ground" is an allusion to the reign of sage-emperor Yao (see previous poem), a time when peace and contentment supposedly prevailed throughout the land. A popular folk song in Yao's time titled "Ji rang ge" (The Ground-Beating Song) was so named because the singers beat time on the ground as they sang. The words to the song ran as follows: "When the sun comes up we work. / When the sun goes down we rest. / We dig wells so that we can drink. / We plow the fields so that we can eat. / The power of the emperor—what does it have to do with us?"
LINE 6: These were hard times for the peasantry, and this edict was intended to provide economic relief. William Wayne Farris observes that the abandonment of paddy land was a common occurrence, a reflection of economic backwardness caused by such problems as epidemic disease, poor technology, and overly "extensive" agricultural practices. See Farris, *Population, Disease, and Land in Early Japan, 645–900*, Harvard East Asian Monographs, 157 (Cambridge, MA and London: Harvard University Press: 1985), pp. 142–44.
LINE 7: The "furthest parts of the emperor's palace" is a reference to the emperor himself.

In My Books, Stories from the Ancient Past

Emperor Ichijō

In my leisure I turn to books to while away the time.
Recorded therein are past events that have left a deep impression.
The splendid deeds of a hundred kings are seen when we open the volumes;
Sages and wise men of countless ages are known when we open the texts.
I learn about the enlightened reign of Emperor Yu long ago.
As I read of Emperor Wen of Han, his greatness causes me shame.
For many years I've explored the past, studying Kong and Mo.
Why, then, is this age of ours not a tranquil time?

SOURCE: HCRS 102, in *Honchō reisō kanchū*, pp. 257–59; octave (heptasyllabic).
LINE 5: Emperor Yu, more commonly known as Shun, was a sage-emperor who ruled during the twenty-third century B.C.
LINE 6: The Japanese emperor by these times was a figurehead who reigned but did not rule, being subject to the decisions of the regent and other power holders at court. This fact may account for Ichijō's manifest sense of inadequacy compared to the powerful Chinese rulers of old, whom the Japanese emperors wished to emulate. Emperor Wen reigned 179–156 B.C.
LINE 7: Kong is Confucius. Mo is Mozi (fifth-fourth century B.C.), a philosopher who preached a doctrine of universal love for all human beings without partiality toward family and friends.

❈ My Thoughts After Stealing a Glance at the Emperor's Composition: Written Using the Basic Rhymes in His Majesty's Poem
Prince Tomohira

Advanced in years, lazy by nature, and neglectful of my studies,
I stole a glance at His Majesty's verse and now offer these trifling thoughts.
Sima compiled a chronology that spanned three thousand years;
Qiuming wrote a history covering two hundred years of events.
It's almost as if you've been conversing with the sages of former times,
So do not say that the past worthies are known to you only by name.
The writings from the days of the Han emperors, from Tang times as well,
Compared to those of Your Majesty are as lowly as an anthill!

SOURCE: HCRS 103, in *Honchō reisō kanchū*, pp. 259–61; octave (heptasyllabic).
TITLE AND AUTHOR: This poem was inspired by poem 102, above. Tomohira does indeed use Ichijō's rhyme scheme, which is seen again in poem 104, immediately below. Prince Tomohira (964–1009) was the seventh son of Emperor Murakami. A literary man, he frequently organized group poetry composition events in his private residence. See ibid., pp. 397–98.
LINE 3: Sima Qian (ca. 145–ca. 85 B.C.) was the famed historian who compiled *Shi ji*, an historical work that became the model for all subsequent dynastic histories in China.
LINE 4: Zuoqiu Ming (or Zuo Qiuming, ?–?) was the putative author of *Zuo zhuan*, a commentary on part of *The Spring and Autumn Annals*, which covers the years 722–468 B.C.

❈ Another Poem
Emperor Ichijō

Reading books in my leisure hours, away from state affairs,
I reflect on myself and feel disturbed over how to rule the realm.
Examining the past, I am abashed by my lack of wisdom and virtue;
At times like these, I bemoan the fact that I am not an enlightened ruler.
My will is strong, but even though I admire the former sages,
I am dull by nature—how could I rank beside the wise men of yore?
Divine words and heroic writings—how could mine compare?
While those men served in the sea of scholars, the ocean waves were calm.

SOURCE: HCRS 104, in *Honchō reisō kanchū*, pp. 261–62; octave (heptasyllabic).
LINE 8: "Those men" refers to the scholars who assisted the emperors.

HONCHŌ MONZUI (LITERARY GEMS FROM OUR COURT)

This renowned collection of Chinese prose and poetry was compiled by the scholar and poet Fujiwara no Akihira (989?–1066), around 1060. A private anthology in fourteen *maki*, *Honchō monzui* contains some 432 Chinese prose pieces and poems by sixty-nine individuals, sixty-five of them courtiers. All of the compositions in the anthology were written between 810 and 1037; especially well represented is the Engi–Tenryaku period, 901–57, which the editor evidently viewed as a golden age for court literature in Chinese. The writers with the most works included are Ōe no Masahira and Ōe no Asatsuna, followed by Sugawara no Fumitoki, Ki no Haseo, Sugawara no Michizane, Minamoto no Shitagō, Ōe no Mochitoki (Yukitoki),[102] Yoshishige no Yasutane, and Prince Kaneakira, all major literary figures who collectively charted the course of *kanshi* and *kanbun* in their time. While the Sugawara and Ōe families are well represented, not a single Fujiwara figures among the authors in the collection, nor do we find works by women or priests. The absence of compositions by Buddhist monks suggests a "Confucian bias to the editorial process," to use Donald Keene's words.[103] Nothing by Akihira himself is included in this anthology, although it has been speculated that the erotic narrative "Tettsui den" (The Biography of Iron Hammer, poem 377), attributed to one Ratai, is most likely the work of Akihira, writing under a pseudonym.[104]

Without duplicating material found in earlier official anthologies, Akihira created a compendium of distinguished verse and prose works to serve as models of documentary, literary, and poetic forms and styles for aspiring writers. Ōsone Shōsuke's research shows that many poems in *Honchō*

---

102. Scholars appear uncertain as to the correct original reading of this poet's name. Other possibilities include Yukitoki, Koreyuki, and Yoshitoki (NKBT, 69, p. 517).
103. Keene, p. 345.
104. NKBT, 69, p. 520.

monzui are the full texts of poems excerpted as couplets in Fujiwara no Kintō's *Wakan rōeishū* (1004–20),[105] which points to an interesting and important connection between the two works that is seldom noted.

The title of this collection was inspired by a Song dynasty anthology of poetry and prose entitled *Tang wen-sui* (Literary Gems from the Tang, compiled 1011). Its organization also reflects Chinese models, with a structure based at least in broad outline on *Wen xuan* (ca. 530), which had 39 subject categories, 12 of which are duplicated in *Honchō monzui*. The latter has 38 divisions (39 if exam questions and answers are treated as two categories), including works both literary and non-literary in character. Like *Wen xuan*, which predated the development of the regulated verse forms, *Honchō monzui* has no examples of verse in regulated form, a striking distinction. In fact, relatively few poems of any kind are found in *Honchō monzui*—there are only 15 *fu* and 28 *zasshi* or *zatsugon* (miscellaneous non-regulated forms of *shi* and a subgenre of *koshi*) in this anthology, pointing to a particular interest on the compiler's part in preserving poems in these particular genres at a time when regulated verse forms were the vogue. Kakimura Shigematsu, a noted *Honchō monzui* scholar, speculates that *kanshi* (especially those in the more contemporary styles) had been so comprehensively collected and preserved in earlier anthologies that the compiler saw no need for yet another large *kanshi* collection. Kakimura also suggests that there were not many *zatsugon* written in the first place,[106] which may explain why the anthology, even while focusing on this subgenre, has relatively few of them.

Among the *shi* poems, we find examples of the following subgenres of *zasshi*: *etchō* (quatrains following a 7/7/6/7 character pattern); *jikun* and *rigō* (both acrostic forms); *kaibun* (palindromes); *sangon* (poems in three-character lines); *ka* (*uta*, "songs," which are relatively free in form); *konankyoku* (folk-style poems); and comedic *kyōka* ("crazy poems"). Many of the poems were doubtless selected primarily for their novelty, an example being the *kyōka* titled "A Poem Satirizing the Efforts of 'Lofty Phoenix' to Blur the Distinctions between Noble and Lowly" (poem 43), composed by Minamoto no Shitagō. The rarity of surviving *kyōka* from the Heian period suggests either that ecccentricity (either formal or thematic) was generally avoided or that such poems, even if commonly written, were not considered worthy of preservation.

A partial inventory of the prose selections in *Honchō monzui* includes the following: 42 *hyō* (memorials), 156 *jo* (anthology prefaces), 27 *ganmon*

---

105. *Wakan rōeishū* is a two-*maki* collection of famous couplets from 588 Chinese *shi* and Japanese *kanshi* and an additional 216 *waka*, including verses by Kakinomoto no Hitomaro and Ki no Tsurayuki. Ōsone's research is summarized in Kojima, *Kaifūsō, Bunka shūreishū, Honchō monzui*, pp. 31–32.

106. Cited in Ōsone and others, *Kanshi, kanbun, hyōron*, p. 30.

(religious petitions), 37 *sōjō* (reports), 3 *iken fūji* (opinion papers), 2 *iki* (appointment documents), 1 *kaibun* (circulars), 3 *kanbu* (directives), 5 *ki* (narratives), 1 *kishōbun* (pledges), 1 *kinseibun* (prohibitions), 6 *shō* (edicts), 26 *taisaku* (civil service exam questions with answers), 2 *rakusho* (lampoons), 1 *san* (encomia), and 3 *saibun* (prayers).

    Honchō monzui had a profound influence upon Japanese medieval letters, inspiring later anthologies such as its sequel, *Honchō zoku monzui* (see below), and *Chōya gunsai* (Collected Works from Around the Land, compiled by Miyoshi no Tameyasu [1049–1139] and completed ca. 1132–35). So influential was this collection that individual pieces therein are often alluded to in medieval war tales, epistolary collections, travel accounts, other *kanshi* collections such as *Honchō mudaishi*, and even *kana* prose narratives of various kinds. Works on composition and rhetoric from later centuries often cite prose and poems from *Honchō monzui*, and even as late as the Edo period writers continued to study and imitate its models.

▨ Prose-Poem on Spring Snow (Using "filled," "foot," "above," and "presage" as the rhyme words)
Ki no Haseo

1   The snow that falls in spring
     Is never deeper than a foot.
     It starts to fall in the mountains and the valleys at the same time;
     The color of sand and pebbles on a river beach.
5   Frozen on the ground,
     Barely deep enough to cover the hoof prints of horses;
     Filling my garden,
     Gradually covering the tracks of birds.
     Sometimes the snow is blown away by the wind, never to return,
10 Resembling the feathers on the flapping wings of cranes in a flock.
     When the weather is fine and snow remains,
     The ground could be taken for a patchwork of fur from a den of foxes.
     Behold! Dazzling white its shimmering brilliance.
     When the snow blows around, its texture is light;
15 Suspended in the sky, its color is white.
     Falling on the ground, without a sound.
     Covering the garden vegetables, making the young shoots wither;
     Blanketing the willows by the gate—what a sight, those aged "catkins."
     All at once, the evening light in my curtained study increases,
20 And my books are illuminated naturally.
     In a flash, it blows into the ladies' chambers, dances in the dawn light,
     And the powder boxes become filled with snow.

The snowflakes whirl around in the warm air;
Fly wildly about, mingling above the clouds.
25 The snow landing on people's heads seems to hasten old age;
When it brushes the window, you'd think it was a moonlit dawn.
Unfastened with a fancy hook and raised, the blinds sparkle like jewels.
Look up at the painted beams—dust whirls gem-like in the air.
The snow swirls downward, tumbling into the water,
30 Quietly joining the scaly creatures beneath the ice;
Gathers and scatters throughout the forest,
As if to seal in the birds in their nests.
Thus, the plants flourish,
The earth is enriched.
35 Everywhere the fields are well watered,
And the underground springs spread afar.
Snow does not just lie in the shade of fences, making for cold evenings;
It can also mingle suddenly with the mild breezes outside of town.
This may happen when we are enjoying the longer late spring days.
40 We know, too, that snow presages an abundant harvest season.

SOURCE: HCMZ 4, in Ōsone Shōsuke, Kinpara Tadashi, and Gotō Akio, annot., *Honchō monzui*, Shin Nihon koten bungaku taikei (SNKBT), 27 (Tokyo: Iwanami Shoten, 1992), pp. 123–24; NKBT, 69, pp. 324–26; *fu* ("celestial phenomena" category), in forty lines.
TITLE: The rhyme words named in the title do not occur in the order in which they appear here. "Foot" appears at the end of line two, "filled" in line 22, "above" in line 24, and "presage[s]" in line 40.
LINE 25: That is, the snow turns their hair white.

▦ Song About a Poor Woman
Ki no Haseo

1 There is a woman, there is a woman, all alone and poor.
The years have slipped away from her, sicker she grows by the day.
Autumn leaves pile high at her gate, people no longer visit;
Nothing there within her walls, hardships aplenty she bears.
5 Born into a wealthy family, she was their beloved daughter,
Raised in seclusion, deep within the confines of their home.
Fine silks, powder, and makeup she wore every single day.
Not a whit less beautiful than Wushan's wisp of cloud.
When she was barely fifteen, her face was like a jewel.
10 Her parents would always say, "Let's give her to a man of quality."
Scions of noble families all competed to win her hand,
Courting her ardently under the blossoms, in the light of the moon.
But her mother and father were deceived by the matchmaker's words,

And had their daughter pledged to a youth from Chang'an city.
15   Though the youth was ignorant and lacking in character,
Her parents honored him, as if he were a god.
They gave him sleek horses, light furs, hawks, and hounds.
Every day he would gather and feast young gallants on banquet mats.
As they chatted, he would tug their arms, pressing them to drink.
20   In a single day, he would manage to spend several thousand cash.
His hunting excursions caused the family estate to gradually decline;
Carousing and drinking, he vainly squandered the fortune of the family.
In the decade past, her mother and father have departed from the world.
All of her brothers have scattered, too, moving to other parts.
25   The gentleman grew tired of his wife and paid her little attention;
He went away and never returned, causing her endless sorrow.
Days turned to months, and in the end she had used up all her money.
Starving and cold, she passes her days, condemned to bitter hardship,
Through autumn winds, rainy nights, and many a miserable dawn.
30   She recalls the past, thinks of the present, kerchief soaked with tears.
Even though she looks like the dead, her mind remains alive.
Embittered, she knows she cannot recapture the springtime of her past.
She dwells alone with just her shadow, no place where she belongs.
Her hair disheveled and in disarray, face all covered with grime.
35   Not a soul is ever seen at her lonely, deserted house.
She longs to unburden herself of her grief but cannot find a way.
To all young girls from noble families, this advice she offers:
In choosing a husband, look at his heart, not at his appearance.
To the parents of all the girls in the world, she would also like to say:
40   "Be sure to write these words of mine upon your daughters' sashes!"

SOURCE: HCMZ 18, in SNKBT, 27, p. 132; NKBT, 69, pp. 344–46; *zatsugon* in the "old style" (heptasyllabic), in forty lines.
LINE 8: "Wushan's wisp of cloud": Wushan is a mountain in Sichuan province and here a reference to a female divinity of great beauty who, according to legend, resided there.
LINE 14: Chang'an: China's capital at various stages in its history.

❈ Seeing Grey Hairs
Minamoto no Fusaakira

1   Having reached the age of thirty-five,
I've seen no sign of physical decline.
But this morning after hanging up my mirror,
I happened to see a couple of grey hairs.
5   Doubting the mirror, not believing what I saw,
I rubbed my eyes, looked at my whiskers again.

But alas, using a pair of silver tweezers,
I managed to pull out several strands of grey.
As autumn nears, there is much upon my mind;
10 And I was all the sadder for finding these hairs.
But my sadness vanished once I'd thought things through.
I believe that now I can grasp the meaning of it all.
At sixteen I was appointed to the fourth rank;
At seventeen became a gentleman-in-waiting.
15 During the glorious years of the Enchō period,
Long did I serve in the courtyard of white jade.
In this Shōhei era, a period untroubled,
I have often held the flag of the palace guards.
Privileged to serve within the imperial house,
20 Holding both court rank and official post.
That noble sage Yan Hui, who lived during Zhou,
Had gone grey before the age of thirty.
And Pan Yue, that famous scholar of Jin,
Wrote "Rhapsody on Autumn Inspirations" while young.
25 Both of them were younger men than I—
I am lucky my first grey hairs have come so late!

SOURCE: HCMZ 20, in SNKBT, 27, p. 132; NKBT, 69, pp. 347–48; *zatsugon* in the "old style" (pentasyllabic), in twenty-six lines.
LINE 15: The Enchō period: 923–31.
LINE 16: A synecdochical reference to the imperial palace, with its stone-paved courtyards.
LINE 17: The Shōhei era: 931–38.
LINE 18: Fusaakira served as a middle captain in the Imperial Bodyguards.
LINE 19: Fusaakira was Emperor Uda's (r. 887–97) grandson but had taken commoner status.
LINES 21 AND 22: According to the "Zhongni dizi liezhuan" (Biographies of the Disciples of Confucius), a section of *Shi ji*, Yan Hui's hair had turned grey by the time he was twenty-nine, and he died when he was thirty-two. We have added the words "had gone grey" for the sake of clarity. The original language in line 22 simply reads, "had not yet reached the age of thirty."
LINE 23: Pan Yue (Pan Anren, 247–300) was a distinguished *fu* poet and official of the Jin dynasty, famed for his handsome appearance. He saw his first grey hairs before the age of thirty-two, a fact often alluded to in *kanshi* on the subject of growing old.
LINE 26: But not lucky enough, for he died less than a year after writing the poem.
COMMENT: This poem is modeled on Bo Juyi's "Looking in the Mirror and Rejoicing in Old Age," as noted in Konishi, II, p. 169.

Deep Feelings on an Autumn Night: Respectfully Presented to Fujiwara, Supernumerary Middle Captain in the Imperial Bodyguards
Tachibana no Aritsura

1 Late at night, the cover of clouds now gone,
Autumn moon suspended in clear skies.

Golden waves dance upon my window,
The Milky Way lights up the trenches and hollows.
5   Moonlight filters through the scattered dryandras,
Shining down upon the withered lotuses.
Melancholy, cold, unable to sleep,
In the depths of night I rise and wander about.
Wander about beneath the shining moon,
10 Shining down upon me here alone.
Watching my shadow, I pace around the garden;
Stepping through moonlight, standing on the steps.
Pure light bathes my breast and sleeves,
Pale dew soaks the hem of my robe.
15 I gaze at the moon, feeling disheartened and sad.
Why is it that I feel disheartened and sad?
A graduate of the Academy am I;
Began my studies at the age of ten.
But for all my studying, nothing have I gained,
20 And now I am more than thirty years of age.
I muddled along, then came back empty-handed;
Now I loll about here in my hut.
My family is poor, acquaintances and relatives few.
Down in the world, I've grown distant from old friends.
25 The Chang'an moon is all that I have now,
Coming each night to visit me in my idleness.

SOURCE: HCMZ 21, in SNKBT, 27, pp. 132–33; NKBT, 69, pp. 348–49; *zatsugon* in the "old style" (pentasyllabic), in twenty-six lines.
TITLE: The identity of Middle Captain Fujiwara is unknown.
LINE 5: The dryandra, Ch. *wutong*, J. *aogiri* (*Sterculia platanifolia*), was considered the national tree of China and, according to legend, the only tree upon which a phoenix would alight.
LINE 25: Chang'an, the capital of China for most of the time from the former Han dynasty to the end of the Tang, is merely a conventional allusion to Heian, the Japanese capital. The layout of Heian was closely modeled on Chang'an.

Autumn Songs in the *Etchō* Mode from a Mountain Dwelling
Ki no Haseo

(No. 1)
I drift about from place to place, disliking empty fame,
Trying to flee the clamoring voices of calumny and praise.
Autumn waters cold; evening mountains clear.
Within this three-roomed hut of mine I'll spend my final years.

SOURCE: HCMZ 22, in SNKBT, 27, p. 133; NKBT, 69, p. 350; *uta* (ballad-style poem) in the *etchō* mode.

TITLE: Eight poems are grouped together under the above title, all of them ballads in the *etchō* mode. *Etchō* poems are quatrains and have heptasyllabic lines, except for the third line, which always has six characters in two feet, each with three words. Some well-known Chinese examples of *etchō* are found in a series called "The Fisherman," by the poet Zhang Zhihe (730-810)

(No. 2)

Here at this remote retreat what occupies my time?
Herb garden overgrown, I plow it by myself.
The valley stream sounds muted; mountain pines seem startled.
These autumn noises intercede, bringing heartbreak and despair.

SOURCE: HCMZ 23, in SNKBT, 27, p. 133; NKBT, 69, p. 351; *etchō* mode.

(No. 3)

Empty mountains quiet, secluded; waters gush and tumble.
Alone I have rested among the clouds for many years on end.
I dream no more of the world; I've broken off all ties.
I just unroll my mat on the moss and sit in meditation.

SOURCE: HCMZ 24, in SNKBT, 27, p. 133; NKBT, 69, p. 351; *etchō* mode.

(No. 4)

I divined a retreat among hills and streams, ceased all schemes of the mind.
No use for debate over right and wrong, away in the world of men.
I lock my valley cottage; close my gate by the pines.
The autumn is cold, a coarse, thin robe the only clothes I wear.

SOURCE: HCMZ 25, in SNKBT, 27, p. 133; NKBT, 69, pp. 351–52; *etchō* mode.
LINE 1: Traditionally, a building site was selected after consulting with a diviner. In poetry, such references to divination are often just a convention, meaning little more than choosing a site for one's house.

(No. 5)

I climb up high and gaze afar—north, south, east, and west.
By nature, I've always been reclusive, without a fixed abode.
Aged autumn cranes; monkeys that cry at dusk.
With them for company, I pass my days in this ancient valley of green.

SOURCE: HCMZ 26, in SNKBT, 27, p. 133; NKBT, 69, p. 352; *etchō* mode.

(No. 6)

Autumn river before my gate, autumn hills behind.
All day long a lonely silence, peaceful the distant view.

No one comes to visit; the road is hard to climb.
I do nothing but watch the evening clouds return in their usual way.

SOURCE: HCMZ 27, in SNKBT, 27, p. 133; NKBT, 69, pp. 352–53; *etchō* mode.

(No. 7)

My dwelling lies beyond the peaks, overlooking a river.
Rushing waters, rustling pines, chilly day and night.
I forget that I am old; peace is all I seek.
Here at leisure idly holding a fishing pole in my hands.

SOURCE: HCMZ 28, in SNKBT, 27, p. 133; NKBT, 69, p. 353; *etchō* mode.

(No. 8)

Lonely silent mountain home in autumn's sunset glow.
Before my gate red maple leaves, seldom swept away.
Content to live here always; I vow I'll never return.
On my pillow, all I hear is the sound of the gushing spring.

SOURCE: HCMZ 29, in SNKBT, 27, p. 133; NKBT, 69, pp. 353–54; *etchō* mode.

▦ Poems in the *Etchō* Mode Written at Leisure on a Summer Day on Three Things in the Courtyard
Minamoto no Shitagō

(No. 1) Pines

Pines in the courtyard, tall and solitary, rustling in the wind.
Throughout the night, the sound surrounds the stars that love the rain.
A pair of white cranes; a single black ox:
How many others are listening now to the clear sound of the wind?

SOURCE: HCMZ 30, in SNKBT, 27, pp. 11–12, 133; *etchō* mode.
TITLE: These *etchō* verses also belong to the *eibutsu* (Ch. *yongwu*, "odes on objects") subgenre, which gained popularity in China during the Southern Qi dynasty (479–502) and was adapted to both *kanshi* and *waka* genres. On the *etchō* mode, see the notes to poem 22, above.
LINE 2: The "stars that love the rain" are the constellation Hyades. This is an allusion to a passage in *Shu jing* (The Book of Documents), which states, "Some stars love the wind, and some love the rain." See James Legge, trans., *The Shoo King or the Book of Historical Documents*, The Chinese Classics, vol. 3 (orig. pub. by Oxford University Press; reprint, Taipei: SMC Publishing, 1991), p. 342. The constellation said to "love the wind" is Ite-za (Miboshi), known to us as the Archer or Sagittarius. Loving the rain and wind may mean that the stars so described appear under these particular weather conditions, or perhaps that the stars were thought to cause such weather conditions to occur.
LINE 3: Pairs of cranes were said to reside in old pines; "black ox" is a metaphor for an aged pine tree.

(No. 2) Bamboo

Pierced by frost, besieged by snow, the bamboo triumphs still,
Vying with the light mist and the moonlight in its beauty.
Cold the misty leaves; frozen the light of the moon.
Just the time to invite Ji and Ruan, friends from ancient days!

SOURCE: HCMZ 31, in SNKBT, 27, p. 12; p. 133; *etchō* mode.
LINE 4: Ji is Ji (Xi) Kang (223–62), a famous poet, essayist, and thinker; Ruan is Ruan Ji (210–63), who was also a poet. Both belonged to the coterie known as the "Seven Worthies of the Bamboo Grove." See KFS 9, above.

(No. 3) Moss

Cool fresh moss growing thick and lush, underneath the trees.
Even in the middle of the day it looks like twilight here.
Covered by shadows of pines; sealing the bamboo roots.
This spot seems even better than the entrance to the cave.

SOURCE: HCMZ 32, in SNKBT, 27, pp. 12, 133–34; *etchō* mode.
LINE 4: The cave reference is associated with Taohua yuan, a mystical fairyland. It was reached through a cave and took one back in time. The best-known account of this legend is in Tao Yuanming's essay "Taohua yuan ji" (A Record of Peach-Blossom Spring).

▨ Word-Gloss Poem (Written in the autumn of the first year of the Kashō period [848])
Kiyohara no Sanetomo

When my rice runs out, I become aware of my stipend.
In my heart, how could I fail to be loyal?
The village fish—carp diving under the waves;
The river birds—wild geese flying through autumn skies.
A fire when it dies turns into embers.
A tall mountain is by nature a lofty peak.
Words as brilliant as colored silk never die.
Common bugs weep as the cold wind blows.

SOURCE: HCMZ 33, in SNKBT, 27, p. 134; NKBT, 69, p. 354; octave, *jikun* (word gloss) mode (pentasyllabic).
TITLE: In this form of parlor-game verse, the first two characters in each of the eight lines are merged to form the fifth and final character in the same line. The resulting poem is often somewhat lacking in coherence, as this example demonstrates.
LINES 3 AND 4: These lines may be drawing a contrast between the recluses of the world ("carp diving under the waves") and the more gregarious types who lead active public lives ("wild geese flying through autumn skies").

LINES 5 AND 6: Here, a further contrast appears intended between the weak (the embers) and the successful or powerful (the tall mountain). See NKBT, 69, pp. 354–55.

⊞ A Palindrome
Tachibana no Aritsura

The chilly dew of dawn moistens the leaves;
The frigid wind of evening rustles the branches.
Faint and feeble the cries of cicadas chirping.
A line of shadows—geese flying through the skies.
Rosy irises adorn the stone-paved path.
Golden chrysanthemums grow throughout the hedge.
Round and full the moon over towering peaks.
Glistening and clear the limpid water in the pond.

SOURCE: HCMZ 36, in SNKBT, 27, p. 134; NKBT, 69, p. 355; octave, *kaibunshi* (palindrome) genre (pentasyllabic).
COMMENT: The poem can be read backwards and still say much the same thing, while also maintaining the requirements for end-rhyme. It can rendered in reverse as follows:

Limpid pond with water clear and glistening.
The moon over towering peaks is full and round.
Throughout the hedge grow chrysanthemums of gold.
Stone-paved path adorned with irises rosy.
Through the skies fly geese, a line of shadows.
Chirping cicadas' cries are feeble and faint.
Branches rustled by evening's wind, frigid.
Leaves moistened by dawn's dew, chilly.

⊞ My Way of Taking Care of My Health While at Ogura
The Former Prince and Minister of Central Affairs [Minamoto no Kaneakira]

1   Upon a hilly stronghold
    By Kameyama mountain,
    Gate made out of brushwood,
    Bamboo lattice fence.
5   Canopy of pines,
    Courtyard paved with stone.
    At the front some trees,
    Behind, a bamboo grove.
    The colors of the spring,
10 The light of the autumn season.
    Blossoms distant and hazy,

Pale the light of the moon.
The mingled calls of warblers,
A line of geese in the sky.
15   The pleasures of the dawn,
The views when evening comes.
High and distant clouds,
Vast and boundless waters.
Poems with two rhymes,
20   Playing music on my *koto*.
What plant is that in bud?
A wild orange, covered in frost.
What things have been picked?
Sunflowers, facing the sun.
25   Bracken in a box,
Bamboo shoots in a basket.
Raw fish—a single slice,
Sake—a single cup.
I lie down and sleep,
30   Then rise and ramble about.
Fragrance of dew on lotuses,
Scent of wind through cassias.
More foolish than Wang Zhan,
And lazier than Xi Kang!
35   I amuse myself as I please,
Meditating, mind miles away.
A place far from the world,
My Never-Never Land.
If my heart remains at ease
40   My life will last forever.

SOURCE: HCMZ 38, in SNKBT, 27, pp. 134–35; NKBT, 69, pp. 356–57; *zatsugon* in three-word lines, forty lines in length.

AUTHOR: Kaneakira's title, Saki no Chūsho Ō, is explained in the title note to FSS 4.

LINE 2: Kameyama is a hill in Kyoto's Arashiyama area adjacent to the Ōi River and southeast of Mt. Ogura.

LINE 33: Wang Zhan lived in the Jin dynasty (265–420) and had a reputation for being simple-minded.

LINE 34: Xi (Ji) Kang (223–62): see HCMZ 31.

✻ While ill, I heard a *zekku* (quatrain) humorously titled "Torikai no Arimi, the Palace Groom Who Wanders About at Night," written by the middle captain of the Imperial Bodyguards. I also read some matching poems in the old style by Fujiwara, governor of Harima, Supernumerary Officer Tachibana, and the presented scholar Minamoto, and I felt by turns moved and grieved. I then wrote the *kyōka* (crazy verse) that follows.

Minamoto no Shitagō

1   The old night watchman:
    Night after night in the old residence, keeping an eye out for fires,
        [A reference to the home of the former Chancellor, who served during the Tenroku era.]
    Calling out, "Watch for fires!" Who is this old man?
    Mindful of danger when all is well, he seems to be so wise.
5   But it is not that he's so very wise, just faithful as can be.
    He is able to keep evildoers at bay—the gods and spirits feel moved.
    Robbers are mortified by his presence and always keep away.
    The God of Fire is on his guard and never causes trouble.
    Torikai, Torikai—this is your family name.
10   Fitting that one called "bird-breeder" belongs to the "Feather Forest"!
    The Captain of the Feather Forest, a man so noble and kind,
    Is aware of your age and poverty, his compassion for you deep.
    Arimi, Arimi—this is your given name.
    But it should be changed from Arimi to Muni—
15   "Muni the Peerless"—we are well aware that your principles are high.
    Whether serving a family or the state, surely the work is the same.
    A servant of this family, your merit is already known.
    Though I have served three emperors, I still haven't reached my goal.
    Long ago, from the Tenryaku age down to the Kōhō period,
20   I served again in the Palace Library, compiling imperial texts.
    Copying manuscripts year after year, my eyesight soon grew dim.
    Now, in the twilight of my life, my ailments are growing worse.
    These legs of mine are withered and thin, I walk all doubled up.
    The hair on my temples has now grown sparse; in the mirror I see frost.
25   There is never a year I'm not laid up with an illness of some kind—
    This condition usually arises three or four times a year.
    Seldom do my ailments clear up, and on rare days when I'm well,
    My legs are heavy and hard to move, I always walk with a limp.
    Visits I make to the homes of officials quickly come to an end;
30   At gatherings with guests and friends, being sociable is hard.
    Alongside my rustic cottage the snowy blossoms gather;
    I would like to go and break off a branch but find myself unable.

By my mountain window birds in flocks twitter noisily;
I'd like to go out and listen to them but cannot go outside.
35 How lonely I am and how forlorn! The empty spring has passed.
Alone I mourn, alone I sigh! Summer and I'm still in bed.
Everyone dislikes me now, believing my ailments are feigned.
The world does not yet grieve for me, for I stubbornly cling to life.
What did *you* do, Arimi, to earn your lord's compassion?
40 Nothing more than call out loudly and go without sleep at night!
Long ago, I served too, forgetting to eat and sleep.
Why am *I* without imperial favor in my declining years?
It is hard for the rays of the sun to reach beneath an upturned dish.
I pray you'll report to His Majesty, high above the clouds,
45 That an old subject from Tenryaku times has sunk to the lowest station
And longs to float in the boundless seas of the Emperor's sagely virtue.

SOURCE: HCMZ 42, in SNKBT, 27, pp. 13–16, 136; *kyōka* in irregular meter; classified also as a *zatsugon*, in forty-six lines.

TITLE: None of the persons mentioned in the title can be identified with any certainty, including the low-ranking palace groom, Torikai no Arimi. The middle captain of the Imperial Bodyguards at this time may have been Fujiwara no Tamemitsu (942–92), according to SNKBT, 27, pp. 14, 411. Tamemitsu was appointed as minister of the right in 985 and chancellor in 991. Tachibana may have been Tachibana no Masamichi (d. ca. 980). Like Tamemitsu, he was a competent poet, composing in both Chinese and Japanese. A student of Minamoto no Shitagō and tutor to Prince Tomohira, he also served as secretary of Saga province in the early 970s. His supernumerary post mentioned here cannot be identified. See NKBT, 27, p. 392. Minamoto, the presented scholar, was possibly Tamenori (941–1011), Minamoto no Shitagō's student. On "presented scholar" status, see the notes to KKBS 1, above. *Kyōka* is a poetic subgenre comprising humorous, unconventional *kanshi*, often with irregular lineation. To the best of our knowledge, the present poem is the earliest extant example.

LINE 1: This line has only three characters.

POET'S NOTE TO LINE 2: The Tenroku period lasted from 970 to 973. The Chancellor was Fujiwara no Koremasa (Koretada), who took office in 971 and died the following year.

LINE 10: Torikai means "one who raises birds." The common Chinese name for the Imperial Bodyguards (Konoefu) was *yulin* (J. *urin*), literally, "Feather Forest," hence the rhetoric seen in this line.

LINE 11: This official may have been the middle captain mentioned in the title of the poem.

LINES 13 AND 14: Arimi means roughly "having three parts" or "having three," whereas Muni, means "without a second," that is, "without a peer."

LINE 18: The emperors he served were Murakami, Reizei, and En'yū.

LINES 19 AND 20: The Tenryaku and Kōhō reign periods spanned the years from 947 to 967. Shitagō was one of the five compilers working on *Gosen wakashū* (The Later Collection of Japanese Poetry), an imperial *waka* anthology completed in 951.

LINES 25 AND 26: We have reversed the order of these two lines in the translation for clarity.

LINE 44: His Majesty—probably Emperor En'yū.

✠ A Poem Satirizing the Efforts of "Lofty Phoenix" to Blur the Distinctions Between Noble and Lowly
Minamoto no Shitagō

1   Lofty Phoenix, Lofty Phoenix:
     Whose son is this man?
     The grandson of one with the senior sixth lower,
     The son of a man with the junior seventh upper.
5   In Shima province, awaiting a post;
     Hoping for a stipend as a palace kitchen steward.
     Plain and unadorned his speech,
     A voice loud, like rolling thunder;
     Possessing the talent of a clay figurine,
10   And a lineage lower than low.
     Look at the leather belt around his waist—
     An old studded Izumo one.
     Take a look at the shoes on his feet—
     Made of rough cloth from Shinano.
15   On his first morning at the Chamberlains' Office
     His cotton breeches earned him a scolding.
     One night as he sneaked past a group of palace guards
     His black cap brought him ridicule.
     Long ago, there was another Lofty Phoenix—
20   We read about his fame as a worthy.
     Now we have this other one—
     Called an "old fool" in the court offense records!
     Lofty Phoenix, Lofty Phoenix:
     Same name, but their natures so different.
25   The one in ancient times a sage,
     This one a fool, an utter fool!
     Why do they only post the names of the successful exam candidates?
     He's not worth talking about,
     He's not worth deriding.
30   But all should deplore that such a dolt has come up in the world!

SOURCE: HCMZ 43, in SNKBT, 27, pp. 16–17, 136; *zatsugon* in irregular meter, lines ranging from three to eight words, thirty lines in length.

TITLE: The identity of "Lofty Phoenix" is unknown.

LINE 1: The word "lofty" (*taka*) may simply be an abbreviation of this person's surname, which is probably Takahashi (see note for line five, below, and SNKBT, 27, p. 16). If this is the case, his sobriquet might instead be rendered as "Taka[hashi] the Phoenix." The phoenix was considered the queen of birds and a symbol of the empress, yet here the word is used ironically to suggest that this man had grandiose pretensions that exceeded his station in life.

LINES 3 AND 4: The court ranks of Lofty Phoenix's father and grandfather were in the lower reaches of the aristocratic hierarchy. This system had eight major rank levels, the lower four of which each had four sub-divisions into senior and junior, upper and lower levels.

LINE 5: Shima province corresponds to the eastern portion of modern Mie prefecture. Members of the Takahashi clan, to which Lofty Phoenix likely belonged, came from Shima province and traditionally served in the Imperial Table Office (Naizenshi).

LINES 11 AND 12: The belt is an *Izumo no ishi*, a leather sash studded with agates and gems. Holders of the sixth rank wore it when in attendance at court. This criticism may have been leveled at Lofty Phoenix because he wore a belt that his rank did not entitle him to wear. To make matters worse, the belt was "old." Whether this means worn-out or outmoded is unclear.

LINES 13 AND 14: The type of shoe mentioned here was made of a coarse, glossy textile from Shinano province supplied to the court as a tax in kind. See ibid., p. 16. Wearing shoes of such material was apparently seen as vulgar.

LINE 15: On the Chamberlains' Office, see the title note to DSKS 48, above.

LINE 16: The cotton breeches, J. *hoko* or *hōko*, were a variety of *hakama*, or trouser skirt. This garment had eight pleats along the midline and was worn with a drawstring at the hem. Court gentlemen never wore such clothing to the morning session, and by doing so, Lofty Phoenix was evidently committing a breach of protocol.

LINE 18: Black cap: from the early tenth century this kind of headgear, called *ebo* or *eboshi*, was worn by upper- and middle-ranking aristocrats as part of their regular court dress. It was typically made of thin silk, over which black lacquer was applied in layers, although soft cloth and later paper were sometimes used instead. The commentator in SNKBT speculates that our subject was wearing the wrong style of *eboshi*, perhaps an *ori-eboshi* (a somewhat squat black cap, which extended backwards beyond the back of the head and was strapped to the chin with cords) instead of the expected *tate-eboshi*, a taller, cordless cap with a bulbous top. See ibid., p 17.

LINE 19: The original Lofty Phoenix was probably one Gao Wentong, fl. first century. From a farming family, Gao devoted himself tirelessly to scholarship. He eventually became a distinguished scholar but declined to serve as an official. Gao taught for several years, then went into seclusion, fishing and living as a hermit until the end of his days. His story is related in *juan* 113 of *Hou Han shu*.

⌗ On Losing My Hair
The Former Prince and Minister of Central Affairs [Minamoto no Kaneakira]

After I became ill, my hair turned completely white, and nearly all of it has fallen out. Moved by Bo Juyi's poem "On Losing My Teeth," I composed this piece called "On Losing My Hair" to console myself. The poem reads as follows:

1   I ask: "You, hair!
      Why have you changed your former appearance?
      You used to look like black clouds,
      Now you are like white snow.
5   Surely you have seen pines and cypresses:
      Autumn frost forms on them time and again,
      But their greenness never changes.

And have you never seen red jade?
Burn it for three days and nights,
10 Its pure beauty remains unaltered.
Could it be that you have a duplicitous heart?
How is it that you have forgotten your pledge?
Did you not make a promise long ago?
Why have you let me down?
15 All right, go! Just go away!
There's nothing that can be done.
The dawn frost sparkles weakly—
You search, but it cannot be found."
    The answer:
20 "When you were young and healthy,
Your veins pulsed with blood, hair long and black.
Now that the decay of old age has set in,
Your flesh has become lifeless, hair grey and unkempt.
This is how things are.
25 Why be upset?
When a fish tires, its tail turns red;
When a tree is ailing, its leaves turn autumnal.
A horse in distress turns a dark yellow;
When a crow feels moved, its head turns white.
30 In the front courtyard of Lord Meng Chang,
Only Feng Huan still resided;
In the residence of General Wei,
Only Ren An was still sleeping.
When your power is gone, it's gone;
35 When guests leave, they don't return.
Once your energy ebbs, it keeps on ebbing;
And when your hair falls out, none remains.
Truly, this is how things are.
Why do you lament?"
40 I respond thus:
"You are absolutely right.
How can there be any doubt?
After my hair has all turned white,
And once it has all fallen out,
45 I shall cut off all ties with officialdom
And return to the seclusion of Buddhist life."

SOURCE: HCMZ 353, in SNKBT, 27, pp. 326–27; NKBT, 69, pp. 402–5; *ji* (Ch. *ci*, lyric) form in irregular meter.

LINE 26: This is a reference to a line in Ode 10, titled "Joo fun" (Ru Fen, The Raised Banks of the Ru), in *Shi jing*, which Legge renders as "The bream is showing its tail all red." The Mao commentary explains the fish's change in color as being due to its thrashing about in water that is too shallow, causing it to become fatigued. See James Legge, *The She King*, pp. 17–18.

LINE 28: This reference to horses in distress derives from Ode 3 in *Shi jing*, "Keuen-urh" (Zhuan er, Mouse-ear). Lines two and three of the third stanza read, "I was ascending that lofty ridge, / But my horses turned of a dark yellow." See Legge, ibid., p. 8. The Mao commentary, quoted in NKBT, 69, p. 403, explains that when dark horses become ill, they turn yellow. The point of the allusion is to suggest that it is natural for all living things to undergo changes in color with aging, illness, or physical discomfort.

LINE 29: The reference to crows comes from a Chinese anecdote relating the story of Prince Dan (d. 226 B.C.), who was being held hostage by the state of Qin. He was informed that he would be released "when the head of a crow turned white and a horse grew horns," in other words, never. Sighing, he gazed upwards, and there above him was a crow with a white head. See NKBT, 69, p. 403.

LINES 30 AND 31: Lord Meng Chang (Meng Changjun, d. 279 B.C., actual name Tian Wen) was an aristocrat who served as minister in the states of Qin and Qi. In his heyday, he had thousands of guest-retainers in his service, but all of them except one Feng Huan deserted him after he was unfairly demoted by the king. Eventually, Meng Chang was rehabilitated and appointed minister of Qi, with the loyal Feng serving as his counselor. Meng Chang is also mentioned in BKSRS 117 and 118.

LINES 32 AND 33: General Wei was Wei Qing (d. 106 B.C.), a cavalry commander who led a series of successful military expeditions against the Xiongnu nomads during the reign of the Han emperor Wu Di. Ren An was one of his guest-retainers. When the prestige of another major cavalry commander named Huo Qubing came to eclipse that of Wei, the latter's retainers left him and sought Huo as their patron. Ren An alone remained loyal. See *Shi ji, juan* 111.

✴ A Song about the Peaceful Retirement of an Old Man
Sugawara no Fumitoki, Holder of the Third Rank

At eighty years of age, during the autumn of the second year of Jōgen (977), a few thoughts occurred to me, and I wrote them down in a leisurely fashion.

1   Days
      Nights
      Come and go,
      Give way to one another.
5   Spring silently slips away,
      And summer quietly passes.
      The bright light of autumn is hard to detain,
      The shadows readily grow long and slanting.
      As night deepens, the dew in the courtyard is cold.
10   As dawn approaches, the mist beyond my window is murky.
      My students have all gone away and no longer enter my house;
      Old friends have grown tired of me and come no more to my door.
      Beside my bed are books—ah!—but I pay them scant attention.
      In my wine-jar there is no wine—ah!—so naturally I am sober.

15 Writing is the family trade; though old, I have not neglected it.
The clamor of the workaday world; though I'm gone, I hear it still.
I can't make a living watering my garden or setting traps to catch fish.
I can't dispel my boredom by playing the *koto* and learning songs.
Why did I leave my post to wander, retiring to these valleys and caves?
20 Why did I dye my robes black, seek the Law in these hills and groves?
I've heard Xiangru was a prolific writer, but his house was little more
than four walls.
I've also heard that when Sun Hong placed high in the exams, he was
eighty years old.
Haven't you seen, in the dusk rain at Beimang, the verdant burial
mounds, one upon the other?
24 And haven't you heard the autumn wind in the eastern suburbs, its
crisp, clear sound in the white poplars?

SOURCE: HCMZ 354, in SNKBT, 27, p. 327; NKBT, 69, 405–7; *kō* (song) form in irregular meter, lines ranging from one to twelve words.

TITLE AND AUTHOR: The *kō* (Ch. *xing*) "song" genre is a variety of *gushi*, "old-style verse." It was considered a kind of *yuefu*, these being folk-ballads or pseudo-folk style poems typically about the lives of the common people. From the Tang dynasty, the *xing* was characteristically a long narrative poem, a famous example being Bo Juyi's "Pipa xing" (Song of the Pipa). The lineation of this verse by Sugawara no Fumitoki is highly irregular. It consists of a series of couplets, each longer than the previous one. The poet's name is actually given here as Kan Sanbon, "Sugawara of the Third Rank," the sobriquet used by Fumitoki.

LINE 21: Xiangru is Sima Xiangru (179–117 B.C.), China's most famous *fu* poet. Among his best-known works is "Shanglin fu" (Prose-Poem on Shanglin Park), a lengthy, dazzling piece which describes in sumptuous detail the splendor of the emperor's hunting grounds.

LINE 22: Sun Hong is Gongsun Hong (d. 121 B.C.), who served as chief minister to the Han emperor Wu Di. He began his career as a scholar late in life, working as a swineherd until his forties. His actual age when he was appointed to the position of professor (*boshi*, J. *hakushi*), after placing first in the palace examinations, was closer to seventy than eighty.

LINE 23: Beimang was northeast of Luoyang and from the Han dynasty the site of a cemetery. The graves mentioned here are those of the wealthy and influential.

LINE 24: Eastern suburbs: these were in Luoyang. The graves of ordinary people were marked with trees instead of grave markers or tombs. The point made here is that death is the great equalizer, coming to everyone, rich and poor alike.

HONCHŌ ZOKU MONZUI (FURTHER LITERARY GEMS FROM OUR COURT)

Conceived in the image of Fujiwara no Akihira's *Honchō monzui*, *Honchō zoku monzui* (Further Literary Gems from Our Court, thirteen *maki*) was compiled sometime after 1140 and may be an unfinished work. Its contents span the years 1018 to 1140. The identity of its compiler is still uncertain; he was perhaps a member of the Shiki-ke Fujiwara or Ōe families.[107] This work consists mainly of some 229 prose pieces, by such leading writers as Ōe no Masafusa, Fujiwara no Akihira, and Fujiwara no Atsumitsu. There are only four poems, all in the *gushi* genre, and five *fu*. The third of these *fu*, translated below, was probably just a routine practice composition written in preparation for an examination. It has been included in the present volume largely because it is Masafusa's earliest known *kanshi*.

❊ The Idle Life on an Autumn Day: A Prose-Poem
Ōe no Masafusa [Student, aged sixteen]

1   The life of the penniless, reclusive scholar:
      He seeks a place remote and quiet,
      Mind devoted to scholarship.
      A garden with but three paths,
5   House nothing more than four walls.
      He closes his door to forget his fields and garden;
      Lowers the blinds so he can ponder the distant past.
      Fragrant oranges growing on a bower—
      Knows them well from Pan Yue's poem.
10 Tall willows at his gate—
      A bond with Tao Qian who lived so long ago.
      Look! Dew covers the deserted lane,

---

107. Honma, *Nihon kanshi*, p. 215.

And rain strikes his remote dwelling.
At leisure he plays a *koto* of pure tone,
15 A cup of green wine in his hand.
Late at night fireflies sparkle in the green marsh;
On frosty days crickets chirp in the blue bedchamber.
Deserted the western garden—visitors scarce.
The moon in the heavens shining brilliantly.
20 Lonesome by the northern door—people few.
Wind through the grotto blowing mournfully,
All the more now that autumn has advanced.
On the grounds of the Emperor's Park,
The year gradually draws to a close.
25 In the back garden, northern geese honk in the clouds,
Awakening him as he lies alone on his pillow.
Marsh cranes warn of the dew, sound piercing the skies afar.
Cold winds harsh, grasses on the border wither;
White mists arise, leaves on the trees turn red.
30 The mountain birds sing in unison.
Head aslant, he gazes: scraggly willows by the twisting stream.
The wild animals have a crazed look in their eyes.
He is grieved to see mugwort fluff flying above the plains.
Ah! Savoring the old classics, reading philosophy and history.
35 Though these men of former generations shunned fame,
Later generations still praise the beauty of their words.
Li Guang, a noble general of the Han court,
Divined for himself a dwelling in Longshan.
Fan Li, a wise minister of Yue,
40 Withdrew from service to live by a lake.
The scholar has inherited something of that ancient dust,
And looks up to these figures in admiration of their lofty deeds.

SOURCE: HZM 3, in Nakatsuka Eijirō and others, eds., *Nihon bungaku taikei*, 24 (Tokyo: Kokumin Tosho Kabushiki Kaisha, 1927), pp. 447–48; Kuroita Katsumi, ed., *Honchō monzui, Honchō zoku monzui*, in [Shintei zōho] *Kokushi taikei*, vol. 29 (pt. 2), p. 3; *fu.*
LINES 8 AND 9: The poet is probably alluding here to Pan Yue's famous prose-poem "Xian ju fu" (Prose-Poem on Dwelling in Idleness), in which a reference to "fragrant orange trees" may be found.
LINES 10 AND 11: On the connection between Tao Qian and willows, see notes to RUS 75, line 6
LINE 37: Li Guang (d.125 B.C.) served the Han court as a cavalry general and was known as the "Flying General of Han."
LINE 39: Fan Li, see notes to HCMDS 5, below.

HOSSHŌJI DONO GYOSHŪ (A COLLECTION OF POEMS BY THE LORD OF HOSSHŌJI)

This small, one-*maki* collection of 102 *kanshi*, known also by the title *Hosshōji kanpaku gyoshū* (The Collection of the Hosshōji Regent), contains poems by the statesman Fujiwara no Tadamichi (1097–1164), who served in the courts of emperors Toba, Sutoku, Konoe, and Go-Shirakawa. Hosshōji was a Pure Land temple in eastern Kyoto founded in 925 by Tadamichi's paternal ancestor Fujiwara no Tadahira (880–949). Tadamichi himself retired there in 1162. The poems in this anthology were selected by Tadamichi, with the assistance of his friend and fellow poet Fujiwara no Sanemitsu (1069–1147), the anthology reaching final form around the Twelfth Month of 1145, the date found in the colophon. The earliest surviving text is dated 1183, and all subsequent editions derive from this version. The *Gunshō ruijū* text is the only modern printed edition and has no commentary. Originally, this collection was simply titled *Gyoshū* (The Collection), but some time after 1148, the year Tadamichi built a residence next to Hosshōji, the title was amended to include reference to this temple.

In these poems, we see Tadamichi as the ideal Heian Confucian official: a self-assured man, calm and contented with his own life, and yet conscious of the less fortunate, as illustrated by poems like "The Old Charcoal Seller," translated below. A lover of nature, Tadamichi is thoughtfully observant of the seasons and natural change, making frequent allusion to the beauty of the moon in particular. His verse titled "Gazing at the Moon, I Forget the Summer Heat" (HDG 19), also translated, shows the poet marveling at how the moonlight possesses the power to make the otherwise sweltering summer night seem cool.

The poems in the first half of the anthology are arranged to follow the order of the seasons and belong to the genre known as *kudaishi*, poems whose title (*dai*) consists of a five-character line (*ku*) or a couplet borrowed from a Chinese *shi*. *Kudai* verse titles (sometimes referred to as "topics") should thus be distinguished from assigned verse topics (*dai*) of a more general nature which are *not* necessarily taken from such Chinese sources, an example being the topic "pines in the valley," which Emperor Saga was assigned in advance of his composing BKSRS 123.

Kudaishi in most instances reproduce all the words that occur in the title within the first two lines of the *kanshi*, either following the original word order or rearranging the individual characters.[108] Sometimes, instead of the original characters, synonymous ones are employed; in other instances, a paraphrase is substituted for the source material. The mid-Heian composition manual *Sakumon daitai* describes three of these indirect borrowing methods as follows: (1) the "fragmented topic form," in which characters synonymous with those in the borrowed poem line are individually distributed in the poem; (2) "the generally-expressed topic form," in which only the general sense of the original borrowed line is incorporated into the poem; and (3) "implied *yūgen* form," in which the borrowed line is alluded to in language that is often even more oblique.[109] *Sakumon daitai* also explains that when it suited their purposes, poets would incorporate words from a *shi* line but create an entirely new title for their verse instead of using the borrowed line as the title.[110]

Popular in China during the late Six Dynasties period, *kudaishi* began to be composed in Japanese poetic circles in the late eighth century, the earliest known examples appearing in *Ryōunshū*. The genre flourished from the mid-ninth century, especially during the reigns of emperors Uda (r. 887–97) and Daigo (r. 897–930), when many *kudaishi* were written at both private venues and official banquets. KKBS and HCRS contain various examples. The genre—in both *kanshi* and *waka* forms—remained popular well into the twelfth century. Since few *kudai*-style *kanshi* are identified as such in their titles, their status as *kudaishi* can go unnoticed by modern readers.

The poems in the second half of *Hosshōji dono gyoshū*, which are not *kudaishi*, are grouped according to category in the following order: human affairs, animals, screen painting inscriptions, *zōtōka* (poetic exchanges), poems on the Chinese classics, books, country retreats, and mountain temples. Tadamichi has given us many simple but charming natural images that linger in our memory—effective in their totality rather than individually novel or unusual in themselves. Overall, the poetic style is straightforward,

---

108. Among the fifty-four *kudaishi* that make up the first half of the anthology, thirty-eight follow this model. However, the remaining sixteen display one or both of the following characteristics: (a) title lines comprise four characters instead of five; or (b) one or more of the characters in the title line do not occur in the opening couplet or elsewhere in the poem. A further, albeit unusual, variation is that occasionally all the words in the title line occur within the first line of the opening couplet—see HDS 18 and 53, for example.

109. Konishi, III, pp. 186–87.

110. See *Nihon kanbungaku daijiten*, the entry titled "*Kudaishi*," pp. 193–94, for a citation of a passage from *Sakumon daitai* explaining this particular practice.

personal, and lucid, showing the influence of Bo Juyi and other Chinese
poets who wrote in a similarly plain and honest manner.

▓ My Mind Is Far Off in the Countryside, Thinking About the Flowers

My mind is far off in the countryside, my spirit feels unsettled.
Endless vistas of floral beauty—the flowers must be newly in bloom.
I'm unable to view the snow-topped trees in the woodlands of the east.
How can I see what spring is like in the villages to the north?
When the peach trees blossom on the hills my thoughts cross the miles;
I ask about their fragrance first when travelers come to visit.
The willows by the pass, the hilltop plum trees—how will I ever see them,
Living a quiet and simple life, here in Chang'an?

SOURCE: HDG 10, in [*Shinkō*] *Gunsho ruijū* 126, vol. 6 (Tokyo: Naigai Shoseki Kabushiki
Kaisha, 1931), p. 402; octave (heptasyllabic). Poem numbers are not present in this edition and
have been supplied by the translators.
LINE 8: Chang'an, in early times the capital of China, stands for Heian, the Japanese capital.

▓ The Spring Is Cold and the Flowers Have Not Yet Come Out

Even though the spring is here, the flowers aren't yet in bloom.
I would guess that this is because the cold still lingers on.
I wonder if the plum trees on the cloudy peaks are fragrant?
The frozen banks are slowly thawing, soft the willow branches.
While snow remains, I well recall, the flowers can scarcely bloom.
I imagine they will open once the warm winds start to blow.
Singing warblers, dancing butterflies—very hard to find.
When will we be able to make a journey out into the woods?

SOURCE: HDG 13, in [*Shinkō*] *Gunsho ruijū* 126, vol. 6, p. 402; octave (heptasyllabic).

▓ Gazing at the Moon, I Forget the Summer Heat

All night long I watch the moon and wander about the tower.
Naturally, I forget the heat while enjoying the pristine light.
That turbid pearl possesses the power to make the night seem cool;
Its snowy light creates the feeling that summer is not yet here.
I go out and gaze at the clear sky, lightly clad for now,
Then go to bed in my darkened room—the sweat again returns.

Wherever the lingering moonlight shines, summer disappears.
Who would feel the need to go and welcome autumn now?

SOURCE: HDG 19, in [*Shinkō*] *Gunsho ruijū* 126, vol. 6, p. 403; octave (heptasyllabic).

The Old Charcoal Seller

May I ask, old charcoal seller, how do you make a living?
"I cut down trees and burn them for charcoal to get through my final years."
On the stormy peaks at dawn his face is covered with dust and grime;
High in the mountains he builds a fire that obscures the light of the moon.
His charcoal worth little, he returns in tears along the frozen road;
His thin garment cannot withstand the cold and snowy weather.
A palace attendant in white robes came and took away his cart.
"Here's half a bolt of red silk gauze—don't treat it as a trifle!"

SOURCE: HDG 88, in [*Shinkō*] *Gunsho ruijū* 126, vol. 6, p. 410; octave (heptasyllabic).
LINES 7 AND 8: The charcoal has been arbitrarily requisitioned by a palace messenger, in exchange for something that the old man probably cannot use.
COMMENT: This poem and the next were inspired by Bo Juyi's "An Old Charcoal Seller." For a translation, see *Sunflower Splendor: Three Thousand Years of Chinese Poetry*, pp. 206–7.

A Poem to Match the Fine One Presented by the Senior Assistant Minister of Ceremonial, Which He Wrote After Reading My Poem "The Old Charcoal Seller"

An old mountain man, down on his luck, there in his hut of thatch.
He knows the routine for a making a living, whether awake or asleep.
What will become of his livelihood on those hot, summer days?
For the sake of his family's welfare he hopes for icy, stormy weather.
Ashamed of the grey hair trailing from his temples, he goes about his work;
Afraid the attendant will take his load away from the southern market.
For more than a thousand catties of charcoal, a single length of damask.
The official reads his proclamation aloud—who is the greedy one?

SOURCE: HDG 89, in [*Shinkō*] *Gunsho ruijū* 126, vol. 6, p. 410; octave (heptasyllabic).
TITLE: The senior assistant minister's poem is not contained in this anthology and probably no longer exists.
LINE 6: "Attendant" is literally "the man in white" and refers to the same white-robed attendant who requisitioned the charcoal-seller's load in the previous poem.
LINE 7: "Single length" is more literally a *zhang*, a unit of length measuring about ten feet.

✖ An Impromptu Poem Written in Summer at the Cassia Retreat

Cassias growing by the water's edge, southwest of the capital.
Scenery beyond compare, in its natural state.
Mountain pines and dark cedars, black clouds trailing low;
Crows and sparrows calling in the forest, the setting of the sun.
My rank and stipend are beyond my due, but I've had a brilliant career;
It's in my nature to live simply and quietly, never striving for power.
What might I have had in mind in seeking out this place?
To explore the area, amuse myself, and bring order to my thoughts.

SOURCE: HDG 93, in [Shinkō] Gunsho ruijū 126, vol. 6, p. 410; octave (heptasyllabic).
TITLE: Tadamichi's Cassia Retreat (Katsura Betsugyō) was probably located along the Katsura
River in the area where centuries later, in 1624, the Katsura Rikyū (The Katsura Imperial Villa)
was built by Prince Toshihito (1579–1629), southwest of Kyoto.
LINE 6: "Never striving for power" is somewhat misleading. In fact, Tadamichi rose to the
highest offices in the land, defeating his half-brother Yorinaga in the Hōgen Uprising to be-
come regent and chancellor.

✖ An Impromptu Poem Written in Early Winter at My Uji Retreat

I am always inspired on my frequent quests for pleasure beyond the city.
The scenery here compels me to stay—I cannot bear to return!
Long I have followed the path of officialdom, lost in the evening mist,
Blundering along the road through life, treading upon spring ice.
Woodcutters in mountain dwellings—sitting with them as a guest;
Water birds in riverside villages—friends of a different species.
Among the things I have seen and heard, what has impressed me most?
The vast expanse of rippling waters, the clear light of the moon.

SOURCE: HDG 94, in [Shinkō] Gunsho ruijū 126, vol. 6, p. 410; octave (heptasyllabic).
TITLE: Uji was a settlement south of Kyoto beside the Uji River. The area was famous for its
scenery and was a favorite spot among the Heian aristocracy for private retreats and excursions.

✖ Stopping at an Old Grotto in the Mist and Worshiping the Buddha on the Last Day of the Ninth Month

High above a lonely temple, beside an ancient grotto.
Grimly I stare off into the distance, dreading autumn's end.
Although I rue the passing of autumn, in my sadness I'm not alone.
A patch of cloud above the mountains casts its pall on me.

SOURCE: HDG 102, in [Shinkō] Gunsho ruijū 126, vol. 6, p. 411; quatrain (heptasyllabic).

HONCHŌ MUDAISHI (POEMS FROM OUR COURT WITHOUT ALLUSIVE TITLES)

With 772 poems divided among ten *maki, Honchō mudaishi* (compiled 1162–64) is the largest collection of eleventh- and twelfth-century *kanshi* ever produced and includes some of the most appealingly down-to-earth verse written during the Heian period. Regent Fujiwara no Tadamichi (1097–1164), who later became a lay priest at Hosshōji, was charged with overseeing the production of this anthology, although some believe that Fujiwara no Chikamitsu most likely compiled it.[111] Only thirty poets are represented; those with forty or more compositions are Fujiwara no Tadamichi, Nakahara no Hirotoshi, Fujiwara no Akihira (the compiler of *Honchō monzui*), Akihira's son Atsumitsu and grandson Shigeakira, Fujiwara no Chikamitsu (Shigeakira's foster brother), and the peripatetic Priest Renzen, Chikamitsu's friend. That the collection has so few poets and that so many of them belonged to the Shiki-ke (Ceremonial) branch of the Fujiwara family makes it somewhat less than representative of the period.[112]

Mudaishi, or "poems without allusive titles," are best defined by what they lack. While *mudaishi* generally have some kind of title, what is missing is a title of a special type, namely, a five-character line or *kudai*, borrowed from a verse by a Chinese poet. The *kudai* has been described earlier in this study, in the *Hosshōji dono gyoshū* introduction where *kudaishi* (poems with *kudai* titles) are discussed. As already mentioned, *kudai* allusion is not merely a feature of the title but typically also extends to the body of the poem itself, where the language of the title is usually reproduced in some fashion.

---

111. Kawaguchi, *Heian-chō Nihon kanbungakushi no kenkyū*, vol. 3, p. 909.
112. Smits, p. 84, based on Ōsone Shōsuke's article "*Honchō mudaishi seiritsu kō*," *passim*, in *Kokugo to kokubungaku* 37, no. 5 (1960): 46–56, and *Kokugo to kokubungaku* 37, no. 6 (1960): 27–38.

The *mudaishi* genre evidently arose around the mid-ninth century as a reaction against *kudaishi*, which had been popular in both the *waka* and *kanshi* traditions. Beyond this lack of an allusive title and the corresponding reference to, or incorporation of, that title in the body of the poem itself, *mudaishi* were generically fairly undistinguished. In comparison to *kudaishi*, they tend to display a rhetorical plainness, and Chinese historical and literary allusions are relatively infrequent. The images are characteristically conventional, even formulaic, only occasionally stimulating the imagination with vivid color or subtle detail. The diction is simple and unaffected, often verging on the prosaic and showing to a greater degree than any earlier *kanshi* the influence of Bo Juyi. One finds much similarity from one poet to another in choice of expression and rhetoric, and little evidence that poets placed a premium on being original. As Konishi writes, *kanshi* poets in the eleventh century had already "moved toward ever more homogeneous expression"; in the twelfth century these poets "constituted a self-contained group" and "adopted little in the way of new poetic styles from China."[113]

But while recycling many of the subjects and styles already known, some poets at this time enjoyed composing on humble or earthy topics—the huts of fishermen, a woman peddling charcoal, puppeteers, and even rats— and had a penchant for the subtle, austere description of natural beauty. Certain poems also evoke what Konishi identifies as a delicate, ethereal faded beauty that is often associated with late Tang poetry and Japanese *waka* of the same period. An example of this style is Minamoto no Tsunenobu's "View from a Farmhouse on an Autumn Day" (HCMDS 283), with its atmospheric middle couplets which read in translation as follows: "On the way through the suburbs, the last flowers were fading; / At my lodge, near the water's edge, bent willows show autumn colors. / Clouds darken the thatched eaves, rain comes from the mountain; / A gale opens the pine door on fields veiled in mist."[114]

All extant manuscripts of *Honchō mudaishi* date from the Edo period, and these may be divided into two main textual traditions: the three-*maki* text bearing the simplified title *Mudaishi*, and the ten-*maki* version, which has the full title. The ten-*maki* text has twelve poems more than the three-*maki* one and in general tends to correct textual errors found in the latter text, suggesting that the shorter version represents an older tradition. The following is an inventory, volume by volume, of the thematic organization of the ten-*maki* text, which we have followed: *maki* (1) imperial excursions, formal palace banquets, and poems composed at gatherings for the Age Veneration Society (Shōshikai), a group which had its beginnings in 877;[115]

---

113. Konishi, III, pp. 3–4.
114. Ibid., pp. 6–8.
115. Minabuchi no Toshina held the first gathering of the society at a mountain retreat. The first such affair in China was in 845, organized by Bo Juyi himself.

(2) celestial phenomena, the seasons, plants, natural features, animals, human affairs, miscellaneous objects, and *byōbu* screen poems; (3) flowers, the moon, and the Tanabata Star Festival; (4) spring and summer; (5) autumn, winter, and miscellaneous irregular verse; (6) pavilions, viewing platforms, and country retreats; (7) mountain homes, country homes, rustic lodges, former homes, mountain villages, countryside and river settings, and inns; (8) mountain temples; (9) mountain temples (part two); (10) mountain temples (part three), miscellaneous temples, zen temples, and mountain grottos. The three-*maki* text shows rather different organization from the above: the first *maki* comprises *maki* 2, 4, and 5 of the longer version; the second *maki*, 3, 6, and 7; and the third *maki*, 1, 8, 9, and 10.

In contrast to the contemporaneous *waka* verse, where we detect at times both historical nostalgia and a fondness for classical allusion, *Honchō mudaishi* rarely exhibits either predilection. Chinese history seems to have receded from the consciousness of *kanshi* poets, historical and literary allusions being far less frequent, especially in the final third of the collection, which comprises mostly temple poems. We also note a diminished interest in the traditional formal topics of the four seasons and annual court events and by contrast considerably more attention being paid to informal, personal topoi such as sojourns to temples for spiritual replenishment. In *Honchō mudaishi* a growing interest in the world outside the palace and capital is apparent; in fact poems with the capital as their setting make up only a small percentage of the total corpus. Poems on the pleasures of excursions to remote, rustic spots, especially Buddhist temples beyond the city, are particularly numerous. As Ivo Smits observes, "If we take recluse poetry to mean isolation in its widest sense . . . nearly 55 percent of the poems in the *Honchō mudaishi* can be grouped together as one category, 'recluse poetry,' which is by far the largest category in this collection."[116]

Indeed, *Honchō mudaishi* shares with the *waka* poetry of the mid-classical age the ideal of pursuing a transcendental rapport with the world beyond human affairs, time, and place.[117] The poet physically removes himself periodically from the capital to seek beauty and peace at temples and rural settings, his uncertainties seeming to compel him to look inward and confront certain disheartening truths, typically Buddhist-inspired, about life. Such poems tend to conclude with an observation—perhaps in some cases merely reflecting poetic convention rather than sincerely held sentiments—concerning the vanity of glory and the futility of a lifetime of striving: "This floating life, glory and dishonor, are no more than a dream," observes Fujiwara no Mototoshi, in HCMDS 645. Similarly, Priest Renzen sadly declares while on a visit to Sōrinji temple: "For half the day I met with priests,

116. Smits, p. 86.
117. See Robert Brower and Earl Miner, *Japanese Court Poetry* (Stanford University Press, 1961), pp. 312–15.

talked about Buddhist Law. / I realize now that all is empty and tears come streaming down" (HCMDS 643). Fujiwara no Chikamitsu strikes a similar chord, with Daoist overtones, when he acknowledges the emptiness of years of hard work while on a visit to Tōkōji: "The mountain clouds and the valley river are surely laughing at me / For seeking fame on the scholarly road and never giving up!" (HCMDS 641).

The prominence of the escapist theme may to some extent reflect the dark, more pessimistic *mappō* (Latter Age of Buddhist Law) consciousness frequently seen in Japanese works written in medieval times. The *mappō* age, commonly reckoned by the Japanese as having finally arrived in the mid-eleventh century, was seen as a time when discord and disorder were bound to prevail. Many writers of the age seem resigned to the notion that their world would never improve, their suspicions confirmed as they witnessed the tragic unfolding of the Hōgen and Heiji uprisings (1156 and 1159–60, respectively). Such events as the burning of Retired Emperor Go-Shirakawa's Sanjō Palace and the taking of Go-Shirakawa himself as a hostage no doubt disillusioned the courtiers and created a sense of personal insecurity. Laments Fujiwara no Tadamichi in HCMDS 622, which was composed during a visit to the temple Kiyomizudera, "Poetry and wine help us forget the miseries of this dreamlike existence; / Fraught with adversity, hard to bear—such is the way of the world."

Thus focused upon his own emotional concerns, the *Honchō mudaishi* poet seems motivated less by the imperatives of literary precedent or the inspiration of past poets than by purely lyrical impulses. References to a failed career or fears for one's future are common refrains in the collection. Expressions of shame over a perceived lack of career success typically occur in the closing couplet of a poem, sentiments reflecting either conventional humility or perhaps genuine emotions shaped by a Buddhist consciousness. A poem that aptly demonstrates this sense of hopelessness and diminished self-worth is one by Koremune no Noritoki, which ends with the lines, "White-haired, in my final years, I'm ashamed of my crane-like hair. / Red-robed, in a lowly post, I sigh, losing heart. / This futile life is slipping away—a man with no achievements. / Slow and irresolute in all affairs, by fortune never blessed" (HCMDS 349, untitled). In poem 642, "Paying a Visit in Late Spring to Sōrinji Temple," Nakahara no Hirotoshi, while enthralled by the scenery, cannot escape apprehensive reflection on the uncertainty of his future: "Gazing, gazing at the misty scenery far off in the distance— / Rivers and mountains in all their splendor fill my heart with joy. / Out of office, with time on my hands and no profession to follow; / Now that I find myself growing old, what will become of me?"

As these excerpts show, the poetry of this collection offers a revealing window into the worldview and personal concerns of aristocrats in the twilight of the Heian age. Situated near the end of the Heian *kanshi* tradition as

Japan entered a period of political upheaval, *Hōncho mudaishi* is a collection of major significance, preserving as it does the straightforward and largely heartfelt reflections of courtiers facing cataclysmic social changes. With some exceptions, such as the eight or so rather novel poems translated immediately below and Priest Renzen's series of travel poems, the topoi favored in *Hōncho mudaishi* are generally more conventional, the language and imagery simpler and more formulaic than is typical in certain earlier collections. And yet the poems succeed admirably in conveying what appears to be the mood of the times, in particular, the formidable quest to find inner peace characteristic of the vast number of temple excursion poems found in this collection. This struggle entailed coming to terms with not only Buddhist notions about human aging, decline, and the ultimate vanity of human endeavors, but also the seeming inevitability of continued conflict, a fear that in subsequent decades would prove to have been justified.

▨ Poem on Strawberries
His Lordship Fujiwara no Tadamichi, Lay Priest of Hosshōji

When summer comes, we love the strawberries more than anything else.
Nothing quite so captures our fancy—our pleasure knows no bounds.
A taste just like the golden peony, deliciousness fills our mouths.
A color unlike the green of the plant, simply the purest red.
Myriad dots like precious pearls, on the ground beside the hedge;
Brazier embers, glowing but cold, piled up in a bowl.
As we pour the wine, recite our verse, sing, and dance about,
These brimming heaps of wondrous fruit will naturally dispel our cares!

SOURCE: HCMDS 44, in Honma Yōichi, annot., *Honchō mudaishi zenchūshaku*, Shintensha chūshaku sōsho, 2, vol. 1 of 3 vols. (Tokyo: Shintensha, 1992), pp. 102–3; octave (heptasyllabic).
TITLE: Strawberries: here, literally "inverted bowls," owing to their shape.
LINE 3: The golden peony was used in Daoist elixirs to promote longevity.

▨ When the Pheasant Encounters a Hawk
His Lordship Fujiwara no Tadamichi, Lay Priest of Hosshōji

The pheasant's thoughts on meeting the hawk we're somehow able to gauge:
It is sure to be panicked and terrified, all tranquility gone.
Furtively hiding in the wild moors, but the springtime grass is short;
Alarmed, winging into the sky, but at dusk there are no clouds.
Yesterday, the pheasant frolicked about in the ancient swamps.
Today, the bird has been made into soup, adding flavor to the banquet.

Roosting alone on its solitary nest, turning its head to listen:
With all those bells ringing left and right, where can the pheasant go?

SOURCE: HCMDS 69, in *Honchō mudaishi zenchūshaku*, vol. 1, pp. 175–77; octave (heptasyllabic).
LINE 8: The bells were around the necks of the hawks, which were used to hunt birds.

Poem About a Rat
Fujiwara no Atsumitsu

Look at the rat—it has no teeth, has nothing but its skin.
Burrows through the hedge, then races off—what's it trying to do?
On cloudless days with kites above, the rat is deeply afraid.
When the lamp is dark and the cat's about, it stands to lose its life.
The rat is like a disgraced official, sense of shame forgotten;
Like someone greedy for a salary, all his dignity lost.
Were the rat to receive the virtuous guidance of Duke Wen of Wei,
The Duke would judge him lacking in talent, conduct remiss as well.

SOURCE: HCMDS 75, in *Honchō mudaishi zenchūshaku*, vol. 1, pp. 188–90; octave (heptasyllabic).
LINE 1: This poem owes much to Ode 52 in *Shi jing*, titled "Seang Shoo" (Xiang shu, Look at a Rat), the first stanza of the James Legge translation reading, "Look at a rat—it has its skin; / But a man shall be without dignity of demeanour. / If a man have no dignity of demeanour, / What should he do but die?" See Legge, *The She King*, pp. 84–85.
LINE 7: Duke Wen was an enlightened ruler who lived during the Spring and Autumn period (722–468 B.C.). He was responsible for restoring the fortunes of the state of Wei and was loved by his people throughout his long and benevolent reign. Among his achievements were the reduction of taxes and the implementation of a fairer penal system.

The Puppeteers
His Lordship Fujiwara no Tadamichi, Lay Priest of Hosshōji

The puppeteers are always traveling, endlessly to and fro,
Over thousands of miles of countryside, always somewhere new.
Divining where to stop, and then singing alone, beneath the mountain moon.
Seek, you will find they have no fixed abode, in the rural mists of spring.
In their prime they were favored ladies, gay their lives in the capital;
In their twilight years, they sit at home in shabby, mugwort shacks.
Travelers and passers-by avert their gaze from afar,
On account of all that greying hair and those hopelessly wrinkled faces.

SOURCE: HCMDS 77, in *Honchō mudaishi zenchūshaku*, vol. 1, pp. 192–94; octave (heptasyllabic).

TITLE: The "puppeteers" (J. *kugutsushi* or *kairaishi*) were itinerant folk who lived on the fringes of society as virtual outcasts. The women practiced prostitution, and the men often worked as butchers.

❊ The Puppeteers
Fujiwara no Sanemitsu

How pathetic the puppeteers, with their sham cavorting about!
The joys and miseries of life in their world are shared by one and all.
They divine for themselves a place to live in the remotest countryside,
Voices and faces showing deeper ill will the older they become.
Traveling around, they almost forget the affairs of the everyday world;
Taking no part in regular work, these sojourners from afar.
Visitors with whom they mingle hems are hardly likely to stay—
At dawn these women will doubtless face the autumn wind alone.

SOURCE: HCMDS 78, in *Honchō mudaishi zenchūshaku*, vol. 1, pp. 194–96; octave (heptasyllabic).
TITLE: The various *Honchō mudaishi* editions we have consulted often provide a title only for the first poem in certain groups of poems on the same subject. For this reason, we have provisionally added the title "The Puppeteers" to this poem and the next one. We have followed this practice for other similar cases which follow, below.
LINE 7: "Mingle hems" means to have sexual relations.

❊ The Puppeteers
Nakahara no Hirotoshi

The puppeteers are totally lacking in manners and decorum.
Among them there are many women, as everybody knows.
The thatched eaves of their houses are close to the forests in the hills.
Always moving their bamboo huts; with the waterweed drifting along.
When people come to pay them a visit, secretly they are pleased.
Travelers who are passing by are peered at with curious eyes.
Their song is "The Broken Willow Branch," this is their stock in trade.
Their livelihood lies not in mulberry leaves—what crop do they sow?
Eyebrows curved like moth antennae, the wispy moon at dawn.
Temple hair charming as cicada wings, dark clouds hanging down.
Ardent pledges of undying love—what husbands and wives are these?
It is fate that after just one night suddenly they part.
In Tanba, the women who sell themselves care not how ugly they are.
  [I say this because the Tanba puppeteer womenfolk are all ugly.]

The well-known ones in Akasaka are whiskery around the mouth.

[Among the female puppeteers of Akasaka in Mikawa province, there are many with moustaches—we call them "whisker dames." Thus, this line.]

Slathering on the rouge and powder, trying hard to look bewitching;
Praying repeatedly to the gods that they'll become popular courtesans.

SOURCE: HCMDS 82, in *Honchō mudaishi zenchūshaku*, vol. 1, pp. 204–7; *pailü* (heptasyllabic), in sixteen lines.

LINE 7: This was a well-known traditional song of parting. The words for "willow" and "remain" were homophonous in Chinese (*liu*); thus, people seeing off a departing friend gave a broken willow branch as a symbolic expression of the wish that the traveler would not leave.

LINE 8: In other words, the "puppeteers," being itinerants, do not practice sericulture or follow any other agricultural pursuits.

LINE 13: Most of the former Tanba province falls into modern Kyoto-fu, the remainder, modern Hyōgo prefecture.

LINE 14: Akasaka was a settlement in Otowa-chō, in modern Aichi prefecture (ibid., p. 206).

❈ On Seeing a Woman Peddling Her Wares
His Lordship Fujiwara no Tadamichi, Lay Priest of Hosshōji

How pitiful, that tired woman in her tattered, worn-out clothes!
As the sun sets she wanders around, peddling her goods.
In front of the steps, she marks up the prices, glad for a chance to sit.
Beyond the gates, she cries out her wares, walks back and forth a while.
At the houses of the poor, no one at all pays her any heed;
At the homes of the rich, she is silent, yet they scramble to buy her things.
Autumn moons and spring flowers are antiquated themes.
The topic I chose on this occasion just piqued my poetic interest.

SOURCE: HCMDS 87, in *Honchō mudaishi zenchūshaku*, vol. 1, pp. 216–18; octave (heptasyllabic).

❈ On Seeing a Woman Selling Charcoal
Prince Sannomiya Sukehito

I learned upon inquiring that the woman selling charcoal
Makes her home in a distant place, away in the Ōhara hills.
Thinly clad, she descends a steep road, accompanied by a storm.
Night arrives, the air is cold; she returns with the moon ahead.
As the white snow falls, her voice seems loud in the alleys of the poor.
When autumn winds blow, she raises her prices, there in the shabby villages.
What she sells is normally sold by able-bodied men.
How moving the sight of this woman, with her head of greying hair!

SOURCE: HCMDS 88, in *Honchō mudaishi zenchūshaku*, vol. 1, pp. 218–20; octave (heptasyllabic).

⚜ An Impromptu Poem Written Under the Moon
Fujiwara no Tomofusa

The moon appears especially bright when the Eighth Month is here.
Every household is making plans for poetry-writing banquets.
At the third watch, I scoop cold water—it's as if I am piercing ice.
In the autumn garden I walk all night, seemingly treading on frost.
Old, I find myself moved by the scenery, shedding melancholy tears.
Alone, I stare at the cloudy sky, feeling deep nostalgia.
Indolent and wracked by illness, meager my share of glory.
Just my medicines and stone needles to see me through my days.

SOURCE: HCMDS 147, in *Honchō mudaishi zenchūshaku*, vol. 1, pp. 334–35; octave (heptasyllabic).
LINE 2: These events would likely be held on the night of the full moon.
LINE 3: That is, the moonlight on the surface of the water has the appearance of ice.
LINE 8: Stone needles (*ishibari*): a kind of Chinese acupuncture needle.

⚜ Treasuring the Last Days of Spring
Fujiwara no Sanenori

Third Month, spring is ending, heavy is my heart.
How long will it last, here in the palace where we treasure its final days?
Who could possibly make spring stay, now that it's almost passed?
Let us give ourselves over to poetry and wine before the season is gone.
If only I could follow my wishes and change the calendar around,
I would surely discard the other seasons, make the whole year spring.
But even if I lacquered and glued, I could not make the flowers stay,
And even if I strung up bird netting, how could I keep the birds?
Wild grasses, deep green, in the districts beyond the town;
City clouds, pale pink, in the skies at this hidden retreat.
Thus I say as I gaze at the sights from here at the Palace Archives:
Do not forget that I was once an immortal for a while!

SOURCE: HCMDS 226, in *Honchō mudaishi zenchūshaku*, vol. 1, pp. 502–4; *pailü* (heptasyllabic), in twelve lines.
LINE 10: "Hidden retreat" is more literally "grotto," normally denoting a place where immortals dwelt, far from the mundane world. Here it is probably a reference to some remote place within the palace precincts, maybe even the Archives.

✖ Two Poems on Summer
His Lordship Fujiwara no Tadamichi, Lay Priest of Hosshōji Temple

(No. 1)
To the east of the river, on the eastern side of town,
In this thatched cottage of three rooms, I do whatever I please.
Cool winds through my bamboo hut—mindless, forgetting the heat.
Nighttime moon by my pine window—it almost feels like autumn.
Throngs of people throughout the temple, praying to the Buddha.
Though crossing the Sea of Suffering, I have yet to reach the shore.
Whenever I see the mountain apes, I begin by asking this:
I wonder, are you aware that I'm the new master of this mountain?

SOURCE: HCMDS 249, in *Honchō mudaishi zenchūshaku*, vol. 1, pp. 554–56; octave (heptasyllabic).
LINE 5: "Throngs of people" is more literally "[people] as numerous as grains of sand in the Ganges River," an expression typically found in the context of popular Buddhist worship.
LINE 6: "Sea of Suffering," J. *kukai*, is a metaphor for the temporal world of transmigration. Reaching "the shore" means attaining Nirvana (enlightenment). Tadamichi, now retired to Hosshōji in the eastern hills of Kyoto, is meditating and undergoing ascetic training in the quest to reach enlightenment.

(No. 2)
The evening cool has found its way inside the robes I wear.
Wind in the eaves beside the pines, moon shining down on the steps.
The cares of the dusty world are gone, here where I live out my days.
A wandering mind so hard to restrain, a life of striving in vain.
I call myself a "worthless tree," dwelling in the mountains—
An old locust tree, generations old, here beside the gate.
My cliffside grotto lonely and desolate, no one comes to visit;
The old path to this place of meditation I allow to be buried by moss.

SOURCE: HCMDS 250, in *Honchō mudaishi zenchūshaku*, vol. 1, pp. 556–57; octave (heptasyllabic).
LINE 5: An allusion to passages in *Zhuangzi* containing discussions of various "worthless" trees, one being an overly large ailanthus, which has escaped being cut down for timber because of the worthlessness of its wood. Being of no use to human beings, the tree has naturally survived to live out its full span.
LINE 6: The locust (Japonica, also known as the pagoda tree) is a traditional Japanese symbol for a family lineage producing influential ministers. See *Honchō mudaishi zenchūshaku*, p. 557. The poet had served as regent and chancellor.

❄ An Impromptu Poem Written in Autumn
Fujiwara no Atsumitsu

As Master of the Right Capital Office, I have no freedom at all.
A public servant, I rarely succeed; my heart is full of cares.
The city gates have been destroyed, the land denuded and bare.
The roads have been turned into farmland, used for growing millet.
Officers bearing imperial edicts are harrying the people.
My own post lacks authority—the Police Chief fields complaints.
The poor folk in the capital bear officialdom's heavy brunt.
Lands allotted to the Kawachi people have been seized by the governor.
Food and clothing provided for the soldiers have almost all run out,
And wood for fixing bridges is becoming hard to find.
What makes me ashamed is that even though I am eighty years of age,
I remain in this post, half-heartedly, unable to retire.

SOURCE: HCMDS 280, in Honma Yōichi, annot., *Honchō mudaishi zenchūshaku*, vol. 2, Shin-tensha chūshaku sōsho, 4 (Tokyo: Shintensha, 1993), pp. 34–36; *pailü* (heptasyllabic), in twelve lines.
LINE 1: The Right and Left Capital Offices, each headed by two officials, exercised nominal authority in urban police affairs, also handling civil suits, household records, commercial matters, and tax collection, and bearing responsibility also for the maintenance of roads and bridges. In reality, by this time these offices had lost much of their authority to the Imperial Police and apparently existed largely in name only, the posts being virtual sinecures for old men in semi-retirement, like the author of this poem.
LINE 8: Kawachi province corresponds to the eastern part of modern Ōsaka-fu. Governors were not the only ones who sometimes confiscated peasant fields. Honma Yōichi writes that officials from the Capital Offices could also seize rice fields allotted to local families if the local governor failed to submit the requisite tax and census information as reported by the householders. See ibid., p. 36.
COMMENT: Honma calculates that Atsumitsu most likely wrote this poem in the autumn of 1142 (ibid.). Some four years earlier, on 1138/3/5, a massive fire started by rampaging monks from Enryakuji had destroyed a large part of Heian.

❄ An Impromptu Poem Written in Autumn
Fujiwara no Michinori

Bustling and busy the workaday world—how could one be lazy?
Oh, to take a thousand in gold and buy a little peace!
Friends close by, conversing, chatting; hearts open, clear as water.
For eluding fame and pleasing oneself, nothing beats the mountains.
Vast and limitless, life's vexations—a million connections and ties.
A career filled with rejection and failure, fleeting as a dream.
I recall the trick that Chen Zun used to make his guests remain:
He'd throw their linchpins into the well, so they wouldn't leave for a while.

SOURCE: HCMDS 290, in *Honchō mudaishi zenchūshaku*, vol. 2, pp. 57–58; octave (heptasyllabic).
LINE 7: Chen Zun (d. 25) was a high official and bon vivant renowned for his wild drinking and conviviality. When guests visited him, he had the linchpins of their carriage wheels removed to prevent them from leaving.

�֍ Thoughts on an Autumn Night, Shown to His Lordship the Ex-Officio Assistant Captain of the Military Guards
Fujiwara no Mototoshi

The autumn night stretches on and on, longer than a year.
Feeling anxious, lost in worry, collar soaked with tears.
Moon obscured, lamp burns dimly, dawn is not yet here.
Many cares and little sleep, the night has far to go.
Gazing ahead at the path to glory, my view is blocked by clouds;
I weep to think of the rest of my days, raindrops fall in my heart.
All the things I've experienced in this life of thirty-nine years—
I assess and ponder them, one by one, and sadly write poems alone.

SOURCE: HCMDS 299, in *Honchō mudaishi zenchūshaku*, vol. 2, pp. 74–76; octave (heptasyllabic).
TITLE: The assistant captain has not been identified.

�֍ An Impromptu Poem Written in Late Autumn
Nakahara no Hirotoshi

Unbearable to see the scenery in this state of ragged decay.
Beneath the bed crickets chirp in the dark, moonlight fills the yard.
Pines and cypresses all year long retain their bushy appearance.
Yet the dryandras grow more shabby and bare with every passing day.
Multitudes of flowering reeds embrace the autumn snow.
Numerous clumps of chrysanthemums capture the starlight of the dawn.
Although I am fifty years of age, do not deride me, please!
Nothing accomplished, I feel chagrined that I'm growing old and feeble.

SOURCE: HCMDS 305, in *Honchō mudaishi zenchūshaku*, vol. 2, pp. 88–90; octave (heptasyllabic).
LINE 4: The dryandra, Ch. *wutong* (J. *aogiri*), is also known as the Chinese parasol tree.
LINE 5: This "snow" is probably the white fluffy seeds of the reeds.
LINE 7: Hirotoshi was born in 1062, so this verse was written around 1111.

�֍ Written While Alone During the Final Hours of the Night
Fujiwara no Atsumitsu

(No. 1)
When the Great Exorcism ceremony ended it was already late at night.
No use begrudging the time that has flown in the year just gone by.
I remain awake in my humble dwelling—everyone else is asleep—
Quietly thinking about the past, by the lamp's remaining light.

SOURCE: HCMDS 336, in *Honchō mudaishi zenchūshaku*, vol. 2, pp. 155–56; quatrain (heptasyllabic).
TITLE: This is a series of three poems, all with the same title.
LINE 1: Originating in China, the Great Exorcism (J. *taina*) was directed at expelling *oni* (evil spirits) and averting epidemics. Judging from contemporaneous historical references, the ceremony usually took place in the Twelfth Month.

(No. 2)
Tonight, the thirtieth year of my life is drawing to a close.
Ruminating about my past makes me feel unsettled.
Lazy by nature, lacking talent, and holding a lowly rank,
I feel ashamed that in my life I have never achieved a thing.

SOURCE: HCMDS 337, in *Honchō mudaishi zenchūshaku*, vol. 2, p. 157; quatrain (heptasyllabic)

(No. 3)
My aged mother lives at home, is in her seventies now.
Joy gives way to deep concern; she is always on my mind.
The calabash is often empty—no salary at all.
How painful that I have trouble keeping her fed with pulse and water.

SOURCE: HCMDS 338, in *Honchō mudaishi zenchūshaku*, vol. 2, p. 158; quatrain (heptasyllabic)
LINE 1: Atsumitsu's mother was the daughter of Taira no Saneshige, Governor of Awa.
LINE 4: Pulse: a variety of legume. The phrase "pulse and water" is a conventional expression from *Lun yu*, denoting the humblest of food.

✖ Thoughts Beside the Brazier
Koremune no Noritoki

I've left my modest dwelling behind to attend a lavish feast.
Warm it feels by the red brazier—for a while I forget it is winter.
Rashly displaying my own poor poems in the lamplight with the others;
Quietly competing with my humble verse, this snowy day in the pines.
White-haired, in my final years, I'm ashamed of my crane-like hair.
Red-robed, in a lowly post, I sigh, losing heart.

This futile life is slipping away—a man with no achievements.
Slow and irresolute in all affairs, by fortune never blessed.

SOURCE: HCMDS 349, in *Honchō mudaishi zenchūshaku*, vol. 2, pp. 182–83; octave (heptasyllabic).
LINE 6: Court protocol specified that fourth-rank holders wore dark red, fifth-rank holders (one rank lower), light red. It is unclear which of the two ranks the poet was holding at this time.

An Impromptu Poem Written at a Pondside Pavilion on an Autumn Day
Prince Sannomiya Sukehito

We've come in search of the rare and unusual; cold and cheerless the scene.
Pausing beside a pondside pavilion, a remote and distant place.
Years come and years go, pines cover the banks.
North of the river, south of the river, lotuses brighten the ripples.
A quiet spot with trees by water; people seldom come.
Sunset at the herbal garden; birds fly about in profusion.
Surely it's more than the lonely bleakness of autumn that saddens my heart.
There is also the song that fills my ears—accompanied by a flute.

SOURCE: HCMDS 372, in *Honchō mudaishi zenchūshaku*, vol. 2, pp. 232–33; octave (heptasyllabic).

On a Summer Day Going North of the City to My Villa
Fujiwara no Chikamitsu

A place with peerless scenery, a villa hidden away.
From here, I stare off into the distance on this summer day.
Peaceful, so I naturally cease to think of worldly affairs.
Feeling inspired, I jot down poems whenever the fancy takes me.
Like fine autumn hair, the distant trees surrounding the outskirts of town.
Sunbeams shine on the clear hills, right before my eyes.
I roam around at night in the darkness, muttering to myself.
For a while, the lurking fish has escaped the bamboo trap in the water.

SOURCE: HCMDS 429, in *Honchō mudaishi zenchūshaku*, vol. 2, pp. 363–64; octave (heptasyllabic).
LINE 8: The fish is the poet himself, temporarily free of the responsibilities of court life.

❈ Autumn Thoughts at a Mountain Home
Nakahara no Hirotoshi

Now that autumn has arrived, there is pleasure in abundance.
I pay a visit to my mountain home, a trip to a peaceful place.
The hedge is all embroidered with red, now that the flowers have bloomed.
The reed blinds are all rolled up; the newly risen moon.
My unkempt hair is growing thin, cold the autumn snow.
My garments of plantain fiber are shabby, fitful the evening wind.
Although I'm acquainted with drunkenness and the happiness it brings,
I cannot forget that in this hovel I have nothing put aside.

SOURCE: HCMDS 452, in *Honchō mudaishi zenchūshaku*, vol. 2, pp. 408–9; octave (heptasyllabic).

❈ At a Mountain Home on a Spring Day, Gazing Afar
Fujiwara no Chikamitsu

Twilight years, autumnal hair, a man now down in the world.
Drawn by the scenery, I linger here, glumly staring afar.
The mist above the hills has parted—I spot the woodcutters' path.
On the southern road the petals fly—glimpsed through meadow mist.
Thoughts of my livelihood disappear once day breaks above the clouds.
Spring melancholy I banish from my heart when the sun sets in the west.
Since fortune has not smiled on me, and I'm tired of the company of others,
I am heading off for the woods and hills, where I'll spend my final years.

SOURCE: HCMDS 454, in *Honchō mudaishi zenchūshaku*, vol. 2, pp. 411–13; octave (heptasyllabic).

❈ At a Mountain Home on an Autumn Day, Gazing Afar
Nakahara no Hirotoshi

Quiet and lonely my mountain home; on a whim I take a walk.
Sights I see as I stare afar bring feelings hard to bear.
A solitary crane, quite used to these woods, I consider as my friend.
A migrating goose flies past the peaks, leading his brothers along.
By my house that faces maple cliffs frosty leaves dot the ground;
Through the window at my cassia retreat shine the clear rays of the moon.
I feel such shame, looking back on this life of trouble and frustration:
Already more than fifty years old and known as a worthless failure.

SOURCE: HCMDS 457, in *Honchō mudaishi zenchūshaku*, vol. 2, pp. 417–19; octave (heptasyllabic).
LINE 8: Hirotoshi (1062–?) turned fifty in the year 1111, so he wrote this poem sometime thereafter. See HCMDS 305, above. At the time, he had a rank but no post. In a poem written that same year (1111) and recorded in *Chūyūki burui shihai kanshishū*, Hirotoshi mentions that he has been nine years without an appointment. See *Honchō mudaishi zenchūshaku*, vol. 2, p. 418.

✠ At a Farmhouse on an Autumn Day, Gazing Afar
Sugawara no Ariyoshi

What place is this I am visiting, this place worth roaming around?
I stare afar, toward the farmlands, lost in deep reflection.
The setting sun shines on the pine trees growing on the peaks;
A distant river flows through a grove of trees in someone's garden.
A scholar, I am alone and poor, and though many years have passed,
My labors with the brush are slow to bear fruit, no sign of autumn yet.
Do not scorn me if my life as a poet is a lonely, solitary one—
Poetry is the treasure bequeathed by my forebears from many ages past.

SOURCE: HCMDS 461, in *Honchō mudaishi zenchūshaku*, vol. 2, pp. 425–26; octave (heptasyllabic).

✠ Three Poems Written at a Traveler's Inn
Fujiwara no Chikamitsu

(No. 1)
At the government office, to welcome spring we have many days off work.
Mild breezes in these parts blowing much more often.
A spot as far from the capital as Hu is far from Yue—
Like the land of the coastal barbarians, where they speak an alien tongue.
The cold has gone, but snow remains atop the mountain range.
The weather is clear, but distant trees are piercing through the mist.
The season has changed, and overhead the spring sun gently shines.
How will I take any notice of my family, once the flowers are in bloom?

SOURCE: HCMDS 472, in *Honchō mudaishi zenchūshaku*, vol. 2, pp. 450–51; octave (heptasyllabic).
LINE 3: Hu and Yue were regions in China's northern and southern extremes, respectively. Where Chikamitsu was serving as an official at this time is uncertain.
COMMENT: The rhyme words in the even-numbered lines are identical in all three poems in this series.

(No. 2)

Whenever I travel, I always find my emotions arise in profusion,
Especially now that I'm old and worn, my sense of ennui growing.
Shady forest, breezes mild; I hear the warblers call.
Mountain vista, snow has cleared; I gaze at the tiger-tooth peaks.
In the world of scholars, who would ever mock the evening moon?
In the land of drunkenness, where might I go to imbibe the springtime mist?
Though I drink and write poems to my heart's content exactly when I please,
I still recall the capital, with its inns of wine and verse.

SOURCE: HCMDS 473, in *Honchō mudaishi zenchūshaku*, vol. 2, pp. 452–53; octave (heptasyllabic).

(No. 3)

A single curtain rolled up high; so much to see this evening.
Since morning I've sat here, legs outstretched, my sense of joy increasing.
Off in the wilds the clouds hide the sun, slanting rain pours down.
Riverside reeds push through the sand, young shoots bursting forth.
The stabled horse neighs in the distance, off on the grassy frontier.
The caged bird, suddenly free, seeks the mist of distant hills.
Even though I've come down in the world, no fetters bind me now.
Roaming free, I have long forgotten those houses of wealth and glory.

SOURCE: HCMDS 474, in *Honchō mudaishi zenchūshaku*, vol. 2, pp. 453–55; octave (heptasyllabic).

▨ Spring Journey by Boat
Priest Renzen

I let myself journey afar by boat, making the most of spring.
A voyage over vast and boundless waters—tiring after so many days.
Trees in blossom on distant hills; we stop our poling to look.
Trailing willows grow on the bank, brushing the sides of the boat.
The sunlit sails follow the wind along the clear watercourse.
The horses make their way through the dew on the green and grassy banks.
In my home village the farming season has already begun.
Is it ever too late to go back home? Let's be on our way!

SOURCE: HCMDS 478, in *Honchō mudaishi zenchūshaku*, vol. 2, pp. 460–62; octave (heptasyllabic).
COMMENT: This poem and others following were composed by Renzen and his friend Fujiwara no Chikamitsu while on a journey by boat. Renzen appears to have spent close to two years, ca. 1143–44, traveling from port to port in northern Kyushu, finally returning to Heian. He was possibly in the company of Chikamitsu for the entire period. For a detailed treatment of the

dating of this journey, see Satō Michio, "Shaku Renzen to Fujiwara no Chikamitsu no kikō shōwa shi no seiritsu jiki ni tsuite," in *Mita kokubun* 1 (1983): 13–20 (cited in *Honchō mudaishi zenchūshaku*, vol. 2, p. 488).

✖ An Impromptu Poem Written While Staying at Uwara in Sesshū During My Journey
Priest Renzen

At the foot of a mountain near the coast, here for a visit.
Remaining for a month or more, accompanied by friends.
Autumn mist enshrouds a line of wild geese in flight.
Nights, the noise of the incoming tide reaches the traveler's hut.
Outside, ears of growing rice, their sweet scent on the wind;
In the shade of the fence persimmon leaves rustle like scattered showers.
"May I ask you local folk, what work is it you do?"
"Our livelihood consists of catching fish here in the bay."

SOURCE: HCMDS 481, in *Honchō mudaishi zenchūshaku*, vol. 2, pp. 466–67; octave (heptasyllabic).
TITLE: Uwara was a seaside district extending along the southern foothills of Mt. Rokkō, in what are now the wards of Ashiya and Higashi in Kōbe (ibid., p. 466).

✖ Moving from My Seaside Lodgings to the House of a Local Resident
Priest Renzen

Green moss on white rocks, a side road steeply rising.
Walking, walking, enjoying the spring, my view at times obscured.
Peasants laughing aloud as they ply their boats along the canal;
The traveler wandering all around, enjoying the hillside flowers.
A drink of wine in the countryside, the taste of it so fine.
A journey by sea of a thousand *li*, as distant as the clouds.
Jie Yu was a crazy man, but I am crazy too.
After I'm back in the Kansai region my feelings of regret will mount.

SOURCE: HCMDS 484, in *Honchō mudaishi zenchūshaku*, vol. 2, pp. 471–72; octave (heptasyllabic).
TITLE: The commentator suggests that the move may have been made on account of a directional taboo.
LINE 7: In poem 498, Renzen writes of pretending to be mad. Jie Yu (Lu Tong), who lived in the Spring and Autumn period, was a famous recluse from the state of Chu, referred to in *Lun yu*. He feigned madness in order to escape the demands of public service and tried to persuade Confucius to cease his attempts to reform the world. See Legge, trans., *Confucius: Confucian Analects, The Great Learning, and The Doctrine of the Mean*, pp. 332–33.
LINE 8: Kansai consisted of the western provinces surrounding the region of the capital, Heian.

✠ Moving from My Seaside Lodgings to the House of a Local Resident
Fujiwara no Chikamitsu

Whipping our nags, riding on and on until the sun goes down.
Riverside village, low and damp, willows enshrouded in mist.
Compassionate the moon by the mountains, escorting me on my way.
Wordlessly they make me tarry, the blossoms on the winding bank.
Water in a dam flowing at night interrupts my dream of returning.
Springtime scene in the countryside, smoke and fire in distant fields.
I happened to meet some farmers today and quietly we conversed;
As I asked about the local conditions, my feelings for them deepened.

SOURCE: HCMDS 485, in *Honchō mudaishi zenchūshaku*, vol. 2, pp. 473–74; octave (heptasyllabic).

✠ A Poem on Sights I Saw in Kashiinomiya
Priest Renzen

The last ten days of the Second Month, during the season of spring.
Staying awhile at a guest house, though it hadn't been my plan.
A red mist obscuring the sun beyond the mountain village;
White egrets watching for fish, right beside the bay.
My servant slices the *mochi* that was kindly given to me.
  [Disciples from a distant district presented me with *mochi*.]
To local folk who came peddling salt I expound on the Buddha's word.
  [Salt-peddlers came to the door and asked jokingly about doctrinal matters. I responded in detail.]
Ancient Chinese reeds on the banks—does spring dew ever cover them?
  [On the ancient banks grow clumps of reeds. The local elders say they were planted long ago and never wither at any time of the year.]
A hedge of wild bamboo from Wu, veiled in dusky haze.
  [Alongside the official residence there is a *mou* of bamboo growing.]
Old fishermen leave their boats and go to the shop for wine.
Kitchen hands head for their stoves, carrying firewood to burn.
Somehow it came over me to gain karmic merit today,
So I went to a nearby temple and made an offering to the Buddha.

SOURCE: HCMDS 486, in *Honchō mudaishi zenchūshaku*, vol. 2, pp. 474–77; *pailü* (heptasyllabic), in twelve lines.
TITLE: Kashiinomiya, located in modern Fukuoka city in Kyushu, was once the site of a country retreat used during imperial journeys. Following the sudden death of Emperor Chūai (who putatively reigned during the third century) at this spot, the retreat was made into a Shinto shrine.
LINE 5: *Mochi* is a kind of dumpling formed from steamed glutinous rice.

POET'S NOTE TO LINE 8: The land measurement *mou* (J. *ho*) varied over time, but it was roughly a seventh of an acre.

◼ Expressing My Thoughts, Having Arrived at Aenoshima
Priest Renzen

If you ask where I've stayed since yesterday, Aenoshima is the place.
    [This is the name of a harbor.]
Blue coastline stretching afar, without a trace of beach.
The ferry did not leave at dawn, for the wind was from the east.
No food at all was served to us till midday had arrived.
    [I was praying until the meal was served to us at midday.]
Willows on the bank met with rain, their catkins quickly lost.
Wheat in the fields awaits the autumn, the grain is slow to grow.
    [The people on this island do not grow rice, many planting wheat instead. The grain ripens in midsummer, which here is like autumn.]
Don't laugh at me if I return to the capital in an impoverished state—
The beautiful scenery of spring itself will enrich me as I travel.

SOURCE: HCMDS 490, in *Honchō mudaishi zenchūshaku*, vol. 2, pp. 483–84; octave (heptasyllabic).
TITLE: Aenoshima is probably the island now known as Ainoshima (a corruption of the original A[w]enoshima), off the coast of Kasuya district in modern Fukuoka prefecture, northern Kyushu. Ainoshima has a sheer coastline and a safe moorage on the south side.

◼ Spending the Night at the Harbor in Ashiya
Priest Renzen

A distant journey over water, sad and vexed my heart.
I stayed here yesterday, also today, cursing the winds of spring.
Warblers call as they fly through the grove beneath the remaining blossoms.
Seagulls sleep upon the peaks in the light of the sinking moon.
Past events are hard to forget—tears fall onto my sleeves;
My uncertain life spins on and on—a dream on a drifting boat.
I pity myself, laugh at myself, as I wet my brush to write.
This is the third occasion that I have visited this place.

SOURCE: HCMDS 492, in *Honchō mudaishi zenchūshaku*, vol. 2, pp. 486–88; octave (heptasyllabic).
TITLE: Ashiya was a village on the Onga River in the district of Oka, Chikuzen province (modern Fukuoka prefecture).
LINE 8: For more on Renzen's association with Ashiya, see poem 499, below.

✠ An Impromptu Poem Written at the Port of Murozumi
Priest Renzen

The boat travels toward the east, drifting along with the current.
This ford, that harbor—famous places all.
In a temple on the hazy outskirts, priests reciting scriptures;
> [In a rustic temple priests recite the *Lotus Sutra*.]

Before a shrine in the port, a shaman divining for a fee.
> [In this port there is an ancient shrine called Hachiman Betsugū. The old shaman living there beats a drum and performs divinations for a fee. Sailors who come and go inquire about the safety of their journeys, paying with grain.]

The tide ebbs past the pines at dusk; vast waters, deep and clear.
Into the peaks the dawn moon sinks, precarious and pale.
Such a shame that catching fish is a serious karmic offense,
But the myriad creatures of the sea must be supplied as tribute.

SOURCE: HCMDS 496, in *Honchō mudaishi zenchūshaku*, vol. 2, pp. 494–96; octave (heptasyllabic).
TITLE: Murozumi village, in old Suō (Suwa) province, is in the modern city of Hikari in Yamaguchi prefecture, western Honshu.

✠ An Impromptu Poem Written at the Port of Murozumi
Fujiwara no Chikamitsu

Long and distant the journey home, so very far indeed.
I've truly grasped that town and country are totally different places.
Low clouds that come and go—the only companions we have.
Safe or not to cross the sea?—in the shaman we place no faith.
Look out at the billowing waves so perilously high:
They're nothing compared to the road through life, so hazardously steep.
At a quiet spot by a seaside village I ask an aged fisherman:
"May I ask you, how much tax do the people pay on their fields?"

SOURCE: HCMDS 497, in *Honchō mudaishi zenchūshaku*, vol. 2, pp. 496–98; octave (heptasyllabic).
LINE 4: Regarding the shaman, see line four in the previous poem.

✠ Expressing My Feelings at the Ferry Crossing
Priest Renzen

Autumn went and now is back, my days all spent in travel.
We suddenly board a boat in the harbor, heading back for home.

Low eaves near noisy waves—the houses in this solitary village.

[Here, the homes are all right next to the harbor.]

A thin column of smoke rises from the stove upon the boat.
A porthole lets the moonlight in—I leave it open wide.
The old trees beside the bay are thin and withered but strong.
Feigning madness, I journey now toward the Kansai region.
Numerous the regrets I have—thousands upon thousands.

SOURCE: HCMDS 498, in *Honchō mudaishi zenchūshaku*, vol. 2, pp. 498–99; octave (heptasyllabic).

LINE 7: On the notion of Renzen's "madness," see also poem 484, above.

My Feelings Upon Arriving at Ashiya Ford

Priest Renzen

Moonlit beach, breezy banks, autumn shimmering white.
Naturally, this traveler keeps his feelings to himself.
Seeking moorings, boats are gathered up and down the river.
On both banks houses are clustered, to the east and to the south.

[There are two villages, one on either bank, and the houses are lined up next to one another.]

The custom here is to start each morning selling vegetables.

[The local folk sell cucumbers and eggplants.]

Fishing continues into the night—how many pine torches burn!
Once again I've come to this place, though it hadn't been my plan.
I recall the past and suddenly the tears roll down my face.

[Once I stayed here with my foster father and now I have returned, thus this line.]

SOURCE: HCMDS 499, in *Honchō mudaishi zenchūshaku*, vol. 2, pp. 500–501; octave (heptasyllabic).

TITLE: For Ashiya's location, see poem 492, above.

LINE 4: There were two settlements on this harbor, one called Ashiya, the other Yamashika. Today both are within the city of Ashiya.

POET'S NOTE TO LINE 8: Scholars have tentatively identified the foster father as Fujiwara no Motozane (1045–1108), who in 12/1105 was appointed governor of Chikuzen. Renzen went with Motozane to Chikuzen, when the latter took up his post the following year, and he remained there until Motozane's death some three years later. The second visit apparently occurred in 1127/1, when Renzen's elder brother Kin'akira (1080?–1133?) himself became governor of Chikuzen. Renzen's third trip to northern Kyushu, the occasion for this sequence of poems, was made with Fujiwara no Chikamitsu, probably in 1143–44.

A Poem Written While Passing Yamashika no Misaki
Priest Renzen

Dense, heavy clouds hang over the sea; I gaze to my heart's content.
I shall not journey afar in search of the famous isle of Peng.
The tide encroaches upon the beach, exposing the roots of the pines.
Huts guard the mountain fields with their ears of autumn grain.
[I stare into the distance and see hills and rivers. There are fields everywhere. The rice is ripe, and there are huts manned by guards.]
Now that I'm old, how can I stand to go traveling here and there?
When the sky is clear I look at the boats—to and fro, one then another.
I've come back to my native village but wear no fancy clothes.
Old friends, please don't laugh at my poor and miserable state.

SOURCE: HCMDS 500, in *Honchō mudaishi zenchūshaku*, vol. 2, pp. 501–3; octave (heptasyllabic).
TITLE: Yamashika no Misaki, the promontory at Yamasaki (known today as Iwayasaki), was on the seacoast, in the modern city of Ashiya, Fukuoka prefecture.
LINE 2: Peng is a reference to the mythical island of Penglai, supposedly located in the Eastern Sea and said to be a place of great beauty inhabited by immortals.
LINE 7: On Renzen's special ties to the Chikuzen area (modern Fukuoka prefecture), which he seems to have considered his spiritual home, see the notes to the preceding poem. Returning to one's native place without wearing fancy clothes harks back to a comment made by the famous general Xiang Yu (third century B.C.). He is quoted in his biography in *Shi ji* as saying, "To not return to one's home district after becoming wealthy and noble is like dressing up in fine clothes and walking around at night."

An Impromptu Poem Written Upon Arriving at Dannoura in Nagato Province
Priest Renzen

From port to port for ten days straight and still we float at sea.
But amidst my gloom, moments of interest; I capture them in verse.
To block out the sun a nearby boat has rigged an awning of hemp.
[One kind of boat is like a small bowl. Using loosely woven cloth, they've put in place a single drape to block out the morning sun and keep away the lingering heat. I mention this as a point of interest.]
At a village shrine they pray for wind, make offerings of mulberry cloth.
[On a distant shore there is a shrine called Ninomiya. People pray to it from afar on their boats. Messengers are sent to the shrine, and soon thereafter prayers for favorable winds are offered.]
Nights, I think of my distant hometown; only then do I sleep.
Clear days—I gaze at that lone island smaller than my fist.
I once went searching in the Saifu area, hoping to find hot springs,
And there I stayed for two years, in order to cure my ills.

SOURCE: HCMDS 502, in *Honchō mudaishi zenchūshaku*, vol. 2, pp. 505–6; octave (heptasyllabic).
LINE 6: This island is unidentified.
LINE 7: Saifu, i.e., Dazaifu, was a town in Chikuzen province. It was the center of government and military administration in Kyushu from around the sixth century. Sugawara no Michizane spent his final years here, in exile. A late eighteenth-century hot spring handbook states that the hot springs alluded to in this poem were those located at Musashi, known today as the Futsukaichi Hot Springs, in the city of Chikushino, in Fukuoka prefecture (ibid., p. 506).

⌘ A Humorous Poem About Life on the Boat, Written While Moored at Port

Priest Renzen

All quiet here on the boat, I lie with my head on my arms.
Everything I see and hear so hard to put into words.
The cook secretly sneers at me as she boils my nighttime medicine.
[My chronic illness has flared up again, so I have been taking a boiled congee made of Job's tears. The house servants are unsympathetic: there is a certain old woman who claps her hands and is particularly derisive.]
All the boatmen feel upset, for at breakfast there's not enough food.
[The boatmen say there are too few people to do the cooking, so they are angry.]
My two sutra volumes I put in a bag, and then I hang it up;
[These are the "Chapter on Daiba (Devadatta)" and the "Chapter on Kannon (Avalokiteśvara)." Over the years, I have had them with me for recitation. I placed them in my scripture bag and then hung it up.]
I sweep the stern, then put in place my portable Buddhist altar.
[In this altar there are two Buddhist statues, which I carry around with me.]
I seek no riches anywhere, keeping just a worn-out broom.
[I have been using this straw broom to sweep the dust from the boat.]
During our journey the grain has run out; the basket sits there empty.
The wind fills our sails as we travel along, clear skies into the distance.
At every port I long for home; the autumn is suddenly cold.
Surely those two sons of mine are laughing at their father:
"Whatever possessed him to journey afar, over the Western Sea?"

SOURCE: HCMDS 506, in *Honchō mudaishi zenchūshaku*, vol. 2, pp. 512–15; *pailü* (heptasyllabic), in twelve lines.
POET'S NOTE TO LINE 3: "Job's tears," *Coix lacryma-jobi* (Ch. *yiyiren*, J. *yokuinin* or *hatomugi*). A maize-like grain from a plant that reaches four to six feet in height, it was taken as a herbal medicine in the form of a gruel or congee made from the hulled seeds. *Coix* was considered useful in reducing fluid retention and arthritis inflammation, relieving fever and pain, alleviating urinary and pulmonary disorders, and treating boils caused by parasites. The nature of Renzen's "chronic illness" is unclear. The curious hand clapping mentioned in this note appears to be a sign of contempt or exasperation.
POET'S NOTE TO LINE 5: "Chapter on Devadatta" (Daibadatta-bon or Daiba-bon) is the title of the twelfth section of the *Lotus Sutra*. It describes the attempt made by Devadatta, a cousin of Śākyamuni and a follower of his teachings, to take control of the Buddhist order and kill the Buddha. The "Chapter on Kannon," also found in the *Lotus Sutra*, was the short, popular name

for the "Chapter on the Universal Gate of the Bodhisattva Avalokiteśvara" (Kanzeon bosatsu fumon-bon).

POET'S NOTE TO LINE 6: Buddhist altar: a small wooden box with a pair of doors on the front, used for housing an icon and for holding offerings. The two images installed in Renzen's altar were likely those of Amida and Kannon (*Honchō mudaishi zenchūshaku*, vol. 2, p. 514).

LINE 11: The annotator conjectures that these two boys were actually the sons of Renzen's older brother, Kin'akira (ibid.)

❋ A Melancholy Poem Written After Arriving in Hajikaminotomari
Priest Renzen

I can hardly bear to bid farewell to autumn on this journey.
Looking left, then gazing right, deeply moved by the scene.
Migrating geese, flying south, call from within the mist.
The traveler's boat is heading east, to the sound of the blowing wind.
As night descends in the coastal village, the new moon pays a visit.
When will I see my old friends in the capital again?
Fragile beings, we cannot tell if we'll perish or survive.
Half-heartedly I write this poem through tears, for posterity's sake.

SOURCE: HCMDS 508, in *Honchō mudaishi zenchūshaku*, vol. 2, pp. 517–18; octave (heptasyllabic).

TITLE: The exact location of the port of Hajikaminotomari is not known. It was somewhere in the province of Suō (Suwa), in Yamaguchi prefecture, near the southern tip of Honshū. Hajikaminotomari is a provisional reading suggested by the Yamaguchi prefectural archivist, Mr. Yamada Minoru, whom we consulted concerning this place-name. His assistance is gratefully acknowledged.

❋ Expressing My Thoughts After Arriving at Akasaki in Aki Province
Priest Renzen

A sandy road stretching on and on, misty and indistinct.
Our craft floated on, going wherever the old singing boatman took us.
Lingering moon over Shiroishi, above the waves at dawn.
    [Shiroishi is the name of a ferry crossing on the border of Suwa province. We passed it this morning.]
Setting sun at Akasaki, the harbor touched by autumn.
    [Akasaki is the name of a port in Aki. This evening we are staying here.]
A view like the marsh at Chumeng, eight or nine vistas in all.
Mountains like those in Wuxing as I gaze both east and west.
Reeds growing by the distant bay, looking just like snow.
A wind pierces my reed hut as I lie down to sleep.
Sharp cries I have long repressed, like the ailing crane.
The traveler's feelings tense and rushed, at one with the migrating goose.

Although I've returned to my old hometown, I have no status at all.
My relatives all dislike me because I'm lowly and I'm poor.

SOURCE: HCMDS 509, in *Honchō mudaishi zenchūshaku*, vol. 2, pp. 518–21; *pailü* (heptasyllabic), in twelve lines.
TITLE: Akasaki (in modern Hiroshima prefecture) probably corresponds to the settlement by the same name in the town of Ōno in Saeki district. See ibid., p. 519.
LINE 5: This marsh, more commonly known as Yunmeng, is actually a vast area of lakes and marshes located in the Hunan-Hubei region of China. References to it typically include the numerical phrase "eight or nine," an allusion to a line in the famous *fu* by Sima Xiangru titled "Shanglin Park," which reads, "Anyone able to swallow eight or nine [swamps] like Yunmeng and hold them in his chest could never hold a grudge."
LINE 6: Wuxing: a county in Zhejiang province, China.
LINE 9: "Ailing crane" derives from Bo Juyi's poem "Looking at an Ailing Crane While I Am Ill."

A Poem on What I Saw While Staying at Michikuchi no Tsu
Priest Renzen

Past many hills, down rivers aplenty, journeying on and on.
The landscape so bleak and dismal I cannot bear to look.
Clear view of mountains, a curtain of peaks where birds come and go.
Autumn tribute in the seaside village, a bounty of fish and salt.
The moon follows the homing boat on its long and distant voyage.
Smoke rises from the stove on the boat in a narrow, wispy plume.
The floating clouds and I possess no place that we call home;
I grieve for myself, laugh at myself, as the tears wet my clothes.

SOURCE: HCMDS 510, in *Honchō mudaishi zenchūshaku*, vol. 2, pp. 521–22; octave (heptasyllabic).
TITLE: Michikuchi no Tsu (Michikuchi Harbor) may be the same place as Mitsukuchi in Yasura-chō in Toyoda district, modern Hiroshima prefecture (ibid., p. 521).

A Poem Written Early in the Day While Passing Through Kōnoura
Priest Renzen

Ever since leaving the Kansai region so much time has passed.
Myriad willows, blue sea, and this tiny reed-like boat.
I stare ahead into the distance—just the moon above the bay.
If there's one thing that angers me, it's the whitecaps on the sea.
Over the years I've despaired to see my friendships growing fewer.
Back in the capital I'm bound to find there are many things to fear.
I've traveled about, to the ends of the earth, and now it is past mid-autumn.
From this point on, who can say what the rest of my life will hold?

SOURCE: HCMDS 513, in *Honchō mudaishi zenchūshaku*, vol. 2, pp. 525–27; octave (heptasyllabic).
TITLE: Kōnoura: a bay on the coast opposite the harbor of Okayama city, western Honshū.

An Impromptu Poem Written at Muro
Priest Renzen

Magnolia rudder, cassia oars, moving quickly through the water.
We moor the boat, and for a while I stare into the distance.
A temple that has seen many years stands by the sandy shore.
[This harbor has an old temple. I do not know when it was founded.]
A boat is tied to an old tree on the bank beside a village.
Daybreak, a windswept bay; gloomily writing this verse.
Sinking moon, autumn lake; red tears of nostalgia for home.
Traveling around for two years now—a wanderer roaming about.
It is up to Heaven what becomes of me in the remaining days of my life.

SOURCE: HCMDS 515, in *Honchō mudaishi zenchūshaku*, vol. 2, pp. 529–30; octave (heptasyllabic).
TITLE: Muro was a coastal settlement in the Iio district of Harima province (modern Hyōgo prefecture). It was on the harbor of Mitsu, which is identified in *Harima fudoki* (ca. 715 or earlier) as the place where the boats of Princess Okinaga Tarashihime once came ashore in early times. See Michiko Y. Aoki, trans., *Records of Wind and Earth: A Translation of Fudoki with Introduction and Commentaries* (Ann Arbor: Association for Asian Studies, 1977), p. 198
LINE 2: The fifth character is missing.
LINE 6: Red tears denotes tears of blood, suggesting great anguish.

Paying a Visit in Late Spring to Sōrinji Temple
Nakahara no Hirotoshi

Stealing some leisure, I grease the wheels, then whip my horses along,
Leaving the mundane world behind, escaping from slander and praise.
Every year I make it my practice to shake off the dust of the world;
And day after day I go flower-viewing, getting out of the house.
Gazing, gazing at the misty scenery far off in the distance—
Rivers and mountains in all their splendor fill my heart with joy.
Out of office, with time on my hands and no profession to follow;
Now that I find myself growing old, what will become of me?

SOURCE: HCMDS 642, in Honma Yōichi, annot., *Honchō mudaishi zenchūshaku*, vol. 3, Shintensha chūshaku sōsho 7 (Tokyo: Shintensha, 1994), pp. 256–58; octave (heptasyllabic).
TITLE: Sōrinji is perhaps modern Sōrinji temple in the Higashiyama ward of Kyoto.

LINE 7: Given that the poet claims to be out of work, the phrase "stealing some leisure" in line one seems rather curious. See also HCMDS 457, above, for information about Hirotoshi's career problems.

�֍ Impromptu Poem Written at Unrin'in
Fujiwara no Shigeakira

The last of the blossoms are scattered about, birdsong all around.
This place with its wondrous scenery is not of the mortal world.
The woodcutters have gone into the clouds, their footprints far away.
Buddhist priests gaze at the moon, their minds calm and at peace.
I should like to keep company with high nobility, but as yet it is not allowed.
It is hard for me to know my fate—perhaps like the goose that was mute?
The hair on my temples year after year turns whiter as I age.
Slander and praise all around me—for whom has my hair become streaked?
My life is coming vainly to an end, as fast as flowing water.
I can't move ahead on the scholarly road—it's steeper than a mountain.
The scenery in this mountain grotto is simply beyond compare.
So I chant this verse and do just as I please, unable to go back home.

SOURCE: HCMDS 688, in *Honchō mudaishi zenchūshaku*, vol. 3, pp. 348–50; *pailü* (heptasyllabic), in twelve lines.
TITLE: The Kyoto temple Unrin'in was established by Priest Henjō, in 879. Located in what is today Shino Unrin'in-chō, it was formerly an imperial residence that belonged to Emperor Junna.
LINE 6: This is a reference to an anecdote from *Zhuangzi* where Zhuangzi has two geese, one of which is mute. When asked which one is to be killed and eaten, he chooses the mute one, because it is of no use as a sentinel. A disciple points out that the goose's fate seems to contradict Zhuangzi's observation that it is safest to be useless. Zhuangzi had previously pointed out that useless trees in forests are never cut down and are left to live out their days.

✖ A Visit to a Mountain Temple
His Lordship Fujiwara no Tadamichi, Lay Priest of Hosshōji

Paying a visit to this mountain temple—what is on my mind?
The look of the rocks, the nature of the water—endless fascination!
Monkeys cry in the heavy rain, the valley shrouded in mist.
Birds sing as the sun sets over rosy mountain peaks.
Glory and wealth in this world of ours as fragile as the blossoms of spring.
The dust and turmoil of the mundane world as empty as a dream at night.
This life of mine I have led in vain, have accomplished nothing at all.
No end to all my karmic hindrances, tears of blood I shed.

SOURCE: HCMDS 712, in *Honchō mudaishi zenchūshaku*, vol. 3, pp. 395–97; octave (heptasyllabic).

✖ Paying a Visit to an Old Temple on a Summer Day
His Lordship Fujiwara no Tadamichi, Lay Priest of Hosshōji

Utterly silent here at the temple, no one comes to visit.
Deer and elk go wandering past together in the forest.
At the temple the bell is tolling; bright moon over the hills.
In the incense brazier the fire is out; lonesome fog on the water.
Wind in the pines—the melody of Rong Qi's zither.
Dew on the lotuses—pearls decorating the robes of the Buddha's disciples.
Everything I see and hear, so much to fill my heart.
I completely forget about journeying home, lingering for a while.

SOURCE: HCMDS 741, in *Honchō mudaishi zenchūshaku*, vol. 3, pp. 447–49; octave (heptasyllabic).
LINE 5: This is a reference to Rong Qiqi, an old man whom Confucius encountered playing the *qin* (zither) and singing. Confucius asked him why he seemed so happy, and Rong explained that it was for three reasons: he was a human being, a man, and had lived for ninety years. This anecdote, probably apocryphal, is related in the Daoist text *Liezi*.
COMMENT: This poem probably dates from 1143.

✖ Paying a Visit to an Old Temple on a Summer Day
Fujiwara no Atsumitsu

Visiting this ancient temple, observing the cheerless scene.
Misty pines and hazy bamboo obscure my field of view.
The sound of water tumbling over stones washes away my dreams.
Clouds cover up my tracks, cloaking the middle of the mountain.
I am sad to see that last night's dew is frozen and slow to melt.
My body is like the bubbles that form then quickly disappear.
More than eighty years of age, my remaining breaths are few.
Will there be another morning when I'll come to these steps again?
  [Owing to chronic illness, I have long been unable to work; thus this line.]

SOURCE: HCMDS 742, in *Honchō mudaishi zenchūshaku*, vol. 3, pp. 449–51; octave (heptasyllabic).
LINE 5: Frozen dew suggests the onset of winter.
COMMENT: Atsumitsu took Buddhist vows about a year after writing this poem.

BIOGRAPHIES OF *KANSHI* POETS OF THE NARA AND HEIAN PERIODS

BIOGRAPHIES OF *KANSHI* POETS
OF THE NARA AND HEIAN PERIODS

✸ *Asano no Katori (774–843)*

Asano no Katori was a native of Yamato province. The son of Oshinoumi-hara no Takatori, he was adopted by his uncle Asano no Sukune Michinaga and thus acquired his surname. Respected for his intellectual gifts, foresight, and sense of propriety, Katori studied in the Academy from a young age, becoming expert in Chinese history and phonology. After completing his education, he was sent to the Tang court as an assistant scribe, returning after about a year. In 810 Katori became Emperor Saga's personal tutor.

In mid-career, Katori seems to have suffered poor health. In 819, on account of illness, he resigned his posts as senior assistant of the War Ministry and vice-governor of Sagami, but within two years he had returned to work, taking up appointments as vice-assistant head of both the Popular Affairs and Central Affairs ministries. Later posts included senior assistant governor-general of Dazaifu (827), consultant (833), left major controller (834), and head of the Popular Affairs Ministry (836). He took part in the compilation of *Nihon kōki* (The Latter Chronicles of Japan, 40 vols., completed in 840), an official history covering the period 792–833, and *Dairi shiki* (Palace Regulations, 821, revised in 833), a body of laws governing court ceremonies, rituals, and posts. Katori's extant poems include six verses in *Bunka shūreishū*. He reached the junior third rank.[118]

---

118. Of the diverse secondary works consulted in the preparation of these biographies, we wish to acknowledge in particular the following valuable reference works as sources for many of the factual details contained in these biographies: *Nihon koten bungaku daiten* (Meiji Shoin, 1998); *Nihonshi jiten* (Kadokawa Shoten, 1996); *Heian jidai shi jiten* (Kadokawa Shoten, 1994); *Heian jinmei jiten: Chōhō ninen* (Takashina Shoten, 1993); *Shinchō Nihon jinmei jiten* (Shinchōsha, 1991); *Nihon kanbungaku daijiten* (Meiji Shoin, 1985); the biographical appendix in *Kaifūsō, Bunka shūreishū, Honchō monzui*, NKBT, 69; and the appended reference materials in Kojima Noriyuki's multi-volume study *Kokufū ankoku jidai no bungaku: Kōnin-, Tenchō-ki no bungaku o chūshin to shite*. For full details, please see the bibliography.

❖ *Priest Benshō (fl. ca. 700)*

Priest Benshō (Shaku Benshō), whose lay name was Hata, was probably of Korean descent. He joined the priesthood at an early age and studied in China ca. 701–4. Benshō was famous for his knowledge of Daoist arts, his wit and humor, and his conversational prowess. He knew the Emperor Xuan Zong (r. 713–56) even before the latter took the throne, and his love of the game *go* (similar to chess) made him a special favorite of the future emperor.[119] Benshō died in China. His two surviving *kanshi* are KFS 26–27.

❖ *Priest Chizō (fl. 690–700)*

Although few details about his life are known, Priest Chizō (Shaku Chizō), an early eighth century Buddhist monk and *kanshi* poet, is believed to have studied in China for a period, returning to the Japanese court during the reign of Empress Jitō (r. 690–97). Curious details about his life and ways may be found in his *Kaifūsō* biography.[120] This source relates that in China, Chizō studied with a learned nun for six or seven years, mastering her teachings. However, he found himself unpopular amongst his fellow priests and suspected they wished to do him harm, so he took on the guise of a madman and wandered about the country aimlessly. Everyone who encountered Chizō scorned his ways, believing him to be a demon and keeping their distance. *Kaifūsō* mentions that he secretly prepared a copy of the essential portions of the *Tripiṭaka*, sealing it for safety's sake with lacquer in a bamboo tube, which he carried around on his back.

A further anecdote relates that upon reaching the shores of Japan after journeying back from China, Chizō and his fellow priests stopped to give their texts an airing, to offset the effects of the humid sea air. Chizō loosened the collar at the back of his robe, where the aforementioned sealed tube was still in place, and proceeded to explain, as he stood in the wind, that he was going to give the esoteric teachings of the *Tripiṭaka* an "airing." His companions laughed at him uncomprehendingly. Chizō then began to lecture, speaking in a manner that impressed everyone present and answering skillfully a number of difficult questions directed to him. Empress Jitō later awarded him the highest rank (*sōjō*) in the priesthood.[121] Priest Chizō lived to the relatively advanced age of seventy-three. Regrettably, only two of his *kanshi* survive, KFS 8–9.

❖ *Priest Dōyū (fl. ca. 730)*

Priest Dōyū (Shaku Dōyū), a scholar and Buddhist monk from Chang'an, immigrated to Japan and adopted the Japanese surname Hata. He began his studies early in life and soon excelled in the composition of Chinese poetry

---

119. For a short biography of Priest Benshō, see *Kaifūsō*, NKBT, 69, p. 95.
120. Ibid., pp. 78–79.
121. Ibid.

and prose. An honest and upright young man, Dōyū became a priest following his mother's death and reputedly reached enlightenment while chanting the *Lotus Sutra*. Dōyū's biography in *Kaifūsō* relates that he quickly mastered the difficult and esoteric *Sifen lüchao* (J. *Shibun risshō*, A Commentary on the *Vinaya* in Four Divisions), a basic text of the Lü (Ritsu) sect written by the Tang high priest Dao Xuan. Dōyū's subsequent teachings on the text were well received by Empress Kōmyō (701–60, the consort of Emperor Shōmu, r. 724–49), who offered him 300 bolts of silk in appreciation of his accomplishments. But Dōyū, ever aware of his moral responsibilities, declined to accept the silk, explaining that his lectures on *Shibun risshō* were delivered "for the sake of the Boddhisattvas," adding, "Only town folk would expect compensation."[122]

Dōyū's abilities were often compared to those of a leading scholar in the Japanese academy named Ōmi no Mifune (722–85). *Kaifūsō* 110 is Dōyū's only extant poem. Originally, four others were also present, according to a notation in *Kaifūsō*, but these have not survived. Poem 110 is followed by two unnumbered anonymous verses whose authorship is uncertain but which are traditionally attributed to Dōyū.

Fujiwara no Akihira (ca. 989–1066)

Fujiwara no Akihira was the son of Fujiwara no Atsunobu, the former governor of Yamashiro and personal tutor to Fujiwara no Yorimichi. He excelled at writing *kanshi*, *waka*, and Chinese prose. Early appointments included supernumerary junior lieutenant in the Left Gate Guards. In the court of Emperor Go-Reizei (1046–68) he held such posts as junior assistant head of the Ministry of Ceremonial (1056), master of the Left Capital Office, professor (1062), teacher of the classics (*gakushi*) in the Crown Prince's Office (1063), and director of the Academy (1066), by which time he held the junior fourth rank lower. He served in the Ministry of Ceremonial until his death and also did a stint as governor of Izumo province.

As the dates of the above appointments indicate, Akihira blossomed rather late in life. He was already over forty years old when he completed his examinations and gained his first significant post, in the Ministry of Ceremonial, when he was in his late sixties. He did not win promotion to the fourth rank until the year before his death, even though he came from a moderately distinguished family and was well positioned for success. It seems likely that Akihira's slow career progress stems from his involvement in two exam scandals, the first occurring in 1034, when he was punished, along with Fujiwara no Sanenori, for giving answers to three candidates while they were taking their civil service exams. The incident disrupted the exam, and Regent Fujiwara no Yorimichi was reportedly so

122. Ibid., pp. 173–74.

incensed that he invalidated all the exam results and made the candidates take a new exam. Akihira was in similar trouble again in 1041, when he incited a student who had failed his exams to demand a re-marking of his paper. (The student failed because he had commited a tonal prosody error while composing a *fu* under test conditions.) The candidate's appeal was referred in due course to Emperor Go-Suzaku for review, and before long Akihira's involvement became known. Both scandals, apparently unprecedented in their day, have been viewed as attempts by Akihira to challenge the civil service system, owing to a supposed personal grudge against the academic establishment for having kept him in relatively lowly positions despite his scholarly prowess.[123]

Akihira's most important and best-known literary undertaking was the compilation of *Honchō monzui*, a massive mid-Heian private collection of Chinese prose and poetry comprising works written between ca. 810 and 1030. It is generally believed that the anthology was compiled toward the end of Akihira's life, during the 1060s, when Akihira would have had the best access to literary materials. Curiously enough, no works by him appear in this collection. In addition to *Honchō monzui*, Akihira has left us various other important works, including his narrative of popular mores known by the title *Shin Sarugaku ki* (A New Account of Sarugaku [literally "monkey music," thought to be a precursor of Noh drama], ca. 1060) and a collection of some 209 of his letters, together with their replies, titled *Meigō ōrai* (Meigō's Letters, 1066).[124] He also compiled *Honchō shūku* (Collection of Outstanding Poetry Couplets from Our Court). More than thirty pieces by him appear in *Honchō zoku monzui*; forty-seven of his *kanshi* are also contained in *Honchō mudaishi*, twelve in *Chūyūki burui shihai kanshishū* (Collection of Poems Written on the Reverse of *Chūyūki*, ca. mid-twelfth century), and others in *Chōya gunsai* (Collected Works from Around the Land, compiled by Miyoshi no Tameyasu [1049–1139] and completed ca. 1132–35). Akihira became ill in 1065 and died the following year.

❖ *Fujiwara no Atsumitsu (1063–1144)*

Fujiwara no Atsumitsu (of the Shiki-ke Fujiwara) was a Chinese studies scholar and is one of the best-represented *kanshi* poets in *Honchō mudaishi*, the largest of the Heian *kanshi* anthologies. The son of Akihira, who served as chief compiler of *Honchō monzui*, Atsumitsu became the foster son of his own elder brother, Atsumoto, after his father's death. Atsumitsu passed his *shūsai* exams in 1094 and in 1107 became a professor at the Academy.[125] He served under the emperors Horikawa, Toba, and Sutoku, holding

123. This account of the scandals follows Ōsone and others, *Kanshi, kanbun, hyōron*, p. 32.
124. Meigō is the sinicized *on*-reading of the name Akihira. The work is also known as *Unshū ōrai* (Letters from Izumo Province).
125. See the note to KKBS 1 for details on the exam system.

such posts as senior private secretary (*dainaiki*) in the Central Affairs Ministry, director of the Academy, and, in 1122, senior assistant head of the Ministry of Ceremonial. He kept the latter position until 1144, at which time he took Buddhist vows, dying that same year. Atsumitsu's highest rank was senior fourth lower, attained in 1131.

Eighty or more of Atsumitsu's *kanshi* and literary compositions survive in such works as *Chōya gunsai* and *Honchō zoku monzui*, a further sixty-one appearing in *Honchō mudaishi*. In 1135 Atsumitsu submitted to Emperor Sutoku an opinion paper heavily laced with Confucian principles on how the court should deal with a variety of social problems, including epidemics, starvation, and crime. This is found in *maki* 2 of *Honchō zoku monzui*. He was a first-echelon literatus in his day and a frequent participant in poetry-composition gatherings. A deeply devout follower of Pure Land Buddhism, like many other aristocrats in these times, Atsumitsu also wrote several Pure Land Buddhist treatises. At the request of Regent Fujiwara no Tadamichi, he compiled *Zoku Honchō shūku* (Further Outstanding Poetry Couplets from Our Court, no longer extant), which was presented to Retired Emperor Shirakawa (1053–1129). Atsumitsu's *waka* are contained in *Kin'yō wakashū* (Collection of Golden Leaves, completed 1127).

Fujiwara no Chikamitsu (1079?–ca. 1170)

Fujiwara no Chikamitsu was the foster son of (Shiki-ke) Fujiwara no Atsumoto (1046–1106), a professor at the Academy. Chikamitsu did not complete his academic training until 1124, by which time he was probably in his mid-forties. He held posts in the Left Gate Guards and the Imperial Police and reached the rank of junior fifth lower in 1142. Chikamitsu was without an appointment for a long period thereafter, but eventually came back to court and was promoted to the junior fifth upper in 1158, when he was around eighty years of age. More than a hundred of his poems appear in *Honchō mudaishi*, making him the best represented of all the poets in this collection. A close friend of Priest Renzen, with whom he exchanged many rhyme-matching poems, Chikamitsu remained active in poetic circles well into his eighties.

Fujiwara no Fuyutsugu (775–826)

Fujiwara no Fuyutsugu (Fuyutsugi) was a prominent and highly accomplished early Heian statesman, imperial confidant, and *kanshi* poet. The second son of former Minister of the Right Fujiwara no Uchimaro, Fuyutsugu was known posthumously as "Minister of the Left of Kan'in," Kan'in being his personal residence, a place often visited by Emperor Saga. A favorite of emperors Heizei and Saga, Fuyutsugu served at court from 806, first as senior secretary and then as vice-master in the Crown Prince's Office (807), also commencing an appointment that year as gentleman-in-waiting to the emperor. In 810, Fuyutsugu became head of the Chamberlains' Office, and later the same year he was appointed master of the Crown Prince's Office and governor of Mimasaka. The following year saw a further promotion to consultant.

Among Fuyutsugu's other major appointments were left major captain of the Imperial Bodyguards (held until his death), middle and major counselor, minister of the right (821), and four years later, minister of the left, Fuyutsugu being the first person to be assigned to this post since 782. By now, Fuyutsugu had risen to the exalted senior second rank. He arranged the marriage of his daughter Junshi (809–71) to the future Emperor Ninmyō, a son of Emperor Saga.

Starting in 819, Fuyutsugu helped to compile *Nihon kōki* and also served as chief compiler of both *Kōnin kyaku* (The Statutory Amendments of the Kōnin Era, presented in 820, no longer extant), and *Dairi shiki*. He is also credited with founding a clinic known as Seyakuin, which was established to provide medicine and treatment for the poor and for orphaned children.[126] In 821, he founded Kangakuin (Institute for the Promotion of Learning), a private boarding facility for Academy students, which later served also as a school for Fujiwara children. Six of Fuyutsugu's *kanshi* appear in *Bunka shūreishū* (818), three in *Ryōun shinshū* (814), and one in *Keikokushū* (827). In 850, during the rule of Emperor Montoku (Ninmyō's son and Fuyutsugu's grandson), Fuyutsugu was posthumously awarded the post of chancellor (*daijō daijin*) and the senior first rank.

▓ *Fujiwara no Maro (695–737)*

Fujiwara no Asomi Maro, the fourth son of Fuhito and the younger brother of Fujiwara no Umakai, occupied a number of important bureaucratic posts, both in the capital and in the provinces, including vice-governor of Mino (717), master of the Left Capital Office (721), consultant (729), and head of the Defense Ministry. In 737, he took up an appointment as a specially commissioned general charged with leading a campaign against the *emishi* aborigines in Mutsu and Dewa. Maro died that same year in a deadly smallpox epidemic, which also claimed the lives of his three brothers. Five of his *kanshi* are preserved in *Kaifūsō*, poems 94–98, and three of his *tanka* are found in *Man'yōshū*, poems 522–24. Maro was the father of Fujiwara no Hamanari, compiler of the first code of Japanese poetic rules, titled *Kakyō hyōshiki* (A Formulary for Verse Based on the Canon of Poetry, 772).

▓ *Fujiwara no Michinaga (966–1027)*

Fujiwara no Michinaga, the fifth son of Chancellor Fujiwara no Kaneie, was a shrewd and powerful mid-Heian courtier as well as a man of letters

---

126. Some sources indicate that Seyakuin was established about a century earlier, in 730.

and patron of literary activities at court. Scholars today especially value his voluminous diary written in variant Chinese, *Midō kanpakki* (Records of the Midō Chancellor), which covers the years 995–1021. Michinaga was virtually a legend in his own time, seen as the most illustrious statesman of the Heian court and conjectured to have been the model for the character Prince Genji in *Tale of Genji*, written by Lady Murasaki Shikibu. His bureaucratic career proceeded through a number of substantial posts that included supernumerary middle counselor (988), supernumerary major counselor (991), minister of the right (995), imperial examiner (*nairan*, 995), minister of the left (996), and regent (1016).

In 999 Michinaga secured for his daughter Shōshi (988–1074) a position in the entourage of Emperor Ichijō, for whom she became consort the following year. In 1012, Michinaga succeeded in having his daughter Kenshi (994–1027) marry Emperor Sanjō. He arranged a third imperial marriage for his daughter Ishi (1000–36), who became the consort of Go-Ichijō in 1018. In 1016 Michinaga resigned his position as minister of the left, then in 1017 left his post as regent to become chancellor, which marked the apex of his political power. Michinaga was the most powerful of all the Fujiwara regents of the Heian age. Remarkably, he became the father-in-law of three emperors, one retired emperor, and one crown prince, as well as the grandfather of two emperors and the father of two regents.

Suffering ill health, Michinaga took Buddhist vows in 1019 and spent his final years in Pure Land devotions, occupied among other things with the establishment of Hōjōji temple in 1020, which he built to the east of his Tsuchimikado Mansion. Seven *kanshi* by Michinaga are found in *Honchō reisō*, and forty-three of his Japanese poems appear in the imperial anthology *Shūi wakashū* (Collection of Japanese Poetic Gleanings, 20 vols.), which was completed around 1007.

▓ *Fujiwara no Michinori (1106–1159)*

Fujiwara no Michinori (Shinzei) was the son of Sanekane, who once served as secretary of Kaga province, but he was adopted as a foster son by Takashina no Tsunenobu. Later in life, Michinori changed his name back to Fujiwara. Michinori served in the courts of emperors Toba, Sutoku, and Konoe as minor counselor and later received a provincial appointment as governor of Hyūga. He took his Buddhist vows in 1144, adopting the name Enkū and later Shinzei. Even after taking his vows, he remained in the former Emperor Toba's inner circle while the latter was senior retired emperor, and he also advised the minister of the left, Fujiwara no Yorinaga.

Later, Michinori, by now better known as Shinzei, enjoyed the favor of Emperor Go-Shirakawa (r. 1155–58), whose side he took with the support of Regent Fujiwara no Tadamichi, Minamoto no Yoshitomo, and Bifukumon'in (the consort of Emperor Toba) in the Hōgen Uprising of 1156. He joined Yoshitomo in defeating Fujiwara no Yorinaga and other supporters of the former Emperor Sutoku, who was intent on regaining control of the imperial succession by means of placing his son Prince Shikihito on the throne. The partisans of Sutoku were defeated, and Sutoku himself was exiled to Sanuki, in Shikoku.

At this point, Shinzei emerged as a powerful political figure in his own right at court, practically running affairs of state. He was instrumental in reinstituting the death penalty and strove to restore the personal authority of the emperor and the authority of the Heian government by adopting administrative and financial reforms embodied in the "Seven Articles of the New Administration." But Shinzei's glory was short-lived. A faction at court headed by Fujiwara no Nobuyori and Yoshitomo greatly disliked Shinzei and wanted to win control over the imperial house for themselves. The stage was set for another intense power struggle: the Heiji Uprising of 1159, a violent clash between supporters of ex-Emperor Go-Shirakawa, who favored Nobuyori's side, and supporters on the side of the reigning Emperor Nijō, who were aligned with Shinzei. In 1159, Shinzei was captured and killed by the Yoshitomo–Nobuyori faction.

Widely read and scholarly, Shinzei was an acclaimed expert in such diverse subjects as astronomy, Buddhist studies, the classics, and mathematics, as well as music and poetry. He was an accomplished master of various Japanese musical instruments and is thought to have written a narrative about the esoteric oral tradition in *biwa* playing. Many of his scholarly works survive, including the important history *Honchō seiki* (Court Annals, 1150), *Shinzei nyūdō-zō sho mokuroku* (Bibliography from the Library of Priest Shinzei), and an annotated text of *Nihon shoki* (Chronicles of Japan, 720). Shinzei was a competent *kanshi* poet and eighteen of his compositions may be found in *Honchō mudaishi*. He was equally adept at *waka* and reportedly enjoyed poetry contests.

Fujiwara no Morokage (?–?)

Morokage is an obscure poet with several compositions in *Fusōshū* (1006). Few facts are known concerning his life and career at court.

Fujiwara no Mototoshi (1060?–1142)

Although a skillful *kanshi* poet, Fujiwara no Mototoshi is best remembered for his *waka*. He was the grandson of the illustrious statesman Michinaga and the son of former Minister of the Right Toshiie. From 1077 to 1082, Mototoshi occupied the post of assistant captain in the Left Gate Guards and held the junior fifth upper rank. This was the highest rank and post he ever held. Following his father's death, lacking influential maternal connections, Mototoshi lost his court post. In 1138, he took Buddhist vows, adopting the name Lay Priest Kongo.

Despite his lack of bureaucratic success, Mototoshi aspired to enter court poetic circles, carving out a firm niche for himself which he held onto steadfastly. He acquired a reputation for being excessively critical of others and had an inflated opinion of his own talents, according to the poetic work *Mumyōshō* (1211). The earliest recorded mention of his participation in a poetry competition dates from 1093, and subsequently he was a frequent and well-established presence in the poetic life of the court of Horikawa. Mototoshi adjudicated some fourteen contests. Together with Minamoto no Toshiyori (Shunrai, 1055–1129), he was considered among the most representative *waka* poets of the Insei period, although originality was not his forté. Mototoshi preferred instead to work within the bounds of the first three Heian *waka* anthologies, deepening the aesthetic color but breaking little new ground in his use of language. Mototoshi was the mentor of the great *waka* poet Fujiwara no Shunzei and was apparently the first Japanese poet to use the term *yūgen* ("depth and profundity") when judging a poetry contest. One hundred and five of his *waka* appear in *Kin'yō wakashū* and other *waka* anthologies. *Honchō mudaishi* preserves fifteen of his *kanshi*, with still others in *Chūyūki burui shihai kanshishū*. A private collection of Mototoshi's poetry, *Mototoshi shū* (The Mototoshi Collection), also survives. Mototoshi was the compiler of *Shinsen rōeishū* (Newly Compiled Songs to Sing, ca. 1133), a collection of exemplary Chinese and Japanese poetry couplets.

❖ Fujiwara no Sanemitsu (1069–1147)

Fujiwara no Sanemitsu was a courtier and *kanshi* poet, with verse preserved in *Honchō mudaishi*. Two Japanese poems by him are also found in *Kin'yō wakashū*. The son of Fujiwara no Arinobu, right middle controller, Sanemitsu became a *monjō tokugōshō* (a highly ranked candidate in literature qualifying to sit the *shinshi* or *shūsai* civil service exams) when he was twenty-three. Sanemitsu held the posts of chamberlain, supernumerary assistant lieutenant in the Left Gate Guards, and left minor controller. By 1144, he had advanced to supernumerary middle counselor, holding the rank of junior second, but in the same year, he ended his court career and took Buddhist vows, adopting the name Saijaku.

❖ Fujiwara no Sanenori (fl. mid-eleventh century, d. ca. 1062)

Fujiwara no Sanenori was a *kanshi* poet and scholar. Descended from the Nan-ke branch of the Fujiwara family, he was the son of Yoshimichi, governor of Tajima. He became a student of Fujiwara no Yoshitada, studying Chinese history and literature. In 1026, Sanenori passed his *taisaku* exams and was employed for a period as secretary in the Ministry of Ceremonial. He gained promotion to the junior fifth lower rank then subsequently lost his secretarial post, for reasons that are not entirely clear. We may speculate that this loss of employment was connected to an incident in 1034/11, when, along with Fujiwara no Akihira (compiler of *Honchō monzui*), he was punished for misconduct in the civil service exams. Sanenori was appointed professor in 1053, then later became director of the Academy. In 1062/10, claiming illness, he resigned his Academy posts and appears to have died soon thereafter. He reached the junior fourth upper rank. Sanenori's *kanshi* are found in *Honchō zoku monzui*, *Honchō mudaishi*, and *Chūyūki burui shihai kanshishū*.

Fujiwara no Sekio (805–53)

Sekio was a *kanshi* and *waka* poet, as well as a distinguished calligrapher and musician. The son of Manatsu, he passed his civil service exams in 825. He served in the courts of Retired Emperor Junna and Emperor Ninmyō. Sekio had a relatively unremarkable career, his highest posts being junior assistant head of the Civil Affairs Ministry and director of the Office of the High Priestess of the Kamo Shrine (Kamo no Itsuki), at the rank of junior fifth lower. He retired early to Higashiyama in Kyoto, where he was known as Higashiyama Shinshi (The Presented Scholar of Higashiyama). His place of retirement later became the site of Zenrinji temple. Two of his *waka* survive in *Kokinshū*, and one *kanshi*, in *Keikokushū*.

Fujiwara no Shigeakira (1093?–1160?)

Fujiwara no Shigeakira was the son of Atsumoto (1046–1106). They belonged to the Shiki-ke branch of the Fujiwara family. Shigeakira studied Chinese history and letters at the Academy and became a *monjōshō* graduate in 1122. He was the grandson of *Honchō monzui* compiler Fujiwara no Akihira and the brother of Fujiwara no Chikamitsu. Shigeakira was originally named Tomoaki and changed his name to Shigeakira some time before 1113. His appointments included junior assistant head of the Ministry of Ceremonial and professor at the Academy. Shigeakira's highest rank was junior fourth upper. He served the courtier and statesman Fujiwara no Yorinaga and in 1151 began teaching Yorinaga's son Chinese history.

In 1154, Shigeakira wrote the preface for a collection of *kanshi* written at a composition event on the theme "Year after Year the Pines Maintain Their Integrity." A small portion of Shigeakira's annotated edition of Bo Juyi poems, titled *Hakushi monjū* (1107), also survives. Shigeakira is one of the most prominent poets in *Honchō mudaishi*, with some fifty-seven poems in that collection. Known for his precocity and erudition, he wrote a poem with the governor of Inaba province titled "Snow Fills the Garden of Pines," in the winter of 1104, when he was only about eleven. This poem is preserved in *Chūyūki burui shihai kanshishū*. The latest known extant composition by Shigeakira, dated 1160, is an obituary for Lady Bifukumon'in

(1117–60), the consort of Emperor Toba. Here, Shigeakira is identified as "Lay Priest Shigeakira." He had evidently taken Buddhist vows by this time.

▓ *Fujiwara no Tadamichi (1097–1164)*

Fujiwara no Tadamichi, son of the influential regent Fujiwara no Tadazane, was the elder half-brother of Yorinaga and the father of regent Kujō no Kanezane, who left us his important private diary *Gyokuyō* (Jewelled Leaves). Tadamichi himself was an influential and important statesman and a fine *kanshi* poet, notable for his charming poems on a wide range of humble subjects, these ranging from prostitutes and rats to strawberries. Tadamichi reached the height of his power after the Hōgen Disturbance, which pitted him against his brothers, Yorimichi and Yorinaga, and his own father. He rose to the court's highest offices, serving as regent and chancellor under the four emperors Toba, Sutoku, Konoe, and Go-Shirakawa. Emperor Sutoku married Tadamichi's daughter Masako. Until his mid-thirties, Tadamichi was much involved in literary compilations undertaken at the request of Retired Emperor Shirakawa, bearing overall responsibility for such projects as the compilation of the couplet collection *Zoku Honchō shūku*, a task he entrusted to *kanshi* poet Fujiwara no Atsumitsu (see above for Atsumitsu's biography).

After Shirakawa's death in 1129, Tadamichi began to focus on his own concerns and projects. A devout Buddhist, he retired in 1162 to a retreat next to Hosshōji, a Pure Land temple built south of Kujō street in 925. His literary activities continued, however, into his retirement. Tadamichi organized the compilation of *Honchō mudaishi*, the largest *kanshi* anthology of the Heian age, delegating the task to scholars of the Shiki-ke branch of the Fujiwara. Tadamichi was called Hosshōji Kanpaku, "The Hosshōji Regent," and Hosshōji Denka, "Lord of Hosshōji." His Buddhist name was Enkan. An outstanding calligrapher, he is credited with establishing the Hosshōji style. His one-volume *kanshi* collection, titled *Hosshōji dono gyoshū* (A Collection of Poems by the Lord of Hosshōji, also known as *Hosshōji kanpaku gyoshū*), survives intact, with 102 verses selected by Tadamichi himself. The anthology bears a colophon with the date 1145/12 and is considered representative of *kanshi* of the Insei period (ca. 1086–1121). Ninety-one other poems by Tadamichi are preserved in *Honchō mudaishi*, with fifty-eight of his *waka* appearing in *Kin'yō wakashū*.

▓ *Fujiwara no Tametoki (fl. mid- to late-tenth century)*

Fujiwara no Tametoki was a mid-Heian courtier and poet and the father of famed female novelist Murasaki Shikibu, author of *The Tale of Genji*. The son of Masatada, he studied with Sugawara no Fumitoki as a young man and from 969 served Crown Prince Morosada, who later came to the throne as Emperor Kazan (r. 984–86). After Kazan's ascension, Tametoki was given a post as secretary in the Ministry of Ceremonial, but he fell on hard times after Kazan, who had been his patron, was maneuvered off the throne by the machinations of Fujiwara no Kaneie and his cohorts. Tametoki's appointment to the governorship of Echizen in 996, which spared him from a less desirable appointment as governor of Awaji, came as the result of a compelling *kanshi* poem he had submitted in a petition to Emperor Ichijō that year expressing his disappointment over his initial selection for the Awaji post. Ichijō ordered Fujiwara no Michinaga to remove the occupant of the Echizen post for Tametoki's benefit. Tametoki went on to become governor of Echigo in 1011. In 1014, following the death of his son, Tametoki resigned his post in the middle of his term and returned to the capital. Two years later, he took Buddhist vows at Miidera and enjoyed good health at least until 1018. Tametoki was an influential and well-connected member of Ichijō's literary salon, frequently participating in poetic contests and poetry-writing banquets. His graceful and delicate verse appears in *Honchō reisō*, *Ruijū kudaishō* (Annotated Classified Poems with Allusive Titles [*Kudai*], 1 vol. extant), and other collections.

✳ *Fujiwara no Tomofusa (?–?)*
Honchō mudaishi poet. No career details are available.

✳ *Fun'ya no Mamuro (?–?)*
A *Keikokushū* poet, he held the junior fifth rank lower in 830. No further career details are known.

✳ *Emperor Ichijō (980–1011, r. 986–1011)*
Emperor Ichijō was the eldest son of Emperor En'yū by the consort Higashi San'jōin (Senshi), a daughter of Fujiwara no Kaneie. Ichijō became heir apparent in 984 and then ascended the throne as a child of six after Emperor Kazan (r. 984–86) was forced to abdicate. His reign marks the very height of courtly and literary splendor in the Heian age. Ichijō was an important patron of literature and a competent *kanshi* poet in his own right, with several compositions in the *kanshi* anthology *Honchō reisō*. Lady Sei Shōnagon was a lady-in-waiting in the salon of Ichijō's consort Teishi (Sadako), while Shōshi (Akiko), Ichijō's other consort had in her entourage such leading female literary figures as Lady Izumi Shikibu and Lady Murasaki Shikibu, author of *The Tale of Genji*. A diary Ichijō kept, titled *Ichijō Tennō shinki* (The Diary of Emperor Ichijō), is no longer extant.

✳ *Prince Inukami (?–709)*
Little is known about Prince Inukami (Inukami no Ōkimi). *Kaifūsō* 21 is his only extant *kanshi*. Inukami apparently served as a funerary official at the funeral of Empress Jitō in 702/12. He was similarly present in an official

capacity at the funeral of Emperor Monmu, in 707. Inukami became head of the Imperial Household Ministry in 708/3 and was dispatched as an offerings emissary to the Grand Ise Shrine in the Tenth Month of that year. Details concerning a further appointment as head of the Civil Affairs Ministry are unknown. *Kaifūsō* gives his rank as senior fourth lower.

Iokibe no Nagauji (fl. mid-ninth century)

Nagauji was promoted to the junior fifth rank lower in 842, but little else is known about his career. He was a minor *Keikokushū* poet.

Ishikawa no Ochindo (?–?)

Keikokushū poet, no further details known.

Isonokami no Otomaro (?–750)

Isonokami no Asomi Otomaro was the third son of Isonokami no Maro. He held the junior fifth rank lower in 724 and was not promoted to junior fifth upper until 732. That same year, he became governor of Tanba. In 738 Otomaro was awarded the junior fourth lower and became left major controller. But his luck soon ran out: the following year, he was exiled to Tosa, in Shikoku, for engaging in illicit relations with Kume no Wakame, the widow of Fujiwara no Umakai, who had died in the smallpox epidemic of 737. Otomaro's affair with Wakame is the subject of an anonymous group of poems in *Man'yōshū*, nos. 1019–23.

Otomaro eventually received a pardon and in 743 was promoted to the junior fourth rank upper. The following year, he became the provincial circuit inspector (*junsatsushi*) for the Saikaidō circuit in Kyushu, reporting to the court on the conduct and administrative efficiency of local officials. In 746, he was appointed head of the Civil Affairs Ministry and governor of Hitachi (the latter post being a sinecure), at which time he held the senior fourth lower. Later the same year, he was appointed right major controller. He reached the junior third rank in 748. Otomaro continued to win promotions, becoming head of the Central Affairs Ministry and middle counselor in 749. Otomaro's biography in *Kaifūsō* indicates that some time during the Tenpyō period (729–49) he was chosen to serve as emissary to the Tang court but in the end did not assume this post, for reasons that are unknown. A private two-*maki* collection of Otomaro's verse, titled *Kanpisō* (Gems of Sorrow), survives in name only. *Kanpisō* was the likely source of the poems by Otomaro found in *Kaifūsō*, nos. 115–18. These were probably composed during his period of exile in Tosa, ca. 739–43.

Emperor Junna (786–840, r. 823–33)

Emperor Junna (former Crown Prince Ōtomo), the fifty-third emperor of Japan, was the third son of Emperor Kanmu (737–806) and the brother of

Emperor Saga, whom he succeeded. He became crown prince in 810, four years after his coming of age ceremony. His administrative accomplishments include revitalizing the operations of the release commissioners (*kageyushi*), officials who supervised transitions from one governor to the next. He also commissioned *Ryō no gige* (A Commentary on the *Yōrō ritsuryō* Legal Code), which was completed in 836 by an editorial committee under Kiyowara no Natsuno (782–837). Before taking the throne, he headed the ministries of War, Civil Affairs, and Central Affairs. With Emperor Saga, Junna was considered one of the most representative palace poets of the Kōnin period (810–24). Eight of his poems appear in the *Bunka shūreishū* collection, five in *Ryōunshū*, and three in *Keikokushū*.

✖ Kamitsukeno no Ehito (766–821)

Kamitsukeno no Ehito (Ebito), son of Ōkawa, attended the Academy, studying Chinese history and literature. During the Enryaku period (782–805), he was sent as a scribe to the Tang court. He later held appointments in the Department of Shrines as a junior and then senior clerk. In 806, Ehito took up a post as senior private secretary in the Central Affairs Ministry and the following year became senior secretary in the Council of State, by which time he held the senior sixth rank upper.

Ehito was promoted to junior fifth rank upper in recognition of his loyal service at the time of the Kusuko Incident in 810. He received the title *ason* in 810 and in 812 became vice-governor of Inaba. Ehito also assisted with the compilation of the genealogy *Shinsen shōjiroku* (Newly Compiled Record of Families), while he was serving as senior secretary in the Council of State and on into his term as vice-governor of Inaba. His name appears in *maki* 4 of *Ruijū fusenshō* (Collection of Classified Edicts and Directives, ca. 1100), a group of court documents dating from the years 737 to 1093, where, in an entry bearing the date 816, his position is given as senior secretary. This suggests that Ehito was still holding the Council of State post late in his career. *Keikokushū* lists Ehito's positions as being tutor to the Crown Prince and senior assistant head of the Popular Affairs Ministry, with the rank of junior fourth lower, the highest level he attained. One *kanshi* of his appears in *Ryōunshū*, one in *Bunka shūreishū*, and two more in *Keikokushū*.

✖ Kasa no Nakamori (?–?)

Nakamori was a minor poet with works in *Keikokushū*.

✖ Ki no Haseo (845–912)

A leading literatus in his time, Ki no Haseo was the son of Sadanori. Early in his career, he held posts as supernumerary junior clerk of Sanuki province, secretary of Sanuki, and junior secretary in the Council of State, while still formally engaged in study at the Academy. His graduation from the Academy therefore came at the relatively late age of thirty-nine. In fact, Haseo was thirty-three before even commencing his literary studies.

Haseo was appointed director of the Bureau of Books and Drawings (Zushoryō no kami) in 890 and the following year became a professor of Chinese history and literature (monjō hakase). He went on to serve in a number of posts, including governor of Sanuki, junior assistant head of the Ministry of Ceremonial, and left and right controllers. In 894, he was appointed Sugawara no Michizane's vice-ambassador to China on a planned mission that was ultimately cancelled. In 895 he became head of the Academy, and in 902, consultant. Haseo received the post of supernumerary middle counselor and was promoted to the junior third rank in 910. The following year he reached the senior third, upon gaining the post of middle counselor. Haseo also served as tutor to Emperor Daigo.

Haseo had the good fortune to study under two of the most renowned scholars of his day, Miyako no Yoshika and Sugawara no Michizane. He was a prolific writer of Chinese, producing poetry, narratives, chronicles, memorials, anthology introductions, and other prose documents, many samples of which survive in Honchō monzui. Although many of Haseo's poems have been lost, sixty-one of his kanshi and fu have survived in Heian literary sources such as Fusōshū, Chōya gunsai, and Ruijū kudaishō. Haseo's personal collection of literature is known as Kikeshū (The Ki Collection, comp. ca. 911–19); only one maki survives intact. Haseo was also an expert waka poet, with four waka appearing in Gosen wakashū (The Later Collection of Waka Poetry, 951). Various stories about his life have come down to us in such narratives as Kokon chomonjū (Stories Heard from Writers Old and New, 1254), Gōdanshō (Excerpts from Conversations with Ōe no Masafusa, early twelfth century), and Konjaku monogatari (Tales of Times Now Past, late Heian period). Haseo's former teacher and lifelong friend Michizane valued his work highly and presented Haseo with his final collection of Chinese poems, Kanke kōshū, shortly before his own death in Dazaifu, in 903.

✖ Ki no Suemori ?–?)

Little is known about the life of Ki no Suemori, son of Ki no Mahito. He was promoted in 825 to the senior sixth rank upper, and six years later held the junior fifth rank upper. Genealogical records indicate that he once served as junior assistant head of the Popular Affairs Ministry. Only one poem by him survives, Bunka shūreishū 28.

✖ Kiyohara no Nakayama (?–?)

A Fusoshū poet, no details available.

※ *Kiyohara no Sanetomo (fl. mid-ninth century?)*

Kiyohara no Sanetomo has one surviving piece in *Honchō monzui*, poem 33, an acrostic verse dated 848. Few facts about his life or career are known.

※ *Koremune no Noritoki (1015?–97?)*

Koremune no Noritoki (known also as Takatoki or Takakoto) was a noted *kanshi* poet and scholar. He hailed from a family with a long tradition of legal expertise. He passed the *taisaku* examination around 1044, after earlier academic failures, and rose to become professor and director of the Academy, commencing in the latter position around 1071. In 1075 Noritoki became the tutor of Fujiwara no Morozane (1042–1101, son of former Regent Fujiwara no Yorimichi), whose patronage helped him to secure the governorships of Nagato, Ise, and Iga in his declining years. He also was employed by Morozane's son Fujiwara no Moromichi (1062–99), lecturing on *Wen xuan* and *Shi jing*. Noritoki helped organize poetry banquets for Moromichi and provided prefaces to poems written at these events. In 1087, Noritoki became custodian of the Office of the Imperial Library (Goshodokoro) and director of the Housekeeping Office (Kanimori no tsukasa) in the Imperial Household Ministry. It appears that he concurrently held a sinecure as senior secretary of Bitchū. With Ōe no Masafusa, he produced a *kunten* annotated text of *Man'yōshū*. His *kanshi* poetry survives in *Honchō mudaishi* and *Chūyūki burui shihai kanshishū*. Noritoki ended his career at the rank of junior fourth upper. The last mention of him in historical records bears the date 1097.

※ *Kose no Shikihito (ca. 795–?)*

Kose no Shikihito was an important poet in the literary circle of Emperor Saga. His lineage is uncertain, but he may have been the grandson of Nutari (Notari). Few facts about his career are known, even though many of his poems are contained in *Bunka shūreishū*. Although Shikihito is listed as rankless in the table of contents in *Ryōunshū* (compiled 814), we know that by 823 he had reached the junior fifth rank upper, having won promotion that year for accompanying Emperor Saga to the mountain retreat of Prince Aritomo. Shikihito was still holding this rank four years later when *Keikokushū* was compiled. Four of his poems appear in the latter collection, with twenty more in *Bunka shūreishū*, making him the next-best represented poet after Emperor Saga.

※ *Priest Kūkai (774–835)*

Born in the Shikoku province of Sanuki to the Saeki family, Priest Kūkai, known posthumously as Kōbō Daishi (The Great Teacher and Promulgator of the Buddhist Law), ranks as one of the preeminent intellectual figures of not only the Heian period but Japanese history as a whole. He became a novice at twenty and two years later was ordained at Tōdaiji in Heian. In 804 Kūkai traveled to Chang'an, the capital city of China, where he remained for two years studying with the abbot of Qinglong Temple, a priest named Huiguo. Upon seeing Kūkai for the first time, the abbot marveled at his appearance and expressed his intuitive belief that here was his long-awaited successor to carry on the doctrine. While in China, Kūkai studied Sanskrit, among other disciplines, and developed a penchant for the highly esoteric Indian Mantrayāna (Tantric) Buddhism. Kūkai returned to Japan in 806 and spent time at Jingoji, a temple northwest of Heian. In 816 he initiated the construction of Kongōbuji monastery on Mt. Kōya, some fifty miles from the capital. This was to become the future center for the study and practice of Shingon Mikkyō (True Word Esoteric) Buddhism. Seven years later, Kūkai became chief priest of Tōji, an important temple in the capital.

Renowned as a philosopher, poet, and linguist, Kūkai is primarily remembered as the founder and intellectual fountainhead of the Shingon sect, which followed a doctrinal system incorporating complex spells, mudras (body postures and hand gestures), and mantras (mystical phrases). Shingon was one of the two major Buddhist sects in the Heian period alongside the Tendai sect, which was founded in 806 by Priest Saichō. Both sects were intimately involved in the affairs of the court and among their concerns was assisting with the preservation of order and the protection of the realm.

Kūkai's earliest known philosophical endeavor was *Sangō shiiki* (Indications of the Goals of the Three Teachings), completed in 797 when he was twenty-four. In this text, the author examines and compares the central ideas of Confucianism, Daoism, and Buddhism, praising the merits of each school but coming down in favor of Mahāyāna Buddhism as the highest level of truth. The text also provides a quasi-apologia for Buddhism, attempting to demonstrate that its core principles are not incompatible with filial piety and other Confucian virtues.

Priest Kūkai's *kanshi* appear in *Keikokushū* and in *Seireishū*, his own private anthology of poetry and prose, which contains some 160 compositions and was edited by his disciple Shinzei (800–60). In 803 Kūkai produced *Jūjū shinron* (Discourse on the Ten Stages of Mind), which describes ten stages of spiritual development, with the doctrines of the Shingon sect as the ultimate stage in the journey toward Buddhist enlightenment. In 819 he completed the poetic treatise *Bunkyō hifuron* (Secret Treasury of Poetic Mirrors), an encyclopedic treatment of Chinese prosody incorporating important Six Dynasties and Tang poetical texts, many of which are now lost.

Kūkai was also a famed calligrapher and sculptor and in the realm of legend is sometimes credited with being the inventor of the Japanese *hiragana* syllabary. His social works were diverse and included the establishment of schools for the common people, the creation of irrigation systems, and performing rainmaking ceremonies and similar services for the protection of the land. Truly a giant figure in the history of Japanese Buddhism, Kūkai brought this religion to a pinnacle of intellectual development perhaps never again surpassed. He was posthumously named Kōbō Daishi in 921.

▓ *Kuwahara (Miyako) no Haraka (789–825)*

Kuwahara no Kimi Haraka (Haraaka) was an early Heian courtier, scholar, and poet. His father Akinari served as vice-governor of Yamato province. For reasons that are unclear, Haraka successfully petitioned in 822 to have his family name changed from Kuwahara to Miyako, with the title of *sukune*. While Emperor Saga was on the throne, Haraka enjoyed a considerable reputation as a poet and was often asked to write poems at court banquets. During the 814 visit of a Parhae mission to the Japanese court, Haraka was called upon to exchange verses with the vice-envoy Gao Jingxiu. In 818, along with Prince Nakao and Sugawara no Kiyokimi (the grandfather of Michizane), he was commissioned to compile *Bunka shūreishū*. Haraka's rank at the time was junior seventh lower, his posts being junior private secretary in the Central Affairs Ministry and concurrently *shōmoku* of Harima, a low-level provincial appointment.

Haraka assisted also with the compilation of *Dairi shiki*, the preface of which indicates that by this time he was a professor of Chinese history and literature holding the junior fifth rank lower, concurrently serving as senior private secretary in the Central Affairs Ministry. When he died, at the age of thirty-seven, he held the senior fifth rank lower. Ten of Haraka's *kanshi* appear in *Bunka shūreishū*, two in *Ryōunshū*, and one in *Keikokushū*. Thirteen of his poems are cited in *Nihon shiki* (A History of Poetry in Japan), written by Ichikawa Kansai (1749–1820).

▓ *Crown Prince Masara—See the entry for Emperor Ninmyō, below.*

▓ *Michi no Nagana (?–?)*
Keikokushū poet, details unknown.

▓ *Minamoto no Fusaakira (904?–39?)*
Minamoto no Fusaakira (Yoshiakira) was the son of Prince Tadayo (tentative reading) and the grandson of Emperor Uda. His mother was a daughter of Sugawara no Michizane. He took the surname Minamoto in his midteens and was granted the fourth rank. At seventeen Fusaakira was appointed gentleman-in-waiting, and later he became middle captain of the Left Imperial Bodyguards. In 927 Fusaakira received the posts of first secretary of the Chamberlains' Office and governor of Harima, while retaining his post in the Imperial Bodyguards. Three years later he left his position as

head of the Chamberlains' Office. Fusaakira's bureaucratic career at around this time began to lose momentum, particularly once his father retired to become a lay priest and he lost the patronage of his grandfather, the former Emperor Uda, after the latter died. It is suggested in the *Gōdanshō* accounts of Fusaakira that he was a flamboyant character and not particularly attentive to his public duties. Nonetheless, his poetry gained him some renown. Four pieces by Fusaakira—two *fu*, a *shi*, and an anthology preface—appear in *Honchō monzui*; twenty or more other poems appear in such collections as *Fusōshū* and *Ruijū kudaishō*. One *waka* by him is found in *Gosen wakashū*. Fusaakira completed a biography of Priest Ennin (794–864) begun by his father and titled *Jikaku Daishi den* (The Biography of High Priest Jikaku).

✖ *Minamoto no Kaneakira (914–87)*

Known also as Saki no Chūsho Ō, "The Former Prince and Minister of Central Affairs," Prince Kaneakira was the sixteenth son of Emperor Daigo and the younger brother of emperors Sujaku and Murakami. At the age of seven, he took the Minamoto surname. In 933 Kaneakira became supernumerary governor of Harima, holding the rank of junior fourth upper. Six years later, he was appointed supernumerary middle captain in the Right Imperial Bodyguards and the following year assumed the additional post of supernumerary governor of Kii. In 942 Kaneakira was made supernumerary left middle captain of the Imperial Bodyguards, and in 944 became a consultant. The following year saw his appointment as supernumerary governor of Ōmi and head of the Civil Affairs Ministry. Other posts included supernumerary middle counselor (955), captain of the Left Military Guards (962), and major counselor (967), by which time he had reached the rank of junior second. During the Anna Incident (Anna no Hen, 969), Kaneakira was temporarily banned from the palace, owing to the banishment of his half-brother Minamoto no Takaakira to Dazaifu, in Kyushu. However, he was soon back at the center of court life, becoming tutor to the crown prince in 970 and minister of the left the following year.

In 977 Kaneakira fell victim to the political machinations of Chancellor Fujiwara no Kanemichi, who hoped to make Fujiwara no Yoritada (924–89) minister of the left. Kaneakira ended up having to relinquish his post as minister of the left to Yoritada. However, that same year, he recovered his former princely status, which he had lost when he was seven, and became head of the Central Affairs Ministry, a position which in Kaneakira's day was reserved for princes of the blood.

Kaneakira resigned from his post as head of the Central Affairs Ministry in 986 and retired to his mountain retreat in Ogura, in the Saga area of western Kyoto. From this location is derived his sobriquet Ogura Shinnō "The Prince of Ogura." His renowned "*Fu* on Tu-qiu" (J. Tokyū no fu,

HCMZ 13), on the subject of retirement, vents anger over the reversal of his fortunes, which he attributed to political abuses committed by the Fujiwara regency. There are stories about Kaneakira in both *Gōdanshō* and *Eiga monogatari* (Tales of Glory, early eleventh century). An important *kanshi* poet, outstanding calligrapher, and leading essayist in his day, Kaneakira also has literary pieces in *Honchō monzui*, *Gōdanshō*, *Wakan rōeishū*, and elsewhere. Along with Prince Tomohira, Minamoto no Shitagō, Ki no Tsurayuki's daughter (name unknown), and others, Kaneakira has been suggested as a possible compiler of *Kokin waka rokujō* (Six Volumes of Poetry, Old and New), a *waka* anthology comprising some 4500 poems and probably dating from the late tenth century.

※ Minamoto no Michinari (?–1019)

Minamoto no Michinari was the son of Masakuni and grandson of *waka* poet Minamoto no Saneakira (910–70). He studied Chinese letters with the *kanshi* poet and scholar Ōe no Mochitoki (955–1010). In 998 Michinari was appointed junior secretary in the Imperial Household Ministry. After leaving the Academy in 1001, he became a chamberlain. Three years later Michinari became secretary in the Ministry of Ceremonial. In 1006 Michinari was holding the junior fifth lower rank and serving as supernumerary governor of Shimōsa. In 1015, he was made governor of Chikuzen and junior assistant governor-general of Dazaifu, and in 1018 he reached the rank of senior fifth lower. His works are contained in such anthologies as *Honchō reisō*, *Ruijū kudaishō*, and *Honchō monzui*. His private collection bears the title *Michinari shū* (Michinari's Collection). Michinari also compiled a work of *waka* poetic theory titled *Michinari jittai* (Michinari's Ten Poetic Styles).

※ Minamoto no Shitagō (911–83)

An important poet, literatus, and lexicographer, Minamoto no Shitagō was one of the acclaimed "Thirty-Six Sages of Japanese Poetry." The third son of Minamoto no Kozoru, assistant director of the Imperial Stables, Shitagō had only an average career as an official but made a great name for himself as a literary scholar and poet. He was the compiler of *Wamyō ruijushō* (A Classified Dictionary of Japanese Glosses), a Chinese-Japanese dictionary-encyclopedia compiled 931–38. He was also one of the five compilers of *Gosen wakashū*, the second official collection of *waka*, completed in 951. Shitagō's career in the bureaucracy following his graduation from the Academy included appointments as scholar in the Bureau of Japanese Poetry (951), release commissioner (956), junior secretary in the Popular Affairs Ministry (962), and chamberlain in the Crown Prince's Office (962). In 963 Shitagō received an official appointment as senior secretary in the Popular Affairs Ministry and in 966 was made supernumerary governor of

Shimōsa, at which time he held the junior fifth rank lower. In 967 he became governor of Izumi; in 979, governor of Noto. Shitagō's own poetry anthology, *Shitagō shū* (The Shitagō Collection), contains the renowned "Ametsuchi" alphabet poem. Thirty-three pieces of his prose and verse are found in *Honchō monzui* and other collections. Shitagō was also the author of *Sakumon daitai*, an important guide to Chinese composition.

✠ *Minamoto no Tamenori (935?–1011)*

Minamoto no Tamenori, a noted man of letters, first became known in poetic circles for his participation in the *Zen shūsai taku shiawase* (The *Kanshi* Contest Held at the Home of *Shūsai* Miyoshi [Michimune, ?–?]), which took place in 963.[127] His posts included chamberlain, junior secretary in the Ministry of Ceremonial, and supernumerary governor of Mikawa. Tamenori went on to serve as governor of Tōtōmi, Mino, and Iga provinces.

Tamenori studied under Minamoto no Shitagō and developed a polished Chinese literary style. He is best known for his Buddhist primer *Sanbō ekotoba* (Illustrated Scrolls of the Three Treasures), which he presented to Princess Sonshi in 984. His other works include *Kūyarui* (A Eulogy for Prince Kūya, compiled ca. 973) and *Kuchizusami* (Recitations, 970), a catalog of useful information designed to be sung aloud to facilitate memorization and intended for young aristocrats. A third work, *Sezoku genbun* (Well-known Sayings, 1007), most of which is no longer extant, consisted of famous phrases derived from Buddhist and Chinese historical anecdotes, events, and popular fables. Tamenori's Chinese prose works and poetry are found in *Honchō monzui*, *Honchō reisō*, *Wakan rōeishū*, and *Ruijū kudaishō*. *Waka* attributed to Tamenori are contained in such anthologies as *Shūi wakashū* and *Gengenshū* (Collection of the Subtle and Mystical, mid-eleventh century), the latter being a private anthology of 167 *waka* by ninety-two poets and compiled by Nōin (Tachibana no Nagayasu, 988–?). His own collection, *Tamenori shū* (The Tamenori Collection), is no longer extant.

✠ *Miyabe no Muratsugu (?–?)*

Miyabe no Muratsugu was a scholar who probably lived around the time of Emperor Saga. He is credited with BKSRS 119. Nothing else is known about his life or career.

✠ *Miyako no Yoshika (834–79)*

Miyako no Yoshika (originally Tokimichi) was the son of Sadatsugu, who once served as the vice-governor of Yamato province. Little is known about

---

127. *Shūsai*, "exceptional talent," is a high academic qualification explained in the notes to KKBS 1.

Yoshika's career, but his posts included appointments as private secretary in the Central Affairs Ministry (870) and as the local contact for the trade mission from the state of Parhae (872). In 875, Yoshika became a professor of Chinese history and literature. He achieved a considerable reputation in the capital for his knowledge of these disciplines, prose being his area of greatest distinction. Yoshika served also as supernumerary vice-governor of Echizen, beginning in 876.

Yoshika drafted many important state documents during his career. He also helped compile *Montoku jitsuroku* (The Chronicles of Emperor Montoku, 879), the fifth of the six official Japanese histories. In the preface he laments that compiling the work took a heavy toll on his health. Indeed, in 879, when the work was completed, Yoshika resigned his post as senior private secretary and passed away soon thereafter, at the age of forty-six. Yoshika's own works of Chinese prose and poetry are collected in *Toshi bunshū* (The Miyako Literary Collection, ca. 879), but only *maki* 3–5 survive. *Honchō monzui* has twelve additional prose pieces by him. Six poems mourning the death of Yoshika's eldest son are among those contained in the *kanshi* anthology *Fusōshū*, and *Kokin wakashū* preserves his only extant *waka* composition. The noted *kanshi* poet Kuwahara (Miyako) no Haraka was Yoshika's uncle.

✖ *Miyoshi no Kiyoyuki (847–918)*
Also known as Zen Shōkō, "Consultant Miyoshi," Miyoshi no Kiyoyuki was the third son of Ujiyoshi, who once served as governor of Awaji. Said to have been a descendant of the Paekche nobility, Kiyoyuki was among the most distinguished Chinese prose writers of his day. He studied under Kose no Fumio and achieved *monjō tokugōshō* status in 874. Kiyoyuki's appointments included supernumerary junior clerk, first in Echizen (877) and then in Harima (880). In 884, he became a junior secretary in the Academy. Two years later, he was appointed junior private secretary in the Central Affairs Ministry, being promoted to senior private secretary the following year, at which point he held the junior fifth rank lower. In 891, he received an appointment as vice-governor of Higo, then was made vice-governor of Bitchū two years later. He remained in the latter post four years before returning to the capital.

In 900 Kiyoyuki became a professor and senior assistant head of the Justice Ministry. The next year saw his promotion to director of the Academy, a post that he resigned three years later. In 903 he became junior assistant head of the Ministry of Ceremonial. Two years later he received an appointment as supernumerary senior assistant head of the Ministry of Ceremonial, becoming the regular senior assistant of the same ministry in 914, by which time he held the junior fourth, upper grade. That same year, he wrote the famous *Iken hōji jūnikajō* ("Opinions in a Sealed Document in

Twelve Articles"), a memorial presented to Emperor Daigo on what he saw as the moral and fiscal decay of the times, urging political reform and a return to high standards of behavior in the court and the priesthood. Kiyoyuki believed that the Academy, too, had fallen into a state of gross neglect and desuetude, particularly in its treatment of students and the overall quality of instruction and examinations. This document is regarded as one of the most distinguished Chinese prose compositions written in the Heian court. In 917 Kiyoyuki became a consultant and the head of the Imperial Household Ministry. The following year, he acquired the additional post of supernumerary governor of Harima. He died that year, at the age of seventy-two.

A devotee of the occult arts, Kiyoyuki wrote stories about the strange and miraculous, but unfortunately they are known today by title only. A one-volume collection of his writings, *Zenkashū* (The Miyoshi Family Collection), is non-extant, as is a biography bearing the title *Zen shōkō* (Minister Miyoshi). Kiyoyuki was one of the compilers of *Engi kyaku* (The Statutory Amendments of the Engi Era, containing documents dated 869–907). Seven of his pieces appear in *Honchō monzui*. Stories about Kiyoyuki appear in *Gōdanshō* and *Konjaku monogatari*, vol. 27. Among his best-known prose works are *Enchin washō den* (The Biography of Priest Enchin) and *Fujiwara no Yasunori den* (The Biography of Fujiwara no Yasunori). A large number of Kiyoyuki's *kanshi* and couplets are contained in such collections as *Fusōshū*, *Gōdanshō*, and *Wakan rōeishū*.

Miyoshi no Kiyoyuki and Sugawara no Michizane had a long-standing bitter rivalry, stemming from Michizane's ungenerous evaluation of Kiyoyuki in the civil service exams when acting as his examiner. Just before Michizane's downfall, Kiyoyuki warned Michizane that he had risen above his station and advised him to retire. It is probable that Kiyoyuki played a role in Michizane's dismissal and exile to Dazaifu in 901.

❀ Emperor Monmu (683–707, r. 697–707)

The second son of Prince Kusakabe (662–89) and Abe (Ahe) no Himemiko, Emperor Monmu was Japan's forty-second sovereign. Earlier known as Prince Karu (Karu no Miko), he came to the throne at the age of fifteen, leapfrogging over his elder brother, the future Emperor Genshō (680–748, r. 715–24). A gentle and mild-mannered but sickly man, Monmu lived only until the age of twenty-five. Upon his death, his mother Himemiko (661–721) came to the throne as Empress Genmei (Genmyō, r. 707–15), then was succeeded by her elder son.

Japan's epoch-making Taihō Code, promulgated in 701, dates from Monmu's reign and represents the culmination of the administrative and political reforms of the earlier Taika era (645–50), providing the underpinnings of the bureaucratic system of government. The retired Empress Jitō directed affairs in Monmu's early years as emperor, and following her death in 702, Monmu was variously advised by Prince Hozumi and by Fujiwara no Fuhito, who was the father of Fujiwara no Miyako, his consort. Prince Obito (Obito no Miko), the son of Monmu and Miyako, came to the throne as the forty-fifth sovereign, Emperor Shōmu, in 724. Monmu in 701 revived the practice of sending emissaries to the Tang court, after a hiatus of thirty-two years. *Man'yōshū* 74, a *tanka*, is attributed to Monmu, as are *Kaifūsō* 15–17, these four pieces being his entire extant poetic corpus.

※ *Nakahara no Hirotoshi (1062–1131)*

Nakahara no Hirotoshi, son of Sadatoshi, a former governor of Etchū, was a student of Chinese history and literature at the Academy and a skilled *kanshi* poet well represented in *Honchō mudaishi*. After finishing his studies, Hirotoshi served as junior private secretary in the Central Affairs Ministry and junior secretary in the Council of State. He reached the rank of junior fifth lower in 1103/1 but never rose any higher. From that point on, he was without a post for many years. In a poem written in 1111 and contained in *Chūyūki burui shihai kanshishū*, Hirotoshi mentions that he had been nine years without an appointment.

Hirotoshi's fortunes eventually improved, however, for in 1112 he was appointed governor of Shimotsuke and later, governor of Hyūga. He was an active *kanshi* poet and kept company with various members of the Shiki-ke branch of the Fujiwara family, including Shigeakira (who married his daughter), Atsumitsu, and Chikamitsu. Fifty-two of his poems are found in *Honchō mudaishi*, making him one of the best-represented poets in that collection. In 1111, Hirotoshi served as reciter for Chinese composition submissions at a meeting of the Promotion of Learning Society (Kangakkai), held at Rokuharamitsuji temple in Kyoto. In 1131, he accepted an invitation from the Age Veneration Society (Shōshikai, founded 877) to compose poems and serve as reciter at a poetry meeting held at Fujiwara no Munetada's (1062–1141) Shirakawa mountain retreat.

※ *Prince Nakao (fl. ca. 825)*

Prince Nakao (Nakao Ō) is one of the main poets in *Bunka shūreishū*, with thirteen *kanshi* to his credit. Despite his noble status and his considerable reputation as a poet, Nakao's genealogy remains a mystery. He is credited with writing the preface to *Bunka shūreishū*, and he may have served as its principal compiler as well. One other *kanshi* attributed to Nakao is found in *Keikokushū*, two more in *Ryōunshū*. When *Bunka shūreishū* was compiled, Nakao was serving as governor of Shinano, concurrently directing the Ōtoneri no Tsukasa (Bureau of Imperial Attendants), an office under the Central Affairs Ministry. He rose to the rank of senior fifth lower (823).

One late Kamakura source lists Nakao as having failed one of the civil service examinations.[128]

�֍ *Emperor Ninmyō (810–50, r. 833–50)*

Known in his youth as Crown Prince Masara, Ninmyō was the fifty-fourth emperor of Japan. The second son of the great literary patron Emperor Saga, Emperor Ninmyō was known for his knowledge of the Chinese classics and history, and during his reign interest in Chinese cultural institutions reached new heights. It was in this period that the last official envoys from the Heian court were dispatched to China. One poem attributed to Masara appears in *Keikokushū*.

✖ *Ono no Ason Minemori (777–830)*

Ono no Ason Minemori was the third son of Nagami (see the next biography), a lieutenant-general in the campaigns to subjugate the *emishi* aborigines to the north. The main compiler of *Ryōunshū*, Minemori also helped compile the third official history of Japan, *Nihon kōki* (completed 840), and a further historical work titled *Dairi shiki* (821, revised in 833), for which he wrote an introduction. Posts held by Minemori include junior secretary in the Council of State (806), junior secretary in the Crown Prince's Office (806), and junior assistant head of the Ministry of Ceremonial (809). Poem 57 in *Ryōunshū* (comp. 814) identifies Minemori as director of the Palace Storehouse Bureau, director of the Left Imperial Stables, and governor of Mino, holding the junior fifth rank upper. He was appointed senior assistant head of the Civil Affairs Ministry in 820.

In 821, Minemori reached the junior fourth rank lower and became master of the Consort's Quarters, serving concurrently as governor of Ōmi. The following year he was made consultant and the senior assistant governor-general of the Kyushu Government Office in Dazaifu. In 823 Minemori memorialized the throne, requesting the establishment of public fields (*kueiden*) in Kyushu, to provide relief grain when there was a poor harvest. Minemori also established a temple, named Shokumyōin, to serve as a hostel for travelers. In 828, he became head of the Justice Ministry, serving also as chief release commissioner. *Ryōunshū* has thirteen of his *kanshi*, *Bunka shūreishū* eight, and *Keikokushū* nine.

✖ *Ono no Nagami (fl. ca. 800?)*

Ono no Nagami was the son of Ono no Kenu, who served as middle counselor and head of the Central Affairs Ministry. Nagami was the father of the *kanshi* poet Ono no Minemori. He took up an appointment as lieutenant general of the Aboriginal Subjugation Force, probably during the Enryaku

---

128. See Kojima, *Kokufū ankoku jidai no bungaku*, vol. 2 (pt. 2), p. 1846.

period (782–805), although some accounts suggest his service occurred sometime after 811. Nagami also had an appointment as vice-governor of Mutsu, at which time he held the junior fifth lower. He was a friend of the *Ryōunshū* poet Kaya no Toyotoshi. Nagami's sole extant poems are *Ryōunshū* 73–74.

✸ *Ōe no Koretoki (888–963)*

Ōe no Koretoki, the third son of Chifuru and grandson of Otondo, was commonly known as "Counselor Ōe." He obtained *monjō tokugōshō* status in 917 and was appointed chamberlain in 921. Koretoki became junior secretary in the Ministry of Ceremonial in 924, senior secretary the next year, and director of the Academy in 928. The following year, he became a professor of Chinese history and literature. Other appointments include junior assistant head of the Ministry of Ceremonial (935), director of the Academy (939), and tutor to the crown prince. Koretoki later served also as senior assistant head of the Ministry of Ceremonial (944), consultant (950), and middle counselor (960). He was tutor to emperors Daigo, Suzaku, and Murakami. Koretoki was also the chief compiler of *Senzai kaku* (A Millennium of Fine Poem Couplets, 2 vols., 947–57), an anthology of selected Tang dynasty *shi* couplets. He was also involved in the editing of *Shin kokushi* (A New History of Our Nation), a non-extant mid-Heian work that was never formally completed. Koretoki was posthumously awarded the junior second rank for his distinguished service as personal tutor to the aforementioned three emperors.

Along with Ōe no Asatsuna (886–957) and Sugawara no Fumitoki (899–981), Koretoki was considered one of the three finest scholars of his age. *Gōdanshō* relates that whereas Koretoki was considered a lesser poet than Asatsuna, he was superior to the latter in his overall scholarship. His literary works are found in *Honchō reisō*, *Honchō monzui*, *Chōya gunsai*, *Honchō bunshū*, *Ruijū kudaishō*, and *Tentoku tōshi*.[129]

✸ *Ōe no Masafusa (1041–1111)*

The son of Shigehira and the great-grandson of Masahira (952–1012), Ōe no Masafusa was a renowned writer of *waka* and *kanshi* and a child prodigy who became absorbed in the Chinese classics at an early age. By the time he was eleven he could write *kanshi* with remarkable skill, so much so that people reportedly were unable to believe that they were the works of a child. He passed his Academy exams at the age of sixteen and achieved *monjō tokugōshō* status two years later. He tutored four emperors: Go-Sanjō, Shirakawa, Horikawa, and Toba. Masafusa also occupied such posts as left

---

129. *Tentoku tōshi* is a record of a Chinese poetry contest held on 959/8/16 by Emperor Murakami at the Seiryōden in the imperial palace.

major controller and senior assistant head of the Ministry of Ceremonial. He became a consultant in 1088 and supernumerary middle counselor in 1094. Some three years later, he was made supernumerary governor-general of Dazaifu in Kyushu, from which time he was known by the sobriquet "Gō no Sochi (Governor-General Ōe)." After 1106, he held this post in name only. Following the premature death of his eldest son, Masafusa spent his final years in ill health, largely at his residence. He became head of the Treasury Ministry just months before his death in 1111.

Together with Fujiwara no Akihira and Fujiwara no Tadamichi, Masafusa is regarded as one of the three greatest scholars and promoters of Chinese literary studies of his time. He prepared commentaries on portions of *Man'yōshū* and compiled *Wakan rōei gōchū* (Ōe's Notes on the *Wakan rōeishū*). Fourteen of his poems appear in the *waka* anthology *Shikashū* (Collection of Flowery Words, ca. 1151). *Gōdanshō* (Excerpts from Conversations with Ōe no Masafusa), compiled by Fujiwara no Sanekane (1085–1112), has made Masafusa one of the better known figures in Heian literary history. At the request of Regent Fujiwara no Moromichi, Masafusa also compiled *Gōke shidai* (Ōe's Correct Procedures, originally 21 vols., ca. 1100), an important source which documents state ceremonies and events, etiquette, and traditional practices. He has also left us *Gōki* (Ōe's Own Record), which narrates the affairs of his family and documents political changes occurring in government in his day. Masafusa's best *kanshi* are found in such collections as *Honchō zoku monzui* and *Honchō mudaishi*.

▓ *Ōmi no Fukuramaro (fl. ca. 800)*

Ōmi no Mahito Fukuramaro was probably a descendent of Emperor Tenchi. Few facts about his life are known, but the records show that in 797 he was promoted to the rank of junior fifth lower, finally rising to the upper grade in 806. The three poems by Fukuramaro preserved in *Ryōunshū* (nos. 75–77) display his unhappiness over the slow progress of his career. At some point, Fukuramaro became junior assistant head of the Civil Affairs Ministry. Other appointments include a post in the Yamatsukuridokoro (The Office of Imperial Mausolea) and supernumerary governor of Hyūga in Kyushu. For reasons unknown, Fukuramaro received an official reprimand while serving in Bungo province, this probably prior to the Hyūga post. In addition to three poems in *Ryōunshū*, two others appear in *Keikokushū*.

▓ *Ōmiwa no Takechimaro (657–706)*

Ōmiwa no Asomi Takechimaro, the son of Tokane, was a loyal official in the court of Emperor Tenmu, whom he supported during the Jinshin Disturbance of 672, a protracted succession dispute that brought Tenmu to the throne. Takechimaro officiated at Emperor Tenmu's funeral in 686. In 692, he remonstrated with Empress Jitō (r. 690–97), urging her not to make a journey to Ise during the busy harvest season, concerned that such a visit would disrupt the peasants' labors. Unhappy that his advice was ignored, he resigned his post as middle counselor. Takechimaro's story is recounted in Priest Kyōkai's *Nihon koku genpō zen'aku ryōiki* (Miraculous Stories of Karmic Retribution for Good and Evil in Japan), vol. 1 (*jō*), no. 25.

Takechimaro's activities between the time of his resignation in 692 and his appointment in 702 as governor of Nagato are unknown; two of his poems, written at a farewell banquet in 702 prior to his taking up this post, are preserved in *Man'yōshū*, nos. 1770–71. Fujiwara no Hamanari's eighth-century poetic treatise *Kakyō hyōshiki* also contains a poem attributed to Takechimaro, this composed in the six-line *sedōka* form. Takechimaro became master of the Left Capital Office in 703, occupying this post until his death in 706, by which time he held the junior fourth rank upper. For his service during the Jinshin Disturbance, Takechimaro was posthumously granted the junior third rank.

▓ Crown Prince Ōtomo—see Emperor Junna, above

▓ Ōtomo Uji no Hime (fl. ca. 810–24)
Ōtomo Uji no Hime (also known as Hime Ōtomo Uji) is an obscure figure whose biographical details are largely unknown. She may have been a lady-in-waiting in the court of Emperor Saga. Hime is one of only a small number of female *kanshi* poets from the court period, *Bunka shūreishū* 50 being her only extant *kanshi* composition. She is mentioned in the headnote to *Bunka shūreishū* 55, a reply-poem written by Kose no Shikihito in response to an earlier, presumably non-extant verse by this lady titled "My Feelings in the Bedchamber on an Autumn Night."

▓ Prince Ōtsu (663–86)
Prince Ōtsu (Ōtsu no Miko) was the third son (or the second, by some accounts) of Emperor Tenmu (r. 673–86) and his consort Princess Ōta, a daughter of Emperor Tenji. As a boy, the prince personally experienced the Jinshin Disturbance of 672, a succession dispute that brought his father Tenmu to the throne in one of the most well-known fraternal usurpations in Japanese imperial history. Much loved by his father and popular throughout the court, Ōtsu became active in affairs of state himself in 684 and two years later was awarded the second rank, with the honorary prefix "Pure and Great."

Ōtsu is remembered not only for his poignant verse, written in both Chinese and Japanese, but also for his untoward political adventures and subsequent forced suicide, ostensibly for treason, at around the age of twenty-four. His death followed an unsuccessful attempt, apparently instigated by Priest Gyōshin and his circle, to have himself crowned emperor ahead of Prince Kusakabe, the heir apparent, following the death of Tenmu in 686. The story recounted in *Kaifūsō* is that Gyōshin divined Ōtsu's future, using physiognomy, declaring that the prince was an extraordinary individual who would likely come to an unnatural end were he to remain merely a courtier. The import of his message was that nothing short of becoming emperor would save Ōtsu, which apparently induced him to mount his rebellion.[130] It seems most likely that the plot supposedly hatched by Ōtsu and Priest Gyōshin was in fact contrived by Tenmu's politically astute primary consort, Princess Uno no Sarara (the mother of Prince Kusakabe but not Ōtsu), who wished to avoid possible challenges from Ōtsu to Kusakabe's accession.[131]

Ōtsu is said to have gone to his death bravely, with his consort Princess Yamanobe at his side. Legend has it that Prince Ōtsu also visited his sister Princess Ōku in Ise shortly before his death. His untimely end was a source of great sorrow and mourning in his day. A brief interregnum followed the deaths of Tenmu and Ōtsu, during which time Tenmu's consort and Kusakabe jointly managed affairs of state, in accordance with death-bed orders given earlier by Tenmu. Prince Kusakabe himself died in 689, whereupon his mother ascended the throne as Empress Jitō, Japan's forty-first sovereign, reigning for seven years.

Described as a tall, brawny man adept at swordsmanship, Prince Ōtsu was deeply admired for his erudition, literary talent, probity, and free-spiritedness. He is credited in *Nihon shoki* with being Japan's first *kanshi* poet, but it is perhaps more accurate to think of him as being primarily one of the moving forces behind the early popularization of Chinese versification in the Japanese court. In any event, only four of his *kanshi*, *Kaifūsō* 4–7, have survived, along with four *tanka* in *Man'yōshū*. The *kanshi* titled "Near the End" (translated in our volume) was written shortly before his death. *Man'yōshū* 416 conveys similar sentiments: "On Iware Pond / (*Fifty of a hundredfold*) / The mallards cry; / Shall I see them only today / And vanish into the clouds?"[132]

❋ *Priest Renzen (1083?–1149?)*

Priest Renzen (Shaku Renzen), born Fujiwara no Sukemoto, was also known as Chikuzen Nyūdō (The Lay Priest of Chikuzen). A peripatetic figure, he is best remembered today for a series of pleasingly idiosyncratic and colorful poems found in *maki* 7 of *Honchō mudaishi*, which describe

130. See NKBT, 69, pp. 73–74, for *Kaifūsō*'s account of the Prince's life.
131. For further details of the plot and its aftermath, see G. Cameron Hurst, "An Emperor who Ruled as Well as Reigned: Tenmu Tennō," in *Great Historical Figures of Japan* (Tokyo: Japan Culture Institute, 1978), pp. 20–27.
132. Trans. by Edwin A. Cranston, *A Waka Anthology, Volume One: The Gem-Glistening Cup* (Stanford: Stanford University Press, 1993), p. 182.

the hardships and occasional pleasures of his travels by sea around Chikuzen province in northern Kyushu and western Honshu, probably during the years 1143–44. Fujiwara no Chikamitsu (see his biography, above) accompanied Renzen on this trip. Renzen had also made two earlier visits to Chikuzen. His foster father, Fujiwara no Motozane (1045–1108), served as governor of Chikuzen from 1106 until his death, and Renzen was apparently with him in Chikuzen for the duration of this appointment. Renzen's elder brother Kin'akira was made governor of the same province in 1127, and Renzen is known to have visited him there.

Although Renzen reached the junior fifth lower rank at court, he retired before he was forty, taking Buddhist vows around 1120 and spending his final years in obscurity. His life was marked by adversity and setbacks, perhaps attributable in part to his losing at a young age the support and protection of both his father Michisuke, director of the Bureau of Carpentry (d. 1095), and his foster father (d.1108).

✖ Emperor Saga (786–842; r. 809–23)

Emperor Saga, the fifty-second emperor of Japan, was the second son of Emperor Kanmu. As Prince Kamino, he succeeded his brother Emperor Heizei (r. 806–9) when the latter abdicated because of illness. Political intrigues marked Saga's early years on the throne. A year after his accession, Fujiwara no Kusuko, the favorite concubine of Emperor Heizei, conspired with her elder brother Fujiwara no Nakanari to reinstall Heizei as sovereign. This event, known as the Kusuko Incident (Kusuko no Hen), was crushed, and Nakanari was condemned to death for his part in the uprising. Kusuko committed suicide with poison, while Heizei and the heir apparent, Prince Takaoka, were made to take Buddhist vows.

Saga's reign was thereafter peaceful, and he proved to be an outstanding ruler as well as a great poet and promoter of Tang culture in the Japanese court. He not only strengthened the Ritsuryō institutions but also greatly enriched the literary climate of his day. Among his many accomplishments was the sponsorship of various important scholarly projects, including the groundbreaking genealogy *Shinsei shōjiroku* (New Compilation of the Register of Families) and codes such as *Kōnin kyaku* and *Dairi shiki*.[133] Saga is also credited with the institution of certain extra-*ritsuryō* offices, including the Kurōdodokoro (Chamberlain's Office) and the Kebiishi (Imperial Police). He retired in 823, after a reign of some fourteen years, living thereafter in the Reizei'in Palace. Later, in 834, he moved to Saga'in, a residence in the western hills of Kyoto. At Saga'in he lived on for another eight years, writing *kanshi*, practicing calligraphy, and promoting the literary arts.

---

133. See our biography of Fujiwara no Fuyutsugu for information on these two legal texts.

A gifted scholar, Saga was deeply respected for his erudition. He was also considered one of the three great calligraphers of his age, along with Priest Kūkai (774–835) and Tachibana Hayanari (?–842). The three were collectively known as Sanpitsu, "The Three Brushes." Saga is renowned for his patronage of Chinese literature, which flourished in the Japanese court during his reign in what has since been regarded as the golden age of *kanbun* literature. Two official *kanshi* anthologies were compiled while he was on the throne: *Ryōunshū*, which was the first imperially commissioned *kanshi* anthology, and *Bunka shūreishū*. A third anthology, *Keikokushū*, followed in 827. In short, Emperor Saga was the imperial family's most distinguished and influential *kanshi* poet—the leading literatus of his day and the primary patron of the literary arts. It is hardly surprising that some twenty percent of the works contained in the above three imperial anthologies were written by Saga himself, ninety-six poems in all.

❊ *Sakanoue no Imiki Imao (fl. ninth century)*
Sakanoue no Imiki Imao, about whom nothing is known, was the putative author of *Bunka shūreishū* 35. The second character in the name Imao may well be a scribal error for "tsugu," which would mean that "Imao" was in fact Sakanoue no Imatsugu, the author of *Bunka shūreishū* 36 and *Ryōunshū* 81–82.[134] *Ryōunshū* identifies Sakanoue no Imatsugu as the left senior recorder in the Council of State. He also served as senior secretary in the Council of State for a period in the 820s, at which time his rank was junior fifth lower. Around the same time he held an appointment as professor of Chinese history and literature, stepping down in 824. Imatsugu later assisted Fujiwara no Otsugu (774–843) with the compilation of *Nihon kōki*, a history covering the period 792–833.

❊ *Prince Sannomiya Sukehito (1073–1119)*
Prince Sannomiya Sukehito (Sannomiya Sukehito Shinnō) was the third son of Emperor Go-Sanjō, who had proclaimed Sukehito his heir. However, following the emperor's death, Sukehito became involved in a protracted succession dispute with his elder half-brother, who eventually won out and took the throne as Emperor Shirakawa (r. 1072–86). After Shirakawa's son succeeded him as Emperor Horikawa (r. 1086–1107), Sukehito lost all hope of ascending the throne himself and retired to the seclusion of Ninnaji temple in the Hanazono area of Kyoto. However, political intrigue continued to follow him. In 1113, Priest Jinkan, a loyal supporter of Sukehito, was found to be plotting the assassination of Emperor Toba (r. 1107–23), who had succeeded Emperor Horikawa. Sukehito lived under virtual house arrest for the next two years, confining himself to literary activities. The father of

134. See NKBT, 69, p. 514.

waka poet Minamoto no Arihito (1103–47), Sukehito was himself an excellent poet, with several *waka* in *Kin'yō wakashū* and *Shinsen rōeishū*. Many *kanshi* by Sukehito appear in *Honchō mudaishi*. A *kanshi* poetry salon, the so-called "Hundred Lords of Sannomiya," formed around him after his retirement to Ninnaji.

🏵 *Sena no Kimi Yukifumi (?–?)*

Sena no Kimi Yukifumi (Gyōmon) was a scholar in the Academy and the son of an immigrant Korean scholar named Sena no Tokufuku, who settled in the Koma district of Musashi province. Few details of his academic career survive. In 721, he held a second-degree professorship of law in the Academy at the rank of senior seventh upper. He was promoted to the junior fifth rank lower in 727 and served as tutor to the crown prince. Yukifumi served as vice-director of the Academy as well, although the years of his appointment are unknown. Two of his *kanshi, Kaifūsō* 60–61, and one *waka, Man'yōshū* 3836, survive.

🏵 *Shigeno no Yoshinaga (fl. first half of the ninth century)*

Little is known about the life of Shigeno no Yoshinaga. He may have served Emperor Saga. *Keikokushū* has three of Yoshinaga's poems, nos. 36, 165, and 213. It is conjectured by Kojima Noriyuki that poem 213 was written on the imperial command of Emperor Ninmyō (r. 833–50) while the latter was still crown prince.[135] Yoshinaga apparently did not hold rank when *Keikokushū* was compiled, although he was eligible under the "shadow rank" system to receive a rank and post at age twenty-one. See the notes to KKS 36, above.

🏵 *Shimada no Tadaomi (828–92?)*

Shimada no Tadaomi was a student of Sugawara no Koreyoshi and studied Chinese history and literature at the Academy. Sugawara no Michizane's first teacher, friend, and later, father-in-law, Tadaomi entered the bureaucracy at a low rank and possibly without taking the civil service exams. At thirty-two, while serving as junior secretary of Echizen, he was chosen to compose poems to match ones written by a visiting ambassador from Parhae. Around this time, Tadaomi was serving under the influential Regent Fujiwara no Mototsune (836–91), with whom he enjoyed a close and enduring personal relationship. Tadaomi was also on friendly terms with Ki no Haseo, an important court scholar-official. In 879 he reached the rank of junior fifth upper. In 886 Tadaomi became junior secretary in the Council of State, responsible for drafting documents. Three years later, he was sent to Inaba as supernumerary vice-governor. Tadaomi also served two years as

135. Kojima, *Kokufū ankoku jidai no bungaku*, vol. 3 (bk. 2), p. 3603.

junior assistant head of the War Ministry during his mid-fifties, and in 892, the year he is believed to have died, he was appointed director of the Bureau of Medicine. Tadaomi had a relatively undistinguished court career compared to his famous student Michizane, spending much of his life serving in lesser provincial posts. However, in the realm of *kanshi* composition he had few peers. Tadaomi's *kanshi* are preserved in the three-volume *Denshi kashū* (comp. ca. 892). This anthology, comprising some 213 poems, is testimony to Tadaomi's considerable skill and appeal as a *kanshi* poet.

❊ *Shimada (?) no Yoshimune (fl. late ninth century?)*

Yoshimune, whose surname is in doubt, was a *Fusōshū* poet. No details concerning his life are known.

❊ *Sugawara no Ariyoshi (1043?–1122?)*

Sugawara no Ariyoshi, a *kanshi* and *waka* poet, was the son of Sadayoshi, sometime Director of the Academy. Ariyoshi studied Chinese history and literature, passing his *taisaku* exams in 1074. In 1077 he was awarded the junior fifth lower rank. Ariyoshi's court appointments included junior assistant head of the Ministry of Ceremonial, senior private secretary in the Central Affairs Ministry, and professor at the Academy. In 1111 he was appointed as a lecturer in the court of Emperor Toba and in the same year became senior assistant head of the Ministry of Ceremonial. He remained in this post for the rest of his life, exercising administrative control over the Academy as well. Ariyoshi rose to the junior fourth upper rank but was posthumously promoted to the junior third rank.

Ariyoshi's *kanshi* are found in *Honchō mudaishi*, and further Chinese works by him are contained in *Honchō zoku monzui*. *Ariyoshi no Ason shū* (The Ariyoshi Collection), his private poetry anthology, preserves many of his *waka*. There are five additional items by Ariyoshi in other anthologies.

❊ *Sugawara no Fumitoki (899–981)*

Sugawara no Fumitoki was a prominent man of letters in his day. He was the son of Takami and grandson of the scholar and courtier Sugawara no Michizane. Fumitoki did not complete his university studies until he was thirty-five, and he sat his *shūsai* essay exams at the age of forty-four. His career included appointments as senior private secretary in the Central Affairs Ministry, middle controller, professor of Chinese history and literature (956), supernumerary governor of Owari, director of the Academy, and senior assistant head of the Ministry of Ceremonial (977). For some reason, he was slow to gain promotion in rank, but he finally reached the junior fourth in 962 and the senior fourth lower in 974. At the advanced age of eighty-three, after repeated application, he was promoted to the junior third rank, dying that same year.

In mid-career, Fumitoki became active in Chinese literary circles, being most influential during the reigns of emperors Murakami (r. 946–67) and Enyū (r. 969–84). He was regarded as one of the pillars of the Chinese literary establishment, his writings becoming models for his peers. Many of his poems, which are characterized by their charm and delicacy, have been preserved in *Fusōshū*, *Ruijū kudaishō*, and *Wakan rōeishū*. In the latter collection he has the most compositions, and some thirty-nine of his literary pieces are contained in *Honchō monzui*. There are various stories concerning Fumitoki's life in *Jikkinshō* (The Miscellany of Ten Maxims, 1252) and *Gōdanshō*. His personal collection, *Bunkaishū* (Collection of Literary Trifles), is no longer extant. Fumitoki was known posthumously by the sobriquet Sugawara Sanbon, "Sugawara of the Third Rank."

✳ *Sugawara no Michizane (845–903)*

A member of a leading family of literati, Sugawara no Michizane stands at the pinnacle of the Japanese *kanshi* tradition. He was the third son of Koreyoshi, who served in the Academy as a professor, as did Koreyoshi's father. Michizane carried on the family's scholastic traditions, beginning his education when he was four and soon distinguishing himself as a gifted student of Chinese studies, poetry in particular. He entered the Academy at seventeen, somewhat earlier than most, obtaining his *monjō tokugōshō* qualification at twenty-three. In 870, at the age of twenty-five, Michizane passed the civil service examinations and began his career as a minor court bureaucrat, drafting documents. Although his official career during this decade was unremarkable, he quickly gained a reputation as a skillful poet and was frequently called upon to compose verse to commemorate state occasions, including palace banquets, imperial excursions, and festivals. While competently crafted, this public poetry was not his best: today Michizane is largely remembered for the impassioned private poems he wrote during periods of adversity in his life.

In 880, when he was thirty-three, Michizane was appointed professor of Chinese history and literature, heading the Academy. But within days he became embroiled in a dispute that saw him accused by students of unfair grading practices. Further strife followed two years later in another scandal, where he was accused of writing an anonymous poem criticizing the influential court figure Fujiwara no Fuyuo (808–90). While the charge was never proven, the insinuations made by contemporaries jealous of his skills left Michizane embittered and cynical about court life, which manifested itself in the poetry he composed as an emotional outlet during these trying times.

Worse, however, was yet to come. In 886, Regent Fujiwara Mototsune engineered a reshuffling of court posts, largely to create vacancies for his own family and followers and further cement the Fujiwara position at court.

This event came soon after the coming of age ceremony of Mototsune's son Tokihira. Michizane and twenty-eight others, considered to be of a lesser pedigree and therefore expendable, lost their positions. Michizane himself was sent to Shikoku to serve as the governor of Sanuki province, a turn of events which left him thunderstruck and filled with gloom. Sanuki was by no means distant from the capital, nor was it a hardship post, but Michizane evidently viewed it as such, all the more so since reaching Sanuki entailed a perilous journey by boat. Throughout the four years he served as governor of this province, Michizane never reconciled himself to being away from the capital. The homesickness he felt, combined with seeing at first hand the harsh realities of life in the provinces, left a lasting impression on him. Indeed, the very unhappiness he experienced made this the most prolific and fruitful period of his poetic career, and some 150 poems from the Sanuki years have survived.

Michizane returned to the court in the spring of 890 to find Emperor Uda (r. 887–97) on the throne. He became a close confident of Uda, flourishing under his patronage, but his position was far from secure because of the suspicion in which he was held by certain Fujiwara courtiers and others at court. His relatively modest lineage was never forgotten as his influence increased, engendering jealousy and a sense in certain quarters that he had risen above his station. In any event, Michizane served in a variety of positions during the Uda years, including head of the Chamberlains' Office (891), left middle controller (891), consultant (893), left major controller (893), middle counselor (895), and head of the Popular Affairs Ministry (896). He was also appointed ambassador to China in 894, but the mission was aborted owing to unrest in China attendant upon the unraveling of the Tang dynasty.

In 897, Uda abdicated and his son Daigo (formerly Prince Atsugimi), then aged twelve, was enthroned in his place. To assist Daigo, who intended to employ Michizane as a buffer against Fujiwara influence, a quasi-regency was established, with Michizane, then fifty-five, appointed minister of the right in 899 and Fujiwara no Tokihira as minister of the left, the higher of the two positions. Michizane had unsuccessfully tried to decline this post, aware of his unpopularity at court and the possible pitfalls that lay ahead. The following year, Miyoshi no Kiyoyuki urged him to retire immediately and go into the mountains, a preemptive step to avoid becoming the victim of a purge, but this advice went unheeded.

Finally, in 901, some two weeks after being elevated to the junior second rank along with Tokihira, Michizane was suddenly stripped of his titles and ordered to leave the capital. A proclamation drawn up by enemies who had engineered his overthrow accused Michizane of excessive ambitiousness and manipulating the emperor to boost his own power. Tokihira and his cohorts alleged that Michizane was scheming to place his own son-in-law, Prince Tokiyo (a son of Emperor Uda), on the throne, deposing Daigo. Although Michizane was declared exempt from severe punishment because of his record of past services to the realm, he was forced to accept a distant appointment as supernumerary governor-general of the Government Head-quarters in Dazaifu, Kyushu. Michizane was escorted from the capital under armed guard and spent the next three years under house arrest in conditions of considerable material hardship, effectively living in exile. Roughly fifty poems, the most poignant and heart-rending he ever wrote, survive from this period. Michizane died in Dazaifu in 903, a broken man.

Some twenty years after his death, Michizane was posthumously reha-bilitated and reinstated as minister of the right, the injustice of his fate being recognized at last by the court. During the ensuing centuries, shrines were established in Michizane's memory, and he was elevated to near mythical status as the patron saint of scholarship. In 993, Michizane was posthu-mously made chancellor. Even today, he is revered by the Japanese people, who worship his deified spirit as Tenjinsama at Shinto shrines throughout the land.

Michizane is perhaps the preeminent *kanshi* poet of the Heian age. His lyrical oeuvre offers penetrating insights into his mind and his checkered official career, as well as glimpses into ninth-century court life, politics, and rural society in those times. Michizane was among the first *kanshi* poets to rise above mere imitation of the Chinese masters and harness the structural and thematic possibilities offered by Chinese poetic models. In so doing, he created a legacy of memorably poignant verse, which, while bearing the imprint of the Tang masters, had its own uniquely Japanese flavor and spirit.

▓ Tachibana no Aritsura (fl. ca. 940s, d. ca. 954)

Tachibana no Aritsura was a respected scholar and minor poet. Accounts differ as to whether he ever completed his Academy studies, but he appears to have gained his first court appointment when he was thirty. Aritsura served as tutor to the literatus Minamoto no Shitagō. His talents were said to have been recognized by such respected intellectuals as Minamoto no Fusaakira. Aritsura was appointed vice-governor of Aki and later, after a series of promotions, rose to become senior assistant president of the Board of Censors.

In 944 Aritsura took Buddhist vows and went to live at Enryakuji on Mt. Hiei under the name of Sonkei. Aritsura particularly loved to compose acrostic verse, enjoying it alongside his more serious compositions. A seven-volume collection of his works compiled by Minamoto no Shitagō and titled *Shamon Kei-kō shū* (The Collected Works of the Monk Lord Kei [Aritsura]) has been lost, although the preface (dated 954), with its details about his life, has been preserved in *Honchō monzui*. A short series of Aritsura's poems exchanged with Minamoto no Fusaakira can be found in

Fusōshū. One poetry anthology preface attributed to Aritsura occurs in *Honchō monzui.* Still other literary pieces and citations of his poetry appear in *Wakan rōeishū, Shinsen rōeishū, Ruijū kudaishō,* and elsewhere.

⌘ *Tachibana no Tameyoshi (?–1017)*
Tachibana no Tameyoshi, eldest son of Michiaki (reading tentative), was known for his expertise in both Chinese and Japanese literature. In 996 he became supernumerary governor of Hizen, at the rank of junior fifth lower. Six year later, he was appointed governor of Iga and became chief of household to Prince Atsuyasu, son of Emperor Ichijō. From this time on, Tameyoshi became a frequent guest at court poetic gatherings. In 1005 he was made supernumerary director of the Imperial Storehouse (Uchinokura), in charge of handling imperial provisions, royal treasures, and daily effects. Later in the same decade, he served in the Imperial Police and in various other court posts. In 1015, Tameyoshi was appointed as Michinaga's chief of household at the rank of senior fourth lower. At the time of his death, he was governor of Tajima, holding the senior fourth lower. Two of his poems are found in *Honchō reisō.*

⌘ *Taira no Satsuki (?–?)*
Biographical details concerning Taira no Satsuki are lacking. Satsuki was the author of *Bunka shūreishū* 95. In the titles of poems 93 and 94 (by Emperor Saga and Fujiwara no Fuyutsugu, respectively) in the same anthology, Satsuki is identified as the clerk (*rokuji*) of Musashi province, a post which carried the eighth rank.

⌘ *Tajihi no Hironari (?–739)*
Tajihi no Mahito Hironari was the fifth son of Tajihi no Shima, minister of the right. He was appointed governor of Shimotsuke in 708 and five years later became lieutenant general (*fuku shōgun*). Hironari went on to gain an appointment as governor of Echizen (719), while also assuming responsibility for the provinces of Nōtō, Etchū, and Echigo, serving in the capacity of *azechi* (administrative overseer for several provinces). In 733, Hironari was sent as an emissary to the Tang court, returning to Tanegashima the following year and then finally to Heian, in 735. Two years later Hironari was made middle counselor and promoted to the junior third rank, finally ending his career as head of the Ministry of Ceremonial. Three of Hironari's *kanshi* appear in *Kaifūsō.*

⌘ *Takaoka no Otokoe (fl. ca. 810)*
Takaoka no Sukune Otokoe (Otoe) is believed to have been a descendant of Korean immigrants from Paekche and Koguryö. In 812, Otokoe received an appointment as vice-governor of Yamashiro at the rank of "second class"

(*ge-i*) junior fifth lower.[136] He was elevated to second class junior fifth upper two years later, winning promotion to regular junior fifth lower the following year. Two poems by Otokoe are found in *Ryōunshū*.

✖ *Tami no Imiki Kurohito (?–?)*

Tami no Imiki Kurohito was of Korean descent, *imiki* being the fourth of eight *kabane* titles created during Emperor Tenmu's reign and awarded primarily to naturalized immigrant families. In records, the prefix "recluse" (*inshi*) often appears attached to Kurohito's name, indicating that he had removed himself at some stage from official life, a fact that is evident in his poetry as well. One source identifies him as senior secretary of Harima province, his rank the junior sixth upper. Kurohiro's place of origin was probably Amuki district in Ise province. *Kaifūsō* contains two of his poems.

✖ *Prince Tomohira (964–1009)*

Prince Tomohira (Tomohira Shinnō), also known as Chigusa-dono (Lord of Chigusa) and Nochi no Chūsho Ō (The Latter Prince and Head of the Central Affairs Ministry), was the seventh son of Emperor Murakami and Princess Sōshi. The founder of the Murakami Genji branch of the Minamoto family, Tomohira was a literary man of talent and broad erudition. He was also expert in Japanese music, medicine, and Chinese composition. He served as the head of the Central Affairs Ministry from his mid-twenties, upon the death of his predecessor, Prince Kaneakira, in 987. In 991 Tomohira produced a four-volume commentary titled *Guketsu getenshō* on works in the Chinese canon, this based on the earlier scholarship of the important Tang dynasty monk Zhan Ran in his work titled *Zhi guan fu xing chuan hong jue*. Tomohira frequently organized poetry composition sessions at his residence. His Chinese prose and poetry are found in *Honchō reisō*, *Honchō monzui*, and *Wakan rōeishū*, his *waka* in *Shūi wakashū*, *Goshūi wakashū* (The Second Collection of Japanese Poetic Gleanings, compiled 1086), and later imperial anthologies. Tomohira's private anthology and a book on poetic style attributed to him are no longer extant.

✖ *Princess Uchiko (807–47)*

Princess Uchiko (Uchiko or Uchishi Naishinnō) was the eighth (third, according to some accounts) daughter of Emperor Saga and one of the few known female *kanshi* poets of the Heian age. She became the first Vestal Virgin of the Kamo Shrine at the age of three, remaining at the shrine for some twenty-three years. In 823, when she was seventeen, Emperor Saga paid her a visit at Kamo Shrine and held a poetry banquet, at which she was

---

136. The *ge-i* ("second class rank") system was reserved for provincial families or persons of lower status than the central aristocracy.

commanded to write seven-character octaves for the assembled guests. Uchiko's compositions were said to have been so distinguished that Saga granted her a one hundred-household enfiefment to supply her with special income for entertaining literati, also awarding her the third imperial rank (*sanbon*), one of four special ranks reserved for imperial princes and princesses. In 833, when Ninmyō came to the throne, Uchiko, who had left Kamo Shrine about two years earlier, was promoted to the second rank.

Upon her retirement, Uchiko went to live at a mountain retreat in the Saga area of Kyoto. Eight of her *kanshi*, most of them rather ordinary, survive in *Keikokushū*, with an additional one in *Zatsugon hōwa* (Irregular-Style Matching Poems) and yet another in *Shoku Nihon kōki* (The Latter Chronicles of Japan Continued, compiled 869). In *Shoku Nihon kōki* it is stated that Uchiko had a superb knowledge of Chinese history and an excellent command of Chinese. Many consider her the best female *kanshi* poet of the Heian period, a view echoed in the seventeenth-century *kanshi* collection *Honchō ichinin isshu* (One Hundred Poems by a Hundred Poets of Our Court, ca. 1660).

Wake no Nakayo (fl. ca. 850)
The son of Wake no Kiyomaro, Nakayo became the governor of Harima in 852 and was known for his loyal and filial nature. A single *fu* (prose-poem) by him, *Keikokushū* 16, has survived. Nakayo was promoted to the junior fifth upper in 826.

Nun Yamato (fl. early ninth century?)
The identity of this minor female poet is unknown, as is the proper reading for her surname, which might alternatively been been "Wake" or another surname beginning with "wa." Several tentative identifications can be found in Kojima, *Kokufū ankoku jidai no bungaku*, vol. 2 (bk. 3), pt. II, p. 2678. One theory is that she may have been a sister of Yamato Niigasa, consort of Emperor Kanmu.

Yoshimine no Ason Yasuyo (785–830)
Yoshimine no Ason Yasuyo was the son of Emperor Kanmu and the father of the *waka* poet Priest Henjō, one of the so-called "Six Sages of Japanese Poetry." A leading scholar and literatus in his day, he is best remembered for having worked with Shigeno no Sadanushi as one of the chief compilers of *Keikokushū*. Four *kanshi* by him are preserved in *Bunka shūreishū*, two in *Ryōunshū*, and seven in *Keikokushū*.

In his youth, Yasuyo developed a passion for falconry and displayed prowess in the martial arts, also showing academic and literary talent. In addition, he was respected for his knowledge of Japanese music and his calligraphic skills. Yasuyo took the surname Yoshimine and the *kabane* title *ason* in 802. During his life, he held an array of court positions, changing posts often and holding many appointments concurrently. His career included service as director of the Bureau of Music (809), right lesser captain of the Imperial Bodyguards (809), left minor controller (810), and left lesser captain of the Imperial Bodyguards (ca. 810). In 810 he also became vice-governor of Tanba, being subsequently promoted to governor of that province in 813. In 811, he was appointed first secretary of the Chamberlains' Office.

Yasuyo went on to hold positions in the Right Bureau of Horses, the Left Military Guards, and the Left Capital Office (815), serving further terms as governor in a number of different provinces, including Ōmi. He was appointed consultant and right major controller in 816. Three years later Yasuyo accepted a commission to compile *Nihon kōki*, the third of the six national histories, working with his maternal half-brother Fujiwara no Fuyutsugu (775–826) and Fujiwara no Otsugu (773–843). In 820 he held the rank of senior fourth lower and had also gained the post of left major controller. The following year he was awarded the rank of junior third and advanced further to become middle counselor, gaining also the position of censor for Mutsu and Dewa provinces. In 821, assisted by Fuyutsugu and Otsugu, he compiled a book of palace laws known as *Dairi shiki*, at the request of Emperor Saga. In 822 Yasuyo assumed duties as master of the Crown Prince's Office and the following year was appointed right major captain in the Imperial Bodyguards and superintendent of the Imperial Police. Finally, in 828, Yasuyo became major counselor, after two years of quasi-retirement, during which time he had declared himself too ill to appear at court. This period of illness appears to have commenced with the death of his half-brother Fuyutsugu, in 826. Upon Yasuyo's premature death at the age of forty-six, Retired Emperor Saga wrote two *kanshi* elegies for him. Yasuyo was also posthumously honored with a promotion to the junior second rank.

BIBLIOGRAPHY

Addiss, Stephen. *Tall Mountains and Flowing Waters: The Arts of Uragami Gyokudō*. Honolulu: University of Hawaii Press, 1987.

———, Jonathan Chaves, and J. Thomas Rimer. *Old Taoist: The Art, Poetry, and Life of Kodōjin (1865–1944)*. New York: Columbia University Press, 2000.

Andō Hideo, comp. *[Shintei] Nihon kanshi hyakusen*. Tokyo: Sōdōsha, 1983.

Aoki, Michiko Y., trans. and annot. *Records of Wind and Earth: A Translation of Fudoki with Introduction and Commentaries*. Ann Arbor: Association for Asian Studies, Inc., 1997.

Arntzen, Sonja, trans. and annot. *Ikkyū and the Crazy Cloud Anthology: A Zen Poet of Medieval Japan*. Tokyo: University of Tokyo Press, 1986.

Aston, W.G., trans. *Nihongi: Chronicles of Japan from the Earliest Times to A.D. 697*. London, 1956; reprint, Rutland, Vermont and Tokyo: Charles E. Tuttle Co., 1972.

Bodman, Richard Wainwright. *Prose and Poetry in Early Medieval China: A Study and Translation of Kūkai's Bunkyō Hifuron*. Ann Arbor, Michigan: University Microfilms, 1978.

Borgen, Robert. *Sugawara no Michizane and the Early Japanese Court*. Orig. Cambridge: Council on East Asian Studies, vol. 120. Cambridge: Harvard University Press, 1986; reprint, Honolulu: University of Hawaii Press, 1994.

Bradstock, Timothy R., and Judith N. Rabinovitch, trans. and annot. *An Anthology of Kanshi (Chinese Verse) by Japanese Poets of the Edo Period (1603–1868)*. Japanese Studies, 3. Lewiston: The Edwin Mellen Press, 1997.

Brower, Robert, and Earl Miner. *Japanese Court Poetry*. Stanford: Stanford University Press, 1961.

Bunka shūreishū. See Kojima Noriyuki, below.

Chang, Kang-i Sun. *The Evolution of Chinese Tz'u Poetry from Late Tang to Northern Sung*. Princeton: Princeton University Press, 1980.

———. *Six Dynasties Poetry*. Princeton: Princeton University Press, 1986.

Chaves, Jonathan, and J. Thomas Rimer, eds. *Shisendō: Hall of the Poetry Immortals*. Tokyo: Weatherhill, 1991.

Cheng, François. *Chinese Poetic Writing with an Anthology of Tang Poetry*. Trans. from the orig. French (1977) by Donald A. Riggs and Jerome P. Seaton; anthology trans. from the Chinese for the English edition by Jerome P. Seaton. Bloomington: Indiana University Press, 1982.

Cranston, Edwin A., trans. *A Waka Anthology*, Volume One: *The Gem-Glistening Cup*. Stanford: Stanford University Press, 1993.

Dai Nihon kokiroku. Comp. Tōkyō Daigaku Shiryō Hensanjo, 1952– (in progress).

Davis, A. R. *T'ao Yuan-ming (A.D. 365–427): His Works and Their Meaning*. 2 vols. Cambridge: Cambridge University Press, 1976.

Eberhard, Wolfram. *A Dictionary of Chinese Symbols*. London and New York: Routledge and Kegan Paul, 1986; [first pub. in German, 1983].

Endō Tetsuo. *Kanshi*. 3 vols. Shinshaku kanbun taikei, vols. 42–43, 52. Tokyo: Meiji Shoin, 1989–92.

Farris, William Wayne. *Population, Disease, and Land in Early Japan, 645–900*. Harvard East Asian Monographs, 157. Cambridge, MA and London: Harvard University Press: 1985.

Frankel, Hans H. *The Flowering Plum and the Palace Lady: Interpretations of Chinese Poetry*. New Haven: Yale University Press, 1976.

Fujikawa Hideo, Matsushita Tadashi, and Sano Masami, eds. *Shikashū Nihon kanshi*. 11 vols. Tokyo: Kyūko Shoin, 1983–84.

———, Matsushita Tadashi, and Sano Masami, eds. *Shishū Nihon kanshi*. 20 vols. Tokyo: Kyūko Shoin, 1985–90.

Fujiwara Michinaga. *Midō kanpaku ki*. 3 vols. In *Dai Nihon kokiroku*, listed above.

Fujiwara Tadamichi. *Hosshōji dono gyoshū*. In *[Shinkō] Gunsho ruijū* 126, vol. 6. Tokyo: Naigai Shoseki Kabushiki Kaisha, 1931.

Fusōshū. See entry for Kawamata Keiichi, below.

Giles, Herbert A., comp. *A Chinese Biographical Dictionary*. 2 vols. Orig. pub. London: Bernard Quaritch, and Shanghai and Yokohama: Kelly Walsh, Ltd., 1898; reprint, Taipei: Literature House, 1962.

Gotō Akio. "Saga Tennō to Kōnin-ki shidan." In *Gobun kenkyū* 28 (1970).

———. *Heianchō kanbungaku ronkō*. Tokyo: Ōfūsha, 1981.

———. *Heianchō bunjin shi*. Tokyo: Yoshikawa kōbunkan, 1993.

Graham, A.C. *Poems of the Late Tang*. Harmondsworth: Penguin Books, 1965.

Hakeda, Yoshito S. *Kūkai: Major Works*. New York: Columbia University Press, 1972.

Hanawa Hokinoichi, comp. *[Shinkō] Gunsho ruijū.* Ed. Sakamoto Kōtarō and others. 24 vols. 1938–39.

Harada Kenyū, comp. *Nihon kanshi sen.* Kyoto: Jinbun Shoin, 1974.

Heian jidai shi jiten. 1 vol. (in 3 parts). Comp. Tsunoda Bun'ei. Tokyo: Kadokawa Shoten: 1994.

Heian jinmei jiten: Chōhō ninen. Comp. Makino Hirozō. Tokyo: Takashina Shoten, 1993.

Hérail, Francine. *Poèmes de Fujiwara no Michinaga, ministre à la cour de Heian (995–1018).* Geneva: Librairie Droz, 1993.

Hightower, James R. *Topics in Chinese Literature: Outlines and Bibliographies.* Harvard-Yenching Institute Studies, vol. 3. Cambridge: Harvard University Press, 1966.

———. *The Poetry of T'ao Ch'ien.* Oxford: Clarendon Press, 1970.

Hirano Hikojirō, and others, comps. *Kanshi meishi hyōshaku shūsei.* Tokyo: Meichō Fukyūkai, 1936.

Inagaki Hisao. *A Dictionary of Japanese Buddhist Terms,* third ed. Kyoto: Nagata Bunshodo, 1988.

Hatanaka Sakae. "Heian-chō kanshijin no bukkyō juyō ni kansuru ikkōsatsu: *Honchō mudaishi* o chūshin ni shite." *Kanazawa daigaku kokugo kokubun* 5 (1976): 42–48.

Honchō monzui. See entries for Kojima Noriyuki, Kuroita Katsumi, Ōsone Shōsuke, and Kakimura Shigematsu, below.

Honchō mudaishi. See Honma Yōichi, below.

Honchō reisō. See Kawaguchi Hisao, below.

Honchō zoku monzui. See Kuroita Katsumi, below.

Honma Yōichi, annot. *Honchō mudaishi zenchūshaku.* 3 vols. Shintensha chūshaku sōsho, vols. 2, 4, 7. Tokyo: Shintensha, 1992–94.

———. "Ōchō kanshi no inshuei kanken: sono goi, koji o meguru oboegaki to shite." *Nihongo Nihon bungaku* 4 (1992): 1–16.

———, annot. *Nihon kanshi: kodai-hen.* Osaka: Izumi Shoin, 1996.

Horikawa Takashi. "Kinsei ni okeru *Honchō mudaishi* no kenkyū to kyōju."*Wakan hikaku bungaku* 13 (1994): 58–69.

———. "Shi no katachi, shi no kokoro: *Honchō mudaishi* no haikei." *Kokugo to kokubungaku* 72, no. 5 (1995): 117–127.

Hosshōji dono gyoshū. See entry for Fujiwara Tadamichi, above.

Hung, William. *Tu Fu: China's Greatest Poet.* Cambridge: Harvard University Press, 1952.

Hurst, G. Cameron. "An Emperor Who Ruled as Well as Reigned: Tenmu Tennō." In *Great Historical Figures of Japan,* pp. 20–27. Tokyo: Japan Culture Institute, 1978.

Ichikawa Mototarō. *Nihon kanbungakushi gaisetsu.* Tokyo: Tōyō Gakujutsu Kenkyūkai, 1969.

Ichiko Teiji, ed. *Nihon bungaku zenshi.* Vol. 2. Tokyo: Gakutōsha, 1978.

Inagaki, Hisao. *A Dictionary of Japanese Buddhist Terms*, third ed. Kyoto: Nagata Bunshodo, 1988, p. 253.

Inoguchi Atsushi, comp. and annot. *Nihon kanshi*. 2 vols. Shinshaku kanbun taikei, vols. 45–46. Tokyo: Meiji Shoin, 1972.

———, comp. and annot. *Josei to kanshi: wakan joryū shi shi*. Kazama sensho, vol. 103. Tokyo: Kazama Shoin, 1978.

———. *Nihon kanshi kanshō jiten*. Tokyo: Kadokawa Shoten, 1980.

———. *Nihon kanbungaku shi*. Tokyo: Kadokawa Shoten, 1984.

———. *Nihon kanshi*. Shinsho kanbun taikei, 7. Tokyo: Meiji Shoin, 1996.

Iritani Sensuku. *Kindai bungaku to shite no Meiji kanshi*. Kenbun sensho, vol. 42. Tokyo: Kenbun Shuppan, 1989.

Iriya Yoshitaka. *Nihonjin bunjin shisen*. Tokyo: Chūō Kōronsha, 1983.

Ishikawa Tadahisa, comp. *Kanshi no sekai: sono kokoro to ajiwai*. Tokyo: Taishūkan, 1975; reprint, 1989.

Iwaki Hideo. *Kanshi bi no sekai*. Bukkyō Daigaku shijō sentā sōsho, 3. Kyoto: Jinbun Shoin, 1997.

Kaifūsō. See second entry for Kojima Noriyuki, below.

Kakimura Shigematsu, and Yamagishi Tokuhei, eds. *Jōdai Nihon kanbungakushi*. Tokyo: Nihon Shoin, 1947.

———. *Jōdai Nihon kanbungaku shi*. Tokyo: Nihon Shoin, 1947.

———, annot. *Honchō monzui chūshaku*. 2 vols. Tokyo: Fuzanbō, 1968.

Kaneko Hikojirō. *Heian jidai bungaku to Hakushi monjū: Kudai waka, Senzai kaku kenkyū hen*. Baifūkan, 1943.

Kanke bunsō, Kanke kōshū. See next entry for Kawaguchi Hisao.

Kawaguchi Hisao, annot. *Kanke bunsō, Kanke kōshū*. Nihon koten bungaku taikei, 72. Tokyo: Iwanami Shoten, 1966.

———. *Heian-chō no kanbungaku*. Nihon rekishi sōsho, 36. Tokyo: Yoshikawa Kōbunkan, 1981.

———. *Wakan rōeishū zen'yaku chū*. Kōdansha gakujutsu bunko, 325. Tokyo: Kōdansha, 1982.

———. *Heian-chō Nihon kanbungaku-shi no kenkyū*, 3 vols. Tokyo: Meiji Shoin, rev. exp. 3rd ed, 1975–88; orig. pub. 1959.

———. *Heian-chō kanbungaku no kaika: shijin Kūkai to Michizane*. Tokyo: Yoshikawa Kōbunkan, 1991.

———, and others, annot. *Honchō reisō kanchū*. Tokyo: Benseisha, 1993.

Kawamata Keiichi, ed. *Fusōshū*. In *[Shinkō] Gunsho ruijū* 126, vol. 6. Tokyo: Naigai Shoseki Kabushiki Kaisha, 1931.

Keene, Donald. *Seeds in the Heart: Japanese Literature from the Earliest Times to the Late Sixteenth Century*. New York: Henry Holt and Company, 1993.

Keikokushū. See Kojima Noriyuki, below.

Kinpara Tadashi. *Heian-chō kanshibun no kenkyū*. Fukuoka: Kyūshū Daigaku Shuppankai, 1981.

Knechtges, David R., trans. Xiao Tong. *Wen xuan, or Selections of Refined Literature*. Vol. 1, *Rhapsodies on Metropolises and Capitals*. Princeton: Princeton University Press, 1982.

——, trans. Xiao Tong. *Wen xuan, or Selections of Refined Literature*. Vol. 2, *Rhapsodies on Sacrifices, Hunting, Travel, Sightseeing, Palaces and Halls, Rivers and Seas*. Princeton: Princeton University Press, 1987.

——, trans. Xiao Tong. *Wen xuan, or Selections of Refined Literature*. Vol. 3, *Rhapsodies on Natural Phenomena, Birds and Animals, Aspirations and Feelings, Sorrowful Laments, Literature, Music, and Passions*. Princeton: Princeton University Press, 1996.

Kobayashi Nobuaki, Ichiki Takeo, and others, eds. *Kanbun binran*. Tokyo: Hyōronsha, 1973.

Kōchū Nihon bungaku taikei. Vol. 24 of 25 vols. Tokyo: Kokumin Tosho, 1927. Contains annotated texts of *Kaifūsō, Bunka shūreishū, Keikoku-shū*, and *Honchō monzui*.

Kōdansha Encyclopedia of Japan. 9 vols. + suppl. vol. Tokyo and New York: Kōdansha International/Kōdansha USA through Harper & Row, 1983 (suppl. 1986).

Kojima Noriyuki. *Jōdai Nihon bungaku to Chūgoku bungaku*. 3 vols. Tokyo: Hanawa Shobō, 1962–65.

——, comp. and annot. *Kaifūsō, Bunka shūreishū, Honchō monzui*. Nihon koten bungaku taikei, 69. Tokyo: Iwanami Shoten, 1964.

——, comp. and annot. *Kokufū ankoku jidai no bungaku: Kōnin-, Tenchō-ki no bungaku o chūshin to shite (hohen exp. ed.)*, 9 vols. (continuous pagination, 4205 pp.) incl. one vol. suppl. Tokyo: Hanawa Shobō, 1968–2002.

——, comp. and annot. *Ryōunshū*. In Kojima Noriyuki, *Kokufū ankoku jidai no bungaku: Kōnin-, Tenchō-ki no bungaku o chūshin to shite*, vol. 2 (bk. 2). Tokyo: Hanawa Shobō, 1979.

——, comp. and annot. *Keikokushū*. In Kojima Noriyuki, *Kokufū ankoku jidai no bungaku: Kōnin-, Tenchō-ki no bungaku o chūshin to shite*, vol. 2 (bk. 3), pt. I; vol. 2 (bk. 3), pt. II; vol. 3 (pt. I); vol. 3 (pt. II); and vol. 3 (pt. III). Tokyo: Hanawa Shobō, 1985–98.

——, comp. and annot. *Ōchō kanshisen*. Iwanami Bunko 30-036-1. Tokyo: Iwanami Shoten, 1987.

——. "Kanshi no uta no aida: ōchō bungaku no mondai." *Bungaku* 55 (1987): 10–22.

Konishi Jin'ichi, annot. *Bunkyō hifuron kō*. 3 vols. Kyoto: Ōyashima Shuppan, 1948–52.

——. Earl Miner, ed. Vol. 1 trans. Aileen Gatten and Nicholas Teele, vol. 2 trans. Aileen Gatten, vol. 3 trans. Aileen Gatten and Mark Harbison. *A History of Japanese Literature*. 3 vols. Princeton: Princeton University Press, 1984, 1986, and 1991.

Kuroita Katsumi, ed. *Honchō monzui, Honchō zoku monzui.* In [Shintei zōho] Kokushi taikei, vol. 29 (pt. 2) of 66 vols. Tokyo: Yoshikawa Kōbunkan, 1965.

Kurozumi, Makoto. "Kangaku: Writing and Institutional Authority." Trans. David Barnett Lurie. In *Inventing the Classics: Modernity, National Identity, and Japanese Literature,* ed. Haruo Shirane and Tomi Suzuki. Stanford: Stanford University Press, 2000.

LaMarre, Thomas. *Uncovering Heian Japan: An Archaeology of Sensation and Inscription.* Durham and London: Duke University Press, 2000.

Legge, James, trans. *Confucius: Confucian Analects, The Great Learning and The Doctrine of the Mean.* Orig. pub. Oxford: Clarendon Press, 1893; reprint, New York: Dover Publications, Inc., New York, 1971.

———. *The She King or the Book of Poetry.* The Chinese Classics, vol. 4. Orig. pub. by Oxford University Press; reprint, Taipei: SMC Publishing, 1991.

———. *The Shoo King or the Book of Historical Documents.* The Chinese Classics, vol. 3. Orig. pub. by Oxford University Press; reprint, Taipei: SMC Publishing, 1991.

Liu, James J.Y. *The Art of Chinese Poetry.* Orig. pub. 1962; reprint, Chicago: The University of Chicago Press, 1966, Phoenix ed.

———. *Major Lyricists of the Northern Sung.* Princeton: Princeton University Press, 1974.

Liu, Wu-chi, and Irving Yucheng Lo, eds. *Sunflower Splendor: Three Thousand Years of Chinese Poetry.* Bloomington and Indianapolis: Indiana University Press, 1975.

Loveday, Leo J. *Language Contact in Japan: A Socio-linguistic History.* Oxford: Oxford University Press, 1996.

Matsuo Yoshiki. "Heian-chō kanbungaku to Tōdai kōgo." *Kokubungaku: kaishaku to kanshō* 55, no. 10 (1990): 26–36.

Matsura Tomohisa. "*Ryōunshū* no shitai (*jō, ge*)." *Kokubungaku kenkyū* 23, no. 24 (1961).

———. "*Bunka shūreishū* kō." *Kanbungaku kenkyū* 10 (1962).

———. "*Keikokushū* ronkō—shi o chūshin to shite." *Chūgoku koten kenkyū* 12 (1964).

———. "Jōdai kanshibun ni okeru rinen to yōshiki—shibun jissaku no imi suru mono." *Bungaku* 34, no. 3 (1966).

McCullough, Helen Craig. *Brocade by Night: 'Kokin Wakashū' and the Court Style in Japanese Classical Poetry.* Stanford: Stanford University Press, 1985.

McCullough, William H., and Helen Craig McCullough, trans. and annot. *A Tale of Flowering Fortunes: Annals of Japanese Aristocratic Life in the Heian Period.* 2 vols. Stanford: Stanford University Press, 1980.

Meli, Mark. "'*Aware*' as a Critical Term in Classical Japanese Poetics." *Nichibunken Japan Review* 13 (2001): 67–91.

Miki Masahiro, comp. *Ki no Haseo kanshi bunshū oyobi kanji sakuin.* Izumi Shoin sakuin sōsho, 27. Osaka: Izumi Shoin, 1992.

———. *Heian shika no tenkai to Chūgoku bungaku.* Osaka: Izumi Shoin, 1999.

Morris, Ivan. *The World of the Shining Prince: Court Life in Ancient Japan.* Orig. pub. Oxford University Press, 1964; reprint, Harmondsworth: Penguin Books, 1969, Peregrine ed.

Mukōjima Shigeyoshi. *Kanshi no kotoba.* Ajia bukkusu, 9. Tokyo: Taishukan, 1989.

Murakami Tetsumi. *Kanshi to Nihonjin.* Kōdansha sensho mechie, 33. Tokyo: Kodansha, 1994.

Nagazawa Kikuya. *Kanbungaku gairon.* Tokyo: Hōsei University Press, 1959.

Nakatsuka Eijirō, and others, eds. *Honchō zoku monzui.* Nihon bungaku taikei, 24. Tokyo: Kokumin Tosho Kabushiki Kaisha, 1927.

Nienhauser, William H., Jr., ed. and comp. *The Indiana Companion to Traditional Chinese Literature.* Bloomington: Indiana University Press, 1986.

Nihon bungaku taikei. See *Kōchū Nihon bungaku taikei,* above.

Nihon jinmei daijiten. 7 vols. Ed. Shimonaka Kunihiko. Tokyo: Heibonsha, 1979.

Nihon kanbungaku daijiten. 1 vol. Comp. Kondō Haruo. Tokyo: Meiji Shoin, 1985.

Nihonshi jiten. 1 vol. Comp. Uno Shun'ichi and others. Tokyo: Kadokawa Shoten, 1996.

Nihon koten bungaku daijiten. See Ōsone Shōsuke and others, below.

Okada Masayuki. *Nihon kanbungakushi.* Tokyo: Yoshikawa Kōbunkan, 1954; rev. exp. ed., 1996.

Ōsone Shōsuke. "Fujiwara no Akihira ron." *Kokugo to kokubungaku* 35, no. 3 (1958): 21–32.

———. "*Honchō mudaishi* seiritsu kō." *Kokugo to kokubungaku* 37, no. 5 (1960): 46–56, and *Kokugo to kokubungaku* 37, no. 6 (1960): 27–38.

———. "*Honchō monzui* no sekai." *Kokubungaku kaishaku to kyōzai no kenkyū* 26, no 12 (September 1981).

———, and others, eds. *Kanshi, kanbun, hyōron.* Kenkyū shiryō Nihon koten bungaku, vol. 11. Tokyo: Meiji Shoin, 1984.

———, Kinpara Tadashi, and Gotō Akio, annot. *Honchō monzui.* Shin Nihon koten bungaku taikei, 27. Tokyo: Iwanami Shoten, 1992.

———. *Ōchō kanbungaku ronkō: Honchō monzui no kenkyū.* Tokyo: Iwanami Shoten, 1994.

———. *Nihon kanbungaku ronshū.* 3 vols. Tokyo: Kyūko Shoin, 1998.

———, and others, comps. *Nihon koten bungaku daijiten*. Tokyo: Meiji Shoin, 1998.

Ōta Seikyū. *Nihon kagaku to Chūgoku shigaku*. Tokyo: Shimizu Kōbundō Shobō, 1968.

Owen, Stephen. *The Poetry of the Early T'ang*. New Haven: Yale University Press, 1977.

———. *The Great Age of Chinese Poetry: The High T'ang*. New Haven: Yale University Press, 1981.

———. *Remembrances: The Experience of the Past in Classical Chinese Literature*. Cambridge: Harvard University Press, 1986.

Ozawa Masao. "*Sakumon daitai* no kisoteki kenkyū (Kōtei *Sakumon daitai*)." *Setsurin* 11 (1963).

Pandey, Rajyashree. *Writing and Renunciation in Medieval Japan: The Works of Poet-Priest Kamo no Chōmei*. Michigan Monograph Series in Japanese Studies, 21. Ann Arbor: The University of Michigan Press, 1998.

Pollack, David. *The Fracture of Meaning: Japan's Synthesis of China from the Eighth Through the Eighteenth Century*. Princeton: Princeton University Press, 1986.

The Princeton Companion to Classical Japanese Literature. Earl Miner, Hiroko Odagiri, and Robert E. Morrell, comps. Princeton: Princeton University Press, 1985.

Rabinovitch, Judith N., and Timothy R. Bradstock, trans. and annot. *The Kanshi Poems of the Ozasa Tanzaku Collection: Late Edo Life through the Poetry of Kyoto Townsmen*. Nichibunken Monograph Series, 5. Kyoto: International Research Center for Japanese Studies, 2002.

Rimer, J. Thomas, and Jonathan Chaves, trans. *Chinese and Japanese Poems to Sing: The Wakan rōeishū*. New York: Columbia University Press, 1997.

Sanford, James Hugh. "The Nine Faces of Death: Su Tung-po's *Kuzōshi*." *The Eastern Buddhist* 21 (n.s.), no. 2 (Autumn 1988): 54–77.

Sansom, George. *A History of Japan to 1334*. Stanford: Stanford University Press, 1958.

Sato, Hiroaki. *Breezes through Bamboo: Kanshi of Ema Saikō*. Translations from the Asian Classics. New York: Columbia University Press, 1997.

Satō Michio. "Shaku Renzen to Fujiwara no Chikamitsu no kikō shōwashi no seiritsu jiki ni tsuite." *Mita kokubun* 1 (1983): 13–20.

———. "*Hosshōji dono gyoshū* kō." In *Chūko bungaku to kanbungaku*. Wakan hikaku bungaku sōsho, vol. 4. Ed. Wakan Hikaku Bungakukai. Tokyo: Kyūko Shoin, 1987.

———. "*Honchō mudaishi* denpon kō." *Wakan hikaku bungaku* 5 (1989): 13–23.

———. "*Honchō zoku monzui* to *Honchō mudaishi*." *Mita kokubun* 12 (1989): 10–14.

———. "Fujiwara Shiki-ke to futatsu no shū: *Honchō zoku monzui* to *Honchō mudaishi*." *Kokubungaku: kaishaku to kanshō* 12 (1990): 123–130.

———. "Shitai to shisō: Heian kōki no tenkai." In Kubota Jun and others, eds. *Jūichi, jūni seiki no bungaku*. Iwanami kōza Nihon bungakushi, 3. Tokyo: Iwanami Shoten, 1996.

Seeley, Christopher. *A History of Writing in Japan*. Leiden and New York: E.J. Brill, 1991.

Seireishū. See entry for Watanabe Shōkō, below.

Shinchō Nihon jinmei jiten. Comp. Ozaki Hideki, Haga Tōru, and others. Tokyo: Shinchōsha, 1991.

[*Shintei zōho*] *Kokushi taikei*. 66 vols. Ed. Kuroita Katsumi, in cooperation with Kokushi Taikei Henshūkai, Tokyo: Yoshikawa Kōbunkan, 1929–65.

Shio Yasuhisa. "*Honchō mudaishi* no henshū ni tsuite." *Kanazawa daigaku kokugo kokubun* 5 (1976): 36–41.

Shirane, Haruo, and Tomi Suzuki, eds. *Inventing the Classics: Modernity, National Identity, and Japanese Literature*. Stanford: Stanford University Press, 2000.

Smits, Ivo. *The Pursuit of Loneliness: Chinese and Japanese Nature Poetry in Medieval Japan, ca. 1050–1150*. Münchener Ostasiatische Studien, Bd. 73. Stuttgart: Franz Steiner Verlag, 1995.

———. "Reading the New Ballads: Late Heian *Kanshi* Poets and Bo Juyi." In *Wasser-Spuren: Festschrift für Wolfram Naumann zum 65. Geburtstag*, ed. Stanca Scholz-Cionaca. Wiesbaden: Harrassowitz Verlag, 1997.

———. "Places of Mediation: Poets and Salons in Medieval Japan." In *Reading East Asian Writing: The Limits of Literary Theory*, eds. Michel Hockx and Ivo Smits. RoutledgeCurzon-IIAS Asian Studies Series. London and New York: RoutledgeCurzon, 2003.

Sugano Hiroyuki. *Heian shoki ni okeru Nihon kanshi no hikaku bungakuteki kenkyū*. Tokyo: Taishūkan, 1988.

Sugano Hiroyuki, and Kunikane Kaiji, comps. *Nihon kanbun*. Kanbun meisakusen, vol. 5. Tokyo: Taishūkan Shoten, 1984.

Sugaya Gunjirō. *Nihon kanshi shi*. Tokyo: Daito Shuppansha, 1941.

Takagi Ichinosuke, and others, eds. *Nihon koten bungaku taikei*. 102 vols. Tokyo: Iwanami Shoten, 1957–68.

Takemura Toshinori. *Kyō no shiseki meguri*. Kyoto: Kyoto Shinbunsha, 1987.

Taninaka Shinichi, ed. *Nihon Chūgoku kanshi kankei ronbun sōmoku sakuin*. Tokyo: Waseda University, 1989.

———, comp. *Fusōshū: kōhon to sakuin*. Fukuoka: Tōka Shobō, 1985.

Tasaka Junko, ed. "*Fusōshū* zenchūshaku," pt. I, in *Sōgō Kenkyūjo hō* (Fukuoka University) 119 (March 1989); pt. II, in *Sōgō Kenkyūjo hō* 120 (February 1990); pt. III, in *Sōgō Kenkyūjo hō* 152 (September 1993).

Tatsumi Masaaki. *Kaifūsō: kanji bunkaken no naka no Nihon kodai kanshi.* Tokyo: Kasama Shoin, 2000.

Thornhill, Arthur H., III. "Typology in Traditional Japanese Poetics: The Reception of Chinese Buddhist Models." In Moore, Cornelia N. and Raymond A. Moody, eds., *Comparative Literature East and West: Traditions and Trends.* Honolulu: University of Hawaii Press, 1989.

Toda Kōgyō. *Nihon kanbungaku tsūshi.* Tokyo: Musashino Shoin, 1957.

Tsunoda, Ryusaku, William Theodore de Bary, and Donald Keene, comps. *Sources of Japanese Tradition.* Vol. 1 of 2. New York and London: Columbia University Press, 1958.

Ury, Marian, trans. *Poems of the Five Mountains.* Tokyo: Mushinsha, 1977.

————. "The Ōe Conversations." *Monumenta Nipponica* 48, no. 3 (1993): 359–380.

————. "Chinese Learning and Intellectual Life." In *Heian Japan*, ed. Donald H. Shively and William H. McCullough. The Cambridge History of Japan, vol. 2. Cambridge: Cambridge University Press, 1999.

Wada Hidematsu. "*Nihon genzaisho mokuroku* ni tsuite." *Shigaku zasshi* 41, no. 9 (1930): 56–69.

Wakan rōeishū, Ryōjin hishō. Ed. Kawaguchi Hisao (*Wakan rōeishū*) and Shida Nobuyoshi (*Ryōjin hishō*). Nihon koten bungaku taikei, 73. Tokyo: Iwanami Shoten, 1965.

Waley, Arthur. *The Life and Times of Po Chü-i.* London: G. Allen and Unwin, 1951.

Watanabe Hideo. *Heianchō bungaku to kanbun sekai.* Tokyo: Benseisha, 1991.

Watanabe Shōkō, and Miyasaka Yūshō, annot. *Sangō shiki, Seireishū.* Nihon koten bungaku taikei, 71. Tokyo: Iwanami Shoten, 1965.

Watson, Burton. *Early Chinese Literature.* New York: Columbia University Press, 1962.

————, trans. *Chuang Tzu: Basic Writings.* New York and London: Columbia University Press, 1964.

————. "Some Remarks on the *Kanshi.*" *Journal-Newsletter of the Association of Teachers of Japanese* 5, no. 2 (July 1968).

————. *Chinese Lyricism: Shih Poetry from the Second to the Twelfth Century.* New York and London: Columbia University Press, 1971.

————, trans. *Japanese Literature in Chinese: Poetry and Prose in Chinese by Japanese Writers of the Early Period.* New York: Columbia University Press, 1975.

————, trans. *The Columbia Book of Chinese Poetry.* New York: Columbia University Press, 1984.

Wen xuan. See David R. Knechtges, trans.

Wixted, John Timothy. "*Kanbun,* Histories of Japanese Literature, and Japanologists." *Sino-Japanese Literature* 10, no. 2 (April 1998): 23–31.

———, comp. *Japanese Scholars of China: A Bibliographical Handbook.* Lewiston: The Edwin Mellen Press, 1992.

Yamagishi Tokuhei. *Nihon kanbungaku kenkyū.* Tokyo: Yūseidō, 1972.

———, ed. *Nihon kanbungaku shiron kō.* Tokyo: Iwanami Shoten, 1974.

Yamanaka Hiroshi. *Heian-chō bungaku no shiteki kenkyū.* Tokyo: Yoshikawa Kōbunkan, 1974.

———. "Ōe no Masafusa." *Kokugo to kokubungaku* 35, no. 10 (October 1957).

Yamano Seijirō. "*Wakan rōeishū* chū no Nihon kanshi ni tsuite." *Chūgoku bunka: kenkyū to kyōiku* 42 (1984): 65–79.

Yoshikawa, Kōjirō. "Chinese Poetry in Japan: Influence and Reaction." *Cahiers d'Histoire Mondiale* 2, no. 4 (1955).

———. *An Introduction to Sung Poetry.* Trans. Burton Watson. Cambridge: Harvard University Press, 1967.

CORNELL EAST ASIA SERIES

275

Order online: www.einaudi.cornell.edu/eastasia/CEASbooks, or contact Cornell East Asia Series Distribution Center, 95 Brown Road, Box 1004, Ithaca, NY 14850, USA; toll-free: 1-877-865-2432, fax 607-255-7534, ceas@cornell.edu